Breaking Anonymity

The Chilly Climate for Women Faculty

The Chilly Collective, editors

Wilfrid Laurier University Press

WLU

for
Louise H. Forsyth
in gratitude
for her courageous and tireless efforts
on behalf of women's equality
within the University

All royalties from the sale of this book will go to a fund dedicated to the support of research and activism on chilly climate issues for those who face racist, ablist, classist, homophobic, and other forms of discrimination in the university environment.

Canadian Cataloguing in Publication Data

Main entry under title:

Breaking anonymity : the chilly climate for women
   faculty

Includes bibliographical references.
ISBN 0-88920-245-1

1. Women college teachers – Ontario – London.
2. Women college teachers – Canada.   3. Sex
discrimination in education – Ontario – London.
4. Sex discrimination in education – Canada.
5. Sex discrimination in employment – Ontario
– London.   6. Sex discrimination in employment
– Canada.   7. University of Western Ontario – Faculty.
8. Universities and colleges – Canada – Faculty.
I. Chilly Editorial Collective.

LE3.W42B74 1995   331.4'8137871326   C94-931445-5

Copyright © 1995

WILFRID LAURIER UNIVERSITY PRESS
Waterloo, Ontario, Canada
N2L 3C5

Cover design by Jose Martucci, Design Communications,
using a detail from "Hours of Women," a mixed-media piece,
copyright © 1991 by Cindy McMenemy

∞

Printed in Canada

Breaking Anonymity: The Chilly Climate for Women Faculty has been produced from a
manuscript supplied in electronic form by the Chilly Collective.

Contents

The Chilly Collective

In the course of assembling *Breaking Anonymity*, several of the contributing authors and a number of the women with whom they had worked on equity issues over the years were involved in ongoing discussions about the manuscript: what form it should take; whether the core of essays written about Western in the late 1980s warrant publication in the 1990s; what revisions they would require; and what impact publication would have on individuals, on the climate in our academic units, and on the institution as a whole. In one of these discussions we conceived the idea of forming a collective to stand with those who were contributing essays and editorial labour to the project. The present Collective includes many of the contributing authors (both from Western and elsewhere) as well as a number of others who have been active on equity issues but whose authorship is not directly represented in the collection.

It goes without saying, given the size of the collective, that this is not an editorial collective in the sense that each member has played a direct and active role either in writing or assembling and editing the manuscript. The support and feedback provided by Collective members has been crucial to the project but, as individuals, our relationship to the manuscript varies a great deal; some have been involved (variously) as authors, as editors, as critics, and as reviewers, while others had little to do with the manuscript until they read it as a prospective member of the Collective. In addition to differences in the degree to which we have been involved in creating the manuscript, Collective members have also differed, sometimes quite sharply, in our response to various components of the collection, to the style of writing and the standpoint of the contributing authors, and to the research and activism they report. Indeed, we differ in our views about the wisdom, success, and value of the project as a whole.

Nevertheless all have been, in our own ways, intensely interested in and supportive of the project. In joining the Collective, we lend our support to the project in quite general terms; we endorse the contributors' right to speak out on climate issues and we make a commitment to stand with those who have been directly involved in creating the manuscript should we have to defend this right.

As of May 1995, the membership of the Chilly Collective is as follows:

Carol Agòcs   Constance Backhouse   Frances Bauer
Kristin Brady   Anne Cummings   Regna Darnell
Nathalie Des Rosiers   Minnette Gaudet   Elizabeth D. Harvey
Winifred H. Holland   Barbara Houston   Gail Hutchinson
Nancy P. Kendall   Madeline Lennon   Jane L. MacDonald
Bonnie MacLachlan   Leela MadhavaRau   Diana Majury
Alice Mansell   Gillian Michell   Patricia A. Monture-OKanee
Kathleen Okruhlik   Ann Schweitzer   Jane Toswell
Aniko Varpalotai   Alison Wylie   Claire Young

Acknowledgments

Chapter 1, "Introduction—Surviving the Contradictions: Personal Notes on Academia," p. 11-28, © Patricia A. Monture-OKanee. Reprinted with the permission of the author.

Chapter 2, "The Contexts of Activism on 'Climate' Issues": Permission to reprint from articles appearing in the May 2, June 10, and June 19, 1988 issues granted by *The London Free Press*.

Chapter 3, "An Historical Perspective: Reflections on the Western Employment Equity Award," originally appeared in the *Canadian Journal of Women and the Law*, 4 (1990): 36-65, and is reprinted here with the permission of the author and the editors of the *Canadian Journal of Women and the Law*.

Chapter 5, "Epilogue: The Remarkable Response to the Release of the *Chilly Climate Report*": Permission to reprint from articles appearing in the November 13, 14, and 17 and December 9, 1989 and the April 30 and May 16, 1991 issues granted by *The London Free Press*.

Chapter 6, "*Reinventing Our Legacy*: The Chills Which Affect Women": Reproduces sections from *Reinventing Our Legacy: Report of the President's Advisory Committee on the Status of Women*, University of Saskatchewan, with the permission of President J.W. George Ivany and the Advisory Committee on the Status of Women.

Chapter 7, "Gender Bias within the Law School: 'The Memo' and Its Impact," was originally published in the *Canadian Journal of Women and the Law*, 2, 1 (1987-88): 362, and is reprinted here with the permission of the author and the editors of the *Canadian Journal of Women and the Law*.

Chapter 8, "Ka-Nin-Geh-Heh-Gah-E-Sa-Nonh-Yah-Gah," © 1988 Patricia Monture, was originally published in the *Canadian Journal of Women and the Law*, 2, 1 (1986): 159, and is reprinted here with the permission of the author and the editors of the *Canadian Journal of Women and the Law*.

Chapter 9, "The Gender Wars: 'Where the Boys Are,'" was originally published in the *Canadian Journal of Women and the Law*, 4 (1990): 66-95, and is reprinted here with the permission of the author and the editors of the *Canadian Journal of Women and the Law*.

Chapter 10, "'Race Relations' Policy Brought to Life: A Case Study of One Anti-Harassment Protocol": Permission to reprint from articles appearing in the September 15, 1992; March 20, 1993; and March 24, 1994 issues granted by *The London Free Press*.

The Epilogue, "Studying Science, Playing Politics," by Deborah Skilliter, was first published in *The Globe and Mail*, July 13, 1994, and is reprinted here with the permission of the author.

Preface

Compiling this manuscript for publication has been a complex and lengthy process. It began as a modest project, indeed, as a series of modest projects. The articles we assemble here were researched and written over a span of more than eight years and reflect concerns that were highly specific to our diverse institutional locations at the time of writing. Few of them were written with any prospect of publication in mind. Many took the form of locally circulated reports and discussion papers written by small groups of concerned women — by ad hoc committees and women's caucuses — or they were drafted by individuals for circulation as a record of experiences that had become too painful or angering to be borne in silence and isolation. One chapter draws on the work of a Committee on the Status of Women that had a mandate from the President of the university in question (the University of Saskatchewan) to investigate the whole range of institutional environments in which women teach and learn and work. Others were written in an effort to ensure that comparable committees at other universities would take climate issues seriously. And still others were written in reaction to the hostility which some of the initial discussions inspired, or in critical response to the range of voices and concerns that had been left out of existing reports on climate issues. If anyone had told us, in 1986 when the first of these essays was being drafted, that the outcome of these disparate projects would be publication in the form of a book, we would have been incredulous. Just writing about climate issues for local circulation and discussion was challenge enough.

The shift in worldview which made it possible for us to draft these essays and, eventually, to propose this manuscript for publication can be marked, at least in Canada, by public distribution of the famous "McIntyre Memo." First circulated in October 1986 by Sheila McIntyre, this memorandum was titled "Gender Bias Within a Canadian Law School."[1] It would later be published in a feminist law journal in 1988,[2] and appears here as chapter 7. In her poignant, richly textured narrative, Sheila McIntyre detailed the patterns of stereotyping, sexualization, overt harassment, exclusion, and devaluation she had experienced during her first year teaching at Queen's University. In the relatively closed community of a law school, the anger and hostility she encountered from a few particularly belligerent students and from some of her colleagues proved incendiary. Each incident built on

1

the last, polarizing those who might have been neutral, isolating any who indicated support or concern for her situation, and intensifying her sense of isolation and vulnerability. This was a climate frozen to the point of being completely dysfunctional.

The courage it took for Sheila McIntyre to give public voice to her experience was inspirational for a great many women who saw in her account elements of their own experience. For women working in academic communities who had, individually and collectively, suffered and witnessed what McIntyre described, the "Memo" was a significant breaking of silence. It established connections between experiences many had assumed were idiosyncratic. It served as a catalyst for discussions in which we began to explore more systematically the commonalities and differences in our situations, to note recurrent patterns and address questions about chilliness as a systemic issue rather than a personal problem. Often this breaking of silence meant breaking the isolation which is a significant part of the chill that many describe. It was the impetus for moving from the personal to the political, in analysis and in action. The bravery of women can be profoundly contagious.

Sheila McIntyre's "Memo" was an especially powerful influence for a number of the women who have contributed to this volume. It was the inspiration for two essays on climate issues at Western which were written in 1987 and 1989, and appear here as chapters 3, "An Historical Perspective on the Western Employment Equity Award" (the *Backhouse Report*), and 4, "The Chilly Climate For Faculty Women at Western" (the *Chilly Climate Report*). These exploratory studies, one historical and the other based on contemporary interviews with a number of women faculty, drew strikingly different and equally surprising responses. The *Backhouse Report* was quietly dismissed as irrelevant to current conditions on campus, while the *Chilly Climate Report* became the occasion for what several members of the senior administration referred to as a "media event," in which the *Report* was denounced as incompetent, the authors irresponsible, and the reports of chilliness implausible and overblown. One recurrent theme in these early critical reactions to the *Report* was that the women whose experiences the *Report* described (whose identities had been carefully protected) were "hiding behind anonymity."

The response of those working in the field of university equity services and with the President's Standing Committee for Employment Equity at Western was less incredulous. They collaborated with members of Western's Caucus on Women's Issues in developing the proposal for an educational video on climate issues which was inspired by the *Chilly Climate Report*. Many of those who had been involved in drafting the original *Report*, as authors and as interviewees, were astonished by the intensity of the reaction that this *Report* drew, from its supporters as much as from its critics. As news of the *Report*, and of the storm of controversy it had generated, reached others in universities and colleges in Canada and abroad, we were inundated with requests for copies of the *Chilly Climate Report* and the earlier historical essay, the *Backhouse Report*, to which it was a Postscript. When the video was released nearly two years later, interest in these essays intensified. Frequently, we learned, the essays and the video played much the same role for women located in other institutions as Sheila McIntyre's "Memo" had played for us.

The idea of publishing a collection of essays was born of this response to our initial reports, and fostered by our own gratitude to Sheila McIntyre and others whose courage had inspired us. It was also born of a certain quiet desperation. Our (often non-existent) copying and postage budgets were overburdened and we thought that a legitimate publisher might be prevailed upon to take over the task of distributing this material. The initial plan was modest. We would assemble the essays we had in hand, write "bridge sections" which would introduce them as historical documents (albeit ones we had already begun to rethink), draft one or two additional essays which would describe the chilly reception of the *Chilly Climate Report*, and set our work in a larger context of research and activism on women's issues in universities and colleges. The results of these efforts appear here as chapters 2 and 5. It was our hope that, despite the partiality and limitations of these essays, they might encourage still others to speak out about the hitherto unspeakable.

Although we were encouraged by the interest expressed in our work and were committed to raising public awareness of climate issues, the decision to seek a publisher for the essays caused us a great deal of anxiety and soul-searching. There were several considerations that weighed against publication. Perhaps the most important, in our view, was our own growing dissatisfaction with the limitations of the essays that were to be the core of the collection. With few exceptions, the focus of these essays was on *gender*, unmediated by the diversifying factors of race, ethnicity, sexual identity, class, or disability. The original studies addressed the experiences of "women" in academia and were conducted without any critical or reflective awareness of ways in which these "women" were assumed, without comment, to be White, gentile, heterosexual, middle-class, and able-bodied. Furthermore, they profiled the experiences of *faculty* women, and did not address the experience of women in the administrative staff or student body of the university. These essays reproduced an artificially "universal" conceptualization of women's experience; they embodied all the partialities of privilege that have compromised the second-wave women's movement and have been the central focus of critical debate within feminism in the last decade.

There are many reasons we might advance to explain why these essays were so flawed. It strikes us, however, that defending gaps in our analyses consumes an extravagant amount of time and energy and is ultimately a waste of precisely the resources we might better use in other ways. What we need are not defensive rationales, endlessly articulated, but a clear understanding of the inadequacies of our past work, and a resolutely creative, forward-looking commitment to make our research and writing fully inclusive of the experience of oppression, in all its diversity. On this principle, we wondered if the limitations of our original essays did not, finally, outweigh their potential usefulness. Perhaps we should set aside the project of publishing these essays. Certainly essays which more fully incorporate considerations of race, ethnicity, sexual identity, class, and disability, and which treat the experiences of women as staff and students, would be far richer, more transformative, and profoundly more challenging to the discriminatory structures of the academy than the reports we had written in the mid- to late 1980s.

These concerns were both reinforced and mitigated by the two referees who were asked to review the initial manuscript by Wilfrid Laurier University Press.[3]

Both noted serious gaps in the manuscript, and articulated more clearly and powerfully than we had been able to do just where the problems lay with our original studies. Nevertheless, both strongly urged an alternative route we had not considered; that we should undertake to address these gaps directly in the manuscript, rather than abandoning the project or publishing it as originally formulated. Despite glaring omissions, both felt that the original essays still contributed in important ways to the literature on sexual harassment and the chilly climate issues they described as "far from settled and far from isolated." It was so rare, wrote one, that *any* women should find themselves able to speak out about oppressive working conditions; here was an institution in which a multitude of voices had broken the silence, enabling a "thick description" of the environment in one organization. The descriptions of isolation, trivialization, and harassment might prove relevant far beyond the individual universities concerned, for other post-secondary institutions (colleges and universities) as well as organizations outside the educational sector where women have not been fully integrated into the work force.

Given this input, and a remarkably rich and detailed set of recommendations for reframing the manuscript, we resolved to pursue the project of publication, treating the original essays as part of an historical record of efforts to bring about change in a Canadian university. These essays exhibit both the flaws and the strengths of the analyses and strategies we adopted, documenting our activities, thoughts, and understandings in the years in which they were written. It seems important not to lose track of women's history, even with all of its obvious misadventures and odious tribulations; if nothing else, these may serve as a valuable negative object lesson for others. We include the essays with which we began, then, in the hope that they will be critiqued, debated, and improved upon in future rounds of engagement.

In the spirit of engaging these essays critically and moving beyond them, we also resolved to take the advice of the referees and broaden the scope of the collection. Such a strategy has both positive and negative aspects. It is fraught with all the dangers of "adding on," of creating tokens, and reinforcing precisely the sense of "centre" we mean to dislodge. We believed, however, that an expanded collection might begin to do some useful work if we were able to integrate into it some of the dynamics of debate that are reshaping how we think about climate issues and, more broadly, how we understand the activist and scholarly commitments of feminism. The most valuable part of the process of creating such a collection is precisely that which is rarely explicit in the finished product of a book: the ongoing critical engagement with one another, with our own previous thinking and work, with women working in other contexts and from very different standpoints than were represented among those active on equity issues at Western, and with women working from standpoints that *were* represented among women at Western but were systematically left out of account.

To this end we began by asking one of the original referees of the manuscript, Patricia A. Monture-OKanee, if she would be willing to write an introductory chapter for the volume. Adding to our already great indebtedness to her, she agreed to do this and has contributed an introduction in which she reflects on post-secondary education from the First Nations perspective of a Mohawk woman (chapter 1). We also asked Leela MadhavaRau to allow us to include an essay she was in the process of writing on the implementation of the "race relations" policy within the University (chapter 10). And we asked Claire Young and Diana Majury to comment on the manuscript and expand on the reports it includes from the perspective of their experiences as lesbians (chapter 11). These authors make it clear how deeply sexism is implicated with racism and with homophobia, and in this they greatly enrich what this collection has to offer. They demonstrate by illustration, by direct critique, and by example, at least some of the range of dimensions on which climate issues must be addressed, providing a point of entry to the growing literature on First Nations' issues, race, sexual identity, and class within post-secondary institutions.[4]

We have not been as successful in addressing disability. Research and analysis in this critical area must transform future projects of the kind we present here.[5]

We have also undertaken to expand the scope of the collection by inviting several reports and discussions which address climate issues as they
arise in Canadian post-secondary institutions other than Western and, to a
lesser extent, for women who are students and administrative staff in these
contexts. We include Sheila McIntyre's essay because it was the catalyst for
many of the other articles here, and because it constitutes a powerful autobiographical account which helps to ground the more abstract discussion of
climate issues by focusing upon the experience of one individual. Patricia
Monture-OKanee has permitted us to reprint an essay originally published
in the *Canadian Journal of Women and the Law* which describes her experience
as a law student within a climate that is chilly with respect to both gender
and race (chapter 8).[6] We include selections from *Reinventing Our Legacy*, a
broad-ranging report on the status of women — all women — at the University of Saskatchewan that provides some important comparisons across different units and diverse positions within university institutions (chapter 6).
Finally, we reprint, as the Epilogue to this collection, an essay originally
published in *The Globe and Mail* in which Deborah Skilliter, a student at
St. Mary's University in Halifax, describes her experiences of chilliness in
the classroom. Her discussion very powerfully focuses attention on ways in
which the climate described by other contributors continues to reproduce
itself, even as the representation of women in the "training pipeline"
changes for the better. Taken together, these essays serve to demonstrate
that a chilly climate for women affects faculty working in a wide range of
university contexts. They also throw into relief some of the ways in which
these accounts are unavoidably partial — unique to women with a certain
specificity of privilege which had gone unremarked in much of the existing
literature on climate issues in academic settings, allowing gender to emerge
as the sole (or primary) dimension of disadvantage.

Throughout this process of thinking and rethinking the shape of the collection, a second consideration has weighed heavily against publishing for
many of those who have contributed to or been involved in assembling the
manuscript. For all the privilege we enjoy, we have been deeply anxious
about the consequences of publishing these articles in a book, for ourselves
and for others who will inevitably be called upon to defend or to deny, to
explain or to justify, the accounts we give of continuing harassment, exclusion, and devaluation. In particular, we feared that we would provoke, yet
again, the vociferous and deeply painful attacks that had been a feature of
previous rounds of debate. We wondered whether we had the strength to
endure, yet again, overt disbelief, anger, and hostility. Some suggested we
would be better off not to draw attention to these issues again; we should let
old wounds heal and work for change more quietly, within the system,
without "rocking the boat." Indeed, some feared that, at this juncture, it

would be counterproductive to speak out again on these issues; it would simply deepen the chill, making the difficult environments with which many have learned to cope intolerably inhospitable.

With the greatest of respect to those who feel differently, we have concluded that these arguments indicate precisely why we should publish these accounts of the chilly climate for women faculty. These fears make it clear that the conditions we documented in the mid- to late 1980s persist. Indeed, in some contexts they have been exacerbated by the hostile and intimidating responses we encountered when we first spoke out against them. Perhaps more important, however, we feel that the writing and publication of these essays make it clear that there do exist, in universities and colleges, vigorous communities of women and men deeply committed to warming the climates in which we work. Members of these communities have found sufficient institutional and collegial support to raise their voices against conditions that perpetuate inequality — conditions which our institutions of higher education are, themselves, officially committed to eradicating.

Taking these considerations into account, we concluded that publishing this collection would represent a positive step forward, marking where we have come from as a measure against which to evaluate future initiatives and opening up a dynamic of discussion and activism which may begin, in itself, to shift the culture of our institutions. We remain stoically optimistic that university administrators will be capable of improving upon their previous records. We hope the publication of this book will permit us all to learn from the past as we collectively negotiate the difficult times that lie ahead.

Finally, a word about our title. Despite the courage of all who have contributed, directly or indirectly, to making possible the projects reported here, the degree to which any of us has been able to "break anonymity" remains sharply circumscribed. There are several chilly climate essays which would have expanded the scope of the discussion in crucially important ways, but which we have not been able to include in this collection. In one case, an author who submitted an essay detailing her experiences of chilly climate practices over a number of years eventually had to withdraw her contribution. She had confronted the university where she worked about her situation and resolved the dispute through legal settlement. The terms of this settlement include clauses which prescribe the ways in which she can publicly discuss her situation. Evidently these are sufficiently restrictive that she was advised by her lawyer that it would be dangerous for her to publish in this collection. In another case, we decided not to include a particular chilly climate report because its authors are under threat of litigation for defamation, and a defamation lawsuit has actually been launched against members of the media who reported on discussions that followed the release of the report in question. Our collection, then, cannot live up fully to its title, of breaking anonymity. For some of us the risks associated with speaking candidly and publicly about our experiences remain too great for us to break the tyranny of silence that is a part of the chill we feel.

We would like to acknowledge the generous support and assistance of the Canada Council, which provided funding towards the publication of this book, and of Wilfrid Laurier University Press. In particular, we are deeply grateful to the director of the Press, Sandra Woolfrey, other members of the editorial board and staff of the Press, and the referees who have provided extremely helpful suggestions and expertise. Their efforts are responsible for much that we consider most valuable about this collection. At many points during the production of the manuscript, Sandra Woolfrey and others at Wilfrid Laurier University Press played a crucial role, not just as editors but as colleagues committed to helping us come to grips with the barriers we felt stood in the way of publication. Their confidence in the project helped us through many difficult passages (literary and otherwise) and stands as an inspiring example of collaborative editorial practice.

Finally, we want to express our appreciation to all the women who have participated in the events, institutions, discussions, and projects chronicled in these chapters. Finding one's voice is a haltingly laborious task, which by necessity builds upon the foundations laid by those who have gone before. All of the women, named and unnamed, whose words and deeds form part of these chapters have contributed to making the publication of this book possible.

Without detracting from the collectivity of this enterprise, we also want to single out one woman whose words and deeds have been especially important to many of those who have contributed to this collection. She is Louise H. Forsyth, currently the Dean of Graduate Studies and Research at the University of Saskatchewan and previously, for 27 years, a Professor in the Department of French at the University of Western Ontario. Louise Forsyth exemplifies the boldness of spirit and imagination that set the stage for many of the events described in this book. An extraordinarily gifted scholar, her research on French Canadian literature and feminist theatre has been described as richly textured "embroidery" creating "multi-faceted tapestries of words."[7]

She was deeply immersed in institutional processes during her tenure at Western, serving as President of the Faculty Association, faculty representative on the Board of Governors, member of the Executive of the Ontario Council of University Faculty Associations and the Canadian Association of University Teachers, treasurer of the Canadian Association of University Teachers, and multiple terms as member of the Senate. She was, in addition, the Chair of the French Department for a period of five years. Her exceptional talents as a teacher and as a sensitive and thoughtful administrator are widely recognized. Her unflagging insistence upon challenging discriminatory institutional practices wherever she encountered them are legendary. She spoke up about sexism within the academy long before most of us ever began to work in these contexts, and continued to do so with vigour, with incisiveness, and with inspiring resolve long after we joined her as faculty colleagues — frequently at critical junctures when the rest of us were either too weary or too fearful to speak. In any institution committed to "excellence" Louise Forsyth would be regarded as a unique and treasured asset to the administrative, pedagogical, and scholarly life of the university. Those of us who were her colleagues at Western deeply regret that she was lured away to the University of Saskatchewan in 1991 and congratulate those who now have the pleasure of working directly with her; their gain is our loss.

We want to pay tribute to the powerful inspiration Louise Forsyth has been for all of us by formally dedicating this volume to her. We hope we may live out the promise that her activism set in motion.

Notes

1 McIntyre's memorandum was published three months later by the Canadian Association of University Teachers' in their newsletter, *CAUT Bulletin* (January 1987), p. 7-11.

2 Sheila McIntyre, "Gender Bias within the Law School: 'The Memo' and Its Impact," *Canadian Journal of Women and the Law*, 2, 1 (1987-88): 362.

3 One reviewer identified herself as Patricia A. Monture-OKanee; the other remains anonymous.

4 For some examples of literature describing some of the problems experienced by racialized faculty and by First Nations faculty, see: Patricia Williams, *The Alchemy of Race and Rights: Diary of a Law Professor* (Cambridge: Harvard University Press, 1991); Joy James and Ruth Farmer, eds., *Spirit, Space and Survival: African American Women in (White) Academe* (New York: Routledge, 1993); Lynn Brodie Welch, ed., *Perspectives on Minority Women in Higher Education* (New York: Praeger, 1992); Y.T. Moses, *Black Women in Academe: Issues and Strategies*, and S. Nieves-Squires, *Hispanic Women: Making Their Presence on Campus Less Tenuous* (Washington DC: Project on the Status and Education of Women, Association of American Colleges, 1988); Benjamin P. Bowser et al., *Confronting Diversity Issues on Campus* (Newbury Park, CA: Sage, 1993); Patricia A. Monture, "Ka-Nin-Geh-Heh-Gah-E-Sa-Nonh-Ya-Gah," *Canadian Journal of Women and the Law*, 2, 1 (1986): 159 [translated into French at *Canadian Journal of Women and the Law*, 6, 1 (1993): 119], and reprinted here as chapter 8; Patricia A. Monture, "Now that the Door is Open: First Nations and the Law School Experience," *Queen's Law Journal*, 15 (1990): 179; Patricia A. Monture-OKanee, *Thunder in My Soul . . . A Mohawk Woman Speaks* (Halifax: Fernwood Books, forthcoming 1995); Fyre Jean Graveline, "Lived Experiences of an Aboriginal Feminist Transforming the Curriculum," *Canadian Woman Studies*, 14, 2 (Spring 1994): 52; Emily Carasco, "A Case of Double Jeopardy: Race and Gender," *Canadian Journal of Women and the Law*, 6, 1 (1993): 142; Roxana Ng, "Sexism and Racism in the University: Analyzing a Personal Experience," *Canadian Woman Studies*, 14, 2 (Spring 1994): 41; Derrick Bell, "The Final Report: Harvard's Affirmative Action Allegory," *Michigan Law Review*, 87 (1989): 2382; Richard Delgado, "Minority Law Professors' Lives: The Bell-Delgado Survey," *Harvard Civil Rights-Civil Liberties Law Review*, 24 (1989): 349; and Indira Karamcheti, "Caliban in the Classroom," *Radical Teacher*, 44 (Winter 1993): 13-17. Ann

duCille, "The Occult of True Black Womanhood: Critical Demeanor and Black Feminist Studies," *Signs: Journal of Women in Culture and Society*, 19, 31 (1994): 591, reports on a conference held at the Massachusetts Institute of Technology in January 1994, entitled "Black Women in the Academy: Defending Our Name 1894-1994." It drew nearly 2,000 Black women from institutions across the country. Conference organizers were overwhelmed by the response to their call for papers. According to duCille, "they were instantly bombarded by hundreds of abstracts, letters, faxes and phone calls from black women describing the hypervisibility, superisolation, emotional quarantine, and psychic violence of their precarious positions in academia" (p. 623).

On class bias within the academy, see Michelle M. Tokarczyk and Elizabeth A. Fay, *Working-Class Women in the Academy: Laborers in the Knowledge Factory* (Amherst, MA: University of Massachusetts Press, 1993).

On issues of sexual identity, see Margaret Cruikshank, ed., *Lesbian Studies: Present and Future* (New York: The Feminist Press at the City University of New York, 1982); Louie Crew, ed., *The Gay Academic* (Palm Springs, CA: ETC Press, 1978); Elly Bulkin, "Heterosexism and Women's Studies," *Radical Teacher*, 17 (Winter 1981): 25-31; Margaret Cruikshank, "Lesbians in the Academic World," in Ginny Vida, ed., *Our Right to Love: A Lesbian Resource Book* (Englewood Cliffs, NJ: Prentice-Hall, 1978); Melanie Kaye, "Anti-Semitism, Homophobia, and the Good White Knight," *off our backs*, 12 (May 1982): 30-31; Judith McDaniel, "Is There Room for Me in the Closet: My Life as the Only Lesbian Professor," *Heresies*, 7 (Fall 1979): 36-39; Julia Stanley and Susan Wolfe, "Crooked and Straight in Academia," in Gloria Kaufman and Mary Kay Blakely, eds., *Pulling Our Own Strings: Feminist Humor and Satire* (Bloomington: University of Indiana Press, 1980); Bianca Guttag, "Homophobia in Library School," in Celeste West and Elizabeth Katz, eds., *Revolting Librarians* (San Francisco: Bootlegger Press, 1972); Adrienne Rich, "Compulsory Heterosexuality and Lesbian Existence," *Signs: Journal of Women in Culture and Society*, 5, 4 (1980): 631; Marilyn Frye, "A Lesbian Perspective on Women's Studies," paper presented at panel on "A Lesbian Perspective on Women's Studies," in Cruikshank, *Lesbian Studies*, p. 194-98; and Sarah-Hope Parmeter and Irene Reti, eds., *The Lesbian in Front of the Classroom: Writings by Lesbian Teachers* (Santa Cruz, CA: Herbooks, 1988).

5 On issues of disability, see the superb article by David Lepofsky, "Disabled Persons and Canadian Law Schools: The Right to the Equal Benefit of the Law School," *McGill Law Journal*, 36 (1991): 636.

6 Monture, "Ka-Nin-Geh-Heh-Gah-E-Sa-Nonh-Ya-Gah."

7 See the comments of Raija Koski, "In Appreciation," UWO Centre for Women's Studies and Feminist Research, *Newsletter*, 3, 2 (1991).

1

Introduction
Surviving the Contradictions:
Personal Notes on Academia

Patricia A. Monture-OKanee[1]

I grew up, for the most part, in London, Ontario. In 1979, I enrolled at the University of Western Ontario as a part-time student.[2] Two evenings a week I studied introductory sociology and economics while I worked full time as a secretary. I received grades in both courses that were far beyond what any of my previous school records indicated was possible. My low self-worth was challenged as a result. The overwhelming sense I had of my first few years of university education was of having finally found a place where I belonged. This is not so much a reflection of the university I attended but of where I was in my personal development. I can always remember being a "thinker." My friends have always told me I am very logical. I was well suited to the requirements of a university life. It was not until years later that I understood that this sense of belonging was a false one. My sense of belonging grew out of my status as a survivor of various incidents of abuse. In university, I did not have to feel, just think. Feelings were what I was trying to avoid. Years later I came to understand that the sense of belonging I felt was really the comfort I took in finding an environment where feelings were not essential.

When I was first approached about writing the introduction to this book, it had not yet expanded to include essays about universities other than the University of Western Ontario. I hesitated initially over the decision to contribute to a book primarily about Western. My hesitation was located in believing I had no University of Western Ontario tales to tell that fit neatly into the theme of this book. How I understood my experiences there were softened by the stage of my personal development when I enrolled in that school. The process of examining my involvement in this text has involved

11

the examination of many experiences I had filed away in the corners of my consciousness. The simple memory of feeling like I belonged at Western has become my window to a more complicated understanding of my experiences there. I do have a number of stories to tell about what I have learned about surviving the contradictions of my life as both a university student and a university professor. These stories, by virtue of the fact that they are not just about Western, provide a larger context in which this book must be understood. Western is not the sole anomaly among Canadian universities where women survive in a chilly and hostile climate. The essays which have been added to the original collection, detailing chilly climate experiences at universities other than Western, make this only too clear. I also believe that the experience of women in universities is not unlike the experience of women in other institutions and professions.

I also hesitated to agree to write this introduction because I was unsure if I was prepared to again bare my soul to the world. There are only a few "women of colour" and Aboriginal women who hold positions within Canadian universities, fewer still who hold tenure-stream positions in Canadian law schools. Obviously, if universities remain a bastion of White male privilege, then it would be difficult for the authors of this book to locate "women of colour" and Aboriginal women who could and/or would write from their current experiences of employment within universities. When I considered my hesitation I realized it was at least partially resistance to the "why ask me again" syndrome!

I am offended by colleagues who would like to ask me to do something but they feel their asking puts an extraordinary burden on me. Not being involved can leave me feeling isolated or inadequate. Not being involved often means that there are no Aboriginal women involved, and that has particular consequences. This is only one of the contradictions where I can be caught. I know that this dilemma is not the creation of my colleagues but that it is the result of the systemic exclusion of Aboriginal women (and other women of colour) from universities. The under-representation of members of equality-seeking communities within Canadian universities has particular consequences for the first few members of these groups to claim previously forbidden positions. This is even more disturbing in institutions that have a commitment to equity. The demands on these few professors sends our quality of life into an irreversible tailspin.

I know that the naming of this contradiction will be unsettling for a number of my colleagues. I do not carry this responsibility well. Recognition of this contradiction results in their understanding that whenever they ask me to participate the delicate balance in my life may collapse. Yet not asking results in my exclusion and, more importantly, not asking likely results in the exclusion of all Aboriginal voices.[3] Only through naming and sharing my experiences and my reflections on those experiences do I believe that we can collectively reach a satisfactory solution.

There is an easy answer which explains why I was asked to participate in the writing of this book. At the time I was asked to participate, in Canada, there were only three Aboriginal people (and I must also point out all three of us are women) who hold tenure-track positions in law faculties.[4] We were all appointed on July 1, 1989.[4] I can be angry and feel that the extraordinary demands on my time are unfair, but that does not change the sad reality that there are only limited choices available to "cover off" issues of race and/or culture (Aboriginality) and gender. I must continually balance my sense of responsibility against feeling like I am perpetuating the silence around certain exclusions by deciding not to participate. Eventually, I decided to write because I have spent a lot of time thinking about my position within the university over the last few years. I have made some important realizations that I need to share, perhaps only to purge my soul.

In purging my soul, I have decided not to name names although I will provide dates, locations, and identify institutions. Although writing is one of the thin strands of sanity that allows me to continue to maintain a grasp on my professional life, it does not come without inner turmoil. I often worry about the pain my writing may inflict upon others when they recognize themselves in the story I just told. I often wonder how this has become my responsibility — your pain — as though I was somehow the author of it. I am getting very tired of "talking back." I am very tired of always being in the position of responding to someone else's agenda rather than participating in the re-creation of our own Aboriginal space.

Things happen and I write them all down, sometimes quite compulsively. Writing — talking back — is the process through which I come to terms with my pain, anger and emotion. It is the process through which I often am able to come to terms with my oppression, the oppression of my people, and the corresponding feelings of helplessness and hopelessness that sometimes ride over me like a tidal wave. In itself my writing is not often within accepted academic traditions, and another contradiction is named. Often only through the process of writing does the feeling of contradiction become actuated. It is real because I can make it appear in bold black letters against stark white paper.

The process I have gone through before making a commitment to write this article is obviously important to me. This is only in part a result of my concurrence with the body of knowledge known as feminist analysis. This body of knowledge often focuses on process, and process is the first thing that is important to me here. Choosing when to participate and when not is one of the least frequently discussed ways that power is exercised in academic circles. Equally important is an examination, both personal and systemic, of what the consequences of involvement are.

I first had the occasion to review this manuscript in the spring of 1993, when it was forwarded to me by Wilfrid Laurier University Press. I devoured the manuscript. Here were teachers telling all. Telling what was in my mind and my heart, almost. Missing from the gendered analysis was an integrated and detailed analysis of the way race and culture have an impact on our gendered lives. I saw my experiences as woman during ten years of schooling and my five years of university teaching reflected on the pages, in neat black type on bold white background. I began reading with pen in hand, taking my reviewer's task very seriously. After a while, I read in the wee small hours of the morning, still clutching the pen but also sitting beside the kleenex box. Taking comfort in the quiet hours of the night — children sleeping — understanding that I was neither alone nor crazy. I sat with these women's words of their own pain and exclusion and I felt empowered by our common experiences. At the same time, I also began to feel invisible. Invisible because race and culture have such a significant impact on my experiences of university and this layer was almost totally absent from the women's storytelling.[5] [See the Preface for a history of the development of this manuscript.]

I know that women teachers from all across the country will read this book and see their own lives. I have studied at three Ontario universities (Western, Queen's, and Osgoode Hall Law School at York University). I have taught law at two other universities (Dalhousie University and the University of Ottawa). My cumulative experience of university indicates that Western is not an ugly exception. The first important step in changing a hostile environment for women in academia is recognizing the nature of the problem. Through the pages of this critical text, it is clear that women (and at least one man) understand what the problem is. When the stories are read together, we see the problem is one of great magnitude. Those who control the administrative realities of universities all too often fail to accept either of these facts. That is a problem of even greater magnitude.

One of my male relatives, a cousin, is a graduate of the medical school at the University of Western Ontario. He is Dr. Michael Monture. My family is very proud of his accomplishments. We attended the university at the same time and often got together to support each other and share our experiences. Once, he told me about the student reception he went to in the first few days of his enrolment at the medical school. The reception was held in a large L-shaped room. He was greeted by the appropriate student dignitaries. They encouraged him to meet some of his colleagues. He was taken to the back corner of the L-shaped room, which was not visible from the entrance, and only introduced to other "people of colour." He interpreted this as a profound message about his place within the institution and whom he was expected to associate with. Perhaps those responsible for the organization of this event bore him no ill will (perhaps they even thought they were being kind) and acted only in their own ignorance, but what they did was clearly wrong. More than ten years later when I talked to my cousin about writing this introduction, about my feelings of ambiguity and contradiction, he recalled the event I just described to you. There is no doubt in my mind that these events may not be remembered by those who perpetuate them, but they are the events that taint our experiences of those institutions.

I remember my second year of law school at Queen's University. It was the first year of the overt "gender wars" at that law school.[6] I still marvel at the imagery that the label "gender wars" instills. Men in trenches; combat clothes; weapons; fighting for their cause. I am also reminded of the Mohawk men, the Mohawk women and their supporters who a few summers ago stood toe to toe with the Canadian military defending a small plot of land. The image of war is a contradictory one for me, as a Mohawk and as a woman. I, as woman, did not feel at war during my tenure as a student at Queen's law school. I felt excluded and battered. My reality and my people's proud history in this country were denied over and over again. Not only did I feel excluded, but that feeling was reality: I *was* excluded. To describe this experience as "gender wars" takes the naming of the experience away from me and other women. This recognition is a reflection of just how powerless women sometimes are; even the popular name for our struggle is not ours. War also implies a battle between equal forces with equal resources. This is not the truth about women's struggles.

While a student at Queen's, in February of 1986, I attended a conference in Winnipeg, Manitoba, sponsored by the National Association of Women and the Law. Five students from my law school were able to secure funds to attend this conference. We all went seeking solace with professional women involved in the law who, we, at least initially, believed shared our common experiences of oppression on the grounds of our gender. At the registration event the night of our arrival, I experienced more conversations than I could count where other women (both lawyers and other students) expressed their concern about our ill fate of having chosen to attend Queen's law school. Many of the women suggested to us that their schools were not bastions of White male privilege and that they were treated with respect within their faculties. At the time, I was more than stunned. I was in no way prepared for this response and found it beyond credibility. It spoke to me volumes about the extent of the denial that many women experience in order to accomplish their goals.

I felt fortunate to be attending Queen's. Even if the institution did little about the gender oppression and the multiple exclusions that women faced, our experience at least was on the table, written in large neon pink letters. For me, that was progress beyond living the denial that seemed to proliferate in the other Canadian law schools. This Winnipeg conference was one of the first times that I felt overpowered by the experience of contradiction. It is an experience that has stayed with me for many years. It is my expression for a state of being that I often run into head-first, and the experience leaves me overwhelmed and motionless. As you will see, there are a number of twists in my story. Usually I think of these twists in terms of the contradictions that I must negotiate. I think of them in terms of contradictions because often I find there is no good solution available. There is often no good solution because what I am experiencing is a clash of my cultural beliefs and the non-Aboriginal legal system of which I choose to be a part. Sometimes the clash is related more closely to non-Aboriginal beliefs about what education is or ought to be.

At the end of my first year of law school, I was very disillusioned. I knew that I would not be able to grow into the role of lawyer and all the assumptions of what a good lawyer is, especially a criminal defence counsel. I felt that there was no sense in continuing on the path I had chosen, because the outcome I had first envisioned was no longer possible. During the eight months after I left the law school, I learned that perhaps I was confused about what was on my path. I wanted very much to be an advocate for my people. I did not like the idea of quitting anything. In the back of my mind I began to formulate a new idea. I wanted to teach law. At the time, I could not say these words out loud. No other Aboriginal person, especially no other Aboriginal woman, had ever secured a career as a law professor. If no one else could, what made me think I could? I quietly returned to law school, not daring to mention my dream. Partially, this dream reflected my desire to change the experience of law school for others as well as a recognition that change can be accomplished by being on the inside of a powerful institution.

In the winter of 1989, I applied to go to graduate school at Queen's. I was worried a little about my marks, but assumed I had a good reputation as a scholar at the school. I had been asked a number of times to make presentations to classes on Aboriginal rights in an effort to augment a sorely lacking curriculum.[7] In the spring of 1989, I learned just how foolish I was. I was denied admission to graduate school at Queen's and was put on the waiting list. The Graduate Studies Committee deemed that I was a "less qualified candidate." I was told this news by a friend and very supportive professor at the school. She gave me the news in person in her office. I was overrun by feelings of betrayal, anger, hatred but finally came to rest on my own foolishness. I bled all over that office. Over the years, I had run away from my past, a typical past of abuse. My experiences growing up in this country mirror what many other Aboriginal women face in this country. I had run from the street. I remember telling the friendly and supportive professor that I longed for the street. I know that she tried but probably did not understand. The street is infinitely honest. If someone bears you ill will, the outcome is direct and obvious, a literal knife in your back. The powers that be at the law school were "packing."[8] The weapons they were carrying were concealed. I never saw the blade before it struck.

It was a very difficult lesson for me, to learn to bring law down from the justice and fairness pedestal on which I had placed it. It was indeed a lofty perch. It is also a lesson that is continually placed before me, one I can never seem to fully grasp. However, I am not going to take full personal culpability for this ongoing struggle. It is one of the continuing contradictions that I negotiate. I went to law school not only to escape the abuse and oppression that came my way solely because I was an Aboriginal woman who was orphaned at an early age. But I also went to school to do something to change that reality for others as well. The hardest lesson that I have had to grapple with in the last few years is that my objectives were fatally flawed.

It is important to document some of the ways in which my experiences and my reality were excluded from my educational experiences. Curricula were not developed with the Aboriginal student in mind. Granted, I could always enrol in a single course in Aboriginal Rights. Law touches the Aboriginal person's experience in a multiple of ways. There are tax problems, child welfare problems, criminal law problems, questions of prisoners' rights, religious issues, personal property issues such as the repatriation of cultural objects, land claim issues, and issues of copyright to songs and stories. There are corporate law problems, environmental questions, questions of matrimonial property, and the issue of who is granted status under the *Indian Act* regime.[9] There are issues of government powers and responsibilities. And the list of Aboriginal issues in Canadian law continues.[10] It is as broad, if not broader, than the problems faced by every other individual or collective domiciled in Canada. Yet all of this is covered in a three-hour per week seminar course for approximately 13 weeks (and some schools do not even offer this course with any regularity from year to year). In the same way, because I have some level of recognized expertise in Aboriginal law, I am expected to understand every Aboriginal legal problem from tax to criminal law, from child welfare to incorporations, from the *Indian Act* to the constitution. No non-Aboriginal person is expected to develop an expertise in all aspects and fields of Canadian law. Yet very few people recognize this imbalance.

The great majority of Aboriginal law courses are offered by non-Aboriginal scholars who have developed an expertise in the area of Aboriginal rights as they are understood in Canadian law. I have often wondered how women professors and women students would respond to the suggestion that men can, could, and should teach courses about law and feminism.

It is so apparent that this would create quite a controversy. But when non-Aboriginal people teach courses on Aboriginal people and how Canadian law is applied to our lives, this is somehow an unrecognizable controversy. This speaks volumes to the power that women have secured within law faculties or, more importantly, the degree that Aboriginal people have not. The courses that are offered are just a small component of what Aboriginal law students need to learn about Aboriginal rights. Curriculum construction reflects the complete ignorance of most law schools about the needs of Aboriginal would-be lawyers and the legal problems that our communities face. The way in which legal education is structured may prepare you for the large corporate firms that occupy plush offices in Canada's large cities. It does not fully prepare us for the practice of Aboriginal law. I suspect that this observation is true for other collectives of "outsiders" across all university disciplines.

Curriculum problems do not reside solely in the construction of the course offerings. Within each course a variety of difficulties arise. When I was at Western, I enrolled in an anthropology course which was a general survey course on the Aboriginal Peoples of Canada. Until the handful of Aboriginal students in the class revolted, all of the materials used in the course were written by non-Aboriginal people. All of the guest speakers were non-Aboriginal people. When we confronted the teacher, we were told that she had no access to materials other than the ones presented. This thin excuse (which seems to be closely related to arguments about academic freedom) completely missed our point. The offering of only non-Aboriginal authorities delegitimized Aboriginal ways of knowing and being. Even after expressing our concerns we were excluded, denied, and marginalized.

As a professor I have often tried to encourage my colleagues to include Aboriginal ideas, materials, issues, and perspectives in their courses. I am frequently met with the same kind of distancing as the anthropology professor provided us years ago. My colleagues tell me that they have no expertise in that area and therefore cannot teach these kinds of materials or present these kinds of issues. Or, there is my favourite excuse: academic freedom. I wonder if I decided to teach only Aboriginal constitutional law problems in the general survey course required of all second-year law students, and justified this decision on my lack of knowledge about White law problems or academic freedom if anyone would take me very seriously! Obviously, both of these arguments are thinly disguised attempts to continue to adhere to the status quo and must be seen as such. Furthermore, they are attempts to steadfastly refuse to examine the way that race and culture have an impact on the power relationships that exist within the university environment.

Problems with curriculum (or the lack thereof) have not disappeared now that I am the teacher and not the student.[11] When I do try to make the materials inclusive of the Aboriginal perspective, it is not necessarily an advantage to the Aboriginal students. Rather than attacking me for forcing them to study materials that they feel are irrelevant, non-Aboriginal students place their immediate anger at the feet of the Aboriginal students in my class. The Aboriginal students are not only more accessible but they also have little power within the institutional hierarchy. There are a number of interesting conclusions that can be drawn from this recognition. It is as though the Aboriginal population of the school is seen as one conglomerate; we are not individuals, but that single Aboriginal "thing" over there. The anger (many would call it backlash) at what I have included in my courses is placed on the backs of those most vulnerable within the institution. It is difficult for me to decide whether it is better to include or exclude Aboriginal perspective (presuming I could exclude my own perspective if I tried!).

There is an interesting double edge in my experience of my teaching position. I am required to carry out the same duties as any other of my colleagues and perhaps it is to their credit that the other professors do not treat me as different (that is, a lessor). However, the reality is that my experience is different. The study of law for me is the study of that which is outside of myself and my community. It requires that I be expert at both the ways in which "White" people do things, as well as continuing to learn as an Aboriginal woman. In fact, my survival of the law school depends on my intimate knowledge of who and what "White" people are. The same does not hold true in reverse. "White" people have the opportunity to fully discard my reality and this is at least one of the significant sources of my marginalization. The result is that my workload, at the intellectual level, is at least double. On top of this recognition, it must be accepted that professors with experiences of "other" are in great demand within the student body, on the conference circuit, and on committees within the school.

This year I was asked to sit on the Admissions Committee, the Aboriginal Advisory Committee, the Equity Committee, the Hiring Committee, one special committee struck to resolve a dispute, and my colleagues elected me to the Executive Committee. This far exceeds the committee responsibilities that the collective agreement requires. This is not a specific complaint about the institution in which I teach. I firmly believe that I teach in the "least worst"[12] law school in the country. When I brought my concerns to the attention of the administration, my suggestions for making this workload bearable were heard and accommodated. My problem is that it was me who had to seek out that accommodation.

The law school I teach in is committed to education equity. Because I belong to and identify with an under-represented and historically excluded group, my particular experiences and expertise are valuable to the work that many of the law school committees conduct. All this is very well as long as the only consideration is the quality of experience of the law school and the students. When the quality of my life is added to the equation, obviously, the commitment to equity is a burden that I disproportionately carry. Equity stops somewhere before my office door and before the door of my colleagues who are members of previously excluded groups. I am excluded from where I most want to be included; the parameters of equity. Contradiction reigns supreme again.

In my lifetime, I have learned more from reflecting on my personal experiences and from my Aboriginal teachers than I have from any educational institution. I spend a good deal of time contemplating my role as professor in a law school. This is the process by which I am able to first name and then examine the contradictions in my life which constantly require mediation. Obviously, any discussion of my personal experiences of law will focus on the law school in which I work. I have already said that I firmly believe that I teach in the least worst law school in the country. I am fond of this least worst idea because I do not feel that any law school yet offers a legal education that is meaningful to Aboriginal individuals (or a teaching position that fully allows us to be who we are). Best is a high standard and we have yet to reach this peak.

As I examined my experiences of law over the last decade, I realized that many of the stories I wished to tell focused on the University of Ottawa. This caused me some concern. I want to say clearly that these reflections are based on the coincidence of my employment and not any kind of ranking of where I believe the most work in legal education needs to be done. In fact, I am not sure that any such ranking would serve a useful purpose. If least worst is the best that we can do, then our energies seem to be better spent on improving the situation for those of us who have been outsiders for too long rather than engaging in a competitive game of who is least worst.

In December of 1991, the Dean of my faculty agreed to hire an outside consultant to interview as many Aboriginal students at the University of Ottawa as could be located, and document their experiences. Several of us had urged my Dean to undertake this study because we felt a lot of inroads had been made since we attended law school and wanted to be certain that, as we mapped out the future of Aboriginal legal education, we were in touch with the current needs of the students. In the few years that had passed since I was a student there were several Aboriginal law professors who could serve as role models, the curriculum offerings had increased, the school had an education equity program, and most importantly, a critical mass of Aboriginal students existed in the student body. The results of the study were daunting. The Aboriginal students still felt extreme alienation during the course of their law studies. This alienation was often expressed in exactly the same words I had used years earlier. All of the inroads we had made amounted to nothing if the standard of success adopted was the experience of the students.[13] It is also worth noting that one of the biggest concerns brought forward by the Aboriginal students interviewed was the near total irrelevance of the courses they were assigned or offered.

Curriculum content and offerings is an important topic and a central concern of a good number of the students whom I have spoken to over the last few years. This is where my story takes another odd twist. I am a law professor. With that comes a certain responsibility. I am a member of the institution, and often the Aboriginal students waste few words in pointing this out to me. When the institution harms the Aboriginal students, I am responsible for that harm as I am a member of that institution. Yet within the structure of the institution, I have little if any immediate power to change the curriculum offerings beyond what I am able to offer in my own courses.[14] This is true even in the face of a very supportive and understanding administration.

The problem that all these examples describe is structural. It includes the assumptions upon which educational institutions are based. It might be helpful to provide a clear example of the way structural assumptions operate within the institution. As a professor, I wield a certain amount of power. I do not deny this. It is true, I decide whether a student passes or fails; if an "A" or a "C" is earned.[15] However, when I stand in front of a class, many of the individuals have more privilege and power than I can ever imagine having. This power is carried as a result of their skin-privilege, or their gender, or their social status, or family income. The law school, however, functions solely on the view that I am the powerful one. Students are protected against any "alleged" bias by any professor by the grade appeal process. However, I am not any professor. I am not male, White, and my family is not economically advantaged. I am heterosexual, able-bodied, and a mother of five. I am Mohawk and follow my ways. There is no protection available to me in any policy of either the law school or the university if the situation arises where I experience a student who discriminates against me based on my gender, culture, or race.

In every class I have taught over the last five years, there are at least half a dozen students who challenge my authority. The easiest way to alleviate the conflict my presence creates (that is, as Mohawk woman) is to delegitimize me. Coupled with the failure of university structures and procedures to recognize that I am not (as others are not) "any" professor, this delegitimation complicates my experience. This is not a problem I encounter only in my exchanges with students. The complexity of my involvement in the institution as professor is not recognized in tenure and promotion processes. Although universities are attempting to diversify their faculties, few attempts are made to alter the policies and practices of the institution to reflect that diversity. There is only one outcome: I am forced to find ways to accommodate my own difference.

I came to this realization through the actual experience of a number of student complaints both directed at myself and other faculty members who are members of other specific collectivities. The details of these complaints are not important for my present purposes. What is important is that I have tried to find ways to insulate myself from as many of the complaints as I possibly can. My teaching has become more conventional. I try to dress to look like a professor more than I did in my first year of teaching. This decision was my response to receiving a teaching evaluation that suggested I wore "too many beads and feathers to class." Try as I may, I can never remember wearing feathers to class. I hesitate to cancel any classes. I make every effort to return assignments immediately. I avoid doing anything that I know the students do not like. I continue to try to find individual ways to protect my difference. I also am aware that many of my colleagues have never had to consider many of these things. At the same time, I know that my individual efforts only operate to partially insulate me from the true problem. My individualized efforts do not remove the structural barriers which give rise to the majority of contradictions and conundrums I encounter. Real change requires a full and systemic institutional response. Such response will never be found unless the institutional commitment to eradicate all barriers is sincere.

In an effort to find a more hospitable environment in which to teach this year, I very excitedly accepted the invitation to teach an Aboriginal women's course in the Women's Studies Department. I naively thought that getting away from a number of conservative factions at the law school would bring me further insulation and an experience that was more rewarding. Over the first month that this course was taught, I was inundated with "White students" (who make up at least two-thirds of a class of close to 40) who feel threatened in the classroom. They are responding to several women of colour who are logically angry and fed up with an education system that has offered them little. The anger of the women of colour is, in my opinion, an expression of a collection of experiences of alienation and exclusion both within the university and in their other life experiences. I understand and identify with the anger of the women of colour even though I recognize that our experiences are not the same. One of the students who came to see me in my office complained to me that the "class unit" was being disrupted and she could not understand how I could let this happen. I was overwhelmed by this comment. In my more than ten years as a student and my five years as a professor, I have never experienced the classroom as a safe place. The gulf between our experience seems to be wider when the criteria is race/culture as opposed to gender. After thinking about my conversation with this student for a long time, it seemed very ironic to me that my efforts to insulate myself by claiming a women's space only highlighted for me the differences of my race/culture experience again.

At the end of the course, many of my women's studies students expressed how much they had learned in the class. For many of them, it had been a good class. For me, it was frequently a lesson in surviving trauma. The solidarity I felt with the anger of the women of colour contradicted the responsibility I felt I carried as professor. In particular, I felt an obligation to provide a safe learning place for all the women in the class. No matter how I taught, someone's sensibilities were outraged (or perhaps only potentially so). This contradiction also manifested itself in my own awareness that I could not fully support a feminist agenda, an agenda which some students felt all professors in a women's studies program would be required to support.[16] Ironically, in the standoff that developed between some of the "White" women and some of the women of colour, the Aboriginal women withdrew. In a class on Aboriginal women, it seemed as though there was no space left for them. I am not sure I understand how to keep this tragic outcome from repeating itself.

When I first read this book manuscript, I was thrilled to know that I was not alone, but I was also deeply angered by what I read on the pages of this text. I hesitate to use that imagery of anger because it is so full of someone else's negative assumptions about my own personal culpability for my anger. Trying to name what I was truly feeling helped lead me to the conclusion that English is a fully inadequate language for the expression of my cultural experiences. English is the language of my colonization. Language is implicitly loaded with a series of cultural presumptions which I do not necessarily share and perhaps may not even be aware of. This, in part, is a result of not sharing the same culture with other speakers of the English language. What I am naming as anger feels more like thunder, thunder in my soul. Sometimes, it is a quiet distant rumbling. Other times it rolls over me with such force that I am immobilized.

None of what I have written so far is meant to suggest that I regret any of the choices I have made in my life. I do not regret my legal education, although sometimes I contemplate denouncing it. My education and subsequent employment have changed the pattern of individualized oppression that I face. But changing my position within Canadian society has done little to change the overall oppression that most Aboriginal people face in this country. I still get the phone calls from people whose children have just been arrested, apprehended by child welfare authorities, or committed suicide. I still hear of the experiences of 40 men in a community abused by one Jesuit priest and the devastation that has been wrought on that community. I know that the women and children are still being abused. I see so much

pain. Others believe that I have the power to change things, and only sometimes can I. Law is often the mop used to clean up the mess. It offers only
rare opportunities to change things before the blood is let. I exist in a contradiction of being expected to be grateful for my success and recognizing that
success reflects a pitiful amount of real change for other Aboriginal people.

This article has been, thus far, pretty serious. I do have a funny story to
share — at least it strikes me as funny. Last year one of my colleagues was
doing some work on a legal problem concerning an Aboriginal community.
During this time, he had occasion to introduce me as one of the least tactful
members of the faculty. This was not done in an offensive way and I was not
offended by an introduction that rang of truth. A few days later, this same
colleague and I were discussing his work on an Aboriginal issue. He expressed frustration that he was getting little cooperation from the Department of Indian Affairs. In fact, he insisted that the only thing he felt that he
had accomplished was to speak to every person within the Indian Affairs
bureaucracy! I was not very sympathetic at his one encounter with such
evasiveness on the part of a bureaucracy charged with the welfare of registered Indians in this country. I asked my colleague if perhaps he now under-
stands how I got to be so tactless, having been weaned on the Department of
Indian Affairs. We had a good laugh.

This story is more than humorous. It is a poignant example of another
shape in which the contradiction appears before me. I do not share with my
colleagues a common view of the world. Nor do I share with them a common personal history. Often, my colleagues do not recognize that we share
little in the way of a common background because they can choose to see me
as a law professor. We have been thrown together as a coincidence of our
chosen profession. The two conversations that occurred between my male
colleague and myself would never have taken place among my Aboriginal
friends, family, or acquaintances. We have all experienced Indian Affairs
"baffle-gab."

Despite all of our differences, I still believe in educational systems as a
site of future social change. I do not cling to the same hope for law as a vehicle for change toward Aboriginally inclusive systems. What I have come
to understand through my last ten years of involvement with the law is that
it is not the answer I am looking for. Every oppression that has been foisted
on Aboriginal people in the history of Canada has been implemented
through laws. This includes child welfare apprehensions, residential
schools, the outlawing of our sacred ceremonies, the prohibitions against
both voting and hiring lawyers, the impact of the criminal justice system — the list goes on. Law is not the answer. It is the problem. My experience of law has been about coming face to face with oppression, both my
own (individual) and that of other Aboriginal people (systemic).

I do not intend to discourage any Aboriginal person from pursuing a legal career. We are in desperate need of more front-line lawyers, the lawyers who spend every day in the trenches of criminal court and child welfare court. We also need good Aboriginal legal philosophers and theorists who will continue to provide the intellectual insight in the reclaiming of our own relationships with one another. I am just concerned that would-be Aboriginal lawyers know exactly what the job is before us. My study of law is the study of my own decolonization. I am reminded of Audre Lorde's warning. You cannot take apart the master's house with the master's tools.[17]

The conclusion that I am able to reach is not a particularly cheerful one. I am where I am today because I decided to make a difference in both my own life and its somewhat tragic beginnings but also in the lives of my Aboriginal relations. Naively, I once believed that if I could just write enough letters behind my name that "White" people would accept me as equal. I no longer subscribe to that theory of equality because it does not significantly embrace my difference or the fact that I choose to continue to remain different. As I climbed that ladder of success I never understood that I could not climb to a safer place. I now understand that the ladder I was climbing was not my ladder and it cannot ever take me to a safe place. The ladder, the higher I climbed, led to the source of my oppression. Being so close to the fire explains for me why I now feel the contradictions and conundrums at a new and heightened level. Although the lessons that led me to this realization were difficult, I do not regret them.

I no longer live in a situation of overt violence, but I still live with the knowledge that overt violence surrounds me. I have found success in my effort to change my personal circumstances even though structural and systemic change can still feel elusive. As a result, I have begun to understand that I am still battered — intellectually battered. But like other women, I am not yet beaten.

This text tells stories of courage. It also exposes experiences that should inspire great shame in the hearts of the perpetrators. It is my hope that by breaking the silence, meaningful and systematic change will begin to occur within education institutions within my lifetime. This change will occur when we all begin to accept our responsibilities and begin to examine more fully the contours of all oppression.

Notes

1 Mother and citizen of the Mohawk Nation. Until June 30, 1994, member of the Common Law Faculty, University of Ottawa. As of July 1, 1994, Associate Professor, Department of Native Studies, University of Saskatchewan. An earlier draft of this paper was reviewed by Sanda Rodgers. I am grateful for not only her comments but the encouragement and support she has kindly and consistently offered me over the last ten years. This article will

never feel done to me. As each day goes by, my reflections on post-secondary education for Aboriginal people and my own personal experiences of post-secondary education continue unabated. It has been difficult for me to let these ideas go in what I feel is only a preliminary form.

2 I have discussed at length the irregular path that I took to university in "Self-Portrait: Flint Woman," in Drew Taylor and Linda Jaine, eds., *Voices* (Saskatoon: University of Saskatchewan, 1992), p. 126-34. The discussion in this earlier paper complements the one presented here.

3 One of the strategies that I have begun to use to combat the exclusion versus exhaustion conundrum is to suggest that people contact other Aboriginal women who can also speak to the issues. This has two effects. It relieves the stress created in my life that is the result of being overextended, and it also opens the door of opportunity for other women. It is a way of redistributing the nominal personal power I have acquired and turning it into something more powerful.

4 As of July 1, 1993, there are several others, three men and two women, who also hold positions within Canadian law faculties. These positions, although at least one is tenured, all involve either an obligation to a special Aboriginal program or are term appointments only. By pointing out that these positions are not "regular" tenure-stream appointments, I do not mean to insult my Aboriginal colleagues. In fact I have great respect for these individuals who carry a greater burden within their respective institutions than I have ever been forced to pick up. This point is made solely to illuminate the unacceptable nature of their appointments within these faculties. The lack of permanency in some of these positions seems to suggest that at some point in time in legal education Aboriginal people and perspectives will no longer need to be included. This is false and, quite frankly, racist.

In fairness, I also want to point out that several Canadian law schools (Osgoode Hall, Queen's, and University of Toronto) have all made concerted efforts during this academic year to hire Aboriginal legal scholars. However, all of the law school hirings to date have been on terms the law schools define. No school has made an effort to involve traditional Aboriginal legal scholars on terms that are acceptable to Aboriginal people or communities. Hiring Elders or traditional teachers to teach courses is not within the current vision of any Canadian legal institution (and perhaps should not be).

5 After five years of teaching law, I have made the decision that it is time to leave the law school fold and venture into a teaching experience within a Native Studies department. I have agonized over this decision for a long time. It rests on the simple principle that remaining full time in the law school takes me too far away from my people — in geographic, spiritual, and intellectual terms.

6 I know that within the dominant culture and especially within the academic tradition the concept of "story" has a negative connotation. Stories are not truth. Experience does not necessarily meet academic standards. I find myself hesitant to use this concept, as it will in some circles, in all likelihood, be misinterpreted and read down. However, storytelling in the Aboriginal tradition occupies a central place within the culture. Perhaps stories are even the central vehicle for sharing knowledge. I use this word "story" in the respectful way of my people.

7 For a detailed accounting of these times, please refer to Sheila McIntyre, "Gender Bias within the Law School: 'The Memo' and Its Impact," *Canadian Journal of Women and the Law*, 2, 1 (1987-88): 62 (reprinted here as chap. 7). During the fall semester of 1985 I was not enrolled at the law school. I had taken a leave at the end of my first year of law because I was so disillusioned by my experiences. It was during this semester that Professor McIntyre wrote her memorandum and circulated it to her colleagues. It was eventually released to the national press (and Professor McIntyre does not know who the individual was that catapulted her to national attention). I returned to school in the winter term of 1986 to confront the fall-out from the memorandum.

8 I have discussed the difficulties of Aboriginal students at law school, including the exclusionary construction of law school curriculums, in "Now that the Door Is Open: First Nations and Legal Education," *Queens's Law Journal*, 15, 1 (1990): 179-91.

9 This is a street slang phrase used to describe someone who is carrying a knife.

10 R.S.C., 1985, c.I-6.

11 It is very important to distinguish between Aboriginal issues in Canadian law and Aboriginal law. Each of the Aboriginal nations has a unique and often complex system of social arrangements. There is a relationship between the two systems. Canadian law has been the tool through which every oppression Aboriginal people in this country have faced has been implemented. The study of Aboriginal issues in Canadian law is a valuable endeavour, but it must be recognized that this is only a partial study. I believe that Canadian law is not the solution; it is the problem. The solution rests in reclaiming our own traditional legal processes.

12 As I worked on this paper, this sentence continued to feel awkward to me. I puzzled for a while over this feeling. I eventually settled on the words "teacher and student." In the way of my people, I am too young to be anything other than a student. There is a constant conflict between my image of myself in a cultural sense and in my professional life. It was not the sentence that was awkward but another contradiction that is nestled between my cultural beliefs and my professional life.

13 It was Professor Sanda Rodgers who first acquainted me with this term.

14 I have not even factored into this discussion the great amount of energy it takes just to maintain the few small successes that we have had against attack from conservative factions within both the law school and the larger legal community. Unfortunately, much of the energy I spend in the law school is spent dealing with "backlash." Backlash is another of those words that I really do not like. Backlash is nothing more than racism, pure and simple.

15 Over the years I have also found myself augmenting course offerings by making myself available to do at least three independent research courses with students. Generally, the students who seek out this opportunity are Aboriginal students. They tend to have interests that are not explored in the courses that are presently being offered. When a student asks me to supervise such a paper course, I am acutely aware that if I say no they have few, if any, options. It is important to me to emphasize that I really enjoy this work with students and plan to continue to encourage them to avail themselves of this opportunity. On the other hand, I am also aware that this obligation is not one that is equally shared across faculty members in the institution where I teach. Another conundrum is located.

16 Interestingly enough, when I do assign a low grade to a paper or examination, I frequently find myself challenged by students. I do not think this is an odd or unfortunate phenomenon. If the challenge is a substantive one, I have no complaint. It keeps the professoriate honest. However, not all of the challenges I face are substantive. Many students challenge my marking in such a way that it is obvious that they do not believe I have the authority to grade their work as anything other than excellent. I believe that some of these challenges, at least, are based on either my gender or race/culture, if not both.

17 I have not ruled out that the fact that I was committed to teaching the course cooperatively, which in my mind includes a responsibility to be non-hierarchical and to let everyone pick up their individual responsibility to learn, complicated the pattern that developed. By this I mean to indicate that I think the fact that I do not assume the role of learned professor, the sole source of wisdom and authority in the classroom, challenged the students in a way that I found very surprising in an institution of higher learning. If I had assumed the classic professor stance, I think that some of the controversy and tension would have only percolated in the undertones of the classroom. As this was a course on Aboriginal women, a topic of great diversity, I did not believe that I had the right to assume sole authority for the experiences of all Aboriginal women because of our great diversity.

18 Audre Lorde, "The Master's Tools Will Never Dismantle the Master's House," in Cherrie
    Moraga and Gloria Anzaldua, eds., *This Bridge Called My Back: Writings by Radical Women of
    Color* (New York: Kitchen Table Women of Color Press, 1983), p. 98.

2

The Contexts of Activism
on "Climate" Issues

Alison Wylie

This essay provides an overview of literature on the chilly climate for women in North American universities and colleges that informed the work on climate issues in Canadian contexts in the late 1980s. It describes the larger context of debate about the reasons for the persistently low representation of women in permanent and senior faculty positions and the circumstances which shaped the projects reported and discussed in the next three chapters.

– Eds.

I. Pipeline Issues and Revolving Doors

The women employed as academics in North American universities and colleges are, without question, an enormously privileged elite — very differently privileged, to be sure, but on a great many counts, enormously privileged. We are, by definition, highly educated professionals who pass our working lives in institutions that conceive of themselves, with pride, as strict meritocracies; on the face of it, this is one context in which we should expect to be treated as peers. Nonetheless, our numbers remain disproportionately low, even as the number of women in graduate and professional schools increases by leaps and bounds, and the proportion of women in the undergraduate population exceeds 50%. In particular, the number of us who are also members of so-called "minority"[1] and otherwise disadvantaged groups remain even more disproportionately small. More striking yet, our numbers have remained low long after overtly discriminatory policies have been struck down and, in some quarters, even after widely publicized employment equity or affirmative action programs have been initiated.[2] Since at least the mid-1980s this situation has led many to argue that we

29

face, to varying degrees and with differing consequences, persistent systemic discrimination which, precisely because of our elite status in other respects, throws into sharp relief the nature and depth of the mechanisms that continue to sustain gender inequity throughout North American society in all its myriad forms — constituted as racist, homophobic, classist, and ablist sexism, to name a few of its variants.

In what follows I offer a summary of reports on the representation of women in academia in Canada and the United States, and then consider the literature on chilly climate issues for women in academia that influenced the work we undertook at the University of Western Ontario (Western) in the late 1980s. I will conclude with an account of the circumstances that gave rise to the various projects reported or discussed in subsequent chapters.

Improvements in the Status of Women in Post-secondary Education

In 1970, the Royal Commission on the Status of Women in Canada reported that "although there had been a gradual increase in female enrolment [in Canadian universities] since 1955, the percentage of graduate students who are female has not yet [by 1970] reached the 1921 figure":[3] in 1921 women accounted for just over 25% of the "post-graduate" enrolment in Canadian universities, but in 1950, their enrolments had reached a low point of approximately 15%. By the late 1960s women still accounted for less than 20% of all students in graduate programs; it was not until the mid-1970s that the graduate enrolments of women reached the levels reported for the early 1920s (in 1973-74 women accounted for 26% of graduate enrolments).[4] In the next decade, however, women's graduate enrolment increased by half again so that, by the mid-1980s, altogether 40% of graduate students in Canada were women (this includes both master's and doctoral level students in all programs).[5] In this same period there were steady gains in undergraduate enrolment. By the late 1960s women had doubled their 1921 representation among undergraduates (moving from 16.3% of all undergraduate enrolments in 1921 to 34.2% in 1967-68);[6] by 1981-82 they were close to 50%,[7] and by 1987-88 they made up just over 50% of full-time undergraduate students in Canada.[8] In 1992 the Canadian Federation of University Women could report that "females now constitute 56.1% of undergraduates."[9]

The proportion of degrees awarded women has kept pace with these increases in their presence in the training "pipeline." In fact, women show slightly higher completion rates than men in many areas. For example, women have received over 50% of the bachelors' degrees awarded each year since 1981.[10] And while the Royal Commission had to report, in 1970, that "since 1955, the percentage of post-graduate degrees earned by women has remained fairly constant" (at approximately 20% of masters' degrees, and 8% of doctorates),[11] these figures had more than doubled by the early 1980s. In 1982 women were awarded 40% of all masters' degrees, and just under 25% of all doctorates.[12] These increases have continued: in 1989 women earned 45% of masters' degrees and 30% of doctorates;[13] and by 1992 these figures had risen again, to 47.8% and 33.2%, respectively.[14]

As Statistics Canada describes these trends in 1990, they represent more than a fourfold increase in the number of women awarded PhDs since 1971, in a period when "the total awarded to men increased by only 15%."[15] This picture looks very much the same for post-secondary education in the United States where, for example, women earned over a third (35.4%) of all PhDs awarded in the United States in 1986.[16] Note, however, that these aggregate patterns may be profoundly misleading when interpreted as evidence that "women" in general have improved their status in academia. There is very little information available that would make it possible to determine whether these aggregate trends hold for women identified as members of "minority" groups including, e.g., visible and ethnic or cultural minorities, immigrant women, First Nations women, lesbians, women with disabilities, or any other category of women who may be multiply disadvantaged in post-secondary educational institutions.[17]

Beyond the Training "Pipeline"

By the mid-1980s, then, the advocates of equity for women in post-secondary education could take pride that their considerable labours were bearing fruit. Dramatic increases were reported in the rates at which women were entering, and successfully completing, university programs at all levels. And in Canada, at long last, it seemed that these gains would be protected and extended by equity regulations at a federal level. The "Act Respecting Employment Equity" and the Federal Contractors Program, instituted in 1986,[18] promised not only clear endorsement of existing initiatives, but also a strong incentive for the vigorous development of equity programs in a number of large institutions, including educational institutions, that had hitherto resisted them. Significantly, this legislation grounds equity principles in our Charter of Rights and Freedoms.[19] Legislation comparable to this (although not so grounded) had begun to appear in the United States more than 20 years ago and despite the challenges it has faced — on grounds of the rights of individuals against "reverse discrimination" — it has been instrumental in eliminating policies and practices that entrench formal discrimination along gender lines, and establishing a number of highly visible "affirmative action" programs.[20]

At the same time, however, there was increasing scepticism about confident assertions (perhaps more typical of the 1970s than the 1980s) that it was just a matter of time before women would work their way through the system: the pronounced male dominance at senior ranks in academia reflected historic, not contemporary, practices; the gender balance would shift "naturally" as jobs came available and the entrenched professoriate was replaced by a new generation of graduates in which women enjoyed much higher levels of representation than ever before. There was growing concern that despite the gains made, especially in getting women into the training "pipeline," they remained disproportionately under-employed, under-compensated, and concentrated in lower-level and temporary or term positions, both within and outside academia.

In the United States, where legal mechanisms and institutional programs for change had been established relatively early, national statistics testified to persistently low rates of representation of women among university and college faculty. Women constituted 26.9% of all full-time faculty in United States academic institutions in 1981-82, compared to 22.7% in the mid-1970s,[21] but they were still concentrated in the lower ranks. Just 10.7% of full professors were women in 1981-82, an increase of .4% since 1974-75, indeed, an increase of just 1.2% since 1958-59.[22] By contrast, women showed their most substantial gains in the lowest, untenured, and untenurable ranks; in 1981-82 they constituted 36% of assistant professors, 47.5% of lecturers, and 51.7% of instructors in United States universities and colleges.[23] M.K. Chamberlain notes one study which concluded that women held non-tenure track posts "almost twice as frequently as men."[24]

In fact, the stability of patterns of distribution, despite changes in the overall representation of women among faculty, is especially clear when you consider the proportion of women faculty who held *tenured* positions in United States post-secondary institutions in the decade 1976-86; the average was 47.8%, with an anomalous high of 53% in 1979-80 and a variance of three percentage points above or below this average in other years. In the same period, between a third and half again as many men were tenured (68%) with a similar pattern of variance over the decade.[25] Although, as many critics of "affirmative action" have been quick to note, women were being appointed to tenurable (i.e., assistant professor) positions at a rate slightly higher than their presence in the relevant pools of trained PhDs,[26] they were still disproportionately absent from tenured positions and were not advancing into more senior positions at the same rates as their male peers. As Chamberlain describes the situation, although "field by field the proportion of women among assistant professors slightly exceeded their presence in the relevant PhD pools ... the rate of promotion for male assistant professors was markedly higher — by more than 50 percent in the case of the top 50 institutions."[27]

These statistics are indicative of what has come to be known as the "revolving door" syndrome. Even when women do make it through the door and begin to establish themselves in a field in substantial numbers, their career paths and levels of compensation and recognition are often very different from those of their male peers. Commenting on library science, where women have a strong presence, Phenix observes that "there is no place, no institution, no level of service, no type of library, and no association in which women are found at the top in equal or greater numbers than men, or where women earn salaries greater than or equal to men's."[28] Most important, as concluded by the authors of a National Research Council survey, "objective factors alone cannot account adequately for the career differences which exist between male and female PhD's";[29] the differentials in levels of appointment and rates of advancement (which are reflected in salary) cannot be attributed in any straightforward way to women's productivity or patterns of participation in academia.[30] Reflecting on the cumulative effects of these patterns of practice in 1982, Lattin observes that,

> Although the number of women faculty grew steadily during the last half of the 1970s decade, that growth stopped abruptly last year, and the percentage of full-time faculty who are women dropped by a full point [at her large university in "mid-America"]. This year saw neither an increase nor a decrease. Keep in mind that this levelling-off comes at a time when the national pool of women doctorates is still growing at a significant rate.[31]

Faced with a "deepening financial crisis in higher education," Lattin predicted that the gains made in the 1970s "will almost surely erode during the next several years," unless the commitment to take strong action which secured these gains, even after the hiring boom was over, is renewed.[32]

This assessment was echoed, four years later, by Simeone, who concludes a general assessment of the progress made by women in academia through the 1960s and 1970s with the observation that, "despite the perception of sweeping changes and dramatic progress, the status of academic women has not improved substantially since Jessie Bernard published *Academic Women* in 1964."[33] To be more specific, "despite [substantial] growth in the pool of qualified women, there has not been much change over the last two decades in the overall representation of women within the faculty ranks."[34] By the mid-1980s women were still "more likely than men to be unemployed, under-employed, or in part-time or nontenure track positions";[35] they were concentrated in less-prestigious institutions; they showed substantially higher rates of attrition;[36] they advanced through the ranks more slowly and, at the same rank, were paid less than their male counterparts.[37]

Although equity legislation came later in Canada, there had been a great deal of research and activism on equity issues for women, the results of which led many to similar conclusions by the mid-1980s. By 1984, the authors of a comprehensive federal report on the status of women in academic contexts, Symons and Page, could draw on literally dozens of institutional and disciplinary analyses of the status of women in the Canadian educational system; they had to hand "at least 32 major university studies, as well as additional supplementary reports" that were commissioned in the 1970s and early 1980s.[38] And yet, for all this outpouring of information and concern, Symons and Page conclude that long-entrenched patterns of gender inequity in rates of advancement, distribution across faculty ranks, and compensation had persisted in Canadian institutions, even as women swelled the ranks of students and the qualified academic candidate pools. In 20 years (from 1960 to 1980), the proportion of full professors who were women had increased just over half a percent (to 4.8%). Perhaps more telling, the proportion of male faculty with doctorates who were full professors was 41%, between twice and three times the proportion for women (16% in 1980-81).[39] Quoting Statistics Canada, Symons and Page report that "in a profession that has a high proportion of males, this [the overall 15.5% proportion of full-time teaching staff at Canadian universities who were women in 1980-81] represents little gain over the ratio of 11 per cent that was recorded 22 years earlier, 1958-59, an increase of 5 percentage points."[40] They conclude that this record of relative stasis in faculty ranks, compared with dramatic gains for women in training programs and among degree recipients, reflects a lamentable squandering of resources:

> One can only conclude that there is a large pool of well-qualified and highly trained talent in Canada that is not being effectively utilized by the universities. One must also conclude that, even though women have become a significant proportion of the university student population, a much lower proportion of women graduates is being encouraged to enter, or being allowed to participate in, university teaching and research.[41]

These worries have since been reiterated in a number of contexts. The Canadian Federation of University Women has recently reported that, despite heartening gains — in 1992 women constituted well over half the undergraduate students, and close to half the master's level students in Canada — the "conundrum" remains that they account for "only 33.2% of Doctoral graduates, ... leading to an even more modest complement of women professors in Canadian universities."[42]

Variants on this pattern are noted in any number of field- and institution-specific reports on the status of women in Canadian universities and colleges. For example, the authors of the 1991 publication, *Women in Science and Engineering*, report a pattern of loss of women from the training "pipeline" which parallels closely that described by Sheila Widnall in her 1988 Presidential Lecture to the American Association for the Advancement of Science (AAAS):[43] "Although the percentage of women earning graduate degrees has increased overall since 1975 . . . the more advanced the degree, the smaller the proportion of female recipients. This is particularly problematic in the natural sciences and engineering."[44]

Even more worrisome are findings reported in the mid-1980s that bear on the employment of those women who do survive through to the completion of advanced degrees. In a 1985 report on the status of Canadian women PhD scientists, Anne Innis Dagg concludes that "although jobs for all highly trained scientists are in short supply [from the second half of the 1970s through the mid-1980s], women particularly have had a difficult time finding permanent jobs. . . . The percentage of women with PhDs form a pool that seems to be at least twice as great as the percentage of women hired as professors."[45]

Residual Questions

It was at this juncture—in the mid-1980s—that the authors of various studies, and reviews of studies, on the status of women began to express a concern that the patterns of under-representation and job segregation they confronted again and again could no longer be explained in terms of a pipeline problem; *viz.*, that women had simply not been in the system long enough to improve their representation as university faculty. Certainly the economic and political crises which secondary education has faced in the last decade, and the demographics of the existing professoriate has limited the rate of possible change. There is a sad irony here: for the most part affirmative action programs in the United States were instituted at the end of the post-war hiring boom; in Canada they were formalized a generation later, in the 1980s, as the prospects for hiring were undercut by a recession-driven economy that sharply limited public funding to universities and colleges. The inroads women made in academia through the 1970s were realized under conditions of deepening constraint which, by the mid-1980s, had been compounded by hiring freezes and cutbacks, precipitated by worsening economic conditions and increasingly conservative political policies. While this may explain why increases in overall representation were painfully slow and levelled off through the 1980s, it does not explain why the rates of advancement and compensation of women who *do* get jobs remain consistently below those of their male peers. The real question is why, as Lattin puts it, "many women faculty and students, who themselves have reaped the benefits of the changes in the 1970s, continue to feel like second-class citizens in academe"[46] and, indeed, why a great many women continue to *be* second-class citizens in a quite literal sense, where they remain disproportionately clustered in the lower and most vulnerable ranks of academic employment.

II. Chilly Climate Research

In order to answer residual questions about why women's gains seemed limited, those concerned with equity issues in post-secondary education increasingly focused, through the 1980s, on the cumulative effects of "environmental" factors: the pervasive culture of the workplaces that women confront when they move through the academic pipeline and to which they seek access as trained professionals. The first of three related factors that Lattin cites in explaining a pervasive sense of dissatisfaction and vulnerability is that "in general the attitudes of male administrators and faculty have not kept pace with the changes the 1970s brought about and . . . women are constantly made aware of this."[47] Women find themselves trivialized, ignored, the butt of sexual joking, their successes attributed to others or to luck, their records of service and academic achievements very differently valued and evaluated than those of male peers, and so on.[48] Symons and Page argue, more generally, and with reference to the Canadian situation, that although "the reasons for the low proportion of women in university teaching are, no doubt, many and varied," the "data" resulting from analyses of their representation in Canadian universities "point inescapably to the conclusion that conscious and unconscious discrimination arising from habit and attitude continues to be a major factor."[49]

Almost a decade later (in 1992; Symons and Page's report appeared in 1983), the authors of the Canadian Federation of University Women report on *Women in Universities* observe that,

> The acknowledged inequitable situation of women in universities is a very complex and multi-faceted problem. It has only recently been recognized that factors such as the 'chilly climate', demanding family responsibilities and the subtle lack of recognition of women's scholarship contribute to the . . . conundrum [of limited gains for women at higher ranks].[50]

Clearly, as Simeone describes it, the "individual and institutional sexism that is woven into the fabric of academic life"[51] continues to operate, perhaps less blatantly than in the 1950s and 1960s but with no less significant effect. It was in 1982 and 1984 that the Association of American Colleges (AAC) produced their reports on "chilly climate" experiences for women students, followed in 1986 by their first report on the experiences of women faculty, staff, administrators, and students, and in 1988 by reports on the status and experience of Black and Hispanic women in academia.[52] The authors of a wide range of other studies have since taken up these issues, turning attention from the statistical evidence of women's continued second-class status to fine-grained experiential studies of the "micro-inequities" that help maintain them in this status, illustrating the forms these take, the mechanisms by which they operate, and the cost they exact both individually and socially.

These analyses often presuppose a distinction between explicit, formally institutionalized policies of discrimination and a range of informal practices and implicit policies which, despite their relative subtlety and the fact that they may not be intended as harmful, do systematically disadvantage women relative to men, members of "minority" groups relative to "dominant" groups, and most especially, all those who find themselves caught in cross-cutting, and multiply reinforcing categories of difference. Such practices and attitudes, which may be referred to as "standing conditions," constitute the essential infrastructure of systemic discrimination and are continuous with (indeed, they derive from) institutionalized sexism, racism, classism, homophobia, ablism, and other oppressive "isms" that pervade the wider culture. Despite variability in the specific forms they take, these conditions seem routinely to be created and maintained through the interdependent mechanisms of stereotyping, exclusion, and devaluation of any who are perceived to be "different" from prevailing norms. In particular, the literature on the chilly climate encountered by women in academia documents how such practices serve to isolate and undermine women even when (or, indeed, especially when) formal barriers to their employment and advancement have been eliminated.

Among the most influential of these studies and reports is Widnall's Presidential Lecture delivered to the AAAS in 1988.[53] She argued that environmental conditions must be recognized as contributing to the disproportionately high rates at which qualified women, and foreign and "minority" students, choose against graduate programs in engineering and the natural sciences or drop out of them midway through their graduate careers. Her motivation was quite explicitly a concern that, with declining numbers of United States citizens in the candidate pools qualified for advanced training in science and technology, the United States simply cannot afford to lose the women and minorities it manages to recruit and train through the master's level in science and engineering programs (the point at which they drop out of the training pipeline).[54] In the AAC reports produced in the mid-1980s, Roberta Hall and Bernice Sandler cast a wider net so far as academic fields, levels of training, and institutions are concerned, although their focus is narrower with respect to foreign and "minority" students. They document, in rich detail, the ways in which the "chilly climate" for women manifests itself on American campuses, cross-cutting standard status and disciplinary boundaries; they report the experiences of women staff, students, administrators, and faculty from a wide range of academic contexts in the United

States.[55] Similarly, in a book-length study of equity cases and climate issues, Nadya Aisenberg and Mona Harrington describe how "sex discrimination" works, "especially when it [is] not blatant," in an effort to address the question why "disproportionately more women than men were ending up with peripheral jobs or none at all."[56] They provide compelling support for the thesis that "the common patterns" they identify, both in the experience of women who have been "deflected" from academic careers and in that of women who hold tenured positions, "consist of the play in all women's lives of social norms that are constructed to cast women in subordinate, supportive roles both in their private and their public lives," enforcing for women in academia the status of "outsiders."[57] Despite the rhetoric of meritocracy, and formal (legal) commitments to equality in both education and employment, the "old norms" defining women's roles and capabilities in the society at large set up incongruities and tensions that constitute insuperable barriers for many women who seek graduate training and employment as university faculty.

Similar themes emerge in a wide range of related studies generated through the 1980s, both published and unpublished.[58] Reports on sexual harassment and safety issues for women on North American campuses routinely acknowledge that these are just the "tip of an iceberg";[59] as Osborne has recently argued, they arise and persist in the context of a deeply entrenched network of sexist practices and attitudes.[60] Similarly, workplace environment figures as a central concern in analyses of the status and advancement of women in non-academic contexts, especially in those dealing with the "glass ceiling" phenomenon that reinforces inequity in the higher levels of corporate structures.[61] Although many see universities and colleges as progressive institutions, their traditions of "academic freedom" seem increasingly to be used against women and "minorities," for example, protecting racist and sexist "speech" and making these institutions breeding grounds for backlash politics.[62]

What the authors of these various climate studies identify as chilly-making factors are a "host of subtle personal and social barriers" which often operate "below the level of awareness of both men and women,"[63] or, when recognized, are perceived as " 'trivial' or minor annoyances," "micro-inequities" whose pervasiveness and cumulative effects are ignored.[64] On my reading of this literature, the specific examples and cases described fall into four main categories of practice. The most basic is that of uncritically imposing stereotypic assumptions about women's roles and capabilities (Aisenberg and Harrington's "old norms"), which all too frequently results in patterns of interaction by which women faculty are systematically isolated and devalued. When women challenge these practices and the assumptions that inform them, they may find themselves revictimized, often through an intensification of the very practices they challenge; they face overt hostility and explicit exclusion and marginalization, where they may earlier have confronted only vague disinterest and dismissiveness. The sorts of practice typically documented in these studies are as follows.[65]

1. *Stereotyping*: the assignment of women to gender-stereotyped roles (often housekeeping, hostessing, nurturing roles), the sexualization of these roles and of the women in them, and the systematic treatment of women differently from men of the same status, in the same roles. For example, women may find themselves subject to a "double standard"; compared with male incumbents in the positions or roles they occupy, their strengths and weaknesses are differentially assessed in ways that reflect the assumption of standard gender stereotypes about women's capabilities and dispositions (e.g., a man may be described as "productive" or "assertive" when the same record or behaviour in a woman is characterized as "busy" or "aggressive," to take two well-worn examples). Similarly, women routinely encounter differential patterns of address and interaction that emphasize the status of men in their positions or roles, but diminish that of comparably placed women. One frequently described practice is that of addressing all the women in a meeting or workplace by their first names while men of the same status are referred to by surname and title.

2. *Devaluation*: the related tendency to explain away women's successes, treating them as an exception or attributing them to circumstance, luck, or the support of a male associate, while failure is accepted as the norm, "all you could expect of a woman." In effect, entrenched stereotypes overwhelm any evidence that counters normative, generalizing assumptions about women, including evidence of differences among women. Women find their credibility and the value or import of their work questioned more readily than that of a man, consistent with widely cited findings that scholarly papers and oral presentations are all routinely accorded greater authority if credited to a man rather than a woman.[66] And they find their authority and expertise routinely discounted by those who are their peers and juniors as well as those senior to them. By extension of this, anything identified as a "woman's issue" is assumed to be of concern only to women, and often to be all that is of concern to women, whatever their record of activism on other issues.

3. *Exclusion*: the isolation of women through standard mixed-gender conversational and interaction patterns. Women routinely find that they are interrupted more frequently than men or by those junior to them (male or female), that their remarks are ignored or attributed to others, and that they are relegated to facilitating, "conversational housekeeping," roles.[67] They may also be systematically alienated through the use of sexist humour, and excluded from informal working groups or social interaction in a professional context (the locker-room and lonely lunch syndrome).

4. *Revictimization*: the targeting of individual women, and supportive colleagues of either gender, who speak out against practices of gender-specific exclusion, devaluation, and stereotyping. These responses take many (often mutually contradictory) forms. On one hand, those who draw attention to climate issues frequently find that the problems they describe are simply denied. Those who feel they have been called to account may insist that such problems could not exist in their workplace because of a good record on these or related issues or, indeed, because they maintain that they themselves have never experienced or witnessed practices that stereotype, devalue, or exclude others. The alleged problems must, therefore, exist in the minds of the beholders, as imaginative, paranoid, or malicious constructions. On the other hand, if accounts of chilly-making attitudes and practices are credited with some accuracy, it may be insisted that they are not (or cannot reasonably be considered to be) disadvantaging in any serious or systematic way. No harm was intended, therefore claims to have suffered harm are entirely unwarranted; those who object that they have been undermined and marginalized are simply (stereotypically) hysterical, thin-skinned, naive, and humourless. Even when harm is acknowledged to have been done, the victims may find themselves blamed for having brought the difficulties they describe upon themselves. In short, the problems identified by critics of a chilly climate are reconstructed as "their" problems in various senses, and they are, as a consequence, further isolated and devalued.

Time and again, those documenting the chilly climate for women in academia observe that it is precisely because these practices are highly localized, and may seem trivial taken on their own that often they are "not seen as discriminat[ory] [either by those who perpetrate them or those who are victimized by them] even though they do make women uncomfortable and put them at a disadvantage."[68] It is the persistence and recurrence of such practices which ensures that they will have non-trivial consequences — that they will reinforce the cycle of progressively eroded confidence, lowered expectations, and compromised ambitions described by Widnall.[69] It is also precisely because of the relative invisibility of these practices that they are so widespread, and so insidious, both in eroding the confidence and capacity of individual women to participate fully in academic settings and in undermining the institutional programs designed to promote equity for them.

This literature on "the chilly climate for women in colleges and universities" has been invaluable in drawing attention to the workplace environment as one fundamental source of the inequity that persists for women in many contexts. It is seriously and pervasively flawed, however. For all the differences in context and perspective it embraces, the contributors to this literature rarely consider the ways in which gender inequities are constituted in and by other dimensions of disadvantage that are widely institutionalized in North America. The experiences they describe are normatively White, middle class, heterosexual, able-bodied, and for the most part, those of relatively young students and faculty; they are the experiences of women who are privileged in every respect but gender. While such women may well predominate in academia — any number of critics have called attention to ways in which equity initiatives serve those who are already privileged — it cannot be assumed that their experience defines a generically *gendered* climate. Their experience is not simply or typically that of "women" but that of women situated in a very specific relationship to the whole range of systems of privilege that constitute universities and colleges as elite institutions. As such, it cannot be assumed that the experience reported by such women, or reported in terms of categories and norms specific to them, can be generalized across other institutionalized systems of difference. There may be many points of contact, but certainly there are important differences that are not explored in the literature on chilly climate issues in academic contexts which appeared in the mid-1980s and influenced the projects we undertook at Western.

These concerns are by no means new or unique to chilly climate research. Throughout the 1980s there was considerable discussion of the ways academic environments embody and reproduce not only racism and classism but, more specifically, racist sexism and heterosexist (homophobic) sexism, for example.[70] More generally, by the mid- to late-1980s the case had been powerfully made, again and again, that in none of its manifestations could "gender" ("sex/gender systems," gendered institutions, categories, identities, ideology, practices) be understood in monolithic terms, as "cross-cutting" or in any other sense autonomous from the range of other institutionalized oppressions that structure North American society.[71] These critical analyses make it clear that the "default assumptions"[72] which may inform the treatment of women who are identified as White will be very different from those affecting women who are perceived to be "of colour," or are identified more specifically as "Black" (African), Asian, or Native, for example. Racialist stereotypes project, for diverse women, quite different expectations about their capabilities, their sensibilities, their credibility. It is also clear that the nature and implications of such stereotypes vary greatly depending on a woman's age, and on assumptions about her class background, her sexual orientation, whether she has disabilities of specific sorts, what her religious or ethnic/cultural affiliation is, whether she is Canadian or in some sense "foreign." Taken together, these stereotypes entail that women will be sexualized in very different ways, that what counts as safe or appropriate (feminine) roles may vary a great deal, that we will have access to quite different communication networks, will have different opportunities for "integration" into the workplace, and will experience very different sorts of exclusion. No doubt stereotypes that differentiate women along these various lines will also make a difference to the kind of shock, disbelief, and anger expressed in reactions that revictimize those who speak out against a multiply chilly climate; for example, reactions against those who identify the effects of unacknowledged racism (or sexist racism) seem, if anything, more virulent than those that target critics of sexism (for example, see chapter 8).

Given that the literature on "difference" was well established in feminist contexts by the mid- to late-1980s, it is profoundly disheartening to see, in retrospect, how little its insights impinged on the analyses of climate issues for women that became influential in Canadian and United States post-secondary institutions through this period. It is especially disheartening that the chilly climate projects undertaken at Western did little to break this pattern. A great deal of important work has since appeared which further illustrates the limitations of exclusively gender-focused studies of climate and demonstrates how much richer are analyses that take seriously "multiple jeopardy" as an integral and structural feature of educational institutions.[73]

III. Western: An Institutional Case Study

It was with a growing awareness of the challenges posed by the workplace environment, albeit conceived in narrowly gendered terms, that a diverse group of faculty at the University of Western Ontario took up the various projects on chilly climate issues for women that are reported and discussed in the chapters that follow. Like many universities in Canada and the United States in the last few decades, Western had had its share of studies, reports, policy proposals, and initiatives in the areas of pay equity, sexual harassment, and employment equity for women.[74] These included a "matched-pair" comparison and pay equity settlement for those faculty women who sought review of their salaries in 1974, the institution of a sexual harassment policy in 1984, the presentation that year of the *Smith Report* (discussed in more detail in chapter 3) on the status of women faculty which included a widely publicized proposal for creating 25 new positions for women across the University,[75] and the approval of a maternity leave policy in 1985. In short, Western was by no means inactive on the equity front; certainly it was no slower or more recalcitrant than other major universities in Canada, or than public universities in the United States of comparable size and with comparably strong profiles in research and in graduate and professional training.[76]

On the other hand, Western was not a strikingly precocious leader in realizing equity for women. There have not been changes in the numbers or status of women at Western that would single it out as especially progressive in any of its relevant comparison groups. The proposals put forward by the *Smith Report* were adopted in such a compromised form that they resulted in the creation of no new positions for women, although provisions were made to facilitate the hiring of excellent women candidates should a department take the initiative in recruiting them and applying for this support. Despite strong interest and a high level of scholarly activity in feminist research and women's studies, no Women's Studies program was seriously considered before 1984. It took two separate proposals before a program was approved in the spring of 1988 and, in both cases, the catalyst was Western's Caucus on Women's Issues, an ad hoc organization consisting of women faculty, staff, and graduate students that had sponsored the publication of a brochure informally advertising courses in Women's Studies since 1981. The two Sexual Harassment Advisor positions proved extremely demanding; turnover was high, they were often unstaffed or under-staffed and, given the demand of the case loads, less and less public education was undertaken as time went on. In addition, the original policy precluded any public reporting of the work done by the advisors, so the University community remained uninformed about the reputedly large and growing demand for their services; a review of the policy was undertaken in the academic year 1989-90. The provisions for maternity leave provide no replacement funding to the unit in which a woman works, so, in many contexts, the local pressures against women taking such a leave are considerable. And, finally, no mechanisms had been established for dealing with the range of problems beyond sexual harassment that women might face in the University. Indeed, until Western joined the Federal Contractors Program in 1988, its administration had issued no institutional statement of commitment to employment equity and had supported no ongoing documentation of the status of women, much less an office or program designed to address equity issues on campus.

Nevertheless, in 1986 Western was nominated for, and won, the Ontario Women's Directorate (OWD) Employment Equity Award; co-recipients that year were London Life, Consumer's Gas, and Ontario Hydro. This award, and especially the fanfare with which it was presented and publicized, came as something of a shock to many of those women faculty and staff who had not been served by the one-time pay equity settlement of 1974, who had witnessed the whittling down of the *Smith Report,* who continued to bear the brunt of resistance to maternity leave, who were then beginning *again* the task of drafting a proposal for a Women's Studies Program, and who were painfully aware that Western's administration had made no official statement of commitment to employment equity.

The *Backhouse Report*

It was in response to the receipt of this award that Constance Backhouse undertook an historical analysis of Western's track record in employment
equity for women, "An Historical Perspective: Reflections on the Western
Employment Equity Award" (see chapter 3). She observes, at the outset,
that Western had not "since 1973 . . . bettered the provincial or national average for percentage of women on faculty,"[77] although its record in recruiting
and retaining women faculty was cited as a factor in its receipt of the OWD
award. Perhaps, she suggested, Western might prove to have offered wom-
en an especially supportive environment in the past; the authors of the
Smith Report had concluded that their investigations had turned up no
"overt evidence of discrimination against women in the University's policies and procedures relating to appointments, promotion, and tenure."[78]
She released her report in April 1988, detailing in it a number of cases of discrimination against women, some of which reflected explicit policies of discrimination.

The *Backhouse Report*, as it came to be known, had special significance,
appearing when it did,[79] because it coincided with a growing awareness
that Western would soon be forced to establish policy and procedures to
deal with gender discrimination if it were to meet the Federal Contractors
Guidelines. The sense that change might be imminent was heightened by
the publication, within a week of the time the *Backhouse Report* was released,
of a *Handbook on Employment Equity for Women* prepared by the Committee
on the Status of Women of the Council of Ontario Universities (COU).[80] This
Handbook set out a series of concrete recommendations for action that would
carry universities beyond mere compliance with the Federal Contractors
Guidelines; many of these recommendations addressed issues and concerns
raised in the *Backhouse Report*. While the media coverage outside the immediate context of London and Western tended to confuse the two documents,
in the local press the COU *Handbook* was described as having substantially
"strengthened" Backhouse's findings, ratifying them and reinforcing her
call for action.[81]

Not surprisingly, under the circumstances, the *Backhouse Report* generated intense discussion within the broad constituency of concerned women
who attended Backhouse's initial presentation of her results and several
meetings that were subsequently convened by the Women's Caucus; these
drew a large complement of women in professional-managerial and staff
positions as well as faculty women. While many of Backhouse's recommendations were controversial — especially those having to do with a review of
tenure that she proposed for faculty, and the specific goals she proposed for
an equity program at Western — there was wide agreement on at least two
points. One was that her summary of the statistical and historical record

confirmed that Western had a very long way to go where equity for women was concerned, notwithstanding the 1986 OWD Award. And the second was that where good faith gestures had proven ineffectual in the past, stronger action must now be taken. In particular, there was a concern that the opportunity to make real change afforded by the Federal Contractors Program should not be squandered; every effort should be made to ensure that the institutional response not be limited to "mere compliance."[82]

These discussions culminated in an open meeting convened by the Women's Caucus on June 13, 1988, and attended by several hundred employees.[83] At this meeting a series of resolutions was presented. The first endorsed Backhouse's findings. Several others urged that the University administration move immediately to make equity initiatives a priority. They called for the creation of a Standing Committee on Employment Equity with a mandate to establish the information base necessary to assess the status of women on campus in a number of employment categories, to produce a public report for discussion by the Senate and Board of Governors, and to put in place measures for improving the status of women at Western and for monitoring their situation on an ongoing basis.[84] These resolutions were drafted as a petition which was signed by 260 members of the University community; they represented all categories of employees in 19 different departments and administrative units. This petition was presented to Western's President in June 1988, within a week of the meeting.

The petition drew no response from the administration. Nevertheless, the momentum it established carried forward into the fall when the Women's Caucus convened two further open meetings to discuss a proposed "baseline for evaluating employment equity at Western" which the Caucus executive hoped might provide a framework for ongoing Caucus input on equity issues as they affect women.[85] Based on a close reading of the COU *Handbook* and the Federal Contractors Guidelines, this baseline called for a clear "communication of commitment" to equity on the part of the administration and for a demonstration, in practice, of a vigorous "institutional commitment" to change. It also identified a number of specific initiatives that would be necessary if the University were to realize the two central goals of employment equity (as characterized by the Federal Contractors Guidelines and the COU *Handbook*): realizing equity in the representation of women at all ranks and in all areas of employment in the university, and eliminating the "chilly climate" created by practices that effectively disenfranchise and marginalize women in these work environments. As these initiatives indicate, the *Backhouse Report* had very effectively mobilized Western's women's community and its supporters; the grass roots response to her report made it clear that status quo responses were no longer acceptable.

Administrative Responses and Initiatives

Not surprisingly, the administration was much less vocal in response to the *Backhouse Report* than members of the constituencies to which it was most relevant. Within a month of the time Backhouse presented her report publicly, and after several public discussions of the *Report* had taken place, the Provost announced that Western had "agreed to become a participant in the Federal Contractors Program" and was thereby committed to "creating and monitoring an Employment Equity Plan."[86] In the media coverage that this development occasioned in late May, the Provost reported that the President had actually signed the certificate of commitment on March 17, but that announcement had been delayed several months "because the complex and far reaching implications of employment equity required detailed study before we could properly explain them."[87]

He also indicated that an Employment Equity Officer had been appointed (although the incumbent was not identified), and summarized the requirements of the Federal Contractors Program which this Officer would be responsible for meeting. With this public statement the senior administration indicated a commitment, in prospect at least, to address many of the demands for action put forward in the June petition presented to the President by the Women's Caucus. Nevertheless, as indicated, there was no acknowledgement of the petition, and in particular, no acknowledgement of the strong endorsement it had given the *Backhouse Report*.

When the President did comment publicly on the *Backhouse Report*, in mid-June 1988, he addressed it in conjunction with the COU *Handbook* in a discussion that was framed as a justification of the 1986 OWD Award.[88] He responded to the "vigorous discussion" occasioned by publication of the COU *Handbook* and the *Backhouse Report*, urging that "Western's record on this issue [employment equity] should be judged within the context of a full historical review."[89] To this end he recapitulated the list of achievements — the various advisory committees, task forces, studies, reports, recommendations, and policies that the University had produced since 1972 — that had figured most prominently in media coverage of the original award two years earlier.[90] He made no mention of the questions Backhouse had raised about this record and offered no rebuttal to the arguments or evidence that led her to conclude that the award was perhaps premature. While acknowledging that "in general" greater progress had been realized in the "professional/managerial area" (perhaps admitting that the record was not all it could be on the faculty front[91]), the President concluded his discussion of the "Pursuit of Equity at Western" with the confident assertion that, "as the record indicates, Western has made substantial progress in the area of employment equity as it relates to women."[92]

With this the senior administration adopted what was, in our view, a stance of studied disinterest in the findings of the *Backhouse Report*. In more informal discussions of the *Report*, a common response was that even if Backhouse's historical account were accurate, the overtly discriminatory policies she had identified and the deeply sexist attitudes and practices that had been reported to her surely all belonged to a bygone era. Western had by now moved well beyond the idiosyncrasies of President Fox (who had systematically forced women to retire at age 60, five years earlier than men), and the misfortunes of women like Madge Macklin (who never advanced beyond the rank of Assistant Professor, despite an exemplary teaching and research record established in the 1920s-40s).[93] Taken together, these responses deflected attention from the issues Backhouse had raised, particularly those having to do with what she believed were persistent (historically rooted) features of the workplace environments in which many faculty women find themselves. Although, in early May, Backhouse had observed optimistically that "we have in place now at Western an administration that is relatively young, relatively new, that has already given some indication that they're sensitive and concerned,"[94] by mid-June, when the Women's Caucus had presented its resolution, she expressed some disappointment. At that time Backhouse still had received no direct response to the *Report* from the administration, a pattern repeated in its treatment of the Caucus' June petition.

While the institutional initiatives following from Pedersen's commitment to join the Federal Contractors Program were encouraging in many respects, this (non-)response to the *Backhouse Report* and to the Caucus resolution was deeply troubling for many who had been actively involved in the Caucus discussions and were following the formulation of an Employment Equity Committee and Program with keen interest. In the discussions that unfolded through the fall and winter of 1988-89, Caucus members reiterated, time and again, the central point that these new initiatives should take seriously the lessons Backhouse and others had drawn from previous failures. In particular, they insisted that it would be crucial to set clear equity goals and not leave improvements to the vagaries of well-intentioned but easily sabotaged procedures.[95] Most important, they were concerned that these initiatives should not be limited to formal measures which would leave untouched the workplace environments that stubbornly reproduce inequities. In this they reaffirmed not only Backhouse's assessment, but the recommendations of the COU *Handbook*.

The *Chilly Climate Report*

One outcome of the discussions that followed the release of the *Backhouse Report* was a strong sense of the need to ensure that climate issues would be high on the agenda of any new employment equity program at Western; this was a central feature of the briefs and resolutions prepared by women on campus for the President's Standing Committee for Employment Equity during the following two years, especially those presented by the Women's Caucus. In this spirit, Backhouse had urged that "a series of public hearings [be] launched on campus this fall (1988)";[96] the original idea, reiterated in Caucus discussions, was to create a forum in which women could make public presentation of their *current* experiences, addressing directly the question of whether the conditions Backhouse described were, in fact, a thing of the past. While this proposal drew no response from the administration, it was the catalyst for the project undertaken by Constance Backhouse, Roma Harris, Gillian Michell, and Alison Wylie, reported in the *Chilly Climate Report* that appeared a year and a half later (included here as chapter 4).

We began with informal inquiries among various of our colleagues, asking whether they thought chilly climate issues were a concern at Western, whether they had experiences like those described in the recently published Association of American Colleges reports,[97] and what they thought we might usefully do to articulate these problems if they perceived them to be important. The response to these first tentative inquiries was overwhelming and, in retrospect, very much like what Aisenberg and Harrington report when, in describing how and why they initiated their research, they noted a striking consistency among the stories they heard, beginning with those told by women who attended an initial meeting of the Alliance of Independent Scholars in Cambridge (Massachusetts):

> Women who had arrived with the sense that the drama and loss in their own academic careers was more or less unique, felt a shock of recognition, hearing their experience in the lives of others previously unknown to them. It seemed clear, as women of highly divergent backgrounds and fields told stories with strikingly similar plot turns, that we were hearing about a generalized experience.[98]

Among those we spoke to early in the summer of 1988, even the most successful, working in what they regarded as supportive environments, described patterns of differential treatment that they found isolating and devaluing to varying degrees, and that closely paralleled the experiences of women who found themselves seriously undermined and marginalized. When we asked whether we should undertake to arrange public hearings as a briefing for those who would be responsible for Western's employment program, the reaction was univocal. None of those we spoke to initially, on an informal basis, were prepared to make public statements about their experiences. The fear that they would face anger, misunderstanding, and possibly direct reprisals if they spoke out was very strong, even among those most secure and well situated. The outcome of these discussions was the alternative suggestion that we interview more widely and write a report that would summarize the experiences described to us by women currently at the University without identifying specific individuals or locales.[99]

As the plan to write such a report began to take shape, we broadened the scope of our interviewing. Each of us took responsibility for several academic units and interviewed as many women in them as could be contacted during the summer of 1988. Ultimately we interviewed women in 12 departments or faculties without departmental structure. These academic units were chosen to represent a range of disciplines and environments; they included departments in the Faculties of Arts, Social Science, and Science, and several professional schools, as well as units with good, bad, and indifferent reputations for their treatment of women faculty. In all but two of the units we interviewed two-thirds or more of the tenured and tenurable women faculty, and in the majority of units (eight of 12) we interviewed over half the women holding term and ongoing part-time teaching positions, as well as those in tenured and tenurable positions.

The result was a report released in early November 1989: *The Chilly Climate for Women at Western: A Postscript to the Backhouse Report* (chapter 4). It describes the experiences of 35 women faculty, organized into sections reflecting key stages in an academic career, the major components of a faculty member's professional life, and a number of specific problem areas that were repeatedly identified as of concern to women on campus by those we interviewed. In the final stages of drafting this report we consulted with each woman we had spoken to about any material we planned to include from her interview. For the most part these inquiries resulted in an elaboration of the details we had included, but in some cases women felt too vulnerable to allow descriptions of their situation to be made public and we revised accordingly.[100]

In its final form the *Chilly Climate Report*, as it came to be known, was initially circulated to the women we had interviewed, members of the senior administration, and key representatives of the Employment Equity Committee and Office. We had contacted most of the senior administrators who might not otherwise have known of the project a week or two before the *Report* was released to let them know what to expect.[101]

The *Report* quickly gained much wider circulation, however, because it drew immediate media attention, largely fuelled by the response with which it was greeted by the senior administration of the University.[102]

Despite a favourable response from members of the Employment Equity Committee and Office, the Provost and President publicly denounced the *Report*. They objected that those whose stories were described in it had "hidden behind anonymity," that the accounts themselves were overblown and unrepresentative, that we had put forward generalizing claims about the University as a whole on the basis of an inadequate sample and, most striking, that we had deliberately produced and used the *Report* to create what the President described as a "media event."

There are several ironies here. One is that if the President and his advisors were serious about repudiating any inquiry in which the identity of informants was protected, virtually all social scientific research would be called into question. Not surprisingly, they subsequently retracted the "anonymity" charge. A second irony is that we had been quite careful to say, at several points in the *Report*, that our aim was specifically not to generalize about the University as a whole; we hoped that the task of collecting the information necessary to do this would be undertaken by the President's new Standing Committee for Employment Equity. Our objective was much more modest; the *Report* was framed as a rebuttal to the claim that chilly climate experiences, like those reported by Backhouse in her historical report, were a thing of the past at Western. The 35 women we interviewed did report such experiences as an ongoing feature of their lives at Western; we hoped this would reinforce the argument, made in the COU *Handbook* and elsewhere, that equity programs in university settings do need to address problems rooted in the workplace environment. A third irony is that the charge of having created a "media event" first appeared as the opening statement of a press release that the President read to an assemblage of reporters before a Senate meeting; the occasion was a press conference on the *Chilly Climate Report* called by the Office of the President just a week after the *Report* had been released. The thesis that, in releasing a report on climate issues, we must be seeking notoriety for ourselves, was deeply puzzling to us. Evidently this was the most plausible explanation the senior administration could give for why four faculty women (two untenured at the time we did the interviews) would undertake over 80 hours of interviews and invest many more hours in writing up and editing the *Report*. It suggested that they were not apprised of the work done elsewhere on chilly climate issues, that what we described was utterly new to them, and that therefore the possibility that the experiences we reported were not made up or exaggerated — that they were a matter of deep and genuine concern to us — was simply too implausible to take seriously.

This initial response and the resulting media coverage were followed by several months of intense discussion of the *Report* in letters to the editor, in columns, and in investigative articles published in both local and university newspapers. Many of these were supportive; their authors indicated disbelief that the senior administration should so strongly condemn the authors of the *Report* for protecting the identities of respondents, and so summarily dismiss both the experiences recounted in the *Report* and the issues they raised concerning the status of women in the University. As unpleasant as it was at the time, in retrospect this highly charged reaction to the *Chilly Climate Report* is most instructive. Clearly it had hit a nerve. In the end, the hostile reaction of the President and the Provost did more to illustrate, graphically and publicly, the problems we had hoped to document than any amount of "anonymous" reporting could have done. And in this the President and Provost engaged a much broader constituency in serious discussion of these issues than we had ever imagined reaching.

Perhaps the most gratifying outcome of this "storm of controversy" was the success of a bid for funding to produce an educational video on *The Chilly Climate for Women in Colleges and Universities* that was initiated by the Women's Caucus that year (1989-90).[103] This video was intended to be the sequel to one on sexual harassment, *Breaking the Trust*, that the Caucus produced in 1985-86, and it was quite directly inspired by the findings of the *Chilly Climate Report*.[104]

Despite the critical stand taken by the Provost and the President on the *Report*, the Caucus received strong support for the video proposal from the President's Standing Committee for Employment Equity and from the Employment Equity Office at Western; these bodies ultimately co-sponsored the proposal and were joint producers of the video. When the video project received generous funding from the Ontario Ministry of Colleges and Universities and the Ontario Women's Directorate in April 1990, we felt it constituted a strong public endorsement of the concerns we had raised in the *Chilly Climate Report*. Certainly, it seemed to stand "in stark contrast to the senior administration's dismissal of the issues earlier this year."[105] Western's President responded that "the administration's criticism of the chilly climate report was not a dismissal of chilly climate issues" and was not intended to "take issue with the examples given or the overall goals of the report,"[106] a retrospective view that appeared, in our opinion, to contradict the public statements he had made on several occasions through the winter of 1989-90. Nonetheless, many of those who had been involved in, or had supported, the *Chilly Climate Report* came away from the year hopeful that this response signalled a recognition that equity initiatives would have to address "climate" issues as an essential part of any equity initiatives.

IV. Conclusions

The very fact that women could collaborate on the projects I have described, and could make their results public in various ways, seems the strongest possible evidence that Western is a comparably humane and supportive university environment. Certainly it is a context in which women have been able to make their concerns public and to work actively for change, and in which we have found some not inconsiderable support for our cause. In speaking out on chilly climate issues, it should be emphasized, our aim was not to vilify Western. Rather it was to draw attention to an issue that we believed would have to be addressed if equity initiatives were to be successful, *viz.*, that it is not enough to attract increasing numbers of women into the training pipeline if they are undermined when they reach the point of taking their place among teachers and researchers within the academy. In this we hoped to illustrate the relevance of recommendations made in such different contexts as the COU *Handbook* and the AAC "Chilly Climate" reports.

More generally, we were committed to documenting experiences of chilliness precisely because they are so systematically erased, so isolating for those who suffer them, and so alien to those who claim not to perpetuate or experience them. Beyond briefing those responsible for employment equity about our concerns, it seemed crucially important to make contact with one another; we wanted to explore the common and political dimensions of experiences of harassment and exclusion that are so often understood as personal and idiosyncratic. It was an essential first step in this process, we felt, that we should draft *not* another statistical summary, but an account of how some of the women represented by these numbers actually experience life in our own academic institution. Striking parallels did, indeed, emerge between the experiences reported to us by women working in very different contexts at Western, and between these and the chilly climate experiences described by women working at a wide range of other universities and colleges in North America through the 1980s; clearly Western was no anomaly where workplace environment was concerned.

What remains to be done, in most general terms, is the work of systematic comparison, not only across institutional contexts within universities and colleges, as critics of the *Chilly Climate Report* suggest, but internally, on a great many dimensions we did not consider. Clearly women in academic contexts confront many different, often multiply chilly climates depending on how they are situated in relation to the whole range of systems of privilege that structure these institutions. As we look back on the projects we took up in the late 1980s we are, above all else, painfully aware of how limited and partial they were, how much they reflect and reproduce the systems of privilege that pervade academic institutions. In many cases it is patently obvious that we systematically failed to interrogate the multiple systems of exclusion that protect us in our contexts of practice, which confer on us (differentially) the privilege of (assumed) dominant race and class positions. In others we reinscribe in our own work differentiating categories and presuppositions by which some of us are ourselves systematically disadvantaged: e.g., those of ablism and ageism, of homophobia, and of ethnic and religious "minority" group affiliation, to name a few. The critical discussions contributed here by Patricia Monture-OKanee, by Leela MadhavaRau, and by Claire Young and Diana Majury,[107] most powerfully name at least some of the silences that compromise our original reports on chilly climate issues for women. Perhaps the greatest value of the essays and reports we contributed to the chilly climate literature of the late 1980s is, then, that they demonstrate how partial are the privileged angles of inquiry that both motivated and informed our work on chilly climate issues.

Notes

1 The term "minority" is deeply problematic. In fact, those referred to, collectively, as "minority" groups are numerically a majority in the world today. "Minority" may accurately portray their relative power and status in some contexts, but it reinforces the sense of these "minority"/majorities being the exception to an entrenched and unquestioned norm. I use it here because it is the language by which our federal (and most other) equity programs designate a range of groups (typically defined ethnically, racially, religiously, or by nation of origin) who have faced discrimination of various kinds and whose claims to equality of access, treatment, and compensation are "targeted" for support by these programs.

2 These patterns of change in the representation of women in universities and colleges will be discussed in detail below. Particularly relevant, in this connection, are a number of overviews and analyses of the statistics available on the training, employment, and advancement of women in academia, for example: the introductory chapter of Nadya Aisenberg and Mona Harrington, *Women of Academe: Outsiders in the Sacred Grove* (Amherst, MA: University of Massachusetts Press, 1988); the discussions in A. Simeone, *Academic Women: Working Towards Equality* (Hadley, MA: Bergin and Garvey, 1987), and in M.K. Chamberlain, ed., *Women in Academe: Progress and Prospects* (New York: Russell Sage Foundation, 1988); and the account Sheila E. Widnall gives of the continuing marginalization of women in science in her 1988 American Association for the Advancement of Science (AAAS) Presidential Lecture, "Voices from the Pipeline," *Science*, 241 (September 30, 1988): 1740-45. Where most of these discussions focus on the situation for women in the United States, comparable statistics have been reported for Canadian institutions in a number of contexts, including Thomas H.B. Symons and James E. Page, *Some Questions of Balance: Human Resources, Higher Education and Canadian Studies* (Ottawa: Association of Universities and Colleges of Canada, 1984); Industry, Science and Technology Canada, Universities and College Affairs Branch, Science Sector, *Women in Science and Engineering: Universities*, Vol. 1 (Ottawa: Industry, Science and Technology Canada, 1991); Mary Saunders, Margaret Therrien, and Linda Williams, *Women in Universities: Survey of the Status of Female Faculty and Students at Canadian Universities* (Ottawa: Canadian Federation of University Women, November 1992); the CAUT *Status Report* on "Employment Equity for Women" (*Status of Women Supplement*); and Statistics Canada, *Women in Canada: A Statistical Report*, 2nd ed. (Ottawa: Statistics Canada, February 1990). These and many other dis-

cussions are striking in their convergence on the thesis that, despite significant improvements in the status of women in universities and colleges, by the mid-1980s these gains had stalled or continued to be limited in a number of key areas. Such conclusions are drawn for the Canadian context, for example, by Susan Donaldson and Will Kymlicka, "Off the Tenure Track," *The Conduit* (1986), p. 22-24. In a similar vein, the analyses offered by authors like Aisenberg and Harrington, Simeone, Widnall, and contributors to Chamberlain call into question the presumption that the continuing problem of women's representation in academia is simply a "pipeline" problem, that it will right itself automatically, over time, as the growing numbers of women in graduate school and entry-level positions advance into the ranks of the tenured and senior professoriate. In short, the findings they report indicate that the rates at which women advance through the system of training and academic employment, and the patterns of their segregation by area and rank, have remained remarkably stable despite dramatic increases in their presence in graduate and professional training school and in entry-level appointments.

3 *Report of the Royal Commission on the Status of Women in Canada* (Ottawa, September 28, 1970), p. 169.

4 Symons and Page, *Some Questions of Balance*, p. 190. Symons and Page report figures for full-time undergraduate and graduate enrolment by gender for 1972-73 to 1981-82 prepared for the Commission by Statistics Canada (1983); the percentages reported here are based on these data.

5 Industry, Science and Technology Canada, *Women in Science and Engineering*, p. 45, 47. Symons and Page report that the increase in female graduate enrolments is consistently much higher than those of men and much more dramatic than in female undergraduate enrolments through the late 1970s; *Some Questions of Balance*, p. 189.

6 *Report of the Royal Commission on the Status of Women*, p. 167.

7 Symons and Page, *Some Questions of Balance*, p. 190.

8 Statistics Canada, *Women in Canada*, p. 45.

9 Saunders et al., *Women in Universities*, p. 1.

10 Symons and Page, *Some Questions of Balance*, p. 189, and Industry, Science and Technology Canada, *Women in Science and Engineering*, p. 3.

11 *Report of the Royal Commission on the Status of Women*, p. 169.

12 Industry, Science and Technology Canada, *Women in Science and Engineering*, p. 44-45.

13 Ibid., p. 5. See also Statistics Canada, *Women in Canada*, p. 47.

14 Saunders et al., *Women in Universities*, p. 1.

15 Statistics Canada, *Women in Canada*, p. 48. The period for which these figures are reported is 1971 to 1987.

16 Chamberlain, *Women of Academe*, p. 258.

17 While the reports providing the figures summarized above frequently offer useful analyses of differences in women's educational attainment by geographical region, type of institution, field, and rank or other status designation, I have found none that provide a breakdown by other major census categories or target-group designations such as ethnicity, race, religious affiliation, First Nations status, or disability, much less by sexual orientation. In fact, it is striking that the authors of the *Report of the Royal Commission on the Status of Women* of 1970 do address the particular needs of "rural women," "women immigrants," and "Native women of the north" in their 1970 discussion of women in "Education" (*Report of the Royal Commission on the Status of Women*, chap. 3, p. 207-16), although they focus here on primary, secondary, and supplementary educational programs in these connections. Fourteen years later, Symons and Page provide statistical summaries of the representation of women in post-secondary institutions by status (as students, faculty, and administrators), by region, and by field, but provide no breakdown, overall or in any of these categories, by race, ethnicity, class background, First Nations status, sexual orientation, age, disability, or any other factor that might make a difference as to who, among all

women in Canada, figure in the ranks of those who have realized at least some success in gaining access to these institutions. The same is true of the discussion of women in colleges and universities provided by Statistics Canada in 1990, in *Women in Canada*, although this publication does include important information about shifts in the enrolment of women in post-secondary institutions by age (p. 46). It is also true of the 1991 CAUT *Status Report* on "Employment Equity for Women" (*Status of Women Supplement*), and the 1992 report issued by the Canadian Federation of University Women, *Women in Universities*. Although it provides commentary on equity initiatives, rather than statistical information, and is not specifically concerned with women in academic settings, the special issue on "Gender Equality and Institutional Change" that appeared in *Canadian Woman Studies*, 12, 3 (1992), is more broadly inclusive. The contributors who focus on the equity concerns of women in universities do address issues of homophobia and the experiences of lesbian faculty at Canadian universities but consider few other dimensions of difference: Anne Innis Dagg, "Feminism Reviled: Academic Non-Freedom at Canadian Universities," *Canadian Women's Studies*, 12, 3 (1992): 89-92, and Kathleen Martindale, "What Is Known about Homophobia in the Classroom and the Limited Applicability of Anti-Homophobia Workshop Strategies for Women's Studies Classes," ibid., p. 95-99. It is to be hoped that, with the requirements for collecting information imposed by the Federal Contractors Program, at least data pertaining to the representation and status of women in the designated target-group categories will begin to be available; these regulations do not, themselves, require public reporting but many institutions governed by them (like Western) have made a commitment to issue public reports on a regular basis. Given the range of factors not addressed by this legislation (e.g., sexual orientation, cultural, ethnic, or religious affiliation), however, no doubt it will fall to advocates for various constituencies of women to collect and publish the information necessary to make a more fine-grained assessment of who, exactly, benefits from gender equity initiatives in Canadian universities and colleges.

18 Employment and Immigration Canada, *Employment Equity: A Guide for Employers* (Ottawa: Minister of Supply and Services Canada, 1987). The Federal Contractors Program applies to any institution that is subject to the *Canada Labour Code* and employs more than 100 people or receives federal contracts worth $200,000 or more; this, of course, includes most Canadian universities and colleges. These regulations identify four "designated groups" — women, visible minorities, Native people, and people with disabilities — and require that employers who have joined the program take measures to ensure that the representation of members of these groups in their work force is proportionate to their presence in the larger work force or in the relevant segments of the work force. The legality of such programs is protected under S. 15(2) of the Charter.

19 Crucial here is S. 15 of the Charter which provides both for the equality of all individuals under the law, including their right to freedom from discrimination "based on race, national or ethnic origin, colour, religion, sex, age or mental or physical disability" *and* for the legality of "any law, program or activity that has as its object the amelioration of conditions of disadvantaged individuals or groups" (*Canada Act, 1982*, Part 1 [Canadian Charter of Rights and Freedoms]). The significance of this second provision under the Charter is that it "provides the constitutional foothold for progressive, strong employment equity initiatives in Canada, including preferential treatment," thus settling in advance (at least until challenged) the legal debates over "reverse discrimination" that have complicated efforts to institute "affirmative action" programs in the United States (Carol Agòcs, Catherine Burr, and Felicity Somerset, *Employment Equity: Co-operative Strategies for Organizational Change* [Scarborough, ON: Prentice-Hall Canada, 1992], p. 95). For a detailed overview of "the legal framework of employment equity," see ibid., chap. 4.

20 This United States legislation includes the *Equal Pay Act* that was enacted in 1963; an Executive Order of 1965, amended in 1967 and 1971, which prohibits employment discrimination on the basis of sex by all employers holding contracts from the federal (United States)

government; Title 7 of the *Civil Rights Act*, adopted in 1964 and amended in 1972, which makes anti-discrimination commitments binding for educational institutions; and the Educational Amendments of 1972 which include, in Title 9, an explicit injunction against sex discrimination affecting students or employees in federally funded education programs and institutions. For further details and discussion of this legislation, see Chamberlain, *Women in Academe*, chap. 8; Patricia Hopkins Lattin, "Academic Women, Affirmative Action, and Mid-America in the Eighties," *Women's Studies International Forum*, 6, 2 (1983): 224; and Simeone, *Academic Women*, p. 39.

21 Chamberlain, *Women in Academe*, p. 261.
22 Simeone, *Academic Women*, p. 33. For comparable Canadian statistics, see chap. 3, especially Appendix A.
23 Chamberlain, *Women in Academe*, p. 261.
24 Ibid., p. 214.
25 Ibid., p. 262.
26 Ibid., p. 214.
27 Ibid.
28 Katharine Phenix, "The Status of Women Librarians," *Frontiers*, 9, 2 (1987): 36.
29 Colin Norman, "Sex Discrimination Persists in Academe," *Science*, 214 (1981), p. 890. As Norman describes this study, "factors other than sex were ruled out by matching each woman in the survey with two men according to race, the year in which the doctorate was awarded, the field of study, and the reputation of the PhD-granting department." It also tracked "changes in the career prospects for women faculty members over time" and considered differences due to marital status and "work orientation" to research as opposed to teaching. None of these factors proved significant in accounting for women's disproportionately slow progress through the ranks and high rates of attrition. Comparing men to women in the same cohort, men who earned their doctorates in the 1960s were "50 percent more likely to have been promoted to full professor than women with the same qualifications . . . and the situation has not improved much in recent years"; a third of the women compared to half the men who earned PhDs in 1970-74 held "senior [tenured] faculty posts" by the early 1980s.
30 This is also argued in detail by Simeone, *Academic Women*, chap. 2. See as well, however, analyses of the "productivity puzzle" by contributors to Harriet Zuckerman, Jonathan R. Cole, and John T. Bruer, eds., *The Outer Circle: Women in the Scientific Community* (New York: W.W. Norton, 1991). Especially useful in bringing out the complexities of the situation is the concluding essay by Jonathan R. Cole and Burton Singer, "A Theory of Limited Differences: Explaining the Productivity Puzzle in Science," p. 277-310.
31 Lattin, "Academic Women," p. 229-30.
32 Ibid., p. 229.
33 Simeone, *Academic Women*, p. 144.
34 Ibid., p. 19.
35 Ibid., p. 45.
36 Esther D. Rothblum, "Leaving the Ivory Tower: Factors Contributing to Women's Voluntary Resignation from Academia," *Frontiers*, 10, 2 (1988): 14-17.
37 For a summary, see Simeone, *Academic Women*, chap. 2.
38 Symons and Page, *Some Questions of Balance*, p. 199.
39 Ibid., p. 191-92.
40 Ibid., p. 190-91.
41 Ibid., p. 191.
42 Saunders et al., *Women in Universities*, p. 1.
43 Widnall, "Voices from the Pipeline."
44 Industry, Science and Technology Canada, *Women in Science and Engineering*, p. 5.
45 Anne Innis Dagg, "The Status of Canadian Women PhD Scientists," *Atlantis*, 11, 1 (1985): 74. A comparable situation is reported for women in astronomy and physics in the

United States (Faye Flam, "Still a 'Chilly Climate' for Women?," *Science*, 252 [1991]: 1604-6). See also Anne Innis Dagg and Patricia J. Thompson, *Miss Education: Women and Canadian Universities* (Toronto: OISE Press, 1988).

46 Lattin, "Academic Women," p. 226.

47 Ibid, p. 227.

48 This is a summary of the examples Lattin presents in ibid., p. 226-28.

49 Symons and Page, *Some Questions of Balance*, p. 193.

50 Saunders et al., *Women in Universities*, p. 1.

51 Simeone, *Academic Women*, p. 143.

52 Roberta M. Hall and Bernice R. Sandler, *The Classroom Climate: A Chilly One for Women?*, Project on the Status and Education of Women (Washington DC: AAC, 1982), and Roberta M. Hall and Bernice R. Sandler, *Out of the Classroom: A Chilly Campus Climate for Women?*, Project on the Status and Education of Women (Washington, DC: AAC, 1984). Sandler subsequently expanded the scope of these previous reports to consider climate issues for women faculty and staff in universities and colleges (Bernice R. Sandler, *The Campus Climate Revisited: Chilly for Women Faculty, Administrators, and Graduate Students* [Washington, DC: Project on the Status and Education of Women, AAC, 1986]), and in 1988 the AAC published two reports on the status and experience of "visible minority" women: Y.T. Moses, *Black Women in Academe: Issues and Strategies* (Washington, DC: Project on the Status and Education of Women, AAC, 1988), and S. Nieves-Squires, *Hispanic Women: Making Their Presence on Campus Less Tenuous* (Washington, DC: Project on the Status and Education of Women, AAC, 1988).

53 Widnall, "Voices from the Pipeline."

54 Ibid. Note Widnall's comparison of the experience of women in the contexts she discusses (for the most part, graduate training programs in science and engineering) with that of foreign students and "minority" men: "the white male students benefit from the self-reinforcing confidence that 'they belong.' The self-identification with the predominantly White male faculty reassures them that graduate school is a step on the way to a productive career in science, and that many others with whom they can identify have done it before them. For women students, minority students, and many foreign students, the environment is not as reinforcing" (p. 1743).

55 Hall and Sandler, *The Classroom Climate*; Hall and Sandler, *Out of the Classroom*; and Sandler, *The Campus Climate Revisited*.

56 Aisenberg and Harrington, *Women of Academe*, p. x.

57 Ibid., p. 3.

58 The Canadian Women's Studies Association is currently involved in a project of documenting "how 'chilly climate' reports have been generated and responded to within [Canadian post-secondary institutions], in order to assess their effectiveness in redressing chilly climates" (Susan Prentice, on behalf of the Canadian Women's Studies Association Chilly Climate project [memo circulated April 20, 1994]). Institution-specific projects in the United States are described by Widnall in "Voices from the Pipeline," and in the AAC "Chilly Climate" publications. See also the range of institutional and environmental factors considered by contributors to Zuckerman et al., *The Outer Circle*.

59 Robert Weyant, "Sexual Harassment: The Tip of a Larger Problem," presentation to the Senate of the University of Calgary (September 30, 1983).

60 Rachel L. Osborne, "Sexual Harassment in Universities: A Critical View of the Institutional Response," *Canadian Women Studies*, 12, 3 (1992): 72-76. Osborne is critical of institutional responses that are individualistic and legalistic. She argues that, so long as sexual harassment is treated as an "individual and isolated experience," a problem between two individuals that requires mediation, what disappears is any consideration of the systemic and political context in which it occurs. It becomes impossible to address the "broader and underlying issue at hand: the sexism and institutionalized sexist practices embedded in

universities" (p. 74-75). See also contributions to "Harassment on Campus," a special issue of *Thought and Action: The NEA Higher Education Journal*, 7, 1 (Spring 1991), and Constance M. Carroll, "Sexual Harassment on Campus: Enhancing Awareness and Promoting Change," *Educational Record*, 74, 1 (1993): 21-28.

61 For a general discussion of these issues as they arise in industry in Canada, see Agòcs et al., *Employment Equity: Co-operative Strategies for Organizational Change*. See also contributions to Rosabeth Moss Kanter, ed., *Discrimination in Organizations* (Washington: Jossey Bass, 1979); Rosalie S. Abella, *Equity in Employment: A Royal Commission Report* (Ottawa: Minister of Supply and Services, 1984); and Carol Agòcs, "Missing Persons: Perspectives on the Absence of Women from Canada's Corporate and Bureaucratic Elites," *Organizational Behaviour*, 6, 5 (1985): 1-12.

62 See, for example, Dagg, "Feminism Reviled."

63 Sandler, *The Campus Climate Revisited*, p. 17.

64 Ibid., p. 3.

65 Others use different categories when describing the range of "factors" or types of practice that make an environment chilly. For example, Joy Parr identifies nine "chilly factors" in "The Chilly Climate — The Systemic Dilemma," *OCUFA Forum*, Supplement, 6, 18 (December 1989): 1-2. Sandler and Hall differentiate roughly five "forms of chilly behavior and practices," one of them a catch-all for practices that don't fall neatly under the categories of "confusion of social and professional roles," "devaluation," "collegiality," and "sexual harassment" (*The Campus Climate Revisited*, p. 4-10). The four categories used here were originally developed through analysis of Sandler and Hall's discussion when formulating a structure for presenting the results of interviews with women faculty at the University of Western Ontario (see chapter 3); the first three categories are meant to capture basic mechanisms involved in gender harassment, all of which may be deployed in the fourth, "revictimization." The examples used to illustrate each of these categories here are generic to the literature on chilly climate issues.

66 For discussion of this literature, see Sandler, *The Campus Climate Revisited*, p. 6.

67 See, for example, Dale Spender, *Man Made Language* (Boston: Routledge & Kegan Paul, 1980).

68 Sandler, *The Campus Climate Revisited*, p. 2.

69 Widnall, "Voices from the Pipeline." This cumulative effect is also captured in the image of death by a million cuts, or by the "ton of feathers" metaphor that Paula Caplan uses in the title of her recent book, *Lifting a Ton of Feathers: A Woman's Guide to Surviving in the Academic World* (Toronto: University of Toronto Press, 1993).

70 For discussions published in the 1980s, see Richard Delgado, "Minority Law Professors' Lives: The Bell-Delgado Survey," *Harvard Civil Rights–Civil Liberties Law Review*, 24 (1989): 349; David Thomas, "Mentoring and Irrationality: The Role of Racial Taboos," *Human Resource Management*, 28, 2 (1989): 331-43; Nellie McKay, "Black Woman Professor — White University," *Women's Studies International Forum*, 6, 2 (1983): 143-47, and the two AAC reports that appeared in 1988: Moses, *Black Women in Academe*; Nieves-Squires, *Hispanic Women*; and Patricia A. Monture, "Ka-Nin-Geh-Heh-Gah-E-Sa-Nonh-Ya-Gah," *Canadian Journal of Women and the Law*, 2, 1 (1986): 159, to take a few key examples. See also general discussions of the experience of Black and "minority" women in academic settings by bell hooks, *Feminist Theory: From Margin to Center* (Boston: South End Press, 1984); Audre Lorde, *Sister Outsider* (Freedom, CA: Crossing Press, 1984); and by contributors to Gloria T. Hull, Patricia Bell Scott, and Barbara Smith, eds., *All the Women Are White, All the Blacks Are Men, but Some of Us Are Brave* (New York: Feminist Press, 1982).

71 Consider, for example, Smith's assessment, in 1983, that "the concept of the simultaneity of oppression is still the crux of a Black Feminist understanding of political reality and, I believe, one of the most significant ideological contributions of Black Feminist thought" (B. Smith, ed., *Home Girls* [New York: Kitchen Table-Women of Color Press, 1983], p. xxxii).

This was the central point of the analysis originally published by the Combahee River Collective in the late 1970s, "A Black Feminist Statement," in *Capitalist Patriarchy and the Case for Socialist Feminism*, edited by Z. Eisenstein (New York: Monthly Review Press, 1979). It has been repeatedly reaffirmed, for example, by Deborah K. King in "Multiple Jeopardy, Multiple Consciousness: The Context of a Black Feminist Ideology" (*Signs*, 14, 1 [1988]: 42-72) and by Patricia Hill Collins in *Black Feminist Thought* (New York: Routledge, 1990). Parallel arguments figure centrally in critiques of mainstream feminist literature that were advanced by the advocates of class analyses (socialist and Marxist feminists), by lesbian activists, by "third world" women, by women with disabilities, by women of minority ethnic, cultural, and religious affiliations, to name just a few influential challenges to "gender only" analyses that were the focus of feminist debate through the 1980s. See, for example, the overviews of "divides" in feminism provided by contributors to the following collections (among many others that could be cited in this connection): Himani Bannerji, Linda Carty, Kari Dehli, Susan Heald, Kate McKenna, eds., *Unsettling Relations: The University as a Site of Feminist Struggles* (Toronto: Women's Press, 1991); Cherrie Moraga and Gloria Anzaldua, eds., *This Bridge Called My Back: Writings by Radical Women of Color* (New York: Kitchen Table Women of Color Press, 1983); C.T. Mohanty, A. Russo, and L. Torres, eds., *Third World Women and the Politics of Feminism* (Bloomington: Indiana University Press, 1991); C.S. Vance, ed., *Pleasure and Danger: Exploring Female Sexuality* (Boston: Routledge & Kegan Paul, 1984); Marianne Hirsch and Evelyn Fox Keller, eds., *Conflicts in Feminism* (New York: Routledge, 1990). "Divides" is a term Ann Snitow uses in "A Gender Diary," in Hirsch and Keller, eds., *Conflicts in Feminism*, p. 9-43.

72 Douglas R. Hofstadter, "Changes in Default Words and Images, Engendered by Rising Consciousness," in Douglas R. Hofstadter, ed., *Metamagical Themas* (Toronto: Bantam Books), p. 136-58.

73 See, for example, Bannerji et al., *Unsettling Relations*; Patricia Williams, *The Alchemy of Race and Rights: Diary of a Law Professor* (Cambridge: Harvard University Press, 1991); Joy James and Ruth Farmer, eds., *Spirit, Space and Survival: African American Women in (White) Academe* (New York: Routledge, 1993); Lynn Brodie Welch, ed., *Perspectives on Minority Women in Higher Education* (New York: Praeger, 1992); Benjamin P. Bowser et al., *Confronting Diversity Issues on Campus* (Newbury Park, CA: Sage, 1993); Monture, "Ka-Nin-Geh-Heh-Gah-E-Sa-Nonh-Ya-Gah"; Patricia A. Monture, "Now that the Door Is Open: First Nations and the Law School Experience," *Queen's Law Journal*, 15 (1990): 179; and Emily Carasco, "A Case of Double Jeopardy: Race and Gender," *Canadian Journal of Women and the Law*, 6, 1 (1993):142.

74 The equity initiatives at the University of Western Ontario summarized here are much more fully described by Constance Backhouse in chapter 3.

75 Denis Smith et al., *Report of the Ad Hoc Senate Committee to Review Appointments, Promotion, and Tenure Policies and Procedures* (London: Office of the Secretary of the Board of Governors and Senate, UWO, 1984).

76 The University of Western Ontario enrols 23,000 full-time students and employs 1,400 full-time faculty in 17 different faculties. It has well-established schools of medicine, dentistry, law, business administration, education, library and information science, and active graduate programs in most core academic disciplines.

77 Constance Backhouse, "An Historical Perspective: Reflections on the Employment Equity Award" (the *Backhouse Report*), London, Ont., manuscript in the possession of the author, 1988, p. 8. This report was later published in *Canadian Journal of Women and the Law*, 4 (1990): 36-65, and appears here as chapter 3; all references here are to the original manuscript.

78 *Smith Report*, p. 7.

79 Detailed discussion of the response to the *Backhouse Report* follows in chapter 5.

80 The Council of Ontario Universities, Committee on the Status of Women, *Employment Equity for Women: A University Handbook* (Toronto: Council of Ontario Universities, 1988).

81 For example, "Hire More Women Teachers, UWO Told," *The London Free Press*, May 2, 1988.

82 These points were made in a summary of "issues for discussion" circulated by members of the Executive of the Women's Caucus in late April (The Executive, Western's Caucus on Women's Issues, "Issues for Discussion: Employment Equity/Backhouse Report" [London, Caucus Archives, April 1988]).

83 This meeting was held on Monday, June 13, 1988, and was advertised as open to the university community in *Western News*, June 9, 1988. It received anticipatory discussion in this issue of *Western News* ("Caucus to Assist University in Employment Equity Steps," June 9, 1988, p. 6).

84 "Campus Group Wants Probe of UWO Women's Pay, Hiring," *The London Free Press*, June 14, 1988, p. B3, and "Study of Hiring Practices Urged," *Western News*, June 23, 1988, p. 3.

85 These and other initiatives are summarized in A. Wylie, "Caucus Update on Employment Equity," *Western's Caucus on Women's Issues: Newsletter*, 9, 1 (1989).

86 "Employment Equity: Western Joins Federal Program," *Western News*, May 26, 1988, p. 1, 4.

87 Ibid., p. 1.

88 "Pursuit of Equity at UWO," *The London Free Press*, June 10, 1988.

89 Ibid.

90 See, for example, "UWO Honored as Exemplary Employer," *Western News*, November 13, 1986, p. 1, 6, and also the handsome brochure produced by the Ontario Women's Directorate, *Employment Equity Award Winners 1986* (Toronto: Ontario Women's Directorate).

91 See, for example, media coverage of a report on faculty appointments that the Provost had presented to the Senate four months earlier: "Improvement Needed in Hiring of Female Academics," *Western News*, February 11, 1988, and "Proportion of Women — 'Virtually No Progress,' " *Western News*, February 18, 1988, p. 4.

92 "Pursuit of Equity at UWO," *The London Free Press*, June 19, 1988.

93 See Backhouse, "An Historical Perspective," chapter 3.

94 "Hire More Women Teachers, UWO Told," *The London Free Press*, May 2, 1988.

95 See recent discussion of the equity program at York which addresses these issues (Ellen Baar, "Using Accountable Self Regulation to Achieve Employment Equity in Universities," *Canadian Woman Studies*, 12, 3 [1993]: 46-52).

96 "Backhouse Report: Female Hiring Record Criticized," *Western News*, May 26, 1988, p. 4.

97 In particular, we drew on Sandler, *The Campus Climate Revisited*.

98 Aisenberg and Harrington, *Women of Academe*, p. ix.

99 The details of how we approached this project, and of reactions to it, are discussed in chapter 5.

100 See Appendix B, chapter 5, for a more detailed description of this process.

101 In fact, in the case of the Provost, this involved a lengthy conversation and the drafting of a summary statement describing the aims of the project and what we hoped it might achieve. This the Provost received several days before the *Report* was released; it was subsequently published in the student newspaper; Alison Wylie, "Some Comments on the 'Chilly Climate' Report," *The Gazette*, November 17, 1989, p. 9. It is reprinted below as Appendix A, chapter 5.

102 The "Epilogue" (chapter 5) describes the media and administrative response in detail.

103 The "Epilogue" (chapter 5) provides a more detailed account of how this video came to be proposed and funded.

104 In fact, as President of the Caucus in 1989-90, I drafted the proposal for this video based on a literature review I had originally undertaken as background for the *Chilly Climate Report*.

105 Quoting Wylie, "Province Funds 'Chilly Climate' Video," *Western News*, April 19, 1990, p. 2.

106 Ibid.

107 Chapters 1, 8, and 9, respectively.

3

An Historical Perspective: Reflections on the Western Employment Equity Award[1]

Constance Backhouse

On November 12, 1986, the University of Western Ontario was awarded the Employment Equity Award by the Ontario Women's Directorate. It was the ensuing public celebration of Western's achievements that inspired the following essay, which came to be known as the Backhouse Report. *Constance Backhouse was one of many women on campus who believed that the award was somewhat "premature." She undertook to examine the University's record in more detail, to compile a more thorough and accurate report on the employment status of faculty women at Western.*

This essay, researched and drafted over many months during 1987 and 1988, considers Western's statistics within a national and historical context, filling out this profile with data from historical records and interviews that bring to life the experiences of women who taught at the University from as early as 1915. In the Report that follows, Backhouse documents a wide range of employment practices bearing on the appointment of faculty women, their compensation, tenure, promotion, and retirement. It seems clear that persistently low levels of representation of women reflect a long history of overt discrimination and of more covert patterns of exclusion and devaluation. Backhouse argues, on this basis, that any effective response to gender inequity on campus must address these root problems, and must, moreover, give up the pious hope that change will come "naturally." Institutional structures and policies require rigorous review; women's concerns must receive strong representation at the highest levels of the University administration; and above all, the University needs to set explicit goals for improving the representation of women, coupled with clearly defined sanctions for those who fail to meet these goals. Given the limited success of previous attempts to improve Western's record on equity, the lesson Backhouse drew in the late 1980s was that more wide-ranging and aggressive strategies would be necessary if progress were to be realized.

When the Report *was complete, but before it was made public, Backhouse made a point of meeting with many senior administrators within the University, presenting each of them, individually, with a summary of her findings. When the* Report *was released, in April 1988, it received wide circulation on campus and intense discussion both at presentations Backhouse had organized and at several large meetings convened by Western's Caucus on Women's Issues. It also received extensive and largely positive media attention.[2] Through all of this, Backhouse's hope was that, by critically assessing the relatively rosy picture painted by the Employment Equity Award, her report might prove to be a catalyst for a clearly focused discussion about strategies for making change.*

– Eds.

The *Backhouse Report*

Faculty Women at Western. Yes, this will constitute yet another report on the abysmally low number of women teaching in full-time[1] faculty positions. One becomes weary of documenting the problem again and again, every time predictably raising the hackles of those who feel uneasy over the presence of *any* women in academia. The reports multiply, the backlash swells, and still there *is* no dent.

So why another report? Let me try to do something a bit different here. First, I do not want to outline the arguments as to *why* more women should be hired. I take the case as self-evident, and, in any event, more than amply discussed in the voluminous scholarly literature on affirmative action.[2] Instead, I want to document the University of Western Ontario's particular history in this field, and then focus on where we might go from here.[3] I am also weary of the stylistically "correct," third-person "neutral" tone of many of these reports, and will thus try to tell this from a more personalized viewpoint.

I should also mention one major *caveat* at the outset. This inquiry does not examine discrimination on the basis of race, disability, or class. It is quite clear that Western is an overwhelmingly White institution as well as a male one. If anything, women and men of colour are less well-represented on campus than White women. Individuals with disabilities and individuals from working-class backgrounds also lack representation. These problems are every bit as serious as sex discrimination, and require immediate investigation and analysis. Not until 1988 did various federal programs begin to require the collection and reporting of data on race and disability. As of the time of writing, no such statistical profile has yet been compiled at Western.[4]

The gathering of statistical information is clearly the first priority. I urge universities to get on with the production of data so that individuals and organizations sensitive to these forms of discrimination can begin to address these critical matters. I would like to stress however, the incompleteness of my report.

I should begin by outlining some of my own experience. I was appointed as an Assistant Professor of Law at the University of Western Ontario in 1979. At that time, there was only one other full-time female faculty member teaching in the law school. In one of my first years there I was asked by a group of women law students to speak as part of a panel on careers for women in law. Naturally, I spoke on the prospect of employment in the academic setting. To prepare for this presentation, I collected statistics on the numbers of women in the faculties of law across the province. The picture, as you can imagine, was not a rosy one. Most universities had at best one or two women law professors each. I told the audience that evening that I felt the statistics were "atrocious," an adjective that I believed aptly characterized the situation. I recommended a strong affirmative action program to remedy the situation. The next day the student newspaper, the *Gazette*, reported my remarks in detail.[5]

The response I received from the University community was truly remarkable. Although the University reveres itself as an institution that prizes academic freedom of thought and expression, such sentiments were far from evident in this case. Some of my colleagues confronted me in my office, loudly demanding that I retract my statements. One male law student wrote to the *Gazette* disputing my comments, and alleging that I was guilty of reverse sex discrimination in connection with my actions inside the law school. One of the senior administrators at the law school took me aside to let me know that he had clipped the article and "placed it on my file." One of the senior administrators at the University personally spoke to me, and I was left with the impression that I should scale down my public activities and spend more of my time publishing scholarly articles. The furore I created with a few short remarks was a clear lesson in the danger of fighting for affirmative action inside the University. It caught me a bit off guard, and I spent the next several years watching with horrified fascination as similar reactions lambasted the other women who spoke out publicly about the need for more women faculty. It is with some trepidation, therefore, that I return to the subject at this time.[6] The incident that forced me to take up the matter once more was the Ontario Government's Employment Equity Award which Western received in 1986.[7]

But let's not get ahead of ourselves. We need to have some contextual information from which to evaluate Western's record. First there is the national picture. Statistics Canada and its predecessor agencies have been keeping records since 1921, although the reliability of the data has been questioned on occasion.[8] In 1921 women could apparently be tallied at 15 per cent of all university faculty in Canada.[9] The numbers peaked in 1944 at 19.9 per cent. (See Appendix A.)

By 1958, hiring committees had pushed the percentage of women faculty back to 11 per cent, revealing the ultimate truism in women's history that progress is not inevitable.[10] With the public reemergence of organized feminism in the mid-1970s, the numbers became something of an embarrassment. Between 1974 and 1982 many universities created committees to inquire into "the problem," and some went so far as to appoint special "Women's Affairs" Officers. A 1984 report commissioned by the Association of Universities and Colleges of Canada concluded "with regret" that these appointments offered no more than "tokenism or window-dressing."[11] The bottom line changed little. By 1985 women represented only 17.0 per cent of the full-time teaching staff. Even Statistics Canada was moved to comment dryly about the university professoriate: "In a profession that has a history of a high proportion of males, this represents little gain over the ratio of 11 per cent that was recorded 26 years earlier . . ."[12]

The bottom line numbers on women professors at Canadian universities are bad enough, but when one looks beneath them, the picture worsens. Men hold most of the permanent senior positions, while women are confined to the temporary, low-status positions. In 1985, for example, only 6.1 per cent of the Full Professors in Canada were female, whereas 44.5 per cent of those ranked below Assistant Professor were female.[13] Women are conspicuously absent from the Faculties of Engineering, Mathematics, and Physical Sciences. What few women there are remain clustered in the traditionally female teaching areas of Education, Nursing, and some fields in the humanities.[14] This translates into dollars and, in 1985-86, the median salary for women in every academic rank was lower than that for men.[15]

But perhaps things look more promising at Western, you say. Certainly one might be tempted to think so, especially after our receipt of the Ontario government's Employment Equity Award in 1986. Western stepped into the limelight along with Consumers' Gas, London Life, and Ontario Hydro. These four organizations were singled out for their "commitment to equal opportunity in the workplace." The UWO President personally travelled to Toronto to accept the award from the Minister responsible for women's issues. Labelling Western a "shrewd employer," the Minister had this to say: "[Western is] aggressive in promoting and communicating their equal opportunity programs to their employees; they have taken a hard look at their organization; and they are committed to a long-term strategy of employment equity."[16] The glossy program that the Ontario Women's Directorate distributed on the occasion singled out women faculty as one of Western's strong points. "One of the university's most aggressive strategies has been to hasten the representation of women on the faculty," it noted enthusiastically.[17]

Underneath the public relations hype, the reality at Western is rather bleak. The latest data (1987-88) show that 14.78 per cent of the full-time faculty at Western are women,[18] lower than earlier levels in the 1930s.[19] Not since 1973 has Western bettered the provincial or national average for percentage of women on faculty.[20] If you concentrate just on tenure-stream positions (the ones that mark out a permanent academic career)[21] the numbers drop. Women represent a mere 9 per cent here.[22] Men make up 95.3 per cent of the Full Professors; women make up 50.7 per cent of the Lecturers.[23] The distribution of women amongst faculties is marked. In 1984 Western released data showing the departments and faculties without any women faculty members: Dentistry, Engineering, Graduate Studies, Journalism, Language Laboratories, Classical Studies, Russian Studies, Cancer Research, Clinical Biochemistry, History of Medicine and Science, Nuclear Medicine, Obstetrics/Gynaecology, Ophthalmology, Otolaryngology, Surgery, Radiation Oncology, Applied Mathematics, Astronomy, Geophysics, Mathematics, Statistical and Actuarial Science, Physics, and Zoology.[24] The overall outlines remained largely unchanged by 1987-88.[25] On top of this, women faculty earned 10 to 20 per cent less than their male counterparts of the same age based on 1987-88 data.[26]

What is there in this record to warrant an award? Well might you ask. Since the Ontario Women's Directorate could not possibly have presented us with the award on the basis of our current statistics, I decided to search for evidence of excellence elsewhere. To make absolutely certain that I was not missing anything, I chose to begin with some historical research about women faculty at Western.

Although books have recently been published detailing the history of women at McGill and at the University of Toronto,[27] none has yet emerged on Western women. There are several published histories of the University, which was first incorporated in 1878,[28] but only one accurately notes the first admission of female students to the campus in 1895.[29] None sees fit to give formal notice to the date of appointment of the first female faculty members.[30]

I have not been able to locate any public records which document the appointment of the first racial minority, Aboriginal, or disabled faculty members at UWO. But I was able to turn to the academic calendar for the year 1915-16 and look for female names as evidence of the appointment of the first female academics at Western: Hilda Baynes was appointed as a Lecturer in French, and Georgia Maud Newbury as Instructor in Elocution and Public Speaking.[31] An increase in funding to the universities during wartime and the prospect of losing male faculty to active service seems to have been the cause of this initiative. The numbers of women slowly increased during the 1920s and 1930s, although as yet no one has undertaken a full statistical analysis of the numbers of women faculty at Western over time, and their ratio to male faculty.[32]

Life as one of the early female academics was not easy, since gender was often the focus for student harassment. Jean Isabel Walker, appointed as Instructor in Public Speaking in 1920,[33] was singled out for special abuse. Ross Baxter-Willis provides details in his historical description of those years. Interestingly, although he wrote this account in 1980, he seems remarkably unaware of the implications of his story:

> During the early period . . . all freshmen were required to take a course in public speaking. By far the greatest number of those caught by this dictum were exposed to a female who prided herself on being a first-rate elocutionist. Each member of the class had to give a speech or two during the year as well as a demonstration. The member of faculty concerned would sit in the front row facing the student who was on the hot seat and men in the class would make faces at the poor unfortunate, hold up signs with such innocent phrases as "your fly is undone. . . ." [. . .] The poor member of faculty who had to cope with these high jinks used to be at her wit's end at times, but she was always ready for further punishment.[34]

There is evidence of institutional discrimination almost from the outset. Dr. Madge Thurlow Macklin, appointed as the first woman on the Faculty of Medicine in 1921, provides a good illustration.[35] She and her husband both came from Johns Hopkins University to take positions at Western. Charles Clifford Macklin, MD was named a Professor of Histology and Embryology, while Madge Thurlow Macklin, MD was appointed at the lower rank of Instructor in Histology and Embryology.[36] Madge Macklin apparently was the victim of a remarkable case of salary discrimination. Dr. Murray Barr, presently of the medical faculty, recalls:

> In those days it was unthinkable for a husband and wife — well they didn't even like them both to be in the university employ let alone in the same faculty. And it was almost unheard of to be in the same department. So she was never on full salary. She was always paid a kind of honorarium every year, on an annual basis. And yet she worked full time and did a lot of teaching and a lot of research work and became pretty well known throughout North America for her research work.[37]

Apparently, during the depression she was not paid at all.[38]

Although Madge Macklin taught from 1921 until 1946, the highest rank she ever obtained was Assistant Professor. Her failure to advance apparently was not due to any shortage of talent or hard work. Barr recalls Madge Macklin as a "superb teacher," and "a brilliant woman" who was "never fully appreciated": her research was widely recognized by the scientific and medical community in North America and abroad. While her passionate commitment to the eugenics movement in the 1930s led her to advance some dangerous social programs, her campaign to establish departments of medical genetics in medical schools was less controversial. In 1938 only one medical school in North America had a compulsory course in the subject, but by 1953, more than half had followed suit. As one historian has noted, the irony was that Madge Macklin, "the country's pre-eminent human geneticist," was never "allowed to offer a course in genetics during the twenty-four years she was at the University of Western Ontario."[39] Barr has charged that "in spite of Dr. Macklin's exemplary teaching and stature as a scientist her years at Western were plagued with difficulties. [. . .] It must be said that Dr. Madge Macklin did not receive from Western the recognition that her contributions deserved."[40]

There is also irrefutable evidence that, for some years at least, members of the administration at Western applied an overt quota system for the hiring of women. Dr. Frances K. Montgomery, who was appointed to the Department of Romance Languages in 1930, received a remarkable admission about the policy. Dr. K.P.R. Neville, Dean of Arts, wrote to offer her a position on the Faculty in July 1930. In his letter, he rather shamelessly exposed the discrimination:

> There is one question in connection with the whole situation that is perhaps disconcerting from your point of view, though my recommendation would be that you borrow no trouble about it. There is already one woman in the Department of Romance Languages and certain members of the administration do not think that it is advisable for us to have the proportion of women greater than one in five in any Department. It may be that idea will work to make your appointment a temporary one. Of course, "temporary" doesn't mean anything less than a year and probably will mean two at the least. If in that time you make yourself so solid in the Department that it will be plainly a distinct loss to attempt to reduce the forty percent feminine to twenty, I can see very plainly that the appointment will not continue to be temporary.[41]

As yet, I have not been able to confirm how long this quota system was in operation, or how many women were excluded from appointments. In Dr. Montgomery's case, despite the cloud hanging over her initial entry, her remarkable talents and energy combined to make her "solid" enough to permit an exception to the "twenty per cent rule." She stayed on at Western, and carved out a highly distinguished academic career until she was forcibly retired at the age of 60, against her wishes.[42] But more about this later.

In the 1940s, female professors were often asked to begin their academic careers as of 1 September.[43] Men were frequently hired two months earlier, as of 1 July, which gave them the advantage of the summer, at full pay, to prepare themselves for fall classes in their first year. The differential starting dates had significant detrimental implications for pension benefits in later years.[44]

Life insurance benefits paid out lower amounts for women faculty than for men in the event of death. A former Professor of Psychology and Dean of Women recalls, "I think women were worth about $3000 dead in the early days. It was appalling."[45] Single men also appear to have received negligible coverage, while married men benefitted from much more extensive life insurance. The discrimination was not wholly based on marital or family status, however. Neither married women nor women with family dependents were entitled to the higher insurance benefits. The same former Dean of Women notes that the University later adjusted this so that insurance benefits were tied to salaries. "But of course our salaries were still lower than men's, so the differential remained," she adds.[46]

The experience of Hanna Spencer is acknowledged by virtually everyone concerned to have been a case of clear and direct sex discrimination. Spencer arrived in London in 1951, accompanying her husband who had been appointed to the federal government's agricultural research centre in the city. Hanna Spencer possessed a PhD degree in Germanic and Slavonic languages from the University of Prague, and had a background in teaching. She presented herself to Professor Herbert Karl Kalbfleisch, the Head of the German Department at Western. He made no offer to Spencer until one of his faculty members quit unexpectedly in the summer of 1959. In late August he offered Spencer a position as a sessional lecturer. As such, she would teach five courses but be paid for eight, rather than 12 months of the year, and there would be no fringe benefits. While Spencer would have preferred a more permanent, full-time position, she agreed. "At that point I was delighted just to be able to teach," she said.[47]

Right from the start there were indications that Spencer would be treated differently. For several years, the Head of the Department refused to provide her with an office. "Kalbfleisch sort of hoped I would operate from my home," Spencer recalls.[48] Travel funds were also withheld. When the German teachers held their first organizing meeting at Carleton, Kalbfleisch suggested that Spencer should attend. When she inquired whether travel funds would be available, Kalbfleisch told her she was "ineligible." She asked Kalbfleisch for his permission to ask the Dean of the College for funding, and he agreed. In fact he phoned ahead to tell the Dean to turn Spencer down.[49] She went and paid her own way; Kalbfleisch attended at University expense.

Two years after Spencer had been hired, Kalbfleisch appointed a man as Associate Professor. Spencer, who had asked to have her rank upgraded and be made full-time, registered her concern about being passed over. In retaliation, Kalbfleisch stripped Spencer of her most interesting courses.[50] She was left to teach only the basic, service grammar courses. She never taught another German literature course until Kalbfleisch retired.

Spencer confronted Kalbfleisch over his refusal to upgrade her position. "There were openings, they were looking for people, why wouldn't he consider me?" she queried. Kalbfleisch was frank. He had a "vision of a greatly expanded German Department that would be all-male," he told Spencer. "If I were not married, if I was a man, I would be eligible to apply."[51] Spencer appealed the decision to the Principal of University College and to Western President G. Edward Hall. Hall dismissed her complaint forthwith. "He told me Kalbfleisch had well-known idiosyncrasies, and that was that."[52] Spencer did not succeed in obtaining her full-time appointment until 1965, when Kalbfleisch retired and John Rowe became the Dean. The situation had significant ramifications for Spencer's salary as well. Hers would later become generally acknowledged as the worst example of salary sex discrimination in the University.

Other cases of salary discrimination at Western never came to public light because those concerned did not raise the issue. A former Dean of Women recounts one instance that affected her personally:

> One year in the 1970s, I was advised by the university that my salary was going to be reduced in the coming year. When I checked into this, I was told that my earlier salary had been a mistake. As Dean of Women I had been listed with the rest of the Deans, and the administration had assumed all the Deans were male. They were running my salary based on the male track. I had to accept an adjustment downward. They told me this was explicitly because of my sex.[53]

Anomalies in fringe benefits, beyond those noted regarding life insurance, also disadvantaged faculty women. Male faculty were entitled to include their wives and children within the scope of the health insurance plan automatically. The husbands and children of female faculty had to be defined as dependent under the federal income tax rules before they qualified for coverage.[54]

Western had also inaugurated a mandatory retirement policy that openly differentiated on the basis of sex. Women were forced to retire at 60, while men could work to 65.[55] John Rowe, former Dean of the Faculty of Arts and Vice-Chair of the Senate, was frank enough to provide particulars. "The policy was developed by the Board of Governors and President G. Edward Hall. They believed that women became more difficult than men at the age of 60." When queried about the meaning of the word "difficult," Rowe expanded. "Difficult meant not doing what you were told. Under the Hall regime, there was a firm understanding about how you ran this place. One way was to keep women from becoming 'difficult.' "[56]

The differential retirement policy was a source of considerable hardship for many women faculty members. Professor Helen Battle, one of the most prominent of the women pushed out early, provides a good example. First hired as a Demonstrator in Zoology in 1923, she embarked upon a brilliant academic career which spanned more than 40 years. Despite Battle's remarkable talent as a scholar and teacher, her promotion was slow, and she did not obtain the rank of Full Professor until 1949. "There was no question about it," she observed. "Promotion was more difficult for women. You had to really show yourself. And that was especially true in the sciences."[57] Battle was forced out of the Department of Zoology in the mid-1960s at the age of 60, then rehired for three years as a part-time instructor and paid by the course at a rate significantly less than her former salary. "I retired but stayed on, you see, at half pay for full work of course."[58] While the reduced salary was insulting, Battle jumped at the chance to earn the extra money. "It helped out with salary. I'd been in at a very low salary in the early years, and my pension was low to start."[59] For two of those post-retirement years, she actually served as acting head of the department.[60]

The early retirement policy was bitterly resented. A former Dean of Women was one who firmly believed the age of retirement should be the same for women and men. "I thought if they were going to retire women at 60, they should retire men at 60 too."[61] A number of faculty women protested the rule to President Hall.[62] But the protest was informal, individualistic, and ultimately ineffective. Hanna Spencer summed up the impact: "President Hall probably dropped the petitions in his waste basket."[63] The policy was retained and enforced until 1 January 1966.[64]

The 1960s and 1970s witnessed a continuation of the discriminatory patterns. The University was growing dynamically, but the representation of women as faculty members was not. John Rowe admits now that it was "deep-seated prejudices" that were responsible for this attitude:

> There were a hell of a lot of bright female academics out there and we just never went after them. Back in the 70s, when we were laying the foundations, we could have brought in some really outstanding, gifted women. If we hadn't missed out on those opportunities, we would have had 35 to 40 percent female representation in the faculty today.[65]

The historical picture reveals many discriminatory practices. There are few instances of traceable collective or individualistic complaint. This is not to suggest that women were not fighting back, however. As someone who has been profoundly influenced by Dale Spender's historical writing,[66] I now customarily assume that as long as women have been present in the institution, there has been some form of active resistance against male domination. That we know little or nothing about most of the women who may have fought for women's rights at Western is certainly no reason to conclude they did not exist.

A few courageous examples of women's resistance at Western are reclaimable. In 1972 Professor Anne Bolgan of the Department of English threatened to sue Western as a result of discrimination with respect to salary, promotion, and entitlement to sabbatical leave. She later received full satisfaction after an external adjudicator reviewed her case in the context of a private arbitration hearing.[67]

Professor Margaret Seguin of the Department of Anthropology also took up the issue of salary discrimination. With the help of the Western Faculty Association she called a public meeting to discuss salary inequities for women generally, in March 1974.[68] After an overflow crowd of 175 turned out, the President established a separate Advisory Committee on Women's Salaries (Academic) to investigate.[69]

Western's Committee examined various options for salary assessment for female faculty. It chose not to use a multiple regression analysis which would check salaries for sex disparities after screening out such variables as highest degree, age, faculty, and rank. Queen's University had recently adopted this method and corrected a $1,961 average salary differential between women and men.[70] The Western Committee chose a "matched peer" technique which plotted a female academic's salary history against a male peer. This allowed for a more individualistic assessment, which may have permitted more accurate adjustments in some cases. But it was also a fairly discretionary methodology, which could not profess to be a systematic, statistical appraisal. Furthermore it amounted to an attempt to assess women's salaries on a case-by-case basis, a misguided effort to apply individual remedies to a systemic problem. Even more importantly, as we shall see, it relied upon the victims of discrimination to initiate the process.

Questionnaires were distributed to 153 female academics above the rank of Instructor. Inexplicably, Instructors and part-time faculty were removed from the scope of the inquiry. The task was to determine whether salary differences were the result of discrimination or lack of merit. Each woman was required to produce evidence of her academic qualifications, teaching experience, research grants and publications, professional activity outside the University, teaching loads, biographical data, and administrative responsibilities. Each was also asked to name a male faculty member whose work was comparable.[71] The male peers were then sent similar questionnaires. Next the Deans were asked to select a male faculty peer for each woman. It was the Committee's task to adjudicate on the appropriateness of the peer selection, and then to plot the salary histories of those involved, searching for discrepancies. When anomalies were identified, the Committee sent its decision for approval to the Deans involved. The rationale: "Because it had reviewed the salaries of female faculty members only, the Committee was very concerned that it did not upset a department that might have a very fine balance in terms of salary ranking."[72] The Committee did note that there was a potential for risk with this procedure: "If discrimination is occurring and is occurring at the level of the dean or the chairman, the review of these salaries with the deans might, in fact, allow such discrimination to continue."[73] Brushing this off as unsubstantiated, the Committee decided to take the risk.[74] Needless to say, the female faculty members were not given similar opportunity to intervene at this point.

The most startling aspect of the entire study was the large number of women faculty members who did not participate. Of the 153 who received questionnaires, a full 49 *did not reply*. Even more remarkably, the University took no further action on these, assuming the 49 women to be "satisfied." The Committee actually declared itself to be both "quite surprised and pleased that such a high number of the female faculty members felt no need to participate."[75] This passive approach by the Committee did nothing for women who may have opted out because of intimidation from male colleagues and academic superiors, or even low self-esteem. Certainly no one ever undertook to examine *why* the 49 had not responded.

Finally, the Report itself noted that the salary positions of instructors and part-time faculty had been deliberately left out of the terms of reference. The Committee firmly recommended to President Williams that a separate study be set up to examine this situation. "I expect there will be quite a widespread interest in this further study, after the release of the Report today," offered the Committee Chair.[76] If further studies were in fact conducted, no public reports were ever issued.

In spite of its shortcomings, some women did benefit from the Committee's 1975 review of salaries. Of the 104 women who proceeded through the inquiry, 21 received salary adjustments totalling $35,887. The actual amounts ranged from $500 to over $2,000.[77] Although many of these cases involved salary discrimination spanning many years, the awards were made retroactive only to 1 May 1974. The long-term implications for pension benefits went unexplored.[78]

In September 1975, the University released a wide-ranging *Status of Women Report*.[79] In an attempt to deal with sex discrimination facing faculty, students, and staff, the document encompassed 111 pages and 96 recommendations. The *Status of Woman Report* was not sanguine about the number of women faculty:

In 1974-5 there were 154 women among the 1,250 full-time faculty members at UWO. This represents 12.3 per cent of the total number. The percentage seems amazingly low when one considers that 43.9 per cent of the undergraduate student body and 23.4 per cent of the graduate body is female. Further, our information shows that while the percentage of women students has increased steadily for the past few years, the percentage of women faculty members has increased less than one per cent since 1971-72. . . . [T]he largest concentration of women faculty members is in the junior ranks. The only level at which women represent a significant percentage of the whole is at Lecturer/Instructor.[80]

Nor was the *Status of Women Report* laudatory about Western salaries:

[M]en on the faculty earn an average salary substantially higher than women at the same rank. This is true in all ranks except Instructor. . . . [T]he average faculty salary for men is $21,027, the average salary for women faculty is $16,371. We note the difference in salaries between men and women is most marked in the upper ranks. . . . We have no data to measure individual performance. However we think these general questions must be addressed: is the average performance of women academics sufficiently weak at the Assistant Professor level to justify the average of a year longer in the rank and $1,204 less in salary? A similar question must also be asked on behalf of women Associate Professors who also spend on average a year longer in the rank and earn $2,231 less than men at the same level.[81]

Professor Louise Forsyth, a member of the Committee, still registers some surprise when she reflects upon the institutional response to the *Report*. "I had expected the administration to be embarrassed by our findings," she related. "Instead, the *Report* seemed to have a sedative effect. The administration showed no interest in making any significant or meaningful change. The university never intended to wade in and really solve the inequities, and the *Report* did little to alter those predispositions."[82]

Unabashed, the University decided in December 1975 to request approval from the Ontario Human Rights Commission to designate itself an "Equal Opportunity Employer."[83] In what I consider to be a serious misuse of the severely limited human rights staff resources, the Commission scrutinized the University's personnel policies to ensure compliance with the Human Rights Code, and the go-ahead was given. Western personnel administrators promptly added the new label to application forms and employment advertisements.

In 1977, Western's President was asked to comment on the implementation of the *Status of Women Report*. He argued that "progress ha[d] been commendable" at Western:[84]

Thirty-one of the 132 new faculty appointments at this university were women, a percentage of 23.5, which compares favorably to the 11.8 per

cent of the full-time faculty in 1976-77 who were women. Although none of
the 31 women hired were at the rank of Associate Professor or Professor,
this may reflect merely the shortage of qualified women candidates at that
level.[85]

The President neglected to add that the percentage of female doctoral
students had been rising steadily from 19 per cent in 1972 to 26.1 per cent in
1977. This trend would continue, with women moving up to 33.5 per cent of
the doctoral candidates in 1984.[86] Despite the President's enthusiasm over
Western's progress, overall women remained only 12.4 per cent of the full-
time faculty.[87]

Furthermore, salary differentials continued at Western unabated. Wom-
en were paid less than men in each rank except the lowest one — Instructor.[88] Indeed the salary gap worsened. A national report on higher education in Canada, the *Symons Report*,[89] examined 42 universities for salary
discrepancies based on 1981-82 data. The median male salary at Western
was $38,759, while for females it was $27,722 (71.5 per cent). This gave Western the dubious distinction of being among the worst universities in the
country for wage gaps. Only the University of Waterloo had a poorer
record.[90] An internal report requested by the Western Faculty Association
Status of Women Committee in 1982 confirmed the problem.[91] Women continued to earn less than men at every academic rank.[92]

The feminists on campus at Western remained concerned about the University's commitment to change. Professor Louise Forsyth, who had been
elected to the Board of Governors, continued to raise the issue at regular intervals. In May 1981 she presented a brief to the Ontario Advisory Council
on Equal Opportunity for Women.[93] She highlighted the abysmally low
number of women faculty, salary inequities, pension inequities, and the
slow rate of promotion for women. She called for the Board of Governors to
adopt an affirmative action program "to provide evidence of the commitment of this university to real change."[94] Western's President was quick to
oppose her suggestion, and he rejected any notion of imposed quotas on
hiring. With some paternalism, he attempted to argue that imposed quotas
could provide "a potential source of danger to the cause of women."[95]

Finally, Nancy Poole and Earl H. Orser, two other members of the Board
of Governors, joined the chorus of questioners and the President was asked
to bring forward a complete report. He had some difficulty explaining the
statistics he had to deliver to the Board of Governors in June 1983. His report
showed women hovering around the level of 10 per cent of probationary
and tenured faculty.[96] Palpably surprised, the Board "encouraged the Senate to consider whether changes ... would be appropriate."[97] In November
1983 the Senate appointed yet another committee to explore this matter. The

"Ad Hoc Senate Committee to Review Appointments, Promotion and Tenure Policies" was to be chaired by Denis Smith, Dean of Social Science.

The "Smith Committee" produced the *Smith Report* in August 1984.[98] As an indication of its generally cautious approach, the *Report* failed to deal with salary anomalies. Noting that it "was not specifically charged with reviewing comparative salaries by sex," the Committee stated that it had "received no evidence, either written or oral, to suggest that this was a current issue in the University."[99] Past history alone should have fostered alarm over such passivity. Instead, the Committee accepted 1983 data compiled by the administration purporting to show that salary anomalies no longer existed.[100]

How Western progressed from notoriously bad salary data in 1981-82 to a clean bill of health in 1983 without any organized institutional intervention in between remains a mystery. To his credit, Dean Smith later expressed concern over the decision not to investigate further. "The salary data were surprising. I'm sure there is a problem, but no one came forward, and we simply felt we couldn't report where we had no evidence. But perhaps we should have pursued this more at the time...."[101] In what I view as a rather surprising statement, the *Report* concluded:

> The Committee looked carefully for any overt evidence of bias or discrimination against women in the University's policies and procedures relating to appointments, promotion and tenure, and could find none.... However, the Committee was told repeatedly of the existence of strong perceptions, both among women faculty members and among women outside the University, that the University's policies and procedures do work to the disadvantage of women, or leave them thinking so. Partly we attribute these perceptions to the lingering tendencies among some male faculty members to speak in language more natural to earlier times; partly to the likelihood that the small number of women faculty encourages a sense of isolation, and means that appointment, promotion and tenure committees and the ranks of senior administration frequently lack the presence of women; and partly to the existence in some University policies of what can be described as "systemic," rather than conscious and deliberate discrimination...[102]

I should be more forthcoming about my sense of surprise here. Men and women would appear to have an equal capacity to contribute as faculty in Canadian universities. Some would argue that since the ratio of men and women is not roughly 50:50, something must be amiss. In fact, the concept of "discrimination," is often used to describe the various factors which operate to create such a skewed population imbalance in the University. Here, instead, "discrimination" was relegated to some "perception" in the minds of women. To couch the issue in terms of "perception" and to suggest that discrimination does not exist is simply not helpful.

Regarding the data and its meaning, I pressed Dean Smith further about our difference of opinion subsequent to the release of the *Smith Report*. By then the Dean was willing to agree that "prejudice" against women did exist at Western. Indeed, he said that he was "quite shocked when he discovered what the general atmosphere was in the administration and in some departments."[103] After the publication of the *Report*, Smith told me he had an opportunity to meet with department chairs to discuss it. "A number made frank, sexist statements," he said. One Chair of a science department, he added, felt no embarrassment in announcing at a meeting with over 20 other Department Chairs "that our recommendations on maternity leave would encourage women faculty to have babies every two years!"[104]

I asked Smith why he had categorized the problem as one of "perception" rather than "discrimination" in his *Report*. "We had no hard evidence we could use," he responded.[105] It may have been that no women came forward with names and dates and details, but that is often the unfortunate result of any process which puts the onus on the victims of discrimination to complain. Given the University's historical record of bias, the Committee should have been instructed to undertake a far more vigilant and activist approach to its task. It should have been given the mandate and the resources to commence an institutional search for any evidence of discrimination towards women faculty — from other faculty, students, and the administration. Without having conducted such a painstakingly thorough investigation, it should never have categorically dismissed the existence of "hard" discrimination.[106] The decision to do so, Smith conceded, "was tactical.... We judged we could achieve more by not laying blame, by encouraging people. I still believe it is better to use incentives than penalties."[107]

The Committee did speak out strongly on the issue of male: female faculty ratios: "We consider a ratio of 9 to 1 among full-time faculty to be one of imbalance because it is so far from the balance of the general population, the undergraduate student population, and the graduate student population in a growing number of disciplines (though not all)."[108]

Shying away from a specific definition of "balance," as most reports of this nature tend to do, the Committee cautioned: "This does not mean, in our view, that the UWO should now aim at a ratio of 50:50, or that there is any magic in it. It does mean that we should aim at a balance which is more reasonable than the present one...."[109] Herein lies another of the major flaws in the *Report*. People seeking change must be very clear about their goals. Refusing to tackle the question of what represents "balance" is fatal. It ensures that subsequent recommendations and their implementation take place in a vacuum. Why is it so difficult for universities to admit that ideally men and women should share faculty positions equally?

The existing imbalances documented by the Committee should have caused considerable embarrassment to Western. It noted that women held a smaller proportion of full professorships than any other rank (4.3 per cent in 1984), and that this proportion had not changed significantly in recent years. Women represented 24.8 per cent of the Assistant Professors and 48.3 per cent of the Lecturers, but these positions were almost wholly limited-term appointments.[110] Women's access to tenure was markedly low. Between 1980 and 1984, men obtained tenure disproportionately to women, leaving the ratio of women tenured faculty at just 8.3 per cent of the total.[111]

The difficulty of rectifying the gender imbalance of faculty in a time of drastically reduced faculty recruitment was of concern. "The policy of stable base complements adopted by Senate in 1981 and applied since 1982, in combination with the existing age profile of tenure-stream faculty, has meant that very few new tenure-stream appointments (for either men or women) have been available in the past four years."[112] What this means is that the University decided not to increase the size of its tenured faculty as of 1982. The large number of male faculty hired in the 1950s and 1960s, when women were not being recruited in fair numbers, show no intention of quitting before regular retirement age. Indeed, some of those men are now challenging in court the University policies requiring mandatory retirement at the age of 65. They would like to stay on even longer! Even if they fail in their litigation, there is still no room left to hire women.

Nor did this problem seem to be of short duration. The Committee actually contemplated a policy which would hire 100 per cent women, but just for the purpose of illustration: ". . . even if a policy were to be applied henceforth which required and achieved the replacement of *every* retiring male with a female, it would take 15.7 years to attain equal numbers of women and men in the tenure stream."[113] The Committee quickly added that such a plan was, of course, an unrealistic proposal.[114] With this sentiment I am in complete agreement. The problem is not that it is too radical, however, but that it is clearly too little, too late. The Committee, on the contrary, had its own notions of realistic reform. Its recommendations were twofold. First, women candidates were to be hired in preference to men, where the two were "of equal qualification" for the academic years 1985-88.[115] This suggestion was eagerly embraced by the administration perhaps because anyone can see how impossible it would be to enforce.[116] The opportunities for evasion are delightfully endless. Western's President would later register surprise that the new policy generated so little hostility from male faculty. "We haven't had a word of dissent," he reported.[117] One would think this alone might have raised some suspicion.

The second set of recommendations entailed a modest affirmative action proposal, although it was not labelled as such. Quotas were expressly rejected, but it was proposed to hire 25 new faculty women over three years time. These were all to be tenure-stream appointments, over and above the static levels set by the administration in 1982. Initial funding was to come from central administration funds, rather than the existing operating budgets of the faculty itself.[118]

This proposal seems to have been one of the key reasons why Western was graced with its Employment Equity Award in 1986, astounding as this might seem. For the program, even if fully implemented, would have done little to alter the overall imbalances at Western. An additional 25 women would be virtually invisible in a full-time faculty of 1,367.[119] The program was deliberately set up as voluntary. Deans had to apply to participate and some of the University's male-dominated Faculties were neither inclined nor convinced. The Dean of the Faculty of Engineering was one of the first to register his views. Despite an unblemished record of 100 per cent male faculty, he boldly told *The London Free Press* that "the lack of women faculty doesn't concern me."[120] Another flaw in the proposal concerned financing — a critical matter in times of budget-shrinkage. No one suggested that these new positions be fully financed on a permanent basis. The departments would be forced to pick up a portion of the costs in the first three years, and the full costs subsequently. This lessened the attractiveness of the offer considerably.

This proposal to create 25 new positions for women faculty was hardly a recipe for radical transformation. Yet the administration still balked. Instead, the Vice-President offered his own proposal, one which was speedily endorsed by Senate. The approved scheme was to operate between 1 January 1985 and 31 December 1989. Faculties were allowed to hire additional women beyond their base complements. The Vice-President had *always* had the authority to permit the temporary lifting of faculty ceilings, but he proposed to use this power in cases where "outstanding women" could be hired.

If the weaknesses of the Smith proposal are obvious, the deficiencies of the fall-back scheme are even more so. First, faculties had to prove that the woman was "outstanding" to the satisfaction of the Provost, and, in some cases, also to the Chair of the Promotions Division or the Tenure Division of the Senate Committee on Promotions and Tenure.[121] Second, these new appointments did not come permanently. Faculties had to show that they could offset the new hire against a retirement before 1 July 1995.[122] In effect they were mortgaging away their future. Third, responsibility for financing was even more firmly allocated to the receiving faculty. Faculties wishing to participate were instructed to "redirect budgetary resources from other uses."[123] Only in exceptional cases, where funds were simply unavailable, did the plan authorize "bridge financing of up to three years."[124] The Vice-

President did not apologize for the backtracking this represented. Instead he told the Senate: "The number of appointments likely to be made under this arrangement cannot be predicted with certainty. However, the total is likely to be significantly more than the 25 proposed by the [Smith] Committee."[125]

The plan was programmed for failure. Dean Smith had obviously been afraid of just such an outcome, for he had recommended in his *Report* that the University be required to report annually to the Senate on its progress.[126] In the first year, the Vice-President reported that six new female appointments had been made under the initiative.[127] By 1986, in the second year, the University boasted to the Ontario government's Women's Directorate that the total number had now reached 12.[128] The government was not informed that there had been no progress in the overall numbers. Indeed, the 1986-87 figures showed women hovering at 14.1 per cent of the overall faculty, whereas they had represented 14.7 per cent in 1984-85, the year before the program started.[129]

After the first year, the administration made no further reports to the Senate or the Board of Governors regarding additional women hired under the initiative.[130] At the November 1987 Board of Governors meeting, Earl H. Orser inquired specifically as to the status of the new program. The new Vice-President (Academic) reported that six or seven appointments had been made in each year of the program, but that funding was "not as ample as it should be to effect change."[131]

Professor Sarah Shorten, President of Western's Caucus on Women's Issues, pursued the issue further in the Senate. In response to her questions, the Vice-President reported that book-keeping had not been done in any systematic way, and that a fully accurate count of the women hired under the initiative could not be produced.[132] Western's failure to monitor the success of the program it used to such artful advantage in the Employment Equity competition concerns me greatly. The decision not to track the impact of the preferential hiring scheme means no one will be able to say for certain whether it succeeded or failed.

Even more upsetting was the information on funding. You will recall that these new positions were, at least theoretically, to have some prospect of central funding. Indeed the Vice-President had made a great fuss in the Senate about his potential generosity here. "The demand for bridge funding is [not] predictable, but I would expect that once the program is in full swing an amount of $250,000 to $300,000 per annum would be involved."[133] In response to Shorten's question about monies expended so far, the new Vice-President reported that a total of 13 women had benefitted to date. He released no figures, and he admitted that there were other needs being given "first priority" for these funds.[134]

The Vice-President did, however, estimate that 21 additional women, over and above those who would have been hired without the program, had been appointed.[135] But the bottom line numbers remained stubbornly unchanged. Women represented 14.74 per cent of the faculty before the program started. The percentage now is 14.78 per cent.[136] The most recent data show Western is continuing to recruit men for approximately two-thirds of its new appointments.[137]

Although the numbers were unimpressive, the new Vice-President appeared to recognize the seriousness of the problem in a way his predecessors had never done. "Frankly the picture is not very encouraging," he stated. "Change has been very modest," he told the Senate, and "much more improvement is still needed."[138] This admission represents a breath of fresh air. One can only hope that this forthrightness indicates an administrative commitment to changes that make a significant difference.

The time has obviously come for a more ambitious, adventuresome approach to the employment of women faculty. None of the mechanisms historically adopted has made much of a dent in the abysmally low ratio of female faculty. The need here is to turn this negative record completely around as quickly as is humanly possible. At issue are results. The bottom line numbers are the only realistic indices of change. I want to challenge the University of Western Ontario to the goal of achieving 50:50 balance between male and female faculty by the year 2000.

I hold no secret formula for procedures and mechanisms to create swift and significant improvement. Indeed, the process by which change occurs is in the hands of the administration, the Deans, and Department Chairs of the University of Western Ontario. They are the people who are best placed to develop agendas for reform, in consultation with feminist, racially sensitive affirmative action specialists.

I cannot leave the issue, however, without offering a few suggestions of my own. These may give University administrators some basis for reflecting upon entirely novel ways in which to accomplish a marked increase in the number of faculty women. My suggestions are basically two-pronged, focusing on a) new appointments which will arise in the regular way as a result of voluntary resignations and retirements from existing faculty, and b) mechanisms to increase the pool of new appointments available.

New Appointment Procedures

1. *The No-Backsliding Rule*: Departments and faculties must not be permitted to lose ground with respect to male-female faculty ratios. Where women faculty resign or retire, they must be replaced with women.

2. *50 per cent Hiring Balance*: All departments and faculties must be expected to hire at least 50 per cent women in new appointments. Those who fail to do so must account for their imbalanced decisions. They should be required to submit detailed reports to a central review panel, containing extensive information on recruitment efforts to attract women, female applicants not selected, and full explanations of why male candidates were considered superior. The review panel must have authority to override initial decisions.

3. *Selected Trusteeships*: Departments and faculties which are notoriously underpopulated with women must be targets of more significant redress. Academic units which have been visibly irresponsible in past recruitment and selection no longer merit autonomous power. They should be placed into temporary trusteeship with respect to hiring. Central officials must assume this responsibility although department and faculty representatives will be permitted to act as advisers to the new hiring committees. There are many faculties and departments which would be obvious candidates for this procedure. Certainly those which have no female academics would qualify for consideration.

4. *Vice-President (Women)*: Western should establish a new senior administrative position at the vice-presidential level to take responsibility for advocacy of women's issues and to encourage affirmative action initiatives. Great care should be taken to ensure that individuals appointed to such a position have previously demonstrated expertise and a public commitment to affirmative action.

Increasing the Pool of New Appointments

Relatively few new appointments are being processed now, a direct reflection of Western's static faculty resources and its current age profile. Without active intervention, even the proposals outlined above will do little to resolve sex imbalances for decades. An increasing proportion of University resources will be diverted towards the salaries of entrenched male academics, while correspondingly few opportunities will open up to newly qualified women. The following proposals would assist in rectifying this inertia. All are designed to make available new and additional openings, above those which would naturally come up. All such positions should be filled by women, since the explicit goal of these affirmative action proposals is to increase the number of women faculty.

1. *Endowed Chairs for Women*: The most obvious method of increasing the number of women is to find more funding specifically earmarked for that purpose. Short-term allocations are not particularly helpful, since they permit only limited-term contractual appointments and offer no real aca-

demic future for recipients. Fund-raising should be mounted to create at least 10 permanent chairs for women faculty. The capital cost of such a commitment is high — approximately $10 million dollars — but certainly no higher than the cost of building new structures and establishing large research projects for which universities have conducted successful fund-raising campaigns in the past.

The prospect of endowed chairs for women is perhaps the most positive proposal that can be put forward. Imagine a woman's Chair in Engineering,[139] named after the distinguished professional engineer from Canadian history, Elsie Gregory MacGill. A Chair in Journalism named for the internationally renowned, first Black woman to found and edit a newspaper in Canada, Mary Ann Shadd. A woman's Chair in the Department of Obstetrics and Gynaecology named for Canada's first White woman doctor and prominent suffragist, Emily Stowe!

2. *Tenure Review*: While tenure is often cited as a critically important feature of academic life, it has not aided males and females equally since women have not been given equal access to its benefits. Men are vastly over-represented among tenured faculty, and the retention of tenure entrenches their status against new female applicants.[140]

Much more research is needed to conclude, from a feminist perspective, whether tenure is, or could be, an academic asset to women faculty.[141] My own inclination is to think it is not. I suspect that at the moment, too few women are given an opportunity to compete for tenure in the first place. In addition, the five to seven year anxiety-ridden process of attempting to place oneself within the context of malestream disciplines in order to seek tenure successfully is enough to knock feminism out of even the most committed woman. Instead of serving as a bulwark for academic freedom, the getting of tenure forces much new thinking underground where it may, or may not, emerge after tenure is obtained. This is no way to begin to transform hostile male-dominated disciplines. My own preference would be to think that the abolition of tenure would be best, coupled with the introduction of a simple industrial relations "just cause" rule. That is, that no one can be fired without just cause. Where disputes arise, an external arbitrator, accepted by both the administration and the faculty member concerned, becomes the final decision-maker. But perhaps such a significant step should be preceded by further analysis and research.

In the meantime, a more moderate process of tenure review should be implemented which would require an assessment of tenured faculty members every five years. Research, teaching, and administrative and community work should all be evaluated, and individuals whose record falls below an acceptable standard should be dismissed. It is possible that discriminatory bias could creep into this process, and that women faculty members might lose their tenure more often than male faculty members for reasons which have nothing to do with their work output. The incentive to create this situation should be diminished however, if positions opened up as a result of this process are filled *only* by women.

3. *Early Retirement*: The University should adopt a new retirement policy which is a mirror reflection of its earlier 60:65 rule. This time male academics will be mandatorily retired at the age of 60, while women are permitted to remain until 65. This will open up a number of additional spots, all of which should be filled by women.

One caveat must be attached to these suggestions. Women hired as a result of these strategies must not be sent in to teach in these faculties and departments alone. They will be entering an almost completely male environment, peopled with individuals who are totally unaccustomed to dealing with women as equals and colleagues. Resentments will no doubt abound. Women who represent the initial appointees in an affirmative action program need all the assistance they can get to surmount the inevitable hurdles and establish themselves securely.[142] They must be hired in twos and threes.[143]

These proposals all have an element of affirmative action in them. Apologists for present-day sex imbalances always begin by arguing that all forms of discrimination are bad. But they insist that one must not try to rectify past wrongs with differential treatment in the present. Their cries for sex-neutral employment practices are both too late and too early. They fail to realize that if women are to make substantial gains in the academic field, men must lose ground correspondingly.

They also conveniently forget that human rights legislation supports affirmative action policies.[144] The Canadian Charter of Rights and Freedoms expressly recognizes the validity of affirmative action programs as well.[145] The Supreme Court of Canada, in *Action Travail des Femmes v. Canadian National Railway Company*, was forthright in its analysis of affirmative action:

> An employment equity program ... is designed to break a continuing cycle of systemic discrimination. The goal is not to compensate past victims or even to provide new opportunities for specific individuals who have been unfairly refused jobs or promotion in the past, although some such individuals may be beneficiaries of an employment equity scheme. Rather, an employment equity program is an attempt to ensure that future applicants and workers from the affected group will not face the same insidious barriers that blocked their forebears. [...] Systemic remedies must be built upon the experience of the past so as to prevent discrimination in the future.[146]

Our statutes, our constitution, and our Supreme Court explicitly support affirmative action. Will Western finally do so as well?

Appendix A

Percentage of Full-time Faculty
Who Are Female[1]

	Nationally	Provincially	UWO
1921	15	—	—
1926	17	—	—
1931	19	12.7	—
1937	13	14.7	—
1941	14.6	17.6	—
1942	18.7	12.3	—
1943	18.2	—	—
1944	19.9	—	—
1946	18.9	—	—
1949	17.3	—	—
1950	17.3	—	—
1951	—	10	—
1953	18	—	—
1958	11	—	—
1964-65	13	—	—
1965-66	12.7	—	—
1969-70	13	—	—
1970-71	12.7	—	—
1971-72	—	12	13
1972-73	13	12	12.3
1973-74	—	13	11
1974-75	13.9	14	12.3
1975-76	14	14	11.8
1976-77	—	14	12.4
1977-78	14	14	13
1978-79	14.8	14	13
1979-80	—	14	12
1980-81	15.5	15	13.2
1981-82	—	15	13
1982-83	16.1	15	13.7
1983-84	16.4	16	13.7
1984-85	16.7	16	14.7
1985-86	17.0	17	13.6
1986-87	—	15.7	14.1
1987-88	—	—	14.7

Notes

Editors' Notes

1 This chapter originally appeared in the *Canadian Journal of Women and the Law*, 4 (1990): 36-65. It is reprinted here with permission of the author and of the editors of *CJWL*.

2 The *Backhouse Report* was the subject of a number of articles and letters to the editor that appeared in *The Globe and Mail*, *The London Free Press*, the *Toronto Star*, *Western News*, and various faculty association and society newsletters from late April through June 1988. See, for example, "Backhouse Report: Female Faculty Hiring Record Criticized," *Western News*, 26 May 1988, p. 4; "Caucus to Assist University in Employment Equity Steps," *Western News*, 9 June 1988, p. 6; "Study of Hiring Practices Urged," *Western News*, 23 June 1988, p. 3; letters to the editor in *Western News*, 12 May 1988, 26 May 1988, 9 June 1988, and 23 June 1988; "Hire More Women Teachers, UWO Told," *The London Free Press*, 2 May 1988; letters to the editor, *The London Free Press*, 6 May 1988 and 16 May 1988; "UWO Has Delayed Hiring Women Too Long," *The Globe and Mail*, 16 May 1988; "University Quotas for Women Faculty," *The Globe and Mail* 11 June 1988, p. D7; and "Western's Record on Job Equity Criticized," *CAUT (Canadian Association of University Teachers) Bulletin*, June 1988, p. 10.

Notes

1 This *Report*, like most of the material available on faculty women in Canada, will focus on full-time appointments exclusively. The omission of part-time women from the study is a serious failing which should be acknowledged at the outset. The small amount of data available tend to suggest that women are represented in higher numbers among part-time faculty than among full-time. The rates of pay, working conditions, and job security are all routinely acknowledged as significantly worse than for full-time employment. However the absence of accessible data on this problem makes the issue extremely difficult to study. See, for example, Helen J. Breslauer, "Women in the Professoriate: The Case of Multiple Disadvantage," in *The Professoriate — Occupation in Crisis* (Toronto: Ontario Institute for Studies in Education, 1985), p. 82, 86. My hope is to leave this question for fuller exploration at a later time.

2 I have chosen deliberately to use the phrase "affirmative action" rather than the newer terminology "employment equity." Frankly I see nothing particularly reprehensible about the earlier phrase, which was coined to describe positive measures adopted to improve the status of a disadvantaged group. The concept of affirmative action has an honourable and lengthy tradition in Canada (see *Roberts v. Ontario Ministry of Health*, [1988] 10 C.H.R.R., D/6353 [Ontario Board of Inquiry]). What could be less offensive than words such as "affirmative" or "action?" I have no quarrel with the professed goals of those who seek to change the terminology. They believe that new phrasing will reduce the amount of opposition to these concepts. These goals are laudable but in my opinion the strategy is unlikely to succeed. The opposition is to the idea and to the programs, not to the phrase. Insofar as "employment equity" programs actually force change, their labels too will come under siege. For my part, I would have preferred to stick with the old terminology, and I will continue to do so. See also Debra J. Lewis, *Just Give Us the Money: A Discussion of Wage Discrimination and Pay Equity* (Vancouver: Vancouver Women's Research Centre, 1988), p. 11, 28-32, and Marjorie Cohen, "Employment Equity Is Not Affirmative Action," *Canadian Woman Studies*, 6, 4 (1985): 23.

3 The present *Report* focuses almost entirely upon easily documented issues such as faculty numbers, salaries, stated university policies regarding retirement, etc. Apart from some anecdotal materials, it does not cover the broader, more subtle issue of sexual harassment. A more comprehensive description of the working environment of faculty women at Western is found in a companion piece, "The Chilly Climate for Faculty Women at Western: Postscript to the Backhouse Report" [the *Chilly Climate Report*], co-authored by Con-

stance Backhouse, Roma Harris, Gillian Michell, and Alison Wylie (November 1989) and reprinted here as chapter 4.

4 On 17 March 1988, the University of Western Ontario became a signatory to the Federal Contractors Program of the federal government's Employment Equity Branch of the Department of Employment and Immigration. This required the University to begin to compile more detailed statistical data on the nature of its workforce, as part of the implementation of an employment equity program. *[Addendum: Subsequent to the publication of this report, the first employment equity census was initiated at Western in the spring of 1990, and showed "visible minority" faculty to account for 5.3% of all faculty, and "disabled" faculty to account for 3.4% of all faculty. Persons of "aboriginal ancestry" represented 0.3% of all regular full-time employees, a number too small to allow for any breakdown of their presence within the faculty alone. Little improvement was indicated by February 1993, when "aboriginal peoples" accounted for < 0.1% of all faculty, "visible minorities" for 5.8%, and persons with disabilities 2.8%. These reports are discussed in more detail in chapter 12. (See "Second Report of the President's Standing Committee for Employment Equity" [London: UWO], June 1992, p. 3 and 32, and "UWO Federal Contractors Program Compliance Review Report, Certificate 60543" [London: UWO], 24 November 1993, Table 2.)]*

5 "Sex Discrimination within Field of Law," *UWO Gazette*, 8 November 1980. It is interesting to note that Western's Faculty of Law has improved upon its statistics considerably: in 1987-88, women represented 23% of the Faculty: Vice-President (Academic) Collins, *Report to the Senate*, 11 February 1988, Senate Minutes, Appendix 1 (on file with Secretary of the Board of Governors and Senate, UWO). While this does not compare with the percentage of women law students (43.2% in 1987-88), it is well above the University average.

6 The Dean of the UWO Faculty of Law at the writing of this paper, Wesley Rayner, has made it somewhat easier for me to begin speaking publicly on this issue once more. Just prior to the release of this paper, he assured me that he believed academic freedom of speech encompassed research such as this, and that regardless of his own viewpoints on the correctness of my arguments, he would personally stand behind my right to make them.

7 This award was announced in the *Employment Equity Award Winners Official Program*, Ontario Women's Directorate (1986).

8 Breslauer, "Women in the Professoriate," p. 82-104. Of equal cause for concern is the fact that the reporting problems that have plagued Statistics Canada have also delayed publication of any national data after 1985. Craig McKie, editor, *Canadian Social Trends* of Statistics Canada, has indicated that until these problems are resolved, we will see no new national figures. He was unable to predict when a resolution might be found (Craig McKie, oral presentation at "The Compensation of Female Academic Staff," workshop co-sponsored by the Ontario Confederation of University Faculty Associations and the University of Toronto Faculty Association, Toronto, 23 September 1988).

9 Dominion Bureau of Statistics, *Salaries and Qualifications of Teachers in Universities and Colleges, 1957-58*, p. 23.

10 See Thomas H.B. Symons and James E. Page, *Some Questions of Balance: Human Resources, Higher Education and Canadian Studies* (Ottawa: Association of Universities and Colleges of Canada, 1984), p. 191.

11 Ibid., p. 209.

12 Statistics Canada, *Teachers in Universities*, 1985-86, p. 13-14. Interestingly, the poor sex ratio lasted despite the fact that the total number of full-time university teachers increased more than sixfold over the 26-year period.

13 Ibid., p. 21.

14 Symons and Page, *Some Questions of Balance*, p. 194.

15 Statistics Canada, *Teachers*, p. 18, 66, 68. More detailed analysis of salary disparity data in 1974-75 concluded that the discrepancies could not be attributed altogether to differences

in age, degree qualifications, and/or the number or years spent at each rank (Gail McIntyre and Janice Doherty, *Women in Ontario Universities; A Report to the Ministry of Colleges and Universities* [Toronto: Ontario Ministry of Colleges and Universities, 1975]).

16 Ontario Women's Directorate, *Employment Equity Award* (1986), inside cover.

17 Ibid., p. 7.

18 Data calculated from *Western Facts, 1988*, p. 62-63. Available from the Office of Institutional Planning and Budgeting, UWO. *[Addendum: Since this* Report *was originally written, the percentage of women faculty has risen at a glacial pace, according to data released annually in* Western Facts: *1989—15.709%; 1990—17.367%; 1991—17.286%; 1992—17.480%; 1993—17.647%; 1994—17.883%. See* Western Facts, 1989; Western Facts, 1990; Western Facts, 1991; Western Facts, 1992; Western Facts, 1993; *and* Western Facts, 1994.]

19 An examination of the annual listings of "Officers of Instruction" from the *University of Western Ontario Announcements*, Faculty of Arts and the Faculty of Medicine, shows the following:

1929-30	30 women of 193 faculty	15.5%
1930-31	36 women of 198 faculty	18.2%
1931-32	29 women of 188 faculty	15.4%
1932-33	39 women of 206 faculty	18.9%
1933-34	35 women of 204 faculty	17.2%
1934-35	42 women of 204 faculty	20.6%

Available at D.B. Weldon Library and Medical Sciences Library, UWO.

20 See Appendix A for details.

21 A tenured position offers job security until retirement; a tenured professor can only be fired for egregious misconduct or in situations of severe institutional financial crisis. A probationary position is one in which the faculty member is given the opportunity to achieve tenure. Once hired on a probationary appointment if the employee continues to demonstrate excellence in her/his field for five to seven years, the chances are that s/he will achieve tenure. Thus both tenured and probationary appointments (tenure-stream) offer real or potential job security and career development. The third type of position is limited term or contractual, which means that the employee has been hired for a specific period of time (generally one to three years) and will be terminated at the end of that period. These jobs do not permit permanent employment.

22 Lynn S. Wilson, "Status of Women Faculty Data for 1983" (April 1984). Available from the office of the Associate Vice-President, Academic Affairs, UWO. There were 1,143 full-time faculty positions, of which 104 were women and 1,039 were men. Expressed as a percentage this works out to 9%. The 1982 data also show women as 9% of tenure-stream faculty. See Lynn S. Wilson, "Report to UWO Faculty Association Status of Women Committee, Contract Types... Men and Women Faculty UWO," 15 November 1982. Available from the office of the Associate Vice-President, Academic Affairs, UWO. There are no more recent data available at this time.

23 *Western Facts, 1988*, p. 62-63. The data available data in *Western Facts, 1990* show men representing 95.9% of the Full Professors and women representing 64.6% of the Lecturers.

24 This information was based on 1983 data. *Report of the Ad Hoc Senate Committee to Review Appointments, Promotion and Tenure Policies and Procedures* (August 1984), Tables 4-8. Available from the Office of the Secretary of the Board of Governors and Senate, UWO.

25 Despite repeated requests it was not until November 1988 that the University again released such full data. The list of departments and faculties without women included Classical Studies, Chemical Engineering, Civil Engineering, Electrical Engineering, Materials Engineering, Astronomy, Geology, Geophysics, Statistics/Actuarial Science, Physics, Clinical Biochemistry, History of Medicine and Science, Otolaryngology, and Radiation Oncology. The list of departments and faculties with one woman included Mechanical En-

gineering, Applied Mathematics, Mathematics, Biochemistry, Medical Biophysics, Pharmacology, Clinical Neuroscience, Diagnostic Radiation and Nuclear Medicine, Obstetrics/Gynaecology, Ophthalmology, Surgery, and Journalism.

26 The following data were compiled by the Western Faculty Association and presented in the UWOFA Salary Brief, 1987-88:

Female Salaries as a Percentage
of Male Salaries Age Band

< 30 yrs.	98.1
30-34	89.9
35-39	81.8
40-44	83.5
45-49	78.4
50-54	91.4
55-59	85.6
60+	80.7

Available from the Faculty Association, UWO. Statistics Canada data for 1986-87 show UWO faculty women earn on average $42,665 while men earn on average $53,925. Statistics Canada, *Salaries and Salary Scales of Full-Time Teaching Staff at Canadian Universities* (1986-87), p. 23.

27 Margaret Gillett, *We Walked Very Warily: A History of Women at McGill* (Montreal: Eden Press Women's Publications, 1981), and Anne Rochon Ford, *A Path Not Strewn with Roses: One Hundred Years of Women at the University of Toronto, 1884-1984* (Toronto: University of Toronto Press, 1985). See also Margaret Gillett and Kay Sibbald, eds., *A Fair Shake: Autobiographical Essays by McGill Women* (Montreal: Eden Press, 1984); Joy Parr, ed., *Still Running. . . . Personal Stories by Queen's Women Celebrating the Fiftieth Anniversary of the Marty Scholarship* (Kingston: Queen's University Alumnae Association, 1987); and, later, the publication of Lee Stewart, *It's Up to You: Women at UBC in the Early Years* (Vancouver: University of British Columbia Press, 1990).

28 William Ferguson Tamblyn, *These Sixty Years* (London: UWO, 1938); James J. Talman and Ruth Davis Talman, *"Western" 1878-1953* (London: UWO, 1953); and John R.W. Gwynne-Timothy, *Western's First Century* (London: UWO, 1978). Other accounts include Ross Baxter-Willis, *Western 1939-70: Odds and Ends* (London: UWO, 1980); Hendrik Overduin, *People and Ideas: Nursing at Western, 1920-1970* (London: Faculty of Nursing, UWO, 1972); Murray L. Barr, *A Century of Medicine at Western* (London: UWO, 1977); and Ruth Helen Davis, "The Beginnings and Development of the University of Western Ontario, 1878-1924" (MA thesis, 1925).

29 Gwynne-Timothy, *Western's First Century*, p. 139, notes that when the University reopened in 1895, after a 10-year hiatus due to lack of funds, there were "several ladies" registered in the Faculty of Arts. Tamblyn (*These Sixty Years*, p. 16) suggests that the first two women students to graduate in Arts were Jessie Murdock (Mrs. Gilmore) and Susan Blackburn, both in 1900. He is wrong. The first female graduated in 1898; her name was Mary L. Cowan (Gwynne-Timothy, *Western's First Century*, p. 152).

30 Gwynne-Timothy, *Western's First Century*, p. 221, is the only author to acknowledge the existence of one of the first women faculty members, Hilda Baynes, but he does not relate that she and Georgia Maud Newbury were the first women appointed.

31 The Western University of London, Ontario, Arts Department, *Calendar* (1915-16), p. 9. Available at D.B. Weldon Library, UWO.

32 Susan Jackel has reported on a recent initiative at the University of Alberta to develop a "full statistical profile of all students and permanent staff by sex" from 1908 to 1985 (Susan Jackel, "Affirmative Action Programs in Canadian Universities and Colleges," *Canadian Woman Studies*, 6, 4 [1985]: 68, 70). This kind of baseline data is sorely needed at Western.

33 The Western University of London, London, Ontario, College of Arts, *Announcement* (1921-22), p. 14. Available at D.B. Weldon Library, UWO.
34 Baxter-Willis, *Western*, p. 56.
35 Gwynne-Timothy, *Western's First Century*, p. 200, provides the appointment date.
36 Western University Medical School Announcements (1922-23). Available at Medical Sciences Library, UWO.
37 *President's Committee on Oral History*, transcripts for Dr. Murray L. Barr, 7 November 1986, p. 12. On file with Professor Jack Hyatt, Department of History, UWO.
38 Barr, *A Century of Medicine*, p. 360.
39 Ibid., p. 359-61. Angus McLaren, *Our Own Master Race: Eugenics in Canada 1885-1945* (Toronto: McClelland & Stewart, 1990), p. 128-45, provides a detailed biography of Macklin, concluding that the University "treated her shabbily throughout her long and distinguished career." See also Daniel J. Kevles, who described Macklin as "one of the pioneers of medical genetics" in "Annals of Genetics: A Secular Faith," *The New Yorker*, 29 October 1984, Part 4 of a four-part series, p. 51, 56.
40 Barr, *A Century of Medicine*, p. 360-61.
41 Letter from K.P.R. Neville, Dean, University College of Arts, to Miss Frances Montgomery, 8 July 1930. On file with the author.
42 The forced early retirement still rankles today. Dr. Montgomery comments: "I could make some tart remarks about the fact that it is over twenty years since I was retired as unfit for university work while men — notably Dr. Neville — went on and on forever, like the babbling brook" (letter from Dr. Frances Montgomery to the author, 17 December 1988; on file with the author).
43 Interview with Mary Wright, Professor Emeritus, Department of Psychology, UWO, 14 September 1987. Wright noted that both she and Leola Neal started work as of September while a number of their male colleagues hired in those years began as of 1 July.
44 Admission to the pension plan was not allowed until an individual had completed two years of service. The date selected for the test of admissibility was 1 July. Thus, while men could join the pension plan after two years of employment, women had to wait three years. Men who had gone into military service were allowed to join the pension plan immediately (Wright interview).
45 Interview with Leola Neal, 21 October 1987. On file with the author.
46 Ibid.
47 Interview with Hanna Spencer, 4 November 1987. On file with the author. See also *President's Committee on Oral History*, transcript of interview with Hanna Spencer, 18 July 1986. On file with Professor Jack Hyatt, Department of History, UWO.
48 Don Kerr, Principal of Middlesex College, apparently took pity on Spencer and provided her with an office in another building with the political scientists (transcript of interview with Hanna Spencer, 18 July 1986, p. 13).
49 Ibid.
50 Ibid.
51 Ibid.
52 Ibid.
53 Interview with Leola Neal, 21 October 1987.
54 Letters complaining of this discriminatory policy were sent to the Status of Women Committee by a number of university women between 1972 and 1975, and remain in the Status of Women files of the Office of the President. Of course this policy had heterosexist implications as well.
55 Interview with Mary Wright, 14 September 1987, and interview with Professor Louise Forsyth, Department of French, UWO, 1 September 1987. On file with the author.
56 Interview with John Rowe, 16 November 1987. On file with the author.
57 Interview with Helen Battle, 16 February 1988. On file with the author.

58 Ibid.

59 Ibid.

60 *President's Committee on Oral History*, transcript of interview with Helen I. Battle, 15 June 1982. On file with Professor Jack Hyatt, Department of History, UWO.

61 Interview with Leola Neal, 21 October 1987.

62 Ibid.

63 Interview with Hanna Spencer, 4 November 1987.

64 Interview with William F. Trimble, Assistant Vice-President Personnel, and Keith Gee, Personnel Manager, Pensions and Benefits, 7 December 1987. On file with the author. Apparently the administration never did bend to the sex discrimination arguments. It never formally conceded that the past practice had been unjust. The policy was changed on the inaugural date of the Canada Pension Plan (CPP). The rationale was administrative efficiency. With the creation of the CPP, Western pension benefits were stacked on top of the CPP payments, and the computers would not program differential starting dates for men and women. Interview with Professor Betty Bandeen, Department of English, 21 December 1987. On file with the author.

65 Interview with John Rowe, 16 November 1987. On file with the author.

66 Dale Spender, *Women of Ideas and What Men Have Done to Them* (London: Routledge & Kegan Paul, 1982).

67 Interview with Professor Anne Bolgan, Department of English, 21 September 1987. On file with the author.

68 Interview with Professor Margaret Seguin, Department of Anthropology, 12 January 1988. On file with the author.

69 My account of the activities of this committee is drawn from W.S Turner et al., "Report of the President's Advisory Committee on Women's Salaries (Academic)," published in UWO *Western News Supplement*, 30 October 1975.

70 Turner et al., "Report on Women's Salaries," p. 2.

71 In some cases, such as the Faculty of Nursing and the Department of Secretarial and Administrative Studies, the Committee maintained that there were no male peers. Refusing to accept the comparisons suggested by the Dean of Nursing, the Committee worked out an alternate methodology here. See Turner et al., "Report on Women's Salaries," p. 1-2, for a description of the altered process.

72 Turner et al., "Report on Women's Salaries," p. 2.

73 Ibid.

74 "The Committee felt that the above objective was worth this risk, and in fact found no evidence that this problem exists in any specific faculty" (ibid.).

75 Ibid., p. 3.

76 *Western News*, 30 October 1975.

77 Turner et al., "Report on Women's Salaries," p. 4. The President appeared relieved by the low number of awards, fewer than "many anticipated" (p. 1). The Committee intimated that a number of Deans had headed them off by using special funds to alleviate inequities prior to the investigation (p. 3).

78 Pension adjustments were made retroactive to 1 May 1974 only. An exception was made in the case of one female who had already retired; it was recommended that an additional amount be purchased above the existing fixed pension. Memo from Alex S. Dobbins, "Salaries," 11 September 1975. Available at Department of Financial Planning and Budgeting, UWO.

79 Betty Campbell, *Status of Women Report*, 1975. Available from the office of the President, UWO.

80 Ibid., p. 10.

81 Ibid., p. 11.

82 Interview with Professor Louise Forsyth, Department of French, 1 September 1987. On file with the author.

83 Information on this application was provided by William F. Trimble, Assistant Vice-President, Personnel, UWO, as part of a public lecture he gave at Western on 24 March 1987 for Western's Caucus on Women's Issues. The request was originally to use the designation with respect to administrative staff, but several years later the University sought and was granted permission to use the designation with respect to academic faculty as well.

84 *Western News Supplement*, "Status of Women Update," 1 December 1977, p. 1.

85 George Connell, *Report on the Implementing of Recommendations of the Report of the President's Ad Hoc Committee on the Status of Women, 1975*, 23 November 1977, p. 7. Available from the Office of the President, UWO.

86 Statistics Canada, *Full-Time Teaching Staff Analysis System, Ontario Universities, Female Doctoral Enrollment against New Faculty Appointments, 1971-72 to 1983-84*. Ontario data from 1986-87 show women as 36.9% of the doctoral candidates, and 26.6% of the recipients of doctoral degrees (*Status of Women in Provincially Assisted Ontario Universities and Related Institutions 1976-77 to 1986-87* [Toronto: Ministry of Colleges and Universities, University Relations Branch, 1988]).

87 *Western News Supplement*, 1 December 1977, p. 2-3.

88 Ibid.

89 Symons and Page, *Some Questions of Balance*.

90 Ibid., p. 197, Table 46.

91 Lynn S. Wilson, "Report to the UWO Faculty Association Status of Women Committee Report on Salaries of the Regular Full-Time Academic and Administrative Staff at UWO in 1982, by Sex" (30 November 1982). Available at the office of the Associate Vice-President Academic Affairs, UWO.

92 Ibid.

93 *Western News*, 7 May 1981, p. 3.

94 Ibid.

95 Ibid.

96 George Connell, "Report on New Appointments 1980-82," to UWO Board of Governors, June 1983. Updates of this information have since been presented to the Board annually, at the Board's request. Reports were delivered in June 1984, June 1985, June 1986, and November 1987. Available at the office of the President, UWO.

97 Denis Smith et al., *Report of the Ad Hoc Senate Committee to Review Appointments, Promotion, and Tenure Policies and Procedures* (August 1984), p. 2. Available at the Office of the Secretary of the Board of Governors and Senate, UWO.

98 Ibid.

99 Ibid., p. 5.

100 Ibid., Table 11.

101 Interview with Denis Smith, 20 August 1987. On file with the author.

102 Smith et al., *Report*, p. 7.

103 Interview with Denis Smith, 20 August 1987.

104 Ibid.

105 Ibid.

106 Couching reports in the language of "perception" contains real dangers. Most crucially, it allows opponents of affirmative action to ridicule remedial programs that are mounted on the basis of spurious complaints. See, for example, my colleague Professor Ian Hunter's categorical denunciation of Smith's subsequent proposals: "Most important, the rhetoric of 'affirmative action' drains language of its meaning. This was aptly illustrated during a recent Senate debate at The University of Western Ontario over a proposal to create an affirmative action program to hire female academics. The debate followed a report of a committee chaired by Social Science Dean Denis Smith. The Smith Committee reported that,

despite a scrupulous examination of university hiring practices, they found not a scintilla of evidence of conscious or intentional discrimination against women. Nevertheless, the proportion of female faculty members was small compared to the proportion of female students, which led to widespread perceptions of discrimination. What was the University's response? Did Western conceive it as its duty to dispel misperception by fact? No, the University chose the path of least resistance, and instituted an affirmative action program to hire more women. For more than a decade, Western has included in every employment advertisement the words 'An equal opportunity employer.' Equal opportunity means that there are no artificial barriers put in the way of a qualified man or a qualified woman. To specifically impose artificial barriers for men, or to create artificial advantages for women, in the name of equality is to debase both logic and language. As one Senator inquired: 'Will Western now be identified as a *more* than equal opportunity employer?'" (Ian Hunter, "When Human Rights Become Wrongs," *University of Western Ontario Law Review*, 23 [1985]: 197, 202).

107 Interview with Denis Smith, 20 August 1987.

108 Smith el al., *Report*, p. 6.

109 Ibid.

110 Ibid., p. 3.

111 "An increasing proportion of the total (88 per cent in 1984 as compared to 81 per cent in 1980) has become tenured, while in the same period the percentage of tenured women among total tenured faculty in both tenured and probationary positions has remained constant at 8.3 per cent. Similarly the balance of women to total faculty in both tenured and probationary positions has remained at 10.1 per cent" (ibid.).

112 Ibid.

113 Ibid.

114 Ibid.

115 Ibid., p. 14-15.

116 Vice President (Academic) J. Clark Leith recommended this initiative to the Senate in November 1984. Memo to Members of SCUP, "Equal Opportunity Committee Report," 26 November 1984. Available at the Office of the Secretary of the Board of Governors and Senate UWO. By 1985 all appointments committees had been notified: *Status Report of the Vice-President (Academic) and Provost Concerning the Recommendations of the Ad Hoc Senate Committee to Review Appointments, Promotion and Tenure Policies and Procedures*, September 1985. Available at the Office of the Secretary of the Board of Governors and Senate, UWO. The potential for avoidance was recognized even by the Vice-President (Academic) J. Clark Leith, who wrote the following to all Deans on 18 February 1985: "While we all recognize the potential difficulties inherent in judging what constitutes 'equal qualifications,' I believe that the intent of the Senate is to consider the term 'qualifications' in the fullest sense of the word and not simply in terms of formal qualifications. At the same time, I believe the intent of Senate is clear that when there is no significant difference between men and women candidates, the woman should be chosen" (J. Clark Leith, "Memo to all Deans re Report on Equal opportunity: Recommendation 21(X)," 18 February 1985. Available at the Office of the Secretary of the Board of Governors and Senate, UWO).

117 Ontario Women's Directorate, *Employment Equity Award*.

118 Smith et al., *Report*, p. 9-10, 13-14. The *Report* suggested that 5 of these positions be at senior levels and 20 at the level of Assistant Professor. The Appendix suggested that funding come from the Academic Development Fund or other central funds at the following rates. For senior positions, 100% first year, 66% second year, 33% third year. For the others, 66% first year, 33% second year (ibid., Appendix 9).

119 *Western Mini-Facts* (1984), p. 1.1. Available at the office of Institutional Planning and Budgeting, UWO.

120 *The London Free Press*, 22 October 1984.

121 "Provost's Proposal," 19 November 1984, p. 3-4. Available at the Office of the Secretary of the Board of Governors and Senate, UWO.

122 Ibid.

123 Ibid.

124 Ibid.

125 Ibid.

126 Smith et al., *Report*, p. 11.

127 *Report of Vice-President (Academic) and Provost Concerning the Recommendations of the Ad Hoc Senate Committee to Review Appointments, Promotion and Tenure Policies and Procedures (Smith Report)*, September 1985. Available at the Office of the Board of Governors and the Senate, UWO.

128 Ontario Women's Directorate, *Employment Equity Award*.

129 The following calculations have been computed from *UWO Mini-Facts 1985, Western Facts, 1986*, and *Western Facts, 1987*:

Percentage of Women Faculty

1984-85	14.7
1985-86	13.6
1986-87	14.1

Different data appear in the University Relations Branch, Ministry of Colleges and Universities, *Status of Women in Ontario Universities* (Toronto, July 1987), Table 4A, which show UWO women at 15.7% for 1985-86 and 15.7% for 1986-87.

130 See Thomas J. Collins, Provost (Vice-President Academic), *Provost's Statistical Summary Report on Regular Full-Time Faculty Appointments and Recruitment Activities Effective 2 July 1985 to 1 July 1986* (21 October 1986). See also Thomas J. Collins, Provost (Vice-President Academic), *Report to the Board of Governors on the Distribution of Male and Female Academic Appointments 1984-86* (26 November 1987). Both reports available at the Office of the Secretary of the Board of Governors and Senate, UWO.

131 Collins, *Report to the Board of Governors*.

132 Tom Collins, Vice-President Academic, Presentation to Senate, 11 February 1988, Appendix 1. Available at the Office of the Secretary of the Board of Governors and Senate, UWO.

133 "Provost's Proposal," p. 3.

134 Collins, Presentation to Senate. Collins provided the following data: 1984 — two women; 1985 — three women; 1986 — three women; and 1987 — five women. The program did not actually commence until 1 January 1985, and so the funding for the two women in 1984 technically cannot be attributed to the Leith initiative. Somewhat confusingly, Collins continued by noting that only four of these individuals had been hired under the Leith program. All funding came from the Academic Development Fund (B). Collins made the following comment concerning budgetary priorities: ". . . the budget is so tight in faculties and departments that we are going to have to give first priority for the use of ADF-B funds to support new Deans and department Chairs." Notes from oral presentation on file with the author.

135 Collins, Presentation to Senate.

136 Data from *Western Facts, 1988*, p. 62-63.

137 Collins, *Provost's Statistical Summary Report*. Sixty-five percent of all full-time appointments went to males and 35% went to females. Data from the Ontario Ministry of Colleges and Universities 1986-87 show even lower statistics. Western's appointment of new full-time female faculty is pegged at 29.2%, a figure lower than that shown for Brock, Carleton, Guelph, Laurentian, OISE, Ottawa, Ryerson, Toronto, Trent, Wilfrid Laurier, and York. OISE leads the group with 100% female hires, while Trent and Laurentian follow up at 50% (*Status of Women in Provincially Assisted Ontario Universities and Related Institutions 1976-77 to 1986-87* [Toronto: Ministry of Colleges and Universities, University Relations Branch,

1988], Table 4e). The latest UWO statistics show the hiring ratio has increased slightly to 38% females and 62% males (*Provost's Statistical Summary*, p. 2).

138 Collins, Presentation to Senate, Appendix 1. See also "Improvement Needed in Hiring of Female Academics: Collins," *Western News*, 18 February 1988.

139 For an example of initiatives following in the wake of the Montreal massacre of 6 December 1989, see Orland French, "National Group to Study Women and Engineering," *The Globe and Mail*, 23 February 1990, p. A10.

140 For further discussion of the effects of tenure, see Leo Groarke, "Beyond Affirmative Action," *Atlantis*, 9, 1 (1983): 13.

141 See Christine Boyle, "Criminal Law and Procedure: Who Needs Tenure?" *Osgoode Hall Law Journal*, 23 (1985): 427.

142 For a remarkable account of the failure of most affirmative action programs to give recipients the support they require to withstand the workplace onslaught, see Marcia McMillan, "How Affirmative Action Programs Fail Women in Non-traditional Jobs," *Canadian Woman Studies*, 6, 4 (1985): 46.

143 Credit for this idea belongs to at least two people — Florence Kennedy, who gave a speech in Toronto in the mid-1970s in which she advised feminists to travel like nuns, in twos, and Sheila McIntyre, who ended her brilliant "Memo on Gender Bias Within the Law School," Queen's University (published as "Gender Bias Within the Law School: 'The Memo' and Its Impact," *Canadian Journal of Women and the Law*, 2, 2 [1987-88]: 362, and reprinted here as chapter 7) with the note that "feminists" (not just women) should be hired at Queen's law school in twos and threes.

144 Section 13(1) of the *Ontario Human Rights Code*, S.O. 1981, c.53, states: "A right under Part 1 is not infringed by the implementation of a special program designed to relieve hardship or economic disadvantage or to assist disadvantaged persons or groups to achieve or attempt to achieve equal opportunity or that is likely to contribute to the elimination of the infringement of rights under Part 1."

145 *Constitution Act, 1982*, Schedule B, Part 1, *Canadian Charter of Rights and Freedoms*, s. 15(2). Section 15(2) of the *Charter* provides that the provisions on equality rights do "not preclude any law, program or activity that has as its object the amelioration of conditions of disadvantaged individuals or groups including those that are disadvantaged because of . . . sex. . . ."

146 *Action Travail des Femmes v. Canadian National Railway Company*, [1987] 1 S.C.R. 1114, per Dickson, C.J. The decision was based on federal legislation and the power of a human rights tribunal to order affirmative action remedies, and thus is not directly applicable to our situation. However, the reasoning of the Court shows a great deal of sensitivity to affirmative action and is an optimistic indicator of the attitudes of the bench on this point.

Note to Appendix

1 It is difficult to provide reliable comparative data, since all who work in this field will report that the numbers are not considered fully accurate. Furthermore, different reports arrive at different results. This chart, while not fully reliable, gives at least some bench-mark figures from which to examine the historical pattern. The numbers have been drawn from the following: Dominion Bureau of Statistics, *Summary of Teaching Staffs at Quinquennial Intervals*, p. 98, Table 15; Jill Vickers et al., *But Can You Type?* (Toronto: Clarke Irwin, 1977), p. 114; Statistics Canada, *Teachers in Universities, 1984-85*, p. 19; Statistics Canada, *Teachers in Universities, 1985-86*; Gail McIntyre and Janice Doherty, *Women and Ontario Universities: A Report to the Ministry of Colleges and Universities* (Toronto: Ontario Ministry of Colleges and Universities, 1975), p. 80, Table B-6; University Relations Branch, Ministry of Colleges and Universities of Ontario, *Status of Women in Ontario Universities* (Toronto: Ontario Ministry of Colleges and Universities, 1984); Ministry of Colleges and Universities, *Status of Women in Provincially Assisted Ontario Universities and Related Institutions, 1975-76 to 1985-86* (Toronto: Ontario

Ministry of Colleges and Universities, 1987); Ministry of Colleges and Universities, *Status of Women in Ontario Universities* (Toronto: Ontario Ministry of Colleges and Universities, 1986); L.C. Payton, "The Status of Women in the Ontario Universities: A Report to the Council of Ontario Universities," June 1975, available from the Council of Ontario Universities, 130 St. George St., Toronto, Ontario; *Western Mini-Facts* (UWO, multiple years); "Report of the Vice-President (Academic) and Provost Concerning the Recommendations of the Ad Hoc Committee to Review Appointments, Promotion and Tenure Policies and Procedures," September 1985, available at the Office of the Board of Governors and the Senate, UWO; Symons and Page, *Some Questions of Balance*, p. 191; Statistics Canada, *Number of Faculty by Age Group*, 1987, Tables 1.1f.1 (1986-87) and 1.1m.1 (1986-87).

4

The Chilly Climate for Faculty Women at Western: Postscript to the *Backhouse Report*

Constance Backhouse, Roma Harris,
Gillian Michell, and Alison Wylie

Despite the great interest that the Backhouse Report *had generated among members of the university community, little of substance appeared to be happening at the level of institutional change. Those seeking real and significant reforms began to wonder whether the* Report *would be ignored because of its historical nature and whether persistent inequities would be explained away as relics of an earlier era, unrelated to current procedures and practices. Given these concerns, a number of women began to think about updating the* Backhouse Report *and about documenting the "environmental" factors which have a negative impact upon women faculty.*

Four faculty members, Constance Backhouse, Roma Harris, Gillian Michell, and Alison Wylie, conducted a series of interviews with a variety of faculty women during the summer of 1988. Their aim was to document the extent to which informal factors were creating problems within the workplace. These interviews were originally intended to serve as the background for testimony presented in public hearings that the University had been urged to hold on employment equity. However, none of the women interviewed was prepared to speak out publicly at the time. Consequently, Backhouse, Harris, Michell, and Wylie undertook to produce a second report which would provide the University community with an account of what they had learned in these interviews without disclosing the identities of the individuals concerned. Released in November 1989, this report came to be known as the Chilly Climate Report.

– Eds.

The *Chilly Climate Report*

I. Introduction: A Cold, Lonely Environment for Women

In April 1988, Constance Backhouse released her report on the history of women faculty at the University of Western Ontario, raising questions about the Employment Equity Award it received in 1986. This report provides an update of Backhouse's study with a focus on recent history — the experiences of women faculty at Western in the last 15 years. It is based on interviews with 35 women, all but two of whom were employed at Western at the time. One had left some years earlier and the other had been interviewed for a permanent academic appointment but not hired. Six of the respondents have since left for more attractive, permanent positions elsewhere. Several others are actively seeking positions elsewhere. Although a number of factors inevitably shape these decisions, all who have left or plan to leave cite chilly climate issues as important. Two were quite clear that these were the primary motivations for leaving.

This report is intended to deal with the issue of gender discrimination, and as such it does not attempt to deal with the very serious problems of discrimination against women and men of diverse races, persons with disabilities, Native people, and other disadvantaged groups. We do not mean to suggest that these groups do not receive as much, if not more discrimination and harassment than White women.[1] However the representation of these groups among the Western faculty is still so negligible and undocumented that it is difficult to chart the extent and manifestations of the differential treatment.

All of the respondents have chosen to remain anonymous, and we have taken pains to ensure that their identity is not revealed by their accounts. There may come a day when those disadvantaged by discrimination feel they can identify themselves without exacerbating the problem. But at present, freedom of speech on these issues seems more like a distant dream. Threats of libel suits, professional stigmatization, and the multiple ways in which colleagues can evidence personal displeasure all combine to silence most discussion of this sort. For now, at least, the information must come by way of confidential sources.

The 35 respondents we interviewed described their experiences in a range of academic units across the campus including four professional or applied faculties as well as eight different departments from the Faculties of Social Science, Arts, and Science. Due to constraints of time, we have not tried to interview every woman in every faculty. We chose departments and faculties to represent a wide range of types of discipline and environment, and then interviewed as many of the women in these units as possible.

Not all women will feel that their experience is entirely captured by this report. However, we were overwhelmed by the number of times that our respondents described incidents that seemed to mirror problems related by other women at Western. In most cases there were three or four women who experienced the individual accounts which follow. Clearly these accounts represent something more than isolated instances of adverse treatment.

The focus of this research was not to unveil overt or intentional policies of discrimination. While examples of deliberate and conscious gender bias continue to exist in universities and elsewhere, not all those who discriminate intend to cause harm. The women who find themselves disadvantaged by differential treatment, however, often find little solace in the more benign motivation of discriminatory actors. It is the negative impact on the victims of discrimination which is the critical variable, not the ideology, understanding, or intentions of the discriminators. Accordingly, in this study, we sought to uncover the more subtle, underlying, pervasive attitudes and practices which systematically differentiate and disadvantage women relative to men. We might refer to these as "standing conditions" rather than explicit policies of exclusion.

We hope to illustrate that, as described in a recent Association of American Colleges (AAC) report, despite a widespread perception that "campus discrimination against women has ended" with the institution of legal provisions for equity, in many respects "things have not changed at all":

> [T]he challenge of truly integrating women into academic life has not been surmounted by the passage of laws and the ending of many overtly discriminatory policies. . . . Men and women working in the same institution, teaching or studying in the same department, often have very different experiences from one another.[2]

There persist what the authors of the *Report* describe as "a host of subtle personal and social barriers" which often operate "below the level of awareness of both men and women." When recognized, they are perceived as "trivial" or "minor annoyances, micro-inequities" whose pervasiveness and cumulative effects are ignored. Most persist in refusing to recognize them as discrimination "even though they make women feel uncomfortable and put them at a disadvantage."[3] These barriers are constituted by conventional practices which communicate a lack of confidence in women, a lack of recognition, or a devaluation of their capabilities and successes. There is a clear understanding that those who deviate from the "norm," who depart from the characteristics of White, able-bodied, heterosexual, middle-class, gentile men, are still outsiders. Despite (indeed, perhaps because of) being informal and unconscious, these practices are particularly pernicious. Their effect is, predictably, that women's self-esteem is undermined and their

authority and credibility subverted in ways which ensure that they will not
have an opportunity to realize their potential. The difficulty of identifying
these barriers and the damage they do is well described by a senior male administrator at the University of Calgary, who says he is "ashamed to admit
that it took me some time to recognize the kind of subtle but systematic discrimination that was being practised":

> I first began to become aware of these attitudes when I saw how my Assis-
> tant Dean, a female, was treated ten years ago at otherwise all male meet-
> ings of Deans of Arts and Science. She received an elaborate courtesy that
> was not born of respect but, rather, of unease, and that made it clear that
> she was not perceived as another academic administrator to be judged on
> the basis of her competence, but as a different kind of creature. She was pa-
> tronized and ignored. Much the same treatment has been recounted to me
> since then by other female academic administrators. The pain lies, as it
> would for any professional, in not being taken seriously.
>
> My first reaction was to be both sad and frustrated, although nowhere
> near, I am sure, as frustrated as my female colleagues. . . . The sadness has
> since given way to impatience and anger. I am tired of watching my male
> colleagues project their own problems and inadequacies on any of my fe-
> male colleagues who show some signs of competence. I have been particu-
> larly frustrated with the waste of talent which this involves.[4]

As this makes clear, the cost of such discrimination is not borne only by the
women who are marginalized and undermined, but by educational institutions and by a society which, as a whole, can ill afford to squander the talents and capabilities of half the population. The Association of American
Colleges *Report* concludes with the observation that the campus environment remains chilly for women "because good will alone is not enough."
Substantial changes must be realized not just in explicit policies and formal,
legal provisions for equity, but in the level of awareness about and concern
with the ways in which "the campus is a different and far less supportive
environment for women than for their male colleagues and peers."[5] Our
aim in compiling information about the "environment" in which women
faculty work at Western is to alert the University community to the
demoralizing conditions that exist for women faculty within some of the departments on campus. It is discouraging that Western has not only an appal-
lingly low percentage of women in full-time faculty positions, but that a
number of women who have held these supposedly desirable appointments have chosen to leave as a result of their unpleasant experiences here.

It is not enough to simply recruit more women into faculty positions at
Western — we have to examine their experiences once they get here, because, as one respondent put it, "For me, it's not solely a hiring issue any
more, it's retaining women." Even if aggressive efforts were made to hire
more women faculty, such efforts would be fruitless if the working environ-

ment remains so marginalizing, undermining, and unpleasant that women are unwilling to stay.

II. The Hiring Process

Interviews: Dispiriting, Perfunctory, and Inhumane

> Before I came I heard comments from [a prominent scholar in her discipline from another Canadian university] and other feminists about Western's reputation for being insensitive to women. "Does she know what she's getting into?" they said. It made for an interesting beginning. [Respondent]

The undermining of women faculty often begins during the hiring process. At Western, as at other universities, hiring is a highly decentralized process. Candidates are recruited and interviewed by members of the department they hope to join, that is, by their colleagues. One respondent, an eminent scholar in her field now at another major Canadian university, described the experience of interviewing for an appointment at Western during the mid-1970s as "an ugly memory": "Gender discrimination is pandemic in academic employment. Its manifestations at [my current university] are virulent. But I have never encountered the disease in so florid and prideful a presentation as at Western."

After having completed her dissertation at a top-ranking American university and teaching there in a junior position, she was pleased to be invited for an interview for a position at Western. Western held special attraction for her because she had grown up in southwestern Ontario. After giving her presentation, which was poorly attended by department members in her area, she spent two days alone in a windowless office waiting for people in the department to come by and speak to her.

On her way to the airport, when she was "dispirited, misguidedly feeling personally responsible," she was told by a senior member of the department not to get her hopes up because "one of the most published scholars in the department had vowed that no woman would be hired so long as he was a member of the university and that the consensus among colleagues was that he was right to stand his ground." She was later offered a one-year job which she turned down — the tenure-track post went to a man.

Another respondent described a more recent recruitment visit. "I interviewed in the Spring of 198- for a teaching job here. Half of the questions I was asked were gendered in nature." One of the most frequently asked questions was: "How would you feel working in a department that is mostly male?" This respondent surmised: "They were trying to find out how feminist I was."

Several years ago, during another interview for a faculty position, one of the respondents recounted how she had been picked up from her hotel by a male faculty member, dropped off in his office, and left by herself with *The Globe and Mail* for an hour. "What was so astonishing about this," she said,

> was that he left without saying anything. I wondered where he had gone, whether some unexpected emergency had arisen. I discovered shortly afterwards that all this time he was chatting next door with a male colleague. I guess his discomfort with a prospective female faculty member was such that he just couldn't bear to sit down and exchange pleasantries with me that morning.

Some respondents reported that their area of speciality had been singled out for sexist comment or derision during recruitment visits. One respondent described the scene after she was brought into the faculty lounge to meet the other members of the academic unit. "Prof. X burst in and said, 'I hear you're in the field of _____. So tell me, what's a nice girl like you doing in a field like that?'"

Where the candidate's field of specialty was a feminist one, this could provoke further abuse. Another respondent told of giving a recruitment seminar on her research on women. Shortly after the lecture, one of the men on the faculty stalked up to talk to her. "He was at pains to show me that he had worn his 'male chauvinist pig' tie (a tie with pink pigs, sporting the letters MCP on their behinds) during the seminar. He was so proud of that. I couldn't believe his arrogance and his insensitivity."

Sometimes these attitudes can appear to have a direct impact on hiring decisions. One respondent described attending the colloquia given by two women candidates competing to teach in one department:

> The first gave an excellent colloquium, had a good curriculum vitae, and handled the questions with great confidence. The second was very nervous, didn't handle questions well, and wasn't nearly as competent or confident. However she was much prettier, and was dressed in a very feminine manner. The latter woman was selected for the job. I think that she was chosen because she was less threatening to the men in the department.

Other women candidates suffered complications that arose, not from their own making, but because they were married to male academics. On occasion, departments assume that an academic couple will only come as a unit. "One woman applied for a position," noted another respondent, "but she didn't get seriously considered. I think she wasn't treated seriously because we didn't want to hire her husband."

Where women are hired at the same time as their husbands, this can prove to be troublesome as well. One respondent had been hired at Western at the same time as her husband. She was the first woman ever hired to teach full-time in her faculty, and some of the professors were uneasy about the development. "The most hurtful comment I heard was that I came in as part of a package deal with my husband," she told us. "One member of the faculty went around saying that the University would never have appointed me otherwise. I was astonished. It simply wasn't true, and furthermore, I never would have come if that had been the basis of the offer."

Another woman was hired while her partner was in the same department. She soon learned that it was widely assumed that she owed her job to her partner's intervention. She was most upset about these allegations, since her partner and the Chair of the Department had publicly specified that he would not be present at any of the interviews or meetings concerning her appointment. "In fact, everyone knew that he hadn't been involved, and yet it was assumed that it was purely my sexual interest that had got me the job; I was incensed."

III. Conditions of Appointment

Limited-Term Appointments

The most sought-after academic positions are "tenure-track" appointments, which entail the possibility of a permanent career in the university. The *Backhouse Report* showed women holding only 9% of these positions at Western. "Limited-term" appointments, which are much less desirable, are generally for a specified period of time (typically one to three years), after which the employee's contract terminates. There is generally no prospect of permanent employment with these latter positions. A disproportionate number of women are found in the limited-term appointments at Western.

For many women on term appointments it is difficult to disentangle their treatment as women from that as members of an underclass, a "caste," as one respondent described it, of temporary but full-load instructors. Several described their departments as appointing as much as a third of their full-time faculty on term positions. It is one thing to justify these appointments as ones to "fill in" for permanent faculty on an occasional basis. It is quite another to set them up as continuously staffed, rotating appointments.

The savings for the department, of course, can be significant. The University avoids making long-term financial commitments. It covers as much as 50% or more of its teaching commitments by issuing rotating, entry-level contracts, thereby retaining considerable flexibility in staffing. However, the consequences for those filling these positions can be devastating.

One respondent was a woman who held a term position for five years (before moving out of the province to take a tenure-track job). She described the situation as one where three-quarters of the permanent faculty were men, but women made up a much higher proportion than this among the term appointments. She clearly perceived an emerging caste system with an obviously gendered dimension. In her department this was coupled with a range of exclusionary and discriminatory practices. Since term appointees were seen as "just passing through," little effort was made to involve them in the life of the department. They frequently arrived to find a heavier teaching load than they had been promised, and collectively they carried a much higher proportion of students than permanent faculty did.

"These sorts of bad practices will back-fire," claimed one respondent. "Soon these departments will find that they have to hire from the pool of those they have 'manhandled'. Western has an especially bad reputation for its treatment of limited-term appointees in my discipline. The word is out and already lots won't take these jobs. We also talk. We may be invisible, but we are not silent."

> There's a woman in [my area] on a one year appointment, who just gradu-ated [with her PhD]. She worked her butt off.... She has a book off to the publisher, and she's giving papers all over the province. We all knew [an-other faculty member] was leaving, and we'd need someone to teach her courses. But when it came down to June, the head of our faculty said there was no money, and he offered to pay [this woman] by the course for three courses, at a total salary that was significantly less than she had been earn-ing.

A number of women who have held limited-term appointments at Western have left to take tenure-track positions at other universities. It was the perception of several of the respondents that when men are in a similar position, their administrative heads often lobbied successfully to have their appointments converted to tenure-track positions. In contrast, little such lobbying was seen on behalf of women.

Part-Time Appointments: Good Enough to Teach but . . .

Part-time faculty members are in an even more precarious position than limited-term people. They face even greater uncertainty over their prospects of continuing employment. Often these instructors are not notified un-til the very last minute that they are needed to teach. They are paid on a per-course basis, a rate of pay that is considerably less than that received by their colleagues who hold regular, continuing appointments. Indeed, some make less money than the teaching assistants they supervise. Generally, they re-ceive no employment benefits whatsoever. In an effort to amass a salary they can live on, many of these individuals carry a much heavier teaching load than full-time professors. Although detailed statistics have never been kept on the University's use of part-time faculty, it is obvious to everyone that women are found in this group in much higher proportion than in full-time positions. One would have thought that this might have presented Western with a golden opportunity to recruit female candidates for tenure-stream positions. However, it doesn't seem to work that way. There appear to be several built-in barriers to faculty hoping for promotion from part-time status to full-time careers.

Many of the part-time women must make a very heavy commitment to teaching. Consequently their rates of publication are lower. Research is not stressed as an integral component of part-time teaching, but for faculty hoping to make the transfer to full-time status, the failure to publish is fatal. The full-time faculty view the research of part-time faculty as second-rate, which in turn may erode self-confidence and further hinder their ability to conduct research.

This cycle is described very well by one respondent in our survey. She completed a master's degree in her Department in the early 1980s. Since then she has taught an average of 2 1/2 courses per year for the Department. Early on, a visiting professor encouraged her to do doctoral work, and he invited her to come and study at another university. She went to her Department head and asked for a letter of support for a graduate scholarship. He talked her out of doing the PhD, stressing how hard it would be for her to commute (she had small children). At the time, she was somewhat suspicious of his real motives. She thought he might be counselling her against the PhD because he needed her around to teach. Nevertheless, she took his advice and stayed on in her part-time capacity at Western.

Shortly thereafter an opening came up in the Department for a one-year, limited-term contract. Our respondent felt she was ineligible to apply because she didn't have a PhD. She pointed out that she certainly wasn't encouraged to apply. Indeed, she has begun to wonder if she will ever have a shot at an academic career. "I don't have anyone to talk to about possible research ideas. I don't publish because I don't feel confident that I'd be taken seriously." She obtained very high teaching ratings, she developed new courses, and students asked to take her courses but "it doesn't seem to mean anything." She felt that her Department did not encourage women students to do graduate work, whereas male students "received really special treatment."

The strong message in these appointments is that "you're good enough to teach but not good enough to be a real faculty member." This is not only demoralizing for the Instructor, but it signals a lack of respect for students, as it clearly indicates that the enterprise of teaching is less worthy of the allocation of the University's resources than those of research and the management of the University. Strangely, these instructors often handle so much of a department's teaching load that without them the department simply could not function. Yet they are seldom seen as potential recruits when full-time appointments become available. Particularly when departments have very few women, if any, in full-time positions, this seems a foolish oversight.

One part-time Instructor we interviewed felt her position was so tenuous that it was not safe to allow her comments to be printed in this report. Even with anonymity, she feared that she might suffer negative reprisals, should someone inadvertently identify her. "I feel so afraid," she explained. "They can simply refuse to renew my contract. They don't have to give me any explanation at all. There are no safeguards if they want to fire me for speaking out."

Double Standards

A number of the respondents reported that there seems to be a double standard for the hiring of women and men. For example, in one faculty, new instructors were often hired without PhDs. The expectation was that professors would earn their PhDs before tenure was granted. But according to one respondent, there was some disparity in the institutional support offered to men and women trying to complete their degrees. The Faculty was much more forthcoming with assistance in the form of "time off" for research leave and scheduling adjustments for men than for women.

Another respondent from a different department stated that, in her opinion, there was significantly different treatment of male and female junior faculty members. She noted that when she won an externally funded post-doctoral fellowship which required that teaching be limited to one course, she encountered considerable hostility from other members of the Department. "They characterized me as 'getting away' with no teaching," she told us. As she saw it, the irony was that junior faculty were strongly encouraged to get such fellowships. And the attitude was considerably different for men. "The men who were successful were seen as assets, as 'serious researchers,'" she pointed out. She has since left this Department for a tenure-track position elsewhere.

Another respondent encountered difficulties over course assignments. Her Department wanted her to teach courses that did not correspond to her area of research. She asked for a change in assignment. This move received an extremely hostile response, which she found very surprising, since she knew the request was perfectly reasonable, given current resources in this Department. If a similar question about teaching assignments were to arise with regard to a male faculty member, she felt the problem would have been approached in quite a different way. Even if the request couldn't be immediately granted, it would have been seen as normal ambition. In her case, however, it was clear from the comments that were made that her request was regarded as selfish. This respondent found it difficult to say whether the situation arose because of her gender or because the professionalism of her male colleagues was being threatened. Nevertheless she felt that they didn't quite see a woman's credentials as equal to a man's.

Broken Promises

A particularly blatant instance of gender discrimination in terms of appointment was described by a woman who had taught at Western on a sessional basis for several years while completing her doctorate. One year another sessional, a man also without a PhD, was hired. She was astonished to learn that the new Chair of the Department had appointed the man at a rank above her and lowered her rank.

She could not think of any explanation for this, since her qualifications were at least as good as the man's in all relevant areas. Furthermore, the outgoing Chair of the Department had made an oral commitment to rehire her at her previous rank. So she asked why this had happened and was told that the male sessional got a higher rank because he was "visiting." When pressed, the new Chair was unable to say in what sense she was not also "visiting." "Evidently the Chair's assignment of rank was completely arbitrary," she said, "and it violated the previous commitments made to me." What added insult to injury was the fact that this woman had competed very successfully on the job market the previous year and had turned down two firm offers in favour of remaining at Western on the terms originally offered.

In a unit in which faculty were regularly appointed without a completed graduate degree, one respondent described having been hired in the early 1970s with the promise that, when she completed a degree which was in process, she would automatically receive a salary increase and a promotion. At the end of her first year, when she had met these requirements, she found that she was not promoted. Over protest, this decision was reversed. Her assessment was that her faculty thought that because she was a woman, she would not put up much of a fuss. Comparing her experience with that of her male colleagues, she stated: "I think they thought I would back down on my request for promotion, but I didn't."

A woman with extensive teaching and research experience reported that she and her husband had agreed to come to the University on the understanding that a position would be coming open in her area within a few years and that, in the meantime, she would hold a research contract. (Her husband, of course, was given a full-time faculty appointment.) To her surprise, when she received the contract from the Faculty, it specified that in addition to doing research, she would have to teach one course. She agreed reluctantly, but was even more taken aback when she discovered that the Faculty then wanted her to teach two courses. At this juncture she contacted the member of the administration who had recruited her and her husband, a man who had since left the Faculty. He supported her and with this backing she took the case to the Dean, and managed to keep her load to one course.

Her teaching ratings were extremely high that year. In fact her students won an internal competition on the basis of work done with her. Thus she was delighted when a job opened up in her area. She actively competed for the position, and was most anxious to learn the outcome of the search. She began to worry when she was repeatedly put off and told that no decision had been made, despite all kinds of awkward interaction that made this seem implausible. Well after an offer been made, she learned that the job had gone to an outside candidate, a man who had never done any teaching and had no publications. The reason given was that the man had 10 years' experience in the field (outside of the University) that she lacked. She was exactly 10 years younger than this man and observed: "Obviously they knew, when they first hired me, that I was too young to have had much (comparable) experience." In any case, she added: "I've never read a study yet showing that such experience is related to success as a faculty member." When she took the matter to the Dean, she was informed that her existing contract would not be renewed for lack of funds. Strangely enough, she was offered further part-time teaching that spring, but told that, as a part-time employee, her contract would have to be terminated over the summer. When she suggested that she would then have to collect unemployment insurance, the Faculty administrators were furious. Evidently one expressed concern that, "with all the heat on about women at Western, what would it look like for a female faculty member to be standing in line to collect UI." She says in retrospect that, "My biggest mistake was to trust their verbal assurances; I thought I had a contract."

One might be tempted to dismiss these accounts as atypical, one-of-a-kind debacles due to human misunderstanding. However, as respondents pointed out, they happen far too frequently to constitute mere mistakes. One respondent emphasized that her experience was not unusual. She pointed out that even in the short time she had been at Western, she had learned of two other women brought to the University under promises of employment that were not kept. "They were given little support, and virtually no recognition for the work they did within the Faculty," she stated. "Their original contracts were terminated, and they were asked to switch over to employment by piecework, teaching course-by-course on a part-time basis."

Compensation

The University of Western Ontario Faculty Association (UWOFA) has published data showing that women faculty members earn on average 10-20% less than their male counterparts of the same age (see chap. 3, p. 65). Many, if not most, women interviewed felt they received unfair compensation relative to their male colleagues. Given the confidential nature of information about salaries, it is often difficult to know if one is underpaid relative to peers. But occasionally hard evidence does surface.

One respondent reported that a colleague who was leaving the University made a chance remark to her about what he was earning at the time. She was astonished to learn that although she was slightly senior to this man, he was being paid more than she was by several thousand dollars. Others told us that they learned of their situation only when their Deans or Chairs singled them out to tell them that their salaries were lower than they should be.

Some speculate that the salary differentials begin at hiring, where professors make one-to-one deals with their administrative head, setting out their starting salary. The theory is that men customarily drive harder bargains at the outset of hiring. Yet even when women try to negotiate the best salary possible, they often come out behind. One respondent described the careful background research she did before starting salary negotiations with the Dean of her Faculty:

> When I was close to being hired, I knew there was no policy, that there were no rules. You negotiate. In preparation I talked to people hired in [the Faculty] last year — there were fifteen of them. I talked to eight of them, four women and four men, seven of them permanent and one woman on a term contract. I found out all about their salary negotiations.

Armed with this information, our respondent began her salary negotiations with the administrative head. He offered her $—. She asked for $15,000 more. She described the process:

> We played broken record back and forth for half an hour. He said he didn't have the money. Finally he came up with $2500 more. It was to the point where I had to say I wouldn't take the job or take that amount. I ended up with $3000 over his original offer. I signed the contract. The day after, I found out that a male had been hired with eleven years' [professional] experience and one publication. I have sixteen years' [professional] experience and two publications. He got a salary of $18,000 more than I did.

This respondent was justifiably angry about this, although she felt there was nothing further she could do. "I keep practising going back to see [the administrative head], but I just know that it wouldn't matter what I said. I just couldn't face it."

Occasionally, administrative heads even disclose sexist reasons for treating women and men differently in this area. One respondent recounted how she had been done out of some extra earnings from a summer school course. "I was next on the rotation to get the opportunity to teach in the summer [for extra income]," she noted. "By rights it was my turn. But they told me I wouldn't be able to teach the course because I didn't need the money." The excuse given was that "I didn't have any alimony payments to meet." "This was by no means an isolated incident," she added.

Benefits

Women often tell of the problems they face in combining career demands with the raising of a family. Instead of recognizing that an academic career spans decades and that colleagues (female and male) should be permitted the flexibility to adjust academic responsibilities around their peak child-rearing years, the University still makes many women feel embarrassed and unprofessional about pregnancy.

One respondent described a situation common to many faculty women, frantically trying to juggle pregnancy around academic calendars. "I tried to have my first baby in May, because I was untenured, so it wouldn't interfere with my teaching." Although she was successful in this, thus inconveniencing the University as little as possible, the birth of the child still had an impact on her research. "I know my research wasn't as strong as it might have been because of my pregnancy," she admitted. "At least six months were gone, and then you're out of date and you have to catch up or switch topics. They tenured me at the rank of Assistant Professor because my research was weak due to this time out." In a tenured position, however, this respondent finally felt secure enough to undertake pregnancy again. "I had my second baby in December," she added. "I got pregnant within two months of getting tenure. The Chair wasn't too happy about it." Men at the same age and stage of their careers are often roundly congratulated when they get tenure and are seen to be starting a family. This is seen as evidence that they are settling down and making a permanent commitment to live in London.

IV. Orientation to Western for the New Woman Faculty Member

"Military Boot Camp"

Many of the academic units at Western seem to have no reliable system for orienting new faculty members. Some encourage a sort of trial by fire for those who are newly hired. Several women described one Faculty as a "vicious," "brutal," and "abysmal" environment for women faculty. All of them mentioned the sexist behaviour of male faculty as well as the harassment of female faculty members by male students. For these women, adjusting to this unit was comparable to surviving "a military boot camp."

A woman in another Faculty described the very specific undermining she was subjected to:

> My first day here, one of my colleagues took me into his office and said, "Well, I'm sure you'd like to know about your predecessor." My predecessor had been a woman faculty member who had apparently been forced out. It was very unsettling to hear about her on my first day. I also learned that there was quite a tradition of not granting tenure to the person who specialized in my area of research.

Another respondent recounted the sense of loneliness she felt when she arrived at Western. "I arrived in London alone, leaving behind all my family and friends in another city. My Faculty expects you to arrive with family in tow and doesn't set up any social introduction to London. It was very alienating, very lonely." These sentiments are no doubt not unique to new women faculty. But women frequently found themselves faced as well with the additional burden of curiosity. They find that their male co-workers think of them as oddities, and even seem to anticipate their failure. This is particularly apparent in faculties which have been unsuccessful in retaining their women members. This same respondent continued: "After I'd been here a few months, one of my male colleagues came by and said 'With all the disasters we've had with women here, I do hope you survive.'" She summed up her impression of the Faculty: "It's abysmal for a woman here. . . ."

Some women describe situations that can only be characterized as vicious environmental harassment. This seems to be particularly true of female academics who do feminist research and teach in the field of Women's Studies. One respondent arrived to teach at Western shortly after publishing a book which was widely acknowledged as a leading feminist publication. She recounted the reception at her Faculty:

> The book had been extensively reviewed, mostly quite favourably. However there had been one predictably vitriolic review in one of the Toronto newspapers, by a journalist who "trashed" it for its feminist perspective. My first day in the Faculty, I arrived in the faculty lounge to get a cup of coffee. To my surprise and discomfort, someone had tacked the column up on the bulletin board. Whoever had done this had evidently enjoyed it, for the most vicious passages were underlined in red.
>
> In some other context, I wouldn't have minded. I'm not afraid of criticism, and I actually thought some of the more far-fetched parts of the article were rather funny. But I didn't really know a soul in the Faculty yet. It was hardly an atmosphere where colleagues could banter back and forth about such things. To have to go in and see that column up there, day after

day, for weeks, gave me the most horrible feeling about the place. It felt like
I was working in a place where people enjoyed seeing my work ridiculed.

Feedback: "Too Little Information, Too Late"

Another respondent held a tenure-track position in her Department. After
four years, during which she published extensively, obtained major research grants, and received satisfactory ratings within her Department, she
resigned and left to take an academic position elsewhere. "I just found the
general climate so isolating," she said. She noted that she had no information network, that is, no way to find out what was "a good or bad thing to
do" in the Department, what committees to get on, or what resources she
was entitled to. She also described feeling that she had no colleagues. There
was no exchange of ideas, she felt no intellectual stimulation, and received
no information about research opportunities from colleagues or suggestions
about projects or granting sources.

Although she got feedback in the form of a terse appraisal letter once a
year, this was all the information she got. She *never* got any personal or face-
to-face feedback and always felt that she was in an information vacuum.
When she returned from a leave of absence of several months during which
she was doing research at another university, she told the Department Chair
that she was leaving. "He had no reaction. He didn't seem to be surprised,
he didn't ask me why I was going and he didn't encourage me to stay." She
summarized her experience in the Department by saying that "I had to be
there for four years before I had enough information to know that I was doing OK in the department. It's a long time to stay in limbo. It was too little information coming too late and I feel a whole lot better since I left." This
sense of isolation was by no means unique to the Department in question
and, as another respondent's account indicates, it has a cost for the University as well as for the individuals involved. One woman in another Faculty
reported that, when she arrived to take a probationary appointment, she
made a point of meeting with the Chair of her Department to discuss the
process of tenure review. When she asked what was expected he said he
could not give her any guidelines, and when she asked if they might set up
some regular procedure for discussing her progress since the requirements
for tenure were so indefinite, he said, "Oh, you'll know how you're doing."
The only assessments she got of her performance in the four years before
she came up for tenure were "telegraphic comments in interviews I requested to discuss my annual SSA (selective salary adjustment) ratings. I was
never able to get any sustained feedback on how I was doing or, indeed, on
what I *should* be doing where tenure was concerned." In the end her tenure
case was unproblematic; nevertheless, she observed that:

It's fine to say "you'll just know ..." if you can expect to be tied into the informal network of the Department. As a woman I felt quite vulnerable; I knew I couldn't take that for granted. I was, in the end, less isolated than many and no problems came up but this sort of attitude is just a recipe for disaster in many contexts.

V. Daily Life at Western: Components of Faculty Responsibility

Several of the women we interviewed reported that during their time at the University they lost confidence in their ability to do scholarly work. Rather than receiving encouragement from administrators and colleagues to develop their skills as teachers and researchers, many found themselves not only unsupported but seriously undermined. The experiences described by these women ranged from isolation and exclusion by colleagues, sexism and harassment on the part of students and colleagues, to threats and intimidation by colleagues and administrators.

Several of the women interviewed stated that the lack of peer support was a major stumbling block. It undermined their confidence in their academic ability, despite external signs that their careers were flourishing. Often this was cited as the reason they left their jobs for other academic institutions. One said that as a result of her experiences, she felt herself losing her sense of professional competence. She reported that it was more than a year after she left that she began to feel better about herself.

Research: Crises in Confidence

One respondent had been teaching on a limited-term position but has also since left for a permanent position elsewhere. She described her initial enthusiasm about coming to the University. There were two senior male colleagues who worked directly in her field and were central to a network of researchers in this area. Her optimism was soon crushed. She said:

> In my five years at Western I found my male colleagues — especially those working in my own area — consistently unwilling to provide any support or even to find out very much about my work and interests. In one instance I was pointedly not invited when an evening reception was held for a researcher in my area who was visiting London. I spent a lot of unproductive time wondering why my colleagues should have so systematically excluded and undermined me, and why the worst offenders should have been those with whom I shared the most by way of academic interest.

In the early years she assumed their lack of interest reflected a negative assessment of her research capability but as time wore on, she realized this was unlikely. Her credibility outside the University grew stronger and she built a strong national reputation with a substantial publication record. She began to wonder if she posed some kind of threat to them. "But this was implausible," she said, "since I was so junior and they were so well established." She finally concluded that an important part of the problem was that they just didn't know how to deal with her as a woman. "They couldn't relate to me as mentors, or see me as a valuable junior colleague the way they do junior men. You see it all the time: they're treated as 'young turks' (junior male colleagues showing signs of success), and everyone takes great pride in their progress."

Feminist Research: No Academic Integrity?

Even more disturbing are the reactions to women who undertake feminist research. For instance, one respondent teaches and publishes in this area; she has a lengthy publication record and has also received prestigious academic awards. She reported that graduate students were actively discouraged from working with her. One senior male faculty member told his class that she was "incompetent" and another cast aspersions on her "academic integrity." Comments such as these were not isolated instances, she noted. Further, her Department Chair had denied her the academic freedom to identify her area of research in the departmental graduate brochure, and she was refused permission to teach graduate courses. This situation continued until it was formally disallowed by more senior administrators in the University.

Another respondent noted that she published some of her scholarly work in a major women's studies journal entitled *Resources for Feminist Research*. "I took all kinds of flak for publishing there," she noted.

One female professor who specializes in feminist scholarship described how she was asked by one of her male colleagues to give a lecture to his class on some of her feminist work. Somewhat surprised, she agreed to do so. When she got to class, she found that he had "no real intention of seeking to understand feminist analysis. He didn't want to hear about the research, the new ways of thinking. He wanted me there as a 'side-show.' He interrupted me, over and over, joking and making snide remarks throughout my presentation." She was beside herself by the end of the class: "I felt entirely marginalized as a woman, completely belittled."

Teaching: Male Students

Male students commonly harass female faculty members. One woman professor reported having pornographic pictures shoved under her office door at night. "It was very frightening," she said, "I felt like someone was really trying to give me a vicious message."

Another respondent referred to the condescending manner in which some male students spoke to her. "I remember having to correct at least two of my young male students because they addressed me as 'dear,'" she said.

Yet another respondent described how women are viewed inside the classroom:

> It's brutal for female faculty. They have to be enormously credible before students will listen to them. Male faculty might be viewed as eccentric, they might be ridiculed or imitated, but they would never be attacked as incompetent. For women, the connotation of incompetence is always tacked on.

Nearly all the women interviewed in one Faculty remarked on the sexist, aggressive behaviour of male students. For instance, two of them reported specifically that male students were unhappy about having women teaching certain subjects, ostensibly because these subjects were supposed to be "male" in orientation. A woman from this Faculty observed that women also "suffer in teaching evaluations. What we say isn't taken as being important."

One woman on a limited-term appointment, who has since left for a permanent position elsewhere in Canada, described her experience as an undergraduate instructor as one of continuous harassment. Each year she taught, several male undergraduates repeatedly demanded extensions of deadlines and reassessments of virtually every component of the course grade she assigned to them. When she was being rehired (a renewal of her original limited-term contract), she was asked by the Department to inform her classes (all undergraduate) that she was being assessed for reappointment so that her students could submit additional documentation to her file if they wished. Two of the male students wrote such extremely vindictive letters they were thrown out by the committee reviewing the file. But none of those privy to her difficulties with these students offered her any support. In fact, it was made clear to her that her teaching ability was in question. She described a double standard that women face as new faculty:

> I had a first year like anyone else's first year. But it was clear to me that, as a woman, I had to be seen to maintain control *on my own*. They'll jump on anything; first year difficulties teaching large classes are played down for men, but for a woman it's immediately seen as evidence of incompetence. You quickly learn not to go looking for help because that would just confirm their suspicion that you can't handle it on your own. It really isolates you.

In response to the pressure to "prove herself," she made teaching a top priority the year her contract was renewed, at the expense of further developing her research strengths.

It is worth noting that the difficulties this respondent faced as a new Instructor were exacerbated by gender bias in the way she was perceived and treated by students. Although the harassment she described did not have any overtly sexual overtones, she was very clear that junior male colleagues would not have been and indeed, were not, a target for such systematically aggressive challenges. She seemed, in fact, resigned to the fact that junior women faculty inevitably suffer such "hazing" and can only hope that as they gain seniority it will be reduced: "I don't have any grey hair and I'm not male," she said pointedly.

Less overt hostility that nonetheless carries the clear message that women faculty are attributed much less authority than their male counterparts was very widely reported during our interviews. One woman, teaching on a probationary appointment in a department she finds quite supportive of women, described a direct comparison she was able to make between the response of first-year students to her and to a junior male colleague:

> Despite having the same name plates on our doors (both were "Professor X" or "Professor Y"), and despite my male colleague looking extremely young for his age and being brand new at the University, I was routinely asked when I would finish my doctorate—whether I was doing an MA or a PhD. The students were just amazed when I said I'd had my doctorate for 8 years already. I asked my male colleague whether he ever got any such inquiries. He'd been out only 1 year when he started teaching and had spoken to me about difficulties he'd had with some of his students. But he said he had never had any such comments. In fact, it was rather gratifying; he was shocked. He couldn't believe a student would challenge a faculty member that way. Clearly, however difficult he found his first years of teaching this was, indeed, no part of his experience!

This same woman reported a much more hostile encounter with a male graduate student when she gave her first graduate seminar in the Department, the second semester after she'd arrived:

> I had prepared my seminar description something like six months in advance. It had been widely circulated and when I met the seminar for the first time in January, there was quite a crowd; lots of senior students as well as ones still doing course work, interested to see the new act in town. When I was part way through laying out the plan for the course, this one (male) student got up and objected to its proposed content as not fully representative in one of the areas to be covered. I pointed out five or six really major figures in the area who were on the syllabus and he then challenged me for lack of material in another, related subfield. I was pretty angry by this point and said I couldn't imagine what he was thinking, pointed out another half-dozen readings on the list in exactly this area, and basically told him that if he had any other complaints he could raise them outside the

class since he didn't seem to be making very much in the way of constructive contributions in the class.

I hated to close down discussion this way, but he was so obnoxious and
hostile I didn't think I had much choice. He didn't bother coming back to
class; it turned out he was an audit anyway, although he had never asked if
I would accept audits in this course! But it took a good month before the
tone of the class loosened up enough that the rest of the students felt comfortable in discussion. It was a real waste of everyone's time. I asked
around and learned that although this student was known to be problematic, he had never pulled anything like this in any of my male colleagues'
classes. In fact, they described him as pretty docile in class.

Even women with years of teaching experience face regular challenges
to their authority. One long-time faculty member observed that these incidents were more frequent early in her teaching career but that she still
does routinely have encounters with students that amount to harassment.
"I wouldn't describe these as specifically sexual, but they are clearly gender-
linked attempts to intimidate." She says she is quite consciously aware that,
at the beginning of classes, she must establish her authority as Instructor in a
way not required of her male colleagues. "Unless they make obvious factual
mistakes or are really poor lecturers, men don't confront as much in the way
of direct challenges as do women faculty of the same age and experience,"
she noted.

She recounted some of the experiences that have made her aware of this
discrepancy. She was once asked when the Instructor would arrive as she
called the class to order. "Maybe the student assumed I was a secretary in to
check chalk . . ." she joked. Another respondent is still routinely asked if she
has taught the course before. "They look utterly shocked when I say I've
taught most of my courses 15-18 years — sometimes longer then they've
been alive!!"

Women Faculty as Administrators

There are very few women serving in senior administrative posts at the University. Women have never been appointed to the top positions of University
President and Vice-Chancellor, or Provost and Vice-President (Academic),
and only a few have been named to the positions of Faculty Dean or Department Chair. Where they do obtain administrative postings, women typically
find themselves assigned to more subordinate positions, as "Associate Vice-
President" or "Assistant Dean." In fact, several of our respondents referred to
this pattern as the "A-job phenomenon." Said one respondent:

A-jobs rarely lead to jobs within the central administrative structure in the
case of women. Women in these jobs are not apprised of or consulted about
what is going on. They tend to learn about decisions in strange ways. And

they find that the jobs tend to become redefined around them into extensions of traditional female roles. They do the major share of the "housekeeping" work: support, counselling, hostessing, mediating. They are not perceived by anybody as being people who are moving in a logical progression toward non-A-jobs.

Some women take pride in their knowledge of how the University works administratively and in their success in having negotiated attractive salaries and terms of appointment. Nevertheless, one who had held several important administrative appointments concluded that it was especially in these positions that she had encountered blatant, offensive, and debilitating sexism. This she found something of an irony, inasmuch as many faculty women feel themselves disadvantaged because they are systematically excluded from administrative positions that have decision-making power. "The persistent use of sexist and sexual language, and the blatant insensitivity to issues having to do with racism and sexism are," she observed, "quite remarkable." She concluded that the culture of the senior administration is, in many respects, even more unapologetically masculinist/sexist than its critics imagine.

Another described the "boys' club" culture she encountered in Faculty and Senate-level committees: "The conversation always runs to sports and cars," she noted, emphasizing that the dissociation she felt in such an environment had gone a long way toward undermining her sense of commitment to the administrative life of the University.

Another respondent spoke of the difficulties for a woman attempting to work within such a male-dominated administrative structure:

> Decisions are taken by an informal network of male buddies that excludes women. A woman in the administration finds that the decision-making structure finds it more logical to work around her. There is a sense that when a woman gets angry or passionate about something, it is obtrusive or lacking in propriety. If a male were to behave the same way, this would be far more acceptable.

Describing the double-bind that this places on women, she continued: "Women administrators must take it easy — or easier than males — in order to be taken seriously. But women also have to push to get any attention. There's a very small range of acceptable behaviour for a woman between speaking out enough to get attention and being seen as an extremist."

Other female faculty, who have sought but not yet obtained administrative appointments, described peculiar responses to their interest in these jobs. One respondent recounted her experience in applying for an administrative post. "A colleague suggested that I apply. I spoke to other members of Faculty and many were quite supportive. Then my colleague told me that

I had a lot of support, but he also revealed that some of the faculty members had said, 'We wouldn't want a man-hater in that position.' "

Nevertheless, this same respondent did apply for the job. Several weeks later, she went to the office of the head of her unit. He said: "I have your application. Are you serious?" She replied as follows:

> I told him obviously I was serious or I wouldn't have applied. He then gave me some "job counselling," using the diminutive of my name which made it doubly offensive, telling me that at this stage of my career it would be a big mistake. I listened, told him I'd thought about it, and wanted to apply. Subsequently I spoke to some of the men who had held administrative positions. They were at a similar or more junior level to me, and I asked them if they had been counselled against taking the position. None had. It was so paternalistic.

She didn't get the appointment. And she summed up her own interpretation of the situation: "Any doubts I had about sexist treatment prior to that point were erased!"

VI. Daily Life at Western: The Features of the Chilly Climate

"We Don't Really Want a Woman Here..."

In some departments simply being female and a faculty member is enough to invite unwelcome comment. "I don't think that there's a day goes by that some kind of comment isn't made about my being a woman," noted one respondent. Another faculty member described her Department as one in which some of her colleagues "aren't very comfortable having women around. They make 'humorous' arguments about how 'we really don't want a woman here' or they keep their distance."

Still another woman recounted an occasion when several of her colleagues were discussing the hiring of women. One of the men asked, "Why do we need another woman, we've already got one," she recalled. She also described another meeting in which members of the Faculty had been conversing about the credentials of a woman applicant. A faculty member had the temerity to say "She's married and she'll just get pregnant anyway." A similar remark was made by a male professor in another Faculty who said "I hope they don't put a woman on the decanal selection committee." One of the respondents in our survey was so astonished to hear this remark made in her presence that she demanded of her colleague: "How do you think that makes me feel?" His reply was even more off-putting. "He actually told me that in his eyes I was not a woman." Another respondent tried to explain the gender barriers:

One of the hardest things about working in my Faculty is that they don't know they have a problem. The majority of my Faculty would say they don't discriminate. Yet they make such obvious sexist comments. I recall a meeting of the women faculty in the 1970s with one of the administrative committees to discuss hiring practices. The meeting had been called in response to the original Western study on the status of women. We came prepared. We asked tough questions about the hiring of women. I remember one male member of the Faculty being so upset at our comments that he said: "all women faculty should be castrated or at home having babies." We wanted that comment minuted but they refused.

Exclusionary and Derogatory Language

The use of sexist language, and of diminutive and derogatory forms of reference is ubiquitous. Virtually all of the women we interviewed reported examples of language which they found exclusionary, offensive, and often indicative of a deep-seated ambivalence about their competence and presence on the faculty. Whether intended or not, the constant and unthinking use of such language is profoundly undermining for women who must live in an environment where it is the norm. What follows is a small selection from among the examples of such language that were reported to us.

Women from many departments reported the constant use of diminutive or derogatory terms by male faculty members. Uninvited nicknames commonly used are terms such as "dolly" and "broad" which are applied to female students and faculty alike. One respondent described it this way: "Ever since I arrived, the head of my Department has called me a diminutive of my name that I would never use myself. Despite my objections, the practice continues. He could not understand why I found this offensive." Several other respondents reported that they have had "cute" suffixes added to their names by male administrators: (name)-"doll," (name)-"love," and so forth, or they are simply referred to as "honey" or "doll." One respondent was called "babe" for her first three years at the University.

Others described treatment that was patronizing, even if not overtly hostile. "There's a certain amount of fatherliness that goes on," advised one respondent. "Young people and women tend to be treated similarly," she added. This respondent found her treatment particularly incongruous and off-putting because she was not young. In fact, she was the age of most of her established male colleagues.

Another respondent attempted to persuade the Chair of her Department to stop referring to the secretaries as "girls" in the Departmental correspondence. When she pointed out to him that even the publication style guidelines within their discipline encouraged the use of non-sexist language, he blew up. In a busy office corridor, he flung her office door open and shouted "who the hell do you think you are anyway?" With the veins throbbing visibly on his forehead, he loudly insisted that she didn't know what she was talking about, because the secretaries in the Department were flattered when he referred to them as "girls."

"Masculine terms are always used here. I hate having to sign university forms on the line labelled 'Chair*man*,'" complained one respondent. "I always stroke it out."

Another noted that after she complained about being referred to as a "chairman," the minutes taken at meetings in which she chaired referred to her as the "chair." However, everyone else, male and female, continued to be referred to as a "chairman." "It singled me out as a crank," she said, "without resulting in any change in the Department's attitude. It's a constant irritant. If those men were always referred to as women, they would be furious."

It was reported that, among a group of senior administrators, a common phrase was, "we've got to keep the big boys happy." When one of the few women privy to these discussions finally called them on this, one of them responded: "And what about the big girls?" Yet there was no recognition that this language might be exclusionary and no effort to change.

Tokenism

One woman told us that she was identified as a strong feminist, from a Department that has always had a strong representation of women. Yet she expressed concern that she was often treated as a "single-issue person," as if her sole concern was women and the position she took on any issue must reflect her feminist commitments, no matter what her record of activism in other areas. Added to this was a tendency on the part of those with whom she dealt to assume that they knew already what she would say. Worse still, she added that they seemed to feel that when they'd heard her out they had "heard from the women." "I am assumed to represent, and to be indistinguishable from, other feminists or women taken as a block," she said.

Another described essentially the same experience, with particular reference to selection committees. She had been involved in a number of such committees (including departmental appointment committees, and search committees for Chairs and Deans) and routinely found that she was "expected, as the token woman, to ask certain questions, as if the consideration of women candidates (and strategies for recruiting them) was my only concern, and as if only I, as a woman, could have any concern for these issues." In one context where the external assessments of the unit in question had specified the lack of women as an issue to be addressed by the new selection committee, she said that she "waited and waited to see if *anyone* else would raise the question 'what do we do about this problem, how do we recruit women?' " When it was clear that no one else would take responsibility for these issues, she finally raised the question herself.

One respondent went on to describe the standard defensive response to such questions:

> The chair went on at great length about how the failure of [our Department] to attract and retain women is all the fault of the women. "Women are so tied to their spouses they won't come to Western," or their emotional ties take over and they won't stay. "Women are emotional and unreliable." Men, of course, have no such conflicts! In the end, they convince themselves they're pure, merely acting out of consideration for all concerned. "We can't hire their husbands, so why bother hiring women."

Devaluation and Trivialization

It is commonplace, in the literature on women's experiences in academia and other professional contexts, for women to find their personal lives scrutinized much more closely than those of their male colleagues. Often this very effectively trivializes the women's achievements by attributing them to the support or capabilities of men with whom they are alleged to be "involved." Although many women reported this, one respondent summed it up best: "Whenever we get anywhere it's assumed we're sleeping with someone who has the power to hand it to us on a silver platter. The idea that we might have made it on our own merits never seems to cross their minds, no matter how baroque a story they have to tell."

One woman described the circumstances of her appointment to a tenure-track position after having taught in her Department for several years both as a sessional and on a probationary appointment. A colleague who contested her appointment couched his objections in blatantly sexist terms, intimating that her position in the Department was entirely due to her "relationship" with a senior member of the Department. She observed that, in addition to these insinuations being completely without basis, the senior male faculty member with whom she had been linked routinely functioned as a mentor for junior men. In fact, given his prominence in the field, his support of them was usually treated as an important indication of their competence and promise.

A long-time member of another Faculty related how, after winning tenure, she faced public comments from colleagues to the effect that the only reason she got tenure was because she must have slept with [the faculty member who had been Chair at the time she was hired]. The bizarre twist here was that the individual cited as responsible for her ultimate success had not been particularly helpful in pursuing her case.

A highly successful member of one Faculty who sustained a commuting relationship with her husband was told by her Dean at a dinner party that he thought it outrageous for a woman to live apart from her husband. The same administrator had the audacity to say to the husband of another faculty member who had transferred jobs to come to London: "What kind of man follows his wife around?"

Isolation

The experience of exclusion — of being "shut out" — is ubiquitous for women faculty. One who had had a successful administrative and political career outside the Department said that the "chilliness" of the climate within her Department really only became apparent to her when she became actively involved in other settings outside the Department and, indeed, the University. She was out of the Department off and on for most of a decade, seconded to an external appointment, and in that period encountered a collegiality "unparalleled" by anything she experienced at Western.

> My external colleagues were not just inoffensive, but in fact deeply sensitive to women's issues and consistently supportive. This included men as much as women. In retrospect, it was an enormous relief. I didn't have to "excuse" being female. I never had to establish my authority as Chair of a committee or council meeting, and I never encountered surprise that a woman might be a competent Chair and Director.

She noted that the contrast was most startling when she returned to the Department. "The tacit agreement to steer clear of me was even stronger but underwritten by an odd deference. Evidently success, even success that reflected well on the Department, wasn't grounds for admission to the boys' club."

Another respondent described her experience as generally very good. She was appointed by a unanimous vote, and was strongly and effectively supported through the tenure process. But despite this she was struck by how little effort members of the Department made to welcome her when she came, or to make her feel comfortable — a part of the Department — since she'd been at the University.

> One small but pretty clear indication: in the first semester I was here I was invited to dinner by just one of my colleagues, and in the subsequent three and a half years, before I came up for tenure, only three others ever asked me over for a meal, or a visit, or any kind of social contact outside official departmental functions.

Furthermore, she noted that generally those who extended a welcome were not the members of the Department working in areas close to her own. She explained,

At first I thought perhaps the Department just wasn't a very social place. Good fences make good neighbours or something like that. But just a couple of years ago we brought in a young man on a sessional appoint- ment, without any prospects of a permanent appointment, and he was treated really well. He was taken out to lunch and dinner by all the mem- bers of the Department working in his area (which overlaps with mine) and by lots of others as well. One of my colleagues who wanted to hire him more permanently made a big point of telling me what a great guy he was. How his wife and family really liked him and loved having him as a house guest. I couldn't believe it. I had never, not ever, been invited to his house in the four years I'd been in the Department.

This respondent continued:

I don't particularly need or want to be best friends with my colleagues, but as a new person in town, no friends to speak of, and as someone with whom they would be dealing for at least the next four or five years if not longer, I would have thought they might make some effort at least to get to know me. Clearly they know what's appropriate. They were really wel- coming to the male sessional. As I've gotten to know women in other de- partments I hear a lot about this kind of treatment and it can be really debil- itating. In my case it wasn't undermining professionally, largely because I already had a large network established before I came. I wasn't dependent on my colleagues. But I often wonder what it would have been like if I'd been drawn into the life of the Department.

Underscoring the career implications of this type of treatment, she not- ed: "I know I don't function as effectively on committees as I could simply because I don't have the sort of ongoing informal interaction with my col- leagues that would keep me really up to date and informed."

Some of this behaviour may be motivated by the attitudes a predomi- nantly male faculty still holds with respect to women. They cannot seem to see them as colleagues, as peers. Instead they are often seen as potential sex- ual partners. One respondent put it this way: "The male faculty here are 'very married.' Single women seem to be perceived of as a threat. When you come, you feel very isolated. You rarely get asked to socialize." As we shall see later, this attitude of aloofness does not protect women faculty from sex- ual harassment at the hands of their colleagues. It merely impedes other forms of social interaction.

Some of the women faculty respond to the "isolation treatment" they get from male colleagues by striking up friendships with the few women teaching at the University. They described themselves as drawn more deep- ly into the community of women academics at the University than into that of their own department or faculty. Others fear even this type of attachment because of the stigma that may be involved. One woman admitted: "When I came, I didn't join the caucus of women, because I didn't want to be identified that way. Knowing what the grapevine had said about this not being a supportive environment for women, I decided not to be politically active."

"At Least We Know She's Straight"

Female faculty who teach in the field of Women's Studies reported an intrusive institutional pre-occupation with their sexual orientation. One respondent noted that when she included academic materials on homosexuality and lesbianism in her courses, the students complained to the Chair that she was "gay." She was very shaken by the situation:

> I hadn't noticed that people were assigning things I talked about to me. I spoke of enforced heterosexuality, and they drew assumptions. It was amazingly upsetting. I don't have biases against people who are gay, but to be labelled something you're not.... My work concerns women, and all sorts of assumptions are made by colleagues and students about my sexuality. I find it very disturbing, because it has nothing to do with my ability to research, teach, and be a colleague. I guess I get labelled because I speak out on women's issues, I share an apartment with a woman, and I don't have a male partner.

Homophobic incidents such as this have serious repercussions for academic work. Many women are intimidated by the pervasive scrutiny of their sexuality, and some find themselves deterred from teaching or doing research in areas that are commonly viewed as challenging to heterosexual or male-dominant stereotypes. The implications for academic innovation are staggering.

One woman pointed out that scrutinizing the sexual orientation of a potential recruit was not uncommon in her field. She had been attending a reception at an academic conference when one of her senior colleagues (and former Dean) came over to speak to her. He told her that he wanted to talk to her because another Canadian university was thinking about making a job offer to one of their female colleagues. He suggested she talk to the Dean of the other university. "I want you to talk to him. He's heard she's a lesbian and wants to talk to you about that."

Our respondent was shocked:

> I told him I couldn't believe he said that. He was surprised at my attitude. I just couldn't believe that a former Dean, with an international reputation, who had been in a position to recommend candidates I don't know how many times, would have thought this an appropriate question. I repeated that it was irrelevant, and he reported this other Dean as having said, "we've got a couple of these [lesbians] on our faculty and they're raising problems. I just couldn't get myself into a position of hiring another." As near as I could find out, the discussion continued elsewhere, questions were asked of other faculty members, and the candidate did not get the job.

Some efforts were made to bring to the attention of another woman in this Faculty that she was suspected of being a lesbian at just the time she was applying for an administrative position. This seemed odd, given that the Dean had made it clear on other occasions that he had "checked her out before he hired her." The woman describing these machinations said that, "it used to be said of XX, 'at least we know she's straight because she's married and has kids.' "

Safety and Sexual Harassment

A number of faculty women we spoke to complained about the insecurity they feel on campus, especially at night or on holidays, despite the fact that many said they have no choice but to be on campus after hours. Those who can frequently avoid campus, as in the case of one respondent, who said: "I don't work nights anymore, which I used to at [another large Ontario university]. I feel that the grounds at Western are simply unsafe for women at night. To get to my car, I would have to walk through two heavily bushed areas, with almost no lighting." Others reported anxiety about the regular appearance of "flashers" inside locked office and classroom buildings on weekends, and about the extremely sexist chants they have to listen to during University orientation week and homecoming celebrations. Both are ongoing problems.

Other respondents reported extreme discomfort in the face of what they described as unwelcome sexual attention and physical molestation by male colleagues. Behaviour frequently cited included unwanted touching, male faculty members draping their arms around women faculty, hugging, "bum patting," and patting the stomachs of pregnant women. One woman even described being bodily lifted up by the shoulders and moved by one of the men on her Faculty who wanted to pass her in the hall.

Another woman described how she found herself singled out for a kind of sexually oriented attention by one of her male colleagues. He regularly put his arm around her and made sexual remarks in the presence of others. One respondent reported: "Within three years of my arriving, a surprising number of male faculty propositioned me, some of whom were married at the time. This all occurred in an environment where other male faculty members tended to hug the women faculty and slap them on the bum. I refused to allow this; all the other women are gone now."

Other respondents noted an unending barrage of sexual jokes, sexual commentary, and sexist humour. One woman said she would never forget sitting in the department lounge on one of her first visits to the University, and hearing some of her colleagues-to-be discussing "the shape of X's ass" (X was a female colleague). The comments ran the gamut from "how good it was looking" to "what she might be doing with it." She says she hasn't heard anything this explicitly sexist since but suspects her colleagues have just become more circumspect.

In other contexts such sexism persists unabated. Sexist jokes are routinely told not only in private, but in departmental meetings and quite public contexts. Often part of the fun seems to be to see how faculty women will respond. One respondent described the patience, tact, and time that she had to spend responding to this type of adolescent behaviour. "It takes so much energy to always be on your toes, always having a snappy come-back. When I put energy into that I can't put energy into teaching and research," she sighed.

Women from five other faculties reported essentially similar experiences, describing the pervasive assumption on the part of their male colleagues that anyone who takes offence at their jokes must be antisocial or have some kind of "personal" problem. All had been ridiculed or feared ridicule for reacting negatively. "You just can't take a joke..." was the standard response of their male colleagues. They described how this put women in a no-win situation. One outlined her three strategies for coping: ignoring it (which doesn't stop it), joking back (which was considered offensive by male faculty members, ironically enough), or assertiveness (which was criticized because it suggested that one was "too sensitive" or "didn't like men"). One result of this was that women felt displaced from lounges and coffee rooms, thus missing opportunities for academic debate and discussion.

VII. The Faculty of Tomorrow: Women Graduate Students at Western

There is widespread interest in increasing the number of women graduate students and ensuring their full integration into university life. It is hoped that upon graduation these women will swell the ranks of Canadian faculties, alleviating some of the gross gender disparities that continue to exist. Yet the chilly climate that exists often spills over to students, tainting their experience at the University.

One particular Department, described by four of our respondents as cold, inhumane, and completely lacking in compassion, has had a deleterious effect on the self-esteem and confidence of both faculty members and graduate students. One of the interviewees said that when she was a graduate student in the Department she felt "totally demoralized ... a failure ... I forget, even now, that I used to be seen as a powerful person. I lost my sense of personal power and self worth in the four years I was there."

She went on to say that as a student she'd felt that she couldn't write, couldn't do research, and that she was stupid — so there was no point in pursuing an academic career. Soon she couldn't remember why she went on to do a PhD in the first place. After she graduated she reported that the only reason she applied for an academic job was because she was invited to do so. She was amazed that anybody thought she could do it. (She now holds a tenure-track position elsewhere in the University and is doing well in both teaching and research.) She described her time in the Department as "the most devastating experience in my entire life."

A comparable but even stronger statement was made by another woman who said that she would never recommend that any woman go into that Department — either as a graduate student or as a faculty member. In fact faculty members from at least three other departments said they feel it is their duty to advise prospective graduate students who want to come to the University to work with them about the unpleasant climate they are likely to encounter.

Another respondent said that in her Department graduate students endured such a negative climate that she had to reassure them constantly. There was no question in her mind that some of her students had definitely suffered in the grades they had received from other professors in the Department because of being her students. When her students asked questions challenging traditional views in other courses, the professors got very upset. One had walked out of class. Another asked a student to leave his office because she was "wasting his time." Other students in the Department had remarked on the tension created in the classroom because of faculty members' unwillingness to entertain critical questions, whether they arose from feminist or other approaches. Because she was associated with these nontraditional views, this respondent felt blamed for any student interventions that reflected them. On another occasion, a student who wanted to take one of her courses was refused permission to do so. Our respondent heard subsequently from a third party that the student's supervisor had said that she would have to choose between taking that course and having him continue to act as her supervisor.

All in all the chilly climate experienced by women faculty is just the tip of the iceberg. One tenured woman observed that she was amazed at the amount of trivializing discrimination visited upon women graduate students. They make "especially vulnerable targets" for male professors who cannot come to grips with the equality of women inside the University.

VIII. Conclusions

Clearly the environmental issues described in the AAC reports of 1982, 1984, and 1986 are a reality at Western in 1989. What happens to women who have these experiences? Not surprisingly, many of us are angered. But, in addition, the result for many women is anxiety, self-doubt, and a loss of confidence. For example, one of the respondents described herself as demoralized and weary, a second-class citizen in her own Department. She noted that without the external recognition she receives (she has achieved national prominence as a scholar), she would lose her self-esteem completely.

Others muster extraordinary courage and determine to succeed against all odds. At the end of one interview, one woman who had described persistent and profoundly undermining harassment concluded:

> I have had a real conversion in the last few weeks. I have decided to set the terms on which I stay and go. I think there is no point in staying silent. I want to stay, to stick in here and make it, but I want to do so on my terms. I want to let the students and the faculty know that the equality of women is the wave of the future, that they have to accept me as an equal. I have decided to make sure I have a positive impact on this place, with new women faculty, to make sure they are less isolated than I was. If I can accomplish that, it will be worth sticking around.

Many of the respondents alleged that Western is a more damaging environment for women than other universities. One noted: "I came from another large Ontario university. There were problems there as well, but gender was not an issue the way it is here." Even women who work in stereotypically male-dominant fields concluded that the University compares unfavourably with other educational institutions. Said one: "My discipline is a male field. There'd probably be difficulties in most departments in my discipline, but this is probably one of the worst cases."

Inevitably there will be critics of this report. Some will complain that the sample of respondents is not representative of all faculty women on campus. Others will be offended that the women who participated are unwilling to be identified. Some will simply dismiss their stories as sour grapes.

In response to our critics we'd like to point out that the women we interviewed independently reported essentially the same kinds of disturbing experiences across a number of different academic units (seven different faculties or schools and six different departments). Furthermore, in view of the very small number of women faculty members at Western (only 227 out of 1,425), 35 respondents constitute a significant sample.

We also want to acknowledge that the environment at Western is not wholly demoralizing or debilitating for women, or equally chilly across faculties, departments, and administrative units. Some women did report supportive relationships with their male colleagues. A strong commitment to equity in some quarters has resulted in attempts to change discriminatory practices. There is some degree of optimism that such warming of the climate is spreading, and can be further spread if a concerted effort is made to foster it.

Our concern is that even if the experiences of stereotyping, devaluation, and exclusion that we heard about were isolated exceptions (which they clearly are not), they would be unacceptable in a university committed both legally and morally to principles of fairness and equity in employment.

Obviously there are personal and collective responses that can be taken to many of the problems described in this report. But they do not represent the institutional solution we seek. Non-institutional responses fail to recognize the influence this chilly climate has on women at the University as a whole. The University of Western Ontario will have to make these problems a primary target of the remedial programs to be instituted in compliance with the federal requirements for employment equity.

We think the following recommendations would be worth serious consideration:

1. The University of Western Ontario should set up procedures for systematically collecting anecdotal, as well as statistical, information on women's status and experience in the University environment. An annual report should be distributed publicly which outlines the quantitative and qualitative findings of these studies.

2. Individual units should be required to establish committees on women's issues whose mandate is to determine the extent of the problem and to propose mechanisms for changing the "chilly" environment. Where necessary, external consultants should be retained to assist these committees in their work. These committees should be subject to institutional review on a regular basis. Provisions should be made for penalizing or censuring those units who fail to realize their own and the University's objectives in changing the quality of the institutional climate for women. A key measure of success in this connection is the ability of individual units to attract and retain women faculty. Failure in this, as well as in other measures of success in improving the climate for women, should be grounds for putting such units under external administration.

3. University-wide programs should be instituted for educating and "sensitizing" administrators and other members of the University campus to the nature of sex discrimination.

4. Formal structures and institutions for the support of women should be established. These might include the following: a mentoring system for

women, a women's centre, a specialized complaint procedure for the reporting and resolution of the sorts of problems detailed in this report.

5. A university-wide policy on non-sexist language should be formulated and enforced for all documents, regulations, and media published in or by the University. This policy should apply not only to the University calendar, departmental brochures, course outlines and University papers and magazines, but also to all internal documents including departmental constitutions and Faculty and Senate policy statements. This would seem to be a minimal expression of the University's commitment to equity for women.

6. Finally, one of the key steps towards "warming" the climate for women will be the appointment of more women to the Faculty and to senior positions in the administration. The intolerably low proportion of women is one of the major factors which permit the continuing isolation and devaluation of women generally. A significant improvement in the gender-balance ratio would do much to dispel the sexism that is still so rampant at the University of Western Ontario.

Notes

1 For examples of literature describing some of the problems experienced by racialized faculty and by First Nations' faculty (some of it published subsequent to the release of this report), see Patricia Williams, *The Alchemy of Race and Rights: Diary of a Law Professor* (Cambridge: Harvard University Press, 1991); Y.T. Moses, *Black Women in Academe: Issues and Strategies*, and S. Nieves-Squires, *Hispanic Women: Making their Presence on Campus Less Tenuous* (Washington DC: Project on the Status and Education of Women, Association of American Colleges, 1988); Joy James and Ruth Farmer, eds., *Spirit, Space and Survival: African American Women in (White) Academe* (New York: Routledge, 1993); Lynn Brodie Welch, ed., *Perspectives on Minority Women in Higher Education* (New York: Praeger, 1992); Benjamin P. Bowser et al., *Confronting Diversity Issues on Campus* (Newbury Park, CA: Sage, 1993); Patricia A. Monture, "Ka-Nin-Geh-Heh-Gah-E-Sa-Nonh-Ya-Gah," *Canadian Journal of Women and the Law*, 2, 1 (1986): 159 (translated into French in *Canadian Journal of Women and the Law*, 6, 1 [1993]: 119); Patricia A. Monture, "Now that the Door is Open: First Nations and the Law School Experience," *Queen's Law Journal*, 15 (1990): 179; Emily Carasco, "A Case of Double Jeopardy: Race and Gender," *Canadian Journal of Women and the Law*, 6, 1 (1993):142; Derrick Bell, "The Final Report: Harvard's Affirmative Action Allegory," *Michigan Law Review*, 87 (1989): 2382; Richard Delgado, "Minority Law Professors' Lives: The Bell-Delgado Survey," *Harvard Civil Rights-Civil Liberties Law Review*, 24 (1989): 349; Indira Karamcheti, "Caliban in the Classroom," *Radical Teacher*, 44 (Winter 1993): 13-17; and Ann duCille, "The Occult of True Black Womanhood: Critical Demeanour and Black Feminist Studies," *Signs: Journal of Women in Culture and Society*, 19, 31 (1994): 591. On class bias within the academy, see Michelle M. Tokarczyk and Elizabeth A. Fay, *Working-Class Women in the Academy: Laborers in the Knowledge Factory* (Amherst: University of Massachusetts Press, 1993). On issues of disability, see M.D. Lepofsky, "Disabled Persons and Canadian Law Schools: The Right to the Equal Benefit of the Law School," *McGill Law Journal*, 36 (1991): 636. On issues of sexual identity, see Margaret Cruikshank, ed., *Lesbian Studies: Present and Future* (New York: Feminist Press at the City University of New York, 1982); Louie Crew, ed., *The Gay Academic* (Palm Springs,

CA: ETC Press, 1978); Elly Bulkin, "Heterosexism and Women's Studies," *Radical Teacher*, 17 (Winter 1981): 25-31; Margaret Cruikshank, "Lesbians in the Academic World," in Ginny Vida, ed., *Our Right to Love: A Lesbian Resource Book* (Englewood Cliffs, NJ: Prentice-Hall, 1978); Melanie Kaye, "Anti-Semitism, Homophobia, and the Good White Knight," *off our backs*, 12 (May 1982): 30-31; Judith McDaniel, "Is There Room for Me in the Closet: My Life as the Only Lesbian Professor," *Heresies*, 7 (Fall 1979): 36-39; Julia Stanley and Susan Wolfe, "Crooked and Straight in Academia," in Gloria Kaufman and Mary Kay Blakely, eds., *Pulling Our Own Strings: Feminist Humor and Satire* (Bloomington: University of Indiana Press, 1980); Bianca Guttag, "Homophobia in Library School," in Celeste West and Elizabeth Katz, eds., *Revolting Librarians* (San Francisco: Bootlegger Press, 1972); Adrienne Rich, "Compulsory Heterosexuality and Lesbian Existence," *Signs: Journal of Women in Culture and Society*, 5, 4 (1980): 631; Marilyn Frye, "A Lesbian Perspective on Women's Studies," in Cruikshank, *Lesbian Studies*, p. 194-98; and Sarah-Hope Parmeter and Irene Reti, eds., *The Lesbian in Front of the Classroom: Writings by Lesbian Teachers* (Santa Cruz, CA: Herbooks, 1988).

2 Bernice R. Sandler, *The Campus Climate Revisited: Chilly for Women Faculty, Administrators, and Graduate Students* (Washington, DC: Project on the Status and Education of Women, Association of American Colleges, 1986), p. 1-2. This 1986 report followed two previous publications that dealt with the chilly climate for women students: Roberta M. Hall with Bernice R. Sandler, *The Classroom Climate: A Chilly One for Women?* (Washington, DC: Project on the Status and Education of Women, Association of American Colleges, 1982), and Roberta M. Hall and Bernice R. Sandler, *Out of the Classroom Climate: A Chilly Campus Climate for Women?* (Washington, DC: Project on the Status and Education of Women, Association of American Colleges, 1984).

3 Sandler, *The Campus Climate Revisited*, p. 2, 3, 17.

4 Robert Weyant, "Sexual Harassment: The Tip of a Larger Problem," excerpted from a presentation to the Senate of the University of Calgary, September 30, 1983.

5 Sandler, *The Campus Climate Revisited*, p. 17.

5

Epilogue: The Remarkable Response to the Release of the *Chilly Climate Report*

Gillian Michell and Constance Backhouse

This essay was written several years after the Chilly Climate Report *was completed as a retrospective summary of the highly volatile and contentious debate that was occasioned by the release of the* Report. *It is based on our files of news clippings, notes, and recollections of the reactions of colleagues, senior administrators, the media, and various other interested parties.*

The essay is accompanied here by two discussions written at the time of the events described (Appendices A and B). Appendix A was published in the Western student newspaper, The Gazette, *shortly after the* Report *was made public. Appendix B, circulated informally several weeks later, was a response to emerging criticisms which we felt misunderstood or misrepresented what we had attempted to do in the* Report. *As difficult and unexpected as the public debate proved to be, it had several constructive outcomes which are described in the conclusion to this discussion.*

– Eds.

The decision to compile the *Chilly Climate Report*, as with the *Backhouse Report*, was taken in response to the awarding of the Employment Equity Award to the University of Western Ontario in 1986. Four of us — Constance Backhouse, Roma Harris, Gillian Michell, and Alison Wylie — believed this award to be seriously misplaced and felt that it was important to make continuing attempts to register our concerns. We decided to release the findings of our research into current conditions at the University on 12 November 1989, the third anniversary of the receipt of the award. None of us anticipated the furore that would erupt in its wake.

Word was out in many quarters that the *Chilly Climate Report* was being prepared. It was discussed openly at meetings of Western's Caucus on Women's Issues (the Women's Caucus), whose membership included senior administrators and members of the recently struck President's Standing Committee for Employment Equity. We had discussed the *Report* with the women we interviewed and many other interested women and men in our departments. Not surprisingly, Wendy McCann, the reporter assigned to cover University affairs for the local newspaper, *The London Free Press*, had also learned of our research some months earlier from her contacts on campus. During an interview with Constance Backhouse about initiatives to reduce sexism at the law school, McCann had asked us to contact her when the *Report* was to be released.

In light of this media interest and the general awareness that the *Report* was imminent, we made efforts to contact members of the administration in advance of releasing the report. Each of us informed the administrative heads of our own units. Alison Wylie also made individual calls to those we thought were most likely to be called upon for a response by the media, including

- the Provost and Vice-President (Academic),
- the Associate Vice-President (Academic Affairs),
- the Dean of Arts,
- the Employment Equity Officer,
- the Chair of the President's Standing Committee for Employment Equity, and
- the Executive of Western's Caucus on Women's Issues (the Women's Caucus).

In all cases the response she received was cordial, ranging from general interest to enthusiasm. Further, after a long and detailed discussion of the genesis and content of the report, the Provost — who seemed most likely to be called on for comment if the *Report* generated public interest — made a point of calling Wylie back to ask if she would provide him with written notes summarizing the various points she had made in their telephone conversation. He thought it might be helpful to have these ready to hand as a basis for constructive response to any calls that might come in from interested reporters. Wylie took that opportunity to write up several pages of discussion of the *Report*, which she delivered to the Provost's office on 7 November, early in the week the *Report* was released (these notes follow as Appendix A).

On Thursday, 9 November 1989, we hand delivered copies of the *Report* to members of the senior administration — the President, the Provost, and the Associate Vice-President (Academic Affairs), as well as to the Deans of the Schools and Faculties whose members we had interviewed. Advance copies were similarly provided to the President of the Faculty Association, the Chair of the President's Standing Committee for Employment Equity, and all of the women interviewed for the *Report*. A copy would also be placed on reserve at the D.B. Weldon Library, Western's main library, on Monday, 13 November, after the University officials had had an opportunity to digest the *Report*.

On Friday evening we contacted Wendy McCann of *The London Free Press*, as she had requested, to inform her that the *Report* was at last released. She drove over to one of our homes to obtain a copy and quickly scheduled a weekend interview with the three authors who were in town at the time. On Saturday morning at the York Street office of *The London Free Press*, McCann grilled us for about an hour and a half on the particulars of our study and our recommendations for change. She was a skilful interviewer who asked astute questions and followed our lines of argument with care. She informed us that she would be contacting representatives of the University for comment before releasing the article in Monday's paper.

We were pleased by McCann's obvious interest in the story, since there had been some question in our minds about whether the *Report* would attract any public attention at all. For the past several months, the press had been carrying stories of blatant and overt incidents of sexism and sexual harassment uncovered at various Canadian universities, including Wilfrid Laurier University, the University of Calgary, Queen's University, the University of Toronto, the University of Alberta, the University of British Columbia, and even at Western.[1] But many of the kinds of experiences our report recounted seemed very subtle to us, and others seemed meaningful only within the rarefied confines of academic life. Indeed, we thought of the study as primarily an internal document at Western, hardly the stuff of national news.

Even closer to home we had limited hopes of news interest. In late September, Alison Wylie had mentioned to a reporter for the *Western News*, the official newspaper published by the University, that the *Report* was forthcoming and asked if he would like to receive a copy. The reporter said we could send him one if we wanted but intimated that coverage was unlikely unless it somehow generated controversy, since it was not an official university report — something of a "don't-call-us-we'll-call-you" response. This lack of interest did not particularly surprise us. After all, what the *Report* did was simply to document *at Western* practices and patterns that had been widely reported and discussed since at least 1983 across a very broad range of universities and colleges in North America.[2]

So naive were we about the potentially explosive media interest that, with one exception, we made no effort to ensure that other media representatives received particulars of the *Report*. George Clark, the news director at London's local television station, CFPL-TV, had expressed a continuing interest in the problems of women faculty at Western after the release of the *Backhouse Report*. As a matter of courtesy, Constance Backhouse informed him that weekend of the new study, and he arranged for two of us to do a segment on the early-morning news program *FYI*, on Monday, 13 November.

Throughout the weekend we awaited the response to the *Report* with mixed feelings and some trepidation. We were surprised and pleased by the level of interest exhibited by the *Free Press* and CFPL-TV. From the outset we had been committed to making this report available to any who might take an interest in it. The attention of the local media, while somewhat unanticipated, would ensure that our message of concern would get out.

We also wondered what the official response of the University would be. Obviously, the news we bore was not good, but the University had already acknowledged that things needed to be changed when it had established the President's Standing Committee for Employment Equity. Further, the stories we had to tell were exactly the kind of information that the Committee needed to collect on a much larger scale in order to know how to develop appropriate strategies for achieving its goals. What we hoped to hear from the senior administrators was twofold: an expression of shock and concern at the range and quality of experiences we had uncovered, and statements about the University's commitment to change. We were afraid that the more likely response would be a routine "yes-thank-you-we've-referred-it-to-our-Employment-Equity-Committee," after which our report would disappear from public view without a ripple. This was essentially what had happened when the *Backhouse Report* was released, and we thought it all too likely that it would happen again.

Bright and early Monday morning, Roma Harris and Constance Backhouse reported to the headquarters of CFPL-TV. They were jointly interviewed by an amiable morning host for an 8:00 a.m. slot on London's *FYI* news program. The 15-minute segment, broadcast live, seemed relatively innocuous, as the two authors of the *Report* and the talk-show host chatted away about some of the difficulties confronting faculty women.

Monday morning's edition of *The London Free Press*, however, came as something more of a surprise. What we had thought was a subtle and reasonably low-key report seemed to transform itself, under the influence of journalism's eye for the dramatic, into potentially sensational copy. On page one of the London section, under the title "UWO Sexism Report," was the headline "One Faculty Rated Brutal and Vicious." The article led off with this statement: "A new report says sexism is 'rampant' at the University of Western Ontario and a female professor compares working in her faculty to 'surviving a military boot camp.'" Six of the complaints we had heard from interviewees were cited in a box, *USA Today*-style. Other headlines and highlighted items followed:

- "The report says unwelcome 'sexual attention and physical molestation by colleagues' are common";
- "SEXISM: Women called dolly, broad, love"; and
- "Bum patting."[3]

Unfortunately, it was never made clear in the article that these statements about women's experiences at the University were quotations from the statements of individual women we had interviewed, rather than broad conclusions drawn by the authors of the *Report*. We had been very careful about making any generalizations at all in the *Report*. This was intended to be an initial attempt to document the experiences of some women at Western, not a sweepingly definitive study. Making a distinction between statements from individual women and broad generalizations was crucial to us, even if it was not essential to the requirements of journalism.

With some relief, we noted that the initial press reaction of Western's Provost was much as we had expected. In the same article, he cited the attempts Western had already made to address problems of sexism, such as the sexual harassment policy, and stated that the President's Standing Committee for Employment Equity would "consider the report." But the Provost claimed, in addition, that he was "powerless" to investigate the complaints because our interviewees had "chosen to go unnamed." This we found strange, given how carefully we had explained the need for anonymity in the *Report*, not only as normal practice in social science research but also, more specifically, in light of the risk of retribution which was all too likely in the climate we were describing.

We each reported to our offices on campus that morning with some anxiety, concerned about the response awaiting us and worried about what newspaper readers, especially within the University community, would make of the story. As the day wore on, it became clear that other news media had picked up the story as a hot topic. A television crew from nearby Kitchener, Ontario, dashed out to interview one of the authors on site. Phone call after phone call began flooding into each of our offices from radio stations urgently requesting statements for airing. Reporters from three separate newspapers demanded follow-up interviews.

Whether it was owing to the mounting media coverage, or the dramatic *Free Press* lead article, or whether it was inevitable from the outset, things were beginning to unravel at the administration building. By late afternoon, television broadcasts revealed an angry and increasingly vehement Western Provost insisting that the *Report* was overblown and unduly critical. His statement for next morning's *Free Press*, in an unusual twist of logic, blamed our study for nullifying the steps the University had taken to combat sexism. "[I]t probably set the issue back five years," he complained, disclosing only too clearly that he understood progress to be a matter of perception rather than reality. He also attacked the credibility of the interviewees: "It's pretty easy to say whatever you want when you hide behind the cloak of anonymity."[4]

Free Press columnist Morris Dalla Costa reviewed the *Report* in his 14 November column, and deplored the broadness of the findings: "[I]t's a horrendous indictment of every male working in the seven faculties and six departments, regardless of their feelings and support of equality. Just as the terms bimbo, babe and broad tar every woman, the report, full of nameless faces, tars every male professor."[5]

In our opinion, the President's response was also defensive. The same edition of the *Free Press* quoted him: "The University of Western Ontario isn't a battleground of sexism and a report suggesting women teachers are under siege 'dramatically overstates the issue,' . . . 'I don't think conditions are as dismal as they are portrayed in this study.'" The President also continued to focus on the matter of anonymity. Questioning the survey results "because the women asked to remain anonymous," he grumbled: "it does leave people open to make any old statement they want."[6]

None of us had ever intended our report to be taken as the basis for drawing final and conclusive generalizations about the University as a whole. In fact, we were careful to represent the work we did as a small pilot study demonstrating that the kind of "climate" problems already well documented in North American universities were to be found at our own university. We hoped and expected that this would give the impetus for a more systematic assessment by University officials. Data gathering on an extensive scale would be one of the first components of this work, a project which we had not been able to undertake as four individuals.

Furthermore, we were astonished by the attack on our decision to keep the names of our interviewees confidential. The women we interviewed had requested anonymity not just out of fear of reprisals but because no constructive purpose would be served by pointing fingers at individual faculties or colleagues. Our objective was not to seek redress for individual cases, but to give voice to a problem that the University needed to address in a broader, institutional manner. In addition, most social scientists and research-granting agencies commonly insist that anonymity be maintained for individuals who participate in their surveys. As Wylie later observed in a response to criticisms of the *Report*: "Subjects are routinely assured that research materials identifying them will be kept under lock and key, and destroyed after a specified period of time; they are guaranteed that the data resulting from studies in which they participate will be published in aggregate form so [individuals] are not identifiable and, in the case of research which focuses closely on particular individuals, pseudonyms are typically used and any identifying details carefully disguised."[7] Given the sensitive nature of the issues we were addressing, it would seem that any survey or set of interviews, pilot or wide scale, should make the protection of subjects' identity a particularly high priority. But whatever the circumstances, "if the anonymity of research subjects was ... ground for dismissing the credibility of social scientific esearch, very little would survive scrutiny."[8]

What was there about the anonymity of participants in our study which had attracted such censure? It seemed as if our detractors were singling out our report and applying special standards that would not have been demanded of other research. Were they implying that the authors had "made it all up"? The President's aspersions on the likely credibility of our sources sounded to us suspiciously reminiscent of the time-worn refrain that women cannot be trusted to tell the truth—a dangerous and unsubstantiated mythology that has haunted generations of rape victims and battered women.

It was also difficult to know exactly what the President meant by his claim that our report dramatically overstated the issue. Was he denying our interviewees' individual stories (since these were the substance of the *Report*)? In fact, as Wylie later observed,

> we took special care to ensure the accuracy of all claims [in the *Report*]. As we completed our final draft, we contacted each woman we had interviewed, ... outlined the context in which her remarks were reported, and asked her to review all the statements attributed to her. ... Frequently interviewees requested that certain details be excised because they were too readily identifiable, but just as frequently they added material to convey more completely and accurately the nature of the difficulties they faced. We incorporated all the revisions suggested. It is a profound insult not just to [the authors], but to the 35 women interviewed, that public critics of the *Report* seemed to find the experiences ... describ[ed] so implausible that ... they questioned the integrity of the accounts [on the ground of anonymity].[9]

Or was the President angered that our survey had included only 35 women? The only generalization that our research supported—and the only one that we made—was that a number of women (approaching 10% of the female faculty) had experiences at Western that diminished them as women and academics, making for a chilly work climate. Was the President claiming that he knew the proportion to be different from this on the basis of some evidence he had available to him? He mentioned no such evidence. Constance Backhouse, when asked to respond in another 14 November newspaper article, called attention to this omission. *Free Press* reporter

Richard Hoffman advised that Backhouse had "urged Western to do its own study if officials find it hard to accept the results of her survey."[10]

Responding to the critique of anonymity, Backhouse placed the responsibility for women's fears of retaliation squarely on the university community: "[T]he women's refusal to be named suggests that despite recent strides there is still an environment of intimidation that keeps women from coming forward. The university could do a lot better than it is doing." Reporter Hoffman added that Backhouse thought it a "travesty" that the Ontario government had given the University an award for its employment equity program.[11]

By late Thursday afternoon, 16 November 1989, things had become increasingly unpleasant. The President was scheduled to preside over a meeting of the Senate, the governing academic body for the University. Much to their bewilderment, members of the Senate arrived to find that the President had issued press notices inviting the media to attend. In front of the assembled throng of faculty, administrators, students, staff, reporters, and camera crews, he lambasted the four authors of the *Chilly Climate Report* for what he characterized as their "recently staged media events." He termed this "effort to debase the achievements of our employees" as "offensive." The President closed with a recital from a prepared text:

> I particularly regret, on behalf of all those women and men who have worked so hard over the last fifteen years to address these sensitive issues, that a report was released at the end of last week for purposes of a media event. It does not help the causes for which so many people have worked to release to the media an unsystematic selection of perceptions formulated into unproven, untestable, and unverifiable complaints and allegations.
>
> Let me be very clear. If there are perceptions of unjust and unequal treatment the University must address them, and do so through all of the mechanisms currently in place. Again, I regret that we have not been allowed to do so in the current circumstances.[12]

The President's statement illustrated only too poignantly how little he understood the contents of the *Chilly Climate Report*. The kinds of experiences we were reporting, by and large, were not amenable to correction under the sexual harassment policy and procedures. No mechanisms for redress of "gender harassment" of a more general sort were in place. Even where the issues seemed quite clear cut — as in the case of gender inequities in starting salaries, in provisions for leave to complete graduate training, and in administrative and teaching assignments — the administrators with the authority to rectify the problems were often those responsible for creating them. The women we spoke to were frequently quite explicit that their difficulties had been compounded by the fact that there was nowhere to turn. Very often, too, the elements that create a chilly climate are not easily identifiable, blatant, concrete acts, but more subtle ones that cause cumulative damage. As one interviewee pleaded: "Tell me, how can I fight a wisp of fog?"[13]

While many of the instances we cited might have fallen under the responsibility of the President's Standing Committee for Employment Equity, at that point the Committee had barely begun its work and was still collecting data. In fact, the Chair of that Committee, Dr. Carol Agòcs, announced that she was pleased to have our report as a resource. As she said to the *Western News*, the *Report* provided "subjective information that raw numbers cannot convey." A noted Canadian scholar in the area of employment equity, Agòcs also described the *Report* as the only work available "that summarizes the experience of women faculty [in Canada] in recent times."

As for the President's charges that we had released the *Report* only to "stage" a "media event," this would have been laughable if things had not become so strained by this point. The President's allegations seemed to imply, at the very least, some element of surprise. Was he suggesting that we had given the media our report before those concerned or affected by it had received it? In fact, the administration had been informed that the *Report* would be available two weeks before it was released, and senior Western administrators received advance copies well before any release to the media.

Was he implying that Western officials were caught off guard by the media interest? As it turned out, the authors of the *Report* learned that Western administrators had actually been forewarned, by a circuitous and largely accidental series of connections, that *The London Free Press* university affairs reporter knew that the *Report* was soon to be released.

The President's comments that our primary goal in releasing the study to members of the media was publicly to discredit and embarrass the University was, in our opinion, extremely irresponsible. The problem, as our report proved only too clearly, was that most victims of sexism are too fearful of retribution to speak out about their situations. A university, which by definition should be dedicated to expanding knowledge about social conditions, ought to welcome previously undisclosed and new sources of information. In our view, the reaction of Western officials amounted to an attempt to squelch any public criticism of themselves, oblivious to the harm they might do to women faculty members who were trying to effect institutional change. They also seemed unwilling to recognize the impact of their actions upon women who might consider bringing forward complaints in the future. "At rock bottom," as Constance Backhouse would state to *The London Free Press*, "we're talking about women's freedom of speech."[14]

The President's complaint of a "staged media event" also implied some large and well-organized press conference, with systematic, wide-ranging press releases. One of the ironies, as one of us mused later, was that if we had truly wanted to attract media attention, or to discredit the University, we certainly would have gone about it differently. We made no overtures apart from the ones listed above; we called no radio stations, no Toronto or national newspapers, no wire services, no press conference.

The *Report* came to public notice in a somewhat unplanned way. As Wylie put it in her response to critics: "It [was] a credit to the energy and attentiveness of local London reporters, not to us, that there was news of the *Report* so soon after it was circulated."[15] Now and again, when we were most disheartened by the frenzied hostility of the administration's response, we jokingly assured one another that we could certainly have created a better "media event" than the haphazard coverage the story initially generated if such had been our intention. It was surely an insult that the President believed this was the best we could do! Certainly there were any number of high-profile reporters we could have contacted, but this was neither our goal nor our expectation. In fact, we had never anticipated the depth or breadth of news coverage our report would generate. And our first assumptions may not have been wildly off the mark. An assignments editor at the *Free Press* subsequently told us that she had not expected the story to run for more than a day. Nor would it have, she added, if the administration had not been so belligerent in attacking the *Report* and its authors.

The single greatest irony was that the media event which did unfold was largely created by the Western administrators who invited television crews and reporters to attend the Senate meeting. It remains, as Wylie observed, "a mystery to us why [at first contact with the media] the President and the Provost did not simply state that they were aware of the problems we describe[d], that [these problems] are generic to universities in North America, and that Western was actively addressing them."[16] With such a response, there would have been no "media event." By contrast, however, the President not only called a press conference to discuss the *Report*, but opened it by denouncing our report as a "staged media event." Not surprisingly, the press eagerly seized on the explosive story of a university president lashing out at four female faculty members. Western's student newspaper, *The Gazette*, described the President as having "minced few words" in an article titled "[President] Slams Report." It also reported the Provost's depiction of the study as "innuendo," along with his reiteration of concern that it could only "counter the process it pretends to support."[17] In the free-for-all that followed the close of the Senate meeting that Thursday afternoon, the President became even more condemnatory. Responding to reporters' questions, he claimed that he refused to take seriously a report that made anonymous allegations, and that he would not order an investigation to see if such conditions really existed. He seemed to imply that evidence of discriminatory treatment could only be voiced within the confines of formal sexual harassment complaint procedures, where named individuals came forward to charge their alleged abusers. Those who purported to study the problems in a larger sense were acting not as legitimate academic researchers, but as some sort of special-interest lobby group. Furthermore, the President seemed to be attacking such wider studies as inherently malicious. He capped off the interview with the extraordinary statement: "It's almost a Joe McCarthy type of research we're doing here."[18]

J.R. McCarthy, a rabidly right-wing United States Senator, achieved historical notoriety in the 1950s Cold War era when he spearheaded a campaign to hunt down suspected Communists and rout them from all positions of power and influence. His was a crusade that relied upon enormous institutional coercion to force individuals to identify suspected Communist sympathizers. Geoffrey Rans, a faculty member of the Department of English, was one of the few men within the Western community who took public exception to the President's remarks. Turning the tables on the President in a letter to the editor published in *Western News* on 7 December, he argued that the President was more deserving of the McCarthy appellation:

> If anything [the President's statement] is exactly what Joe McCarthy did; [the President] holds up a report which few in the room had read and was not included in the Senators' documentation for the meeting, and delivers an ex cathedra judgment upon it. The largely male Senate held its collective tongue. Not a sound. Not one senator had the heart to question this act of demagoguery.[19]

We were terribly dismayed by the escalating hostility of the University officials. The *Free Press* describes Roma Harris' response:

> Roma Harris, a library science professor who helped write the report, said [the President] should recognize that the women asked to be anonymous because they're afraid of what would happen to them if they were identified. She said [the President's] reaction shows they were probably right in expecting they'd "get dumped on for naming the problem."[20]

Despite the President's vilification, Gillian Michell tried to continue to maintain a positive perspective. Speaking to reporters from the *Western News*, Michell emphasized that all the authors remained "committed to Western": "It's a good university overall, but there are some things which we must work at to make it a better place to work, especially for women," she insisted.[21]

None of us had even remotely anticipated being labelled "McCarthy-like" for our attempts to make visible the barriers to women's equality within the University. To be called such in the press by the President of the University was frightening in the extreme. Reached for comment late in the day on 16 November, at a conference for sexual harassment officers in Windsor, Ontario, where she was speaking, Constance Backhouse was startled and angered by the inflammatory characterization. As she told *Free Press* reporter, Wendy McCann, the contrast between the vehemently critical treatment of the four authors of the *Chilly Climate Report* and the kid-glove handling of Western Psychology Professor J. Philippe Rushton, was very revealing.[22] That contrast was remarked on by many observers and is worth further comment.

In January 1989, Rushton had delivered a paper to the annual meeting of the American Association for the Advancement of Science (AAAS) in San Francisco. In this remarkable document, Rushton purported to rank "Orientals," Whites, and Blacks in descending order in terms of intelligence, sexual restraint, and respect for the law. Rushton's theory ignited an incendiary debate, enraging academics and the public alike, and landing him international headlines and widespread publicity on such pop-culture television shows as *Geraldo*.

In a response to Rushton's work closer to home, a racially diverse group of Western students formed the Academic Coalition for Equality to call for a boycott of Rushton's classes, claiming that a man who produced such "research" was incapable of treating students of different races equally. The University's student newspaper, *The Gazette*, backed their call, citing the numerous professors and scientists who had denounced Rushton's research in an editorial headlined "Rushton Not Fit to Teach."[23] Forced by 10 days of media barrage to issue an institutional statement, the President repudiated racism but explicitly refused to attack Rushton's research itself.[24]

As *London Magazine* described it, the President "effectively blacked out" the debate, defending Rushton's presence on the grounds of "academic freedom." Academic freedom, he claimed, guaranteed that "such ideas can be expressed without fear of interference or repression from University administrators, politicians or others." On this matter, the President was unequivocal: "This is a final statement of the university," he announced tersely.[25]

Yet such academic protection was remarkably far from his mind as he cast about for ways to undermine the credibility of the *Chilly Climate Report* and its authors. In a private interview with *Western News* which appeared on 23 November 1989, he characterized the *Report* as "shabby work," taking great pains to register his official disgust. "If this had been done as a second-year undergraduate social science paper, it would get a failing grade," he insisted, adding that it was "disappointing and embarrassing to have work of such poor quality by faculty members passed off as reputable research."[26] "Academic freedom," as *London Magazine* would later remark, "was no longer an institutional buzzword."[27]

We were shocked by the failure of most of the academic community to express concern over the lack of due process or systematic peer review. The administration took the position that we were incompetent and irresponsible researchers, and their statements were published without any respect for the kind of review process that was scrupulously adhered to in the case of Philippe Rushton, whose credibility the administration was careful never to question or to challenge.

On Friday, 24 November 1989, Wylie attempted some damage control with the publication in *The Gazette* of the notes she had written for the Provost prior to the release of the *Report*. Emphasizing that the *Chilly Climate Report* was intended merely as a "pilot study," a "first step," in coming to terms with subtle, environmentally based barriers to equity, she pleaded for cooler heads to prevail (see Appendix A). In a second paper, titled "A Response to Some Criticisms of the Chilly Climate Report," Wylie addressed the three main criticisms levelled against the *Report:* (1) the anonymity of the interview subjects, (2) the selection of interviewees and their representativeness of the population of faculty women, and (3) the "media event" charge. Although it was not published at the time, this paper was widely circulated to those who inquired about our views on these matters (it is included here as Appendix B). Certainly the allegations were cause for serious concern. But we decided as a group not to publish any formal response. We believed the attacks on us were politically motivated and did not arise from genuine concerns about the reliability and validity of the research. A defensive rebuttal would simply have made it easier to keep up the attacks on us.

The President would eventually be forced to concede the anonymity point. After Western employment equity expert Carol Agòcs and Faculty Association President Sarah Shorten made repeated attempts to draw his attention to the errors inherent in his castigation of anonymous surveys, the President subsequently wrote to the authors on 17 December 1990: "I was quite incorrect in any comments which I made about the anonymity of respondents and for that extend to you and your colleagues an unqualified apology."[28] He continued to refuse, however, to apologize on other fronts:

> My own experience in social science research and the advice which I have received from others continue to leave me with serious misgivings. There is no need to repeat these concerns in detail here, but they relate to the generalizations which have been drawn, particularly with respect to the sampling procedures and the nature and format of the interview schedule.[29]

Wylie had already addressed the complaints about the representativeness of the survey in her *Gazette* essay of 24 November 1989. There Wylie was unequivocal on the point that "questions about the extent of the problem and its variability" required "much more wide-ranging and systematic research than we were able to undertake." Congratulating the women who could claim, in good faith, never to have had such experiences or observed such practices, she continued:

> I would be delighted to learn that we had, by dint of remarkable sampling error, spoken to all the women faculty at Western who had ever had such experiences, but would still maintain that the number of problems reported to us are too many to be tolerated in an institution that has made the sort of commitment this one has to employment equity.[30]

Somehow this and all the other careful disclaimers, clarifications and statements of objective that we included in the *Report* and its related documents were overlooked throughout this entire affair. Conceding that change would necessitate "an unsettling process of candid self-criticism directed not just at some amorphous 'other' ... but at ourselves, our own units, our immediate colleagues," Wylie urged the University community to move towards a more egalitarian environment. This was, she argued, something that was "absolutely essential if this institution is to continue to play a vital role in an increasingly diverse society."[31]

At about this time another line of attack was initiated. An unnamed member of the university community was said to have contacted the Research Office to ask if we had received ethics clearance to interview the women to whom we had spoken. On 26 January 1990, Backhouse received a letter from the Chair of Western's Review Board for Social Science and Humanities Research Involving Human Subjects (the committee charged with ensuring that ethics guidelines are observed by all faculty members whose academic research involved human subjects) who had by then investigated the matter. The letter read as follows:

> I have been directed by the Review Board for Social Sciences and Humanities Research Involving Human Subjects to inform you and your colleagues that it is the opinion of the Review Board that the study by you and others, (the Chilly Climate Report), should have received ethical review. Since it was substantiated that the study did not receive ethical approval, the Board has informed the Vice-President (Research) of its opinion and has recommended that he take any disciplinary action he deems appropriate.[32]

Wylie, who had long sat as a member of this Review Board, was astonished. As she noted in her letter of reply dated 1 February 1990, guidelines and procedures appropriate to this sort of unfunded study had not yet been established by the University. In fact, the Review Board had only begun to formulate such guidelines in the previous year (well after the time the *Chilly Climate* interviews had been undertaken and completed), and they were still under active consideration at the time the Review Board ruled against the authors of the *Chilly Climate Report*. The retroactive nature of this decision is particularly striking, since the *Chilly Climate Report* was quite clearly represented as an "institutional study," not as "academic research" (funded or otherwise). The question of whether administrative officers, employee associations, unions, and the various clubs on campus should be required to seek formal ethics approval for any studies they might undertake of their members and constituencies was, at the time, hotly debated. The framework for delivering a decision against the authors of the *Report* was not in place at the time the Review Board ruled against them. Moreover, the reference to disciplinary action was problematic. We were informed by the President of the Faculty Association that there were no provisions in the conditions of appointment for faculty members outlining the circumstances under which "disciplinary action" could be taken, the forms this could take, or any procedure for appeal.[33]

By now, debate over the *Report* was rapidly spreading beyond the authors and Western officials. Perceptions and responses within the university community were varied. Fifteen women from the Faculty of Education signed a letter to the *Western News* objecting to the administration's "shrill" and "accusatory tone." "Ironically," they noted, "such a response further enhances the credibility of the report by providing yet another example of the ways in which women's attempts to be heard are denigrated. [W]e found much in the report with which we could identify."[34]

Western women's studies student Karen McCaffery wrote, tongue-in-cheek:

> Well! It seems there really is no sexual harassment of female faculty at Western! Our fearless leader, [the] President, . . . has spoken. . . . He says so in *The London Free Press*, right on page B2 in the November 17th edition, so he must be sure, eh? He knows all about sexual harassment. . . . [There is no] sexism at Western, no hostility towards wimmin. Of course not! And there is no racism here either. Everybody knows that. . . . we should all just bust out and rename the place Shangri-la.[35]

Law student Jane Hegney expressed her astonishment that the President had characterized the *Report* as "akin to McCarthyism." Pointing out the comparison that was increasingly being drawn between Rushton and the *Chilly Climate* authors, Hegney noted that the President's version of "academic freedom" apparently had "different meanings when applied to male and female academics." She wrote:

> I have a plea for the President of Western: . . . your statements speak volumes about your ignorance of these matters. If you care about this university, or more pragmatically, if you want to retain a shred of credibility, you will educate yourself — quickly. You can start by believing what the people in the university community are trying in good faith to tell you instead of

ridiculing them and calling them names. Do some basic reading on the
subject. (Why do I have to say this to a professor?)

Until you start treating these concerns seriously, the person who most
debases this university in the public eye is you.[36]

Louise Forsyth, a senior faculty member of the Department of French,
courageously identified herself in the *Western News* as one of the 35 previously unnamed interviewees. One of the key members of Western's first
President's Advisory Committee on the Status of Women 15 years earlier,
she had considerable experience and authority on the basis of which to comment. Noting that many of the 92 recommendations made in the 1975 *Report*
had still not been implemented, she called the current administration's denunciation a "disdainful, uncomprehending and defensive condemnation"
that was "symptomatic" of a glacial pace of change.[37]

Michael Bennett, one of Western's Sexual Harassment Officers and a
Professor of Computer Science, spoke out in support. Claiming that the *Report* was "one of the best" he had seen, Bennett termed it "an excellent start
for examining this whole problem of the 'chilly climate,' to eradicate it and
then extend the concept to other areas where it might exist."[38] Where people
work in an environment of sexism and harassment, claimed Bennett, "they
will not come forward publicly. The report has offered an opportunity for
those voices to be heard."[39]

Not all of the correspondence published about the *Report* was so supportive. One male Professor of philosophy complained that no men had been
interviewed. "What might these wrongdoers have had to say for themselves?" he queried. "What might any male professor at Western have to say
for himself — for is he not implicated by having remained at this university
of unusually rampant sexist practice?"[40] This challenge raises several crucial questions. Why are the oppressed not believed without proof from their
oppressors? And why are the experiences of women not important in and of
themselves? Do we require the testimony of the beneficiaries of sexual discrimination to validate women's accounts of sexist practices? For the most
part male colleagues do not decide to freeze their female colleagues out;
they simply don't think of them as equals and they act accordingly. The effect, more than the intention, is what chills.

A female subscriber to *The London Free Press* from Port Stanley, Ontario,
wrote that she feared that demands for employment equity programs
would result in reverse discrimination. "Has it occurred to Constance Backhouse that many women at the University of Western Ontario aren't afraid
to speak out without the veil of anonymity?" she exclaimed. "They may just
be having a hard time trying to verbalize the way they feel without coming
across as prejudiced and discriminatory themselves. It's boisterous,

unthinking, sexist statements by so-called feminists that make me sometimes embarrassed to be a woman."[41]

A professor emeritus from the University of Calgary was perhaps the
most vehement. His letter to *Western News*, published on 23 November 1989,
was direct and to the point. Labelling the authors "the gang of four," he
used gleefully vitriolic prose:

> The accusations made by four female persons of rampant sexism in West-
> ern are the most sexist orientated statements I have encountered in any
> University in 40 years of academic life. Without presenting any evidence
> they accuse male faculty of sexual misdemeanours ranging from the ab-
> surdly trivial to the very serious.
>
> Do they expect to be accepted uncritically? The methodology is ludi-
> crous and a disgrace to any academic institution. Their behaviour in releas-
> ing this to the press is a serious breach of academic good manners. It is all
> the more reprehensible that they include at least one Faculty of Law mem-
> ber who should surely be expected to understand the meaning of evidence,
> the unacceptability of hearsay evidence and no doubt the use of leading
> questions. It is quite clear from their attitude and their behaviour that they
> are in the wrong jobs and are most assuredly unsuitable as role models for
> students. . . . The four can clearly be classified into what I call "uneducated
> literates," a very dangerous group in our society.
>
> Perhaps in self protection, male faculty members should refuse to have
> any communication with the four. Who knows if in saying "hello" they
> might be written up as potential seducers.[42]

The offensiveness of the letter is somewhat offset by the rich scope it offers those wanting to understand the anti-feminist perspective more thoroughly. Like the Western administrators, this professor emeritus seems
completely unable to distinguish between studies that begin to give voice to
women's problems within the University and procedures appropriate for
the formal litigation of sexual harassment complaints — the exclusion of
hearsay evidence, the use of leading questions during cross-examination,
and the like. Furthermore, his use of the phrase "potential seducers" reveals
his understanding of chilly climate issues as rooted in male sexuality. This is
clearly not how the women victimized by gender harassment perceive it.
That male apologists seem wedded to metaphors of coercion, aggression,
and sexuality provides much pause for thought.

This critic's rant about our disgraceful breach of scholarly manners and
decorum implies that it was we who had chilled the climate. The obvious
conclusion, according to this professor, is that we were "in the wrong jobs"
and logically "unsuitable" for the academy. After all, how better to improve
the climate than to remove the rain clouds? The serious danger we posed
emanates from our status as "uneducated literates." We should either educate ourselves to conform to the rules and perspectives he enunciates, or re-

frain from writing. The concept of free speech unfettered by male conventions goes right out the window.

Our *Report* also provoked censure from some female colleagues, some of which we found very disheartening. While we knew that the various women who taught and studied at Western would not all accept our depiction of gender inequality, we had not fully anticipated the extent of the disagreement. A female faculty member of the Department of Pharmacology and Toxicology was one of the first to write to *Western News*. While she allowed that "undoubtedly sexism exists at Western," she was anxious to disassociate herself from the *Report*:

> I am concerned that the report issued on the "chilly climate" has left the impression that sexism and unequal treatment have been the universal experience of female faculty at this institution. This is not the case. Just as those who were interviewed felt that anonymity was essential to protect them from possible negative repercussions arising from their statements, those of us who were not interviewed and have not been subjected to the types of harassment described in the report now feel obliged to distance ourselves from its conclusions.[43]

This letter singled out, by peculiar juxtaposition, the contrasting positions of women who felt themselves to have experienced discrimination and women who did not. The former needed to cling to the blanket protection of anonymity, the latter claimed public voice. The obvious rationale for the divergent responses — that the forces of institutional retribution awaited the first group while more beneficent behaviour welcomed the second — seemed lost on Western's President. He cited his personal receipt of "numerous telephone calls from women faculty members upset at the report and its allegations" as authority for impugning the reliability of the original study.[44] In doing so, curiously, he failed to apply to his own analysis any of the methodological and sampling critiques with which he so vigorously assailed our *Report*.

The most systematic denunciation was led by Western's Associate Dean of Medical Research, who wrote a statement of rebuke on behalf of some 30 women with whom she had been in contact. As she wrote to the *Free Press* on 9 December 1989, she was both "bothered" and "dismay[ed]" by the tone of "hostility and extremism" in the *Chilly Climate Report*. The following passages have been excerpted from her lengthy letter:

> That view of the atmosphere on the campus is not shared by the first 30 women I happened to see in two days, and asked if their experiences were those described in the report. Some of the women surprised me by the depth of their anger and irritation, because they felt that the report belittled and denigrated them and portrayed them as victims.

We do not come to work in fear; do not find the atmosphere chilling; do not find ourselves put down, harassed, ignored or insulted by our male colleagues.

The report's tone of bristling hostility doesn't help the cause of women. [T]he great majority of the many men I personally interact with daily are reasonable, pleasant to deal with, and often most helpful. I consider many of them to be valued colleagues and good friends.

I take exception to the assumption that the authors of this report speak for all women on the campus. The report and the publicity surrounding it have served to distort the situation at Western, which does not deserve to have its good name tarnished.[45]

While we were greatly upset by this effort to discredit the *Report*, misrepresenting again the scope and generality of the claims we were making, the four authors made the collective decision not to respond publicly to any of our detractors. The author and the other women she claimed had never experienced discrimination may indeed have been able to flourish unscathed within the predominantly male academy. Alternatively, they may have survived by systematically ignoring such sexist treatment as came their way, denying the existence of gender-related barriers in their work.[46]

Rather than respond publicly, we sought to meet privately with the Associate Dean of Medical Research and the women she spoke for, as well as with several other influential women who had taken umbrage at our report. One of the meetings we scheduled with a senior female administrator at the University seemed, at first blush, to have lessened hostilities somewhat and accorded greater opportunity for future communication. In later months we would be disappointed to observe that in public our positions remained sharply separated.

One of the most unsettling responses from a female academic came from a professor from the Department of Microbiology and Immunology. A prominent advocate for women's equality within Western's Faculty of Science, she too was upset about our report. She argued, in the *Western News* of 7 December 1989, that our focus on matters such as "gender-neutral language" and the "deep-seated, subtle attitudinal difficulty which may afflict the occasional faculty member of either sex," was seriously misplaced. Attention to these issues would detract from what she viewed as far more pressing concerns: the low number of female faculty members, especially in the sciences; the decreasing representation of women in postdoctoral positions and amongst applicants for faculty positions in science; the clash between tenure opportunities and women's reproductive biology; and the exploitation of part-time faculty members, particularly those with child-rearing responsibilities.[47]

Not for one minute would any of us have thought to belittle the importance of the issues this Professor cited. In other documents, under other circumstances, we had all argued for measures to address these important problems. A great many of the experiences outlined in the *Chilly Climate Report* had to do with such matters. In contrast to the Professor's dismissal of more subtle issues, biologist Sheila Widnall, in her 1988 Presidential Lecture to the American Academy for the Advancement of Science (AAAS), had pinpointed the workplace climate as the precise reason why women disappear from the training "pipeline" feeding the sciences. Yet our critic had been so offended by our environmental approach that she felt compelled to disassociate herself from our initiative. Stunned by this reproach from a woman we had thought of as sharing similar goals, we realized that divergent opinions about how to improve the status of women would continue to make positions of broad solidarity tenuous.

While critiques of this sort were deeply unnerving, we were gratified to learn that many others were eager to hear more about the *Report*. We were invited to give presentations about the *Report*, and its reception, to various groups: to interested members of the Faculty of Nursing and King's College, and to the University chaplains. Off campus, we spoke before a number of learned societies and professional associations and at various conferences and symposia in Canada, Australia, Norway, the UK, and the United States. In none of these settings did we encounter the kind of hostility meted out to us by the administration, or by various of our colleagues.

On a more personal note, the four of us found it, in varying degrees, very difficult to continue to work on campus after the *Report* came out. Professional and social relations with many of our colleagues, numbers of whom manifested various degrees of hostility and paranoia, were strained beyond repair. Our apprehensions and anxieties were intensified by the horrific events of 6 December 1989, when Marc Lepine gunned down 14 female engineering students on University of Montreal's Ecole Polytechnique, shouting "You are all a bunch of feminists!" Feminists across the nation, numbed by the Montreal massacre, were shocked to the core by the misogynist backlash which followed, as media pundits and community leaders banded together to insist with increasing hyperbole that this was the isolated act of a lone madman, bearing no particular meaning for women, which feminists were "using" to promote their own "narrow, political interests."[48] They adamantly refused to recognize the extreme and catastrophic consequences of the hatred and distrust of women within Canadian society, in much the same way that Western administrators had refused to listen to more subtle variations on this theme.

Along with other feminist university women across Canada, in the wake of the massacre we felt our position at Western to be particularly precarious. We felt that as the authors of the *Chilly Climate Report* we had been left dreadfully exposed by orchestrated attacks on our motives, our methodology, and our recommendations for change. Disappointed and unnerved by the reaction of the senior administrators of the University, we reflected upon the telling irony that their response had served to replicate many of the mechanisms that produce a chilly climate in academic contexts: stereotyping, devaluation, exclusion, revictimization. If there had ever been any question about the currency of sexist and misogynist attitudes and behaviour on campus, it had been decisively and conclusively laid to rest — most powerfully by the example, in action, of those who most vehemently denied the seriousness of these issues.

Significantly, this point was not lost on a good many of our male colleagues: people who had sat on the fence and been inclined to dismiss the *Report* as generalized belly-aching, or as idiosyncratic to specific units or individuals. Some found their thinking turned around first by the administrative response to the *Chilly Climate Report* and then by the enormity of the Montreal massacre. Suddenly it was graphically clear just how deep and pervasive the problem was. In a couple of cases our male colleagues made a point of telling us that, where they had previously seen sexist behaviour as simply bad taste which was best ignored, the events of the fall of 1989 made it clear to them that they had a moral obligation to take active steps to oppose such behaviour.

The four of us had originally hoped to conduct annual, continuing studies on the status of women at Western, branching out to examine such additional matters as the plight of part-time faculty and the situation of non-academic staff. But coping with the fall-out from the *Chilly Climate Report* proved significantly more draining and time consuming than any of us had anticipated. In fact, we have not met as a group for quite some time now, and we have no active plans for further follow-up studies.

One particular project did move forward, however, under the aegis of Western's Caucus on Women's Issues. When the *Report* drew such a hostile response, Alison Wylie (as President of the Women's Caucus) and the Executive of the Women's Caucus were reinforced in their commitment to a project that was already in the works: a video on chilly climate issues. Our experience with hostile reactions to the *Report* made it clearer than ever just how important an issue climate was, especially as employment equity programs were getting under way in the province. In April 1990, supported by Western's Caucus on Women's Issues, Western's Employment Equity Office, and the President's Standing Committee on Employment Equity, Wylie successfully made application for funding to underwrite a video on chilly climate issues. The sum of $55,200 from the Ontario Ministry of Colleges and Universities and the Ontario Women's Directorate was granted to fund the creation of a 28-minute video and an accompanying facilitators' manual. Ironically, the success of the grant was greeted enthusiastically by the President of the University, who stated that the issue was "tremendously important."[49]

Produced by London's Kem Murch Productions, the video was described in *The London Free Press* as "deeply mov[ing]" after its premiere showing at an anti-discrimination conference in London on 29 April 1991. Based on interviews with female and male students, faculty, staff, and administrators from London's Fanshawe Community College, Toronto's York University, and the University of Western Ontario,[50] the video reached beyond the original *Chilly Climate Report* to include a welcome and important focus on race and disability. With emotion, humour, and rich irony, it described the subtle features that operate to thwart the full participation of women, persons with disabilities, and individuals of diverse races within post-secondary educational institutions. The market for the video and manual has rapidly expanded beyond provincial borders to include purchasers from across Canada and the United States and beyond. In a gesture which held great meaning for all of us, the authors of the manual generously dedicated it to the *Chilly Climate* authors, "for their vision and courage." The more appropriate dedication, however, would have been to all of the women at Western who have striven, for many decades and through many generations, for greater acceptance of women's perspectives within the academy.

Appendix A
Some Comments on the *Chilly Climate Report*
Alison Wylie

This commentary was published in The Gazette, *17 November 1989, p. 9.*

– Eds.

Preface

In the week before the *Chilly Climate Report* was circulated I set down a few thoughts about my hopes and expectations for its reception. They were circulated to members of the administration and those responsible for the development of employment equity programs on campus, in the hope that they would provide a fuller sense of the spirit in which the *Report* was drafted. Unfortunately, they have not mitigated what has been described as a "nasty exchange" in the external press in which the credibility of the *Report* has been called into question on the grounds that we undertook to protect the identities of the 35 women we interviewed and because it is considered unrepresentative of the conditions under which women faculty work at Western.

In fact, it is clearly stated in the introduction to the *Report* that those we interviewed requested anonymity not just out of fear of reprisals but because no constructive purpose would be served by pointing fingers at individual units or colleagues. Our objective was not to seek redress for individual cases, but to characterize, with reference to Western, a problem that has been widely documented on campuses across North America against which effective action can only be taken if it is named and understood. Clearly, questions about the extent of the problem and its variability require much more wide-ranging and systematic research than we were able to undertake; we consider this report a first step in the process of coming to terms with the subtle, environmentally based barriers to equity which have been found to persist even when formally discriminatory policies are struck down. The key conclusions of our report are that the chilliness of the climate at Western varies a great deal across the departments and faculties from which we drew our samples of interviewees, but that there are a number of common themes (i.e., similar actions or mechanisms which make the climate chilly, such as stereotyping, isolation or exclusion, and systematic devaluation of women) which cross-cut this variability and replicate the conditions that have been documented, in the past decade, on campuses across the United States.

What follows is the text of the "comments" that were circulated two weeks ago; they amplify these points in a way that I hope may put discussions of the *Report* and the problems it describes on a more constructive track.

Comments Circulated 7 November 1989

I see this report as, above all, a contribution to efforts to realize equity for women at Western that are being made on a number of fronts. In particular, the President's Standing Committee for Employment Equity has made a clear commitment to address exactly the sorts of chilly climate issues that we set out to document in our report. With this committee in its first year of operation and engaged in a process of familiarizing itself with the concerns of the four target groups covered by its mandate, the timing for release of such a report couldn't be better. This is in part, a matter of luck rather than design. The President's Committee didn't exist when we began our study, nor did the University's policy or the President's statement of commitment to employment equity. At the time, the most we could have hoped for was that our results would underline the need for such a committee and policy. Now, however, they can enter directly into a process of designing and implementing a program for realizing equity at Western that has already been set into motion. My hope is that this report will reinforce the Committee's resolve to make climate issues one chief target of a pro-active program for change, because it is only with change at this level — in effect, in the culture of the institution — that changes in formal policy and procedures will have any sustained effect.

What this study has to offer, more specifically, is the demonstration that women at Western encounter essentially the same kinds of difficulties that have been widely recognized to persist in other contexts, even when strong action is taken to eliminate overt discrimination. It replicates the sorts of results established by a number of studies of climate issues that have been undertaken on campuses across the United States. While this is, in one sense, a depressing result (we might have hoped, rather unrealistically, that things were different at Western), it is extremely valuable in situating our local problems in a larger context. And it provides, in a preliminary and exploratory way, some indication of the context-specific form that these problems take at Western. My hope is that, in making these results available to everyone concerned with employment equity at Western, we will have accelerated the process of program design and implementation. With a qualitative pilot study in hand, complementing the quantitative "audit" of target groups now in the final stages of development, there is the basis for beginning the process of education and for designing more encompassing surveys that will ascertain the extent of the problems described to us by those we interviewed.

I expect that the main negative reaction to the *Report* will be the objection that it is "anecdotal" and unrepresentative. In response to this I can only repeat what we say in the *Report*: as an institution we (collectively) have a problem if *anyone* feels as demoralized and excluded as did many of the women with whom we spoke. I would be delighted to learn that we had, by dint of remarkable sampling error, spoken to all the women faculty at Western who have ever had such experiences, but would still maintain that the number of problems reported to us are too many to be tolerated in an institution that has made the sort of commitment this one has to employment equity. In fact, the way we proceeded was to identify departments and faculties that represent a range of different kinds of disciplines and environments, and then interview as many women faculty in each unit as possible. In this, several of the units in which we conducted interviews were chosen precisely because they had a reputation for supporting women, so such a happy error would be quite remarkable. I was, in fact, delighted to learn that there is a great deal of variability in the experience of women faculty at Western: as indicated in the *Report*, some of the 35 we spoke to did feel that, overall, they had been treated well. But every one of them described ways in which their own effectiveness and productivity, or their ability to participate in the life of the institution had been compromised by gender-specific patterns of treatment that they felt devalued and isolated them as women. However widespread or broadly "representative" these negative experiences prove to be, for the target population as a whole or for individuals, they result in an unacceptable waste of talent and person-power in an institution whose main asset is undeniably its employees.

It is worth noting that the cost of squandering these human resources (e.g., those of the four key target groups) is quickly becoming unsupportable, not just in universities but in society as a whole. *The Toronto Star* ran a story in August under the headline, "U.S. Employers Face Boggling Demographics." These "boggling demographics" were that, while "white males . . . as few as five years ago represented 45 per cent of the U.S. work force, [they] will comprise only 15 per cent of the entering work force by 1995." *The Star* goes on to conclude that "U.S. businesses will be *forced to turn to women, minorities and immigrants* if they expect to compete in the global economy of the 1990s and beyond" (*The Toronto Star*, Monday, 28 August, B2; emphasis added). Whatever the peculiarities of the situation in Canada, the fact remains that we can ill afford to allow the persistence of practices that exclude, devalue, and undermine members of traditionally marginalized groups; taken together, these are rapidly emerging as the majority of the entering workforce. As a primary focus of training for members of this entering workforce, particularly managers and professionals, universities have a special responsibility to be on the cutting edge of change in this area, and a special potential to realize the sorts of positive change that will be necessary if we are to capitalize on diversity.

I have every expectation that the new employment equity initiatives at Western will make a real difference, not just for women (or, more narrowly, for women faculty), but for all target groups. There is no question, however, that this will require the hardest kind of change: changes in attitudes and in patterns of everyday practice that are so widely taken for granted they are never even acknowledged, much less questioned. Although this necessitates an unsettling process of candid self-criticism directed not just at some amorphous "other" ("the administration," "the decision makers") but at ourselves, our own units, our immediate colleagues, it is absolutely essential if this institution (indeed, if any post-secondary institution) is to continue to play a vital role in an increasingly diverse society.

Appendix B
A Response to Some Criticisms of the *Chilly Climate Report*
Alison Wylie

Drafted for circulation on 24 November 1989.

– Eds.

The criticisms levelled against the *Report* we drafted on the chilly climate for women faculty at Western fall into three categories: 1) interviewees were not identified (we, and they, "hid behind anonymity"), 2) the chilly climate experiences we report are not "representative," and 3) the *Report* was used to create a "staged media event." I respond to each in turn.

1. Anonymity

It is difficult to know why protection of the identities of research subjects would be considered grounds for questioning the credibility of the reported results of interviews with them. Virtually every professional association of social scientists and most credible granting agencies enforce codes of ethics which not only allow, but in fact require, that social scientists guarantee their subjects' anonymity. Subjects are routinely assured that research materials identifying them will be kept under lock and key and destroyed after a specified period of time; they are guaranteed that the data resulting from studies in which they participate will be published in aggregate form so they are not identifiable and, in the case of research which focuses closely on particular individuals, pseudonyms are typically used and any identifying details are carefully disguised. If researchers do plan to publish material in which their subjects are identified, they must get written permission to do this, the only exception being cases where the subjects are public figures who are being interviewed in their official capacities. If the anonymity of research subjects was, indeed, ground for dismissing the credibility of social scientific research, very little would survive scrutiny.

The reason we have been criticized for such standard research practice seems to be a worry that, in not identifying those we interviewed, we (or the subjects) could have "made it all up." In fact, we took special care to ensure the accuracy of all claims made about the experiences women reported to us. As we completed our final draft, we contacted each woman we had interviewed whose experiences were described in the *Report*, outlined the context in which her remarks were reported, and asked her to review all the statements attributed to her, including both direct quotes and summary descriptions. Frequently interviewees requested that certain details be excised because they were too readily identifiable, but just as frequently they added material to convey more completely and accurately the nature of the difficulties they faced. We incorporated all the revisions suggested. It is a profound insult not just to us, but to the 35 women we interviewed, that public critics of the *Report* seem to find the experiences we describe so implausible that, *in this particular case*, they take anonymity to be grounds for questioning the integrity of the accounts given, indeed, for intimating that we (and they) may have falsified the data we report.

2. Representativeness

Two separate issues are raised in this connection. The first has to do with the sample of women we interviewed, and the second with the kinds of incidents and experiences we reported on the basis of these interviews. The crux of both seems to be a suspicion that what we report is not representative of women's experiences at Western considered either collectively or individually, and that therefore any conclusions we have drawn are false generalizations.

It has first to be noted that we did not, in fact, undertake to establish general conclusions about the extent or degree of the problems we documented in the University as a whole. Our aim was to characterize some of the mechanisms by which a chilly climate can be created for women, following the lead of numerous studies done at other institutions in North America and nationally in the United States. To this end we were most concerned simply to describe the experiences of the women we interviewed. The conclusions we drew were that there is, in this sample, great variability in the degree to which women find the climate chilly at Western. As we indicate repeatedly, we did speak to women who felt they had been treated well overall and that their units had been relatively hospitable, but even they had encountered the same sorts of chilly climate practices which, in more extreme forms elsewhere, were described as creating an extremely hostile environment. There were consistent themes in the treatment of women, as women, which are comparable to those that have been identified in the surveys reported by the Association of American Colleges. As we said in the *Report* and elsewhere, we would be overjoyed to learn that we had interviewed the only 35 women faculty at Western who have encountered the sorts of problems that were described to us, and we congratulate those women who can claim, in good faith, never to have had such experiences or observed such practices. Our report shows, however, that Western is not an anomaly among North American universities; the problems identified elsewhere do exist here. In fact, we had assumed that the President's creation of a Standing Committee on Employment Equity was informed, at least in part, by an appreciation that climate issues are crucial, as acknowledged in the Federal Contractors Guidelines, and that the mandate of this committee would include investigation of the extent — the distribution and seriousness — of exactly the sorts of subtle and informal, as well as formal (and now illegal), barriers to employment equity that were described by the women we interviewed.

Despite the fact that generalization was not our objective we did make a concerted effort to speak to a range of women working in a number of different sorts of academic disciplines and environments. As indicated in the *Report*, we proceeded by drawing a sample of academic units (either departments, or faculties without departmental structure) and then undertook to interview as many women within these units as possible. Where the choice of units was concerned, we felt it important to maximize variability on two dimensions: the type of discipline and the reputed warmth or chilliness of the climate for women. We chose 12 units altogether. Four can be broadly defined as "professional schools," and the rest are distributed across the "core faculties" of Arts, Social Science, and Science. Two had a strong reputation for supporting women and two we understood to be problematic in this regard, while the rest (i.e., two-thirds of them) had no particular reputation in either direction. In all but two of the units we achieved coverage of two-thirds of all the tenured and tenurable women faculty, and in the majority of units (eight of them) we were able to interview over half the women faculty holding term appointments and ongoing part-time positions, as well as tenured and tenurable positions. None of the women we contacted declined to speak to us, although two asked that none of their experiences be included after having been interviewed. Although our assessment of the "reputation" of units was necessarily impressionistic, the fact remains that we did undertake to interview women in contexts where we believed the climate might be relatively warm and, in the end, women from such units were proportionately better represented in our sample than women from the other units. We interviewed 80% of the women in the two units we identified as supportive environments; none of them felt it necessary to withdraw their accounts and, in the end, they constituted just under a quarter of the reported sample. Insofar as our sample is skewed, then, it is definitely not skewed in the direction of a concentration on women working in what we understood to be inhospitable contexts.

In short, contrary to the allegations of our critics, we did not speak to a sample of 35 women whom we knew in advance would have negative stories to tell about their experiences at Western. We interviewed a great many women we knew hardly at all and many we believed would have had relatively good experiences at Western, given their location in units supportive of women. Given this, we were interested to learn that the climate for women varies a great deal at Western, although all of those we interviewed report various forms of differential treatment as women that they find irksome at best, and profoundly debilitating at worst.

The second sense in which our account seems to be considered unrepresentative is that we are suspected of having included only the worst experiences reported to us or that we manipulated our subjects (using "leading questions") into reporting their bad experiences in an unrepresentative way. In fact, the way we proceeded in interviews was to ask, in as open-ended a manner as possible, whether the woman in question felt that gender had made a difference, or had affected the way she was treated in her unit, in her capacity as teacher, researcher, and administrator (the three areas covered by our contracts as faculty). More often than not we were overwhelmed by the response we got to this initial inquiry; for many women, especially those we knew least well or who were relatively isolated in their units, we presented an opportunity to talk about an enormous range of experiences that they found problematic and puzzling, but felt quite alone in addressing. In several cases what began as an hour-long interview went on for three, even four or five hours, and a number of interviewees made a point of keeping in touch with us after the interviews, calling back to add observations about the experiences they had initially described to us, or adding new incidents as they came to mind or unfolded around them in subsequent weeks and months (these include five women with whom contact through the project, as interviewees, was their primary connection with the interviewer). We certainly did not have to employ "leading" questions to elicit the enormous volume of interview material on which we based our report. All we had to do was indicate a willingness to listen and we encountered, over and over, a great desire to break the silence and isolation and to talk to others about what we quickly came to see as common problems. We can only hope the President's Employment Equity Committee will provide more women with the opportunity to discuss their experiences, concerns, and hopes for change with regard to chilly climate issues.

As this suggests, we came away from the interview process with vastly more material than we could hope to summarize in a manageable report. The selection process proved less difficult than we expected, however, because a great deal of this material proved unusable by virtue of being so specific to individual women and their situations that there was no possibility of reporting it without revealing their identities. In fact, for this reason, we left out at least as many incidents and examples of chilly climate practices as we included. Moreover, as might be expected, the experiences we did not report include the worst, most explicit cases of sexist and discriminatory behaviour we heard about, as well as many of the accounts given by women whose positions are so tenuous that they felt they could not allow us to report any but the most sanitized descriptions of their experiences. The incidents we were able to include are, for the most part, generic enough that they could be described without specific references that would expose individuals. In short, if there is any bias in our selection of material from the accounts women gave us of their experiences at Western, it is certainly not in the direction of emphasizing the worst aspects of this work environment.

Finally, a question often raised is whether the incidents reported are representative of recent and ongoing practices, rather than relating to the environment of 15 or 20 years ago. In fact, 60% of the women we interviewed had been appointed to positions at Western in the 1980s (21 women) and well over half of these had been at Western less than five years when we contacted them in the summer of 1988. Given this, it is to be expected that the vast majority of the incidents reported are recent history. And, in fact, only a handful (specifically, six) of the incidents described were reported to us as having occurred in the 1970s. Another 10 occurred in the early 1980s but most of them (eight) were described as practices or problems that originated at that time and have continued to the present. All the rest are current either in the sense that, as discrete events, they occurred within the past five years, or they constitute features of the environment — what we referred to as "standing conditions" — that are ongoing problems. It is perhaps significant that all the incidents concerning compensation (e.g., lower starting salaries) date to within three years of the interviews, with the one exception being the case reported by a woman who had been denied summer teaching on the grounds that she had no alimony payments to meet.

I conclude, then, that the experiences we describe are not, in any of the senses identified, "unrepresentative" of the kinds of difficulties that at least 35 women currently face at Western. From the point of view of developing an effective employment equity program, it would be most interesting and useful to characterize this variability in greater detail, to establish a data base that will support generalizations about the climate at Western as a whole and, most important, to determine what factors make a difference in the environment for women. Our point has always been that our study should be treated as a contribution to this larger investigative and policy-making enterprise — it provides some preliminary information on the basis of which more extensive surveys could profitably be based. The proposal that our report be used as a point of departure for further research was, in fact, the first of the six recommendations with which we concluded the *Report*.

But whatever follow-up research is undertaken at Western, and whatever its results, we maintain that the problems reported to us by the 35 women we interviewed are too numerous, too serious, and too consistent thematically (both among themselves and with those reported in other con-

texts) to be dismissed as unproblematic because they are unrepresentative
of the population as a whole.

In addition, I would argue that, whatever the results of this follow-up research, our interview data do establish a clear and present need for the sorts
of response to problems of climate that we recommended in the conclusion
of the *Report*. In particular, it is crucial that some kind of mechanism be
established for handling complaints about the various types of discriminatory behaviour reported to us which do not fall within the mandate of the
Sexual Harassment Officers. There is no individual or office empowered to
handle these complaints comparable to the Sexual Harassment Officers
and, as many of the stories reported indicate, women frequently find themselves in positions where those to whom they might properly report their
difficulties are part of the problem. This concern was addressed by our
fourth recommendation. In addition to dealing more effectively with more
or less overt cases of discriminatory practice, it is crucial to sensitize the university community to the damage done by the sorts of informal, often inadvertently compromising practices that exclude and devalue women (recommendations three and five) and, most important, that every effort be made
to increase the number of women on faculty and in administrative positions
at Western (recommendation six with provisions for implementation in recommendation two). The President's Standing Committee for Employment
Equity presumably has a mandate to take action in each of these areas and,
as we indicate in our conclusion, we did see evidence that a commitment to
equity has begun to change the environment for women in some quarters:
we came away from the study with "some degree of optimism that such
warming of the climate is spreading, and can be spread if a concerted effort
is made to foster it" (p. 37).

3. The "Staged Media Event"

The allegation that we "staged" a "media event," evidently with the deliberate aim of discrediting the University, is one of the most puzzling features
of the defensive reaction that our report has provoked. We were, from the
outset, committed to making the *Report* public, in the sense that we were
committed to making it available to any who might take an interest in it. It
was originally distributed to the women we interviewed, to the senior administration, and to those appointed by them to address employment
equity issues, and a copy was put on reserve at D.B. Weldon Library where it
would be accessible to others. It is not clear what it means to say that a media event has been "staged." At the very least it would seem to imply some
element of surprise—that the media were given the *Report* before those
concerned or affected by it knew it was coming or had themselves received

it — and it would seem to suggest some large and well-organized press conference or systematic press release involving a range of media. In fact, many members of the administration were informed that the *Report* would be available two weeks before it was released and that the local *Free Press* reporter responsible for university news also knew that the *Report* was coming. In the event, this reporter drove over to one of our houses on the weekend after the *Report* was released to get a copy, and very quickly did interviews with the three of us who were in town at the time. The electronic media likewise made arrangements, that weekend, to interview two of us early on Monday morning. There was, then, no element of surprise and, far from "staging" a press conference or arranging a systematic, wide-ranging press release, the *Report* came to public notice in an extremely haphazard way. It is a credit to the energy and attentiveness of local London reporters, not to us, that there was news of the *Report* so soon after it was circulated.

It is a mystery to us why the President and the Provost did not simply state that they were well aware of the problems we describe, that these problems are generic to universities in North America, and that Western is actively addressing them, deferring any further questions to the highly professional staff and faculty they have appointed to positions of responsibility for these initiatives. With such a response there would have been no story, and no "media event." The only real media event we can identify, using the criteria of surprise (or, failure to inform those involved) and deliberate solicitation of media attention, was created by the invitation of TV crews and reporters to cover the Senate meeting at which, ironically, the President issued the statement denouncing *our* report as a "staged media event."

It has finally to be noted that this charge of having "staged a media event" is puzzling in another sense. If we had, in fact, intended publicly to discredit and embarrass the University or, more specifically, its administration, is it really plausible that we would have limited the scope of our activities to local news outlets? With the current national interest in sexism and sexual harassment on Canadian campuses it would not have been hard to draw much wider attention had that been our aim. Our concern is that in focusing on this highly questionable allegation about our motivations and objectives, the administration trivializes and obscures the real issues which require our attention and which were our primary concern: the variety of chilly climate issues raised by the 35 women to whom we spoke.

Notes

Notes

1 See, for example, Cathryn Motherwell, "Just Saying No Doesn't Always Work," *The Globe and Mail*, 6 November 1990, which discussed male students' mocking of anti-rape activists at Queen's University, sexual harassment of two female medical students by five faculty members at the University of Calgary, and violent and sexually explicit notes placed under female residence doors by male students at the University of British Columbia. See also Debora Wilson, "Brothers No More at UBC Dorms," *The Globe and Mail*, 18 October 1990, and Frances Bula, "Hostility between the Sexes: Crude Note Exchange Got Out of Hand, Male Students Ponder their Complicity," *The London Free Press*, 27 October 1990, p. E-5.

   See also accounts of "student panty raids" at Wilfrid Laurier University: Michele Landsberg, "University 'Sanctions' Student Panty Raids," *The Toronto Star*, 25 October 1989; Frances Kelly, "Panty Raids Banned at Wilfrid Laurier," *The Toronto Star*, 29 October 1989; and Michele Landsberg, "Students Learn Sexist Lesson at Universities," *The Toronto Star*, 11 November 1989.

   See also an account of death threats delivered to the female editors of a Queen's University newspaper, "Death Threat Sent to Female Editors," *The Globe and Mail*, 7 November 1991, p. A-6.

   Additional comment appears in Susan Donaldson and Will Kymlicka, "No Thaw in Chilly Campus Climate," *The Globe and Mail*, 17 November 1989; Katherine Govier, "A Time to Be Just," *Queen's Alumni Review* (March-April 1990), p. 12; and Tom Kierans, "Where Are the Guardians?" *The Globe and Mail's Report on Business* (May 1990), p. 47.

2 Roberta M. Hall and Bernice R. Sandler, *The Classroom Climate: A Chilly One for Women?* (Washington, DC: Project on the Status and Education of Women, Association of American Colleges, 1982); Roberta M. Hall and Bernice R. Sandler, *Out of the Classroom: A Chilly Campus Climate for Women?* (Washington, DC: Project on the Status and Education of Women, AAC, 1984); Bernice R. Sandler, *The Campus Climate Revisited: Chilly for Women Faculty, Administrators, and Graduate Students* (Washington, DC: Project on the Status and Education of Women, AAC, 1986); Sarah Nieves-Squires, *Hispanic Women: Making their Presence on Campus Less Tenuous* (Washington, DC: Project on the Status and Education of Women, AAC, 1991); and Yolanda T. Moses, *Black Women in Academe: Issues and Strategies* (Washington, DC: Project on the Status and Education of Women, AAC, 1989).

3 Wendy McCann, "UWO Sexism Report: One Faculty Rated Brutal and Vicious," *The London Free Press*, 13 November 1989, p. B-1.

4 Richard Hoffman, "UWO Sexism Report: Findings Overstated, President Counters," *The London Free Press*, 14 November 1989.

5 Morris Dalla Costa, "UWO Sexism Report Lacks a Real Punch," *The London Free Press*, 14 November 1989.

6 Hoffmann, "UWO Sexism Report."

7 Alison Wylie, "A Response to Some Criticisms of the 'Chilly Climate' Report," 24 November 1989 (Appendix B).

8 Ibid.

9 Ibid.

10 Ibid.

11 Ibid.

12 President K.G. Pedersen, Statement to the Senate, 16 November 1989. Copy on file with the authors of the *Chilly Climate Report*.

13 For an excellent overview of this problem, see Mary P. Rowe, "Barriers to Equality: The Power of Subtle Discrimination to Maintain Unequal Opportunity," *Employee Rights and Responsibilities Journal*, 3, 2 (June 1990): 153-63.

14 Alan Bass and Wendy McCann, "Sexism Report, Pedersen Assails 'Anonymity,' " *The London Free Press*, 17 November 1989.
15 Wylie, "A Response to Some Criticisms."
16 Ibid.
17 Jane Milburn, "Alleged Harassment Disputed by Western," *UWO Gazette*, 17 November 1989.
18 Bass and McCann, "Sexism Report."
19 Geoffrey Rans, " 'Fear and Loathing' on the Hill: A Male Professor Speaks," *Western News*, 7 December 1989.
20 Bass and McCann, "Sexism Report."
21 James Anderson, " 'Chilly Climate' at UWO Alleged," *Western News*, 23 November 1989, p. 6.
22 Bass and McCann, "Sexism Report."
23 For reference to *The Gazette* article, see Keith Risler, "Behind the Purple Curtain," *London Magazine* (April 1990), p. 43. See also John Sloan, "Academic Racism Debated," *Western News*, 1 November 1990, p. 9; "Canadian Politics: Rise in Racism Blamed on Shift to the Right," *The London Free Press*, 14 November 1990, p. A-19; Silvia Valdman, "MP McCurdy Speaks Out against Rushton, Racism," *The Gazette*, 16 November 1990, p. 5; Lynn Marchildon, "Rushton Cancels Another Lecture," *The London Free Press*, 1 February 1991, p. B-34; "Professors Urge UWO to Fire Rushton," *The London Free Press*, 2 May 1991, p. B-7; "Motions Include Call for Dismissal Action," *Western News*, 9 May 1991, p. 7; and Greg Van Moorsel, "Human Rights: Backlog May Delay Complaint against Rushton," *The London Free Press*, 25 May 1991.
24 Continuing demands from members of the Western student body finally forced the administration to require Professor Rushton to provide his lectures through a televised format for a defined period of time, ostensibly to avoid risks of confrontation in the classroom. Students who protested Rushton's views publicly on campus were threatened with suspensions and trespass charges. Rushton was never prohibited from teaching. For details of the human rights complaint lodged against Western in this matter, see Van Moorsel, "Human Rights."
25 Risler, "Behind the Purple Curtain," p. 43.
26 John Sloan, "Report on Sexism Blasted by Senior Administrators," *Western News*, 23 November 1989, p. 1.
27 Risler, "Behind the Purple Curtain," p. 43. Freelance writer Risler's article was generally critical of Western's handling of the Chilly Climate affair, depicting its response as "on the verge of losing control of its media agenda" and "reactive self-defence ... indicative of the chasm between Western and its sustaining society" (p. 26, 43-44). In a somewhat contradictory stance, *London Magazine*'s November 1990 issue acclaimed President George Pedersen as one of "The People Who Make London," depicting him as "dealing with alleged on-campus sexual harassment that, if substantiated, must be curtailed without a McCarthyist witch hunt" (p. 38-40).
28 Letter from Pedersen to Wylie et al., 17 December 1990. Copy on file with the authors.
29 Ibid.
30 Alison Wylie, "Perspective: Everyday Attitudes, Practices Must Warm Chilly Climate," *The Gazette*, 24 November 1989 (Appendix A).
31 Ibid., p. 9. See also Wylie, "A Response to Some Criticisms."
32 Letter from W.J. McClelland to Constance Backhouse, 26 January 1990. Copy on file with the authors.
33 Letter from Alison Wylie to W.J. McClelland, 1 February 1990. Copy on file with the authors. In the end, the recommendation to take disciplinary action seems to have been dropped by the Vice-President (Research). Neither Wylie nor any other author of the *Report* received acknowledgement of, much less a reply to, any of the objections and responses Wylie addressed to the Review Board concerning both the inquiry and its ruling. In fact,

when Wylie and one other member of the Review Board subsequently resigned, protesting the arbitrariness of applying guidelines retroactively before they had received public review or had even been adopted by the Review Board itself, neither received any response to their concerns, not even a formal acknowledgement that they had resigned.

34 Rebecca Coulter, Maryann Ayim, and 13 other signatories from the Faculty of Education, Teaching and Research Unit on Women and Education, "Report 'Opens the Door' to Look at Strategies," *Western News*, 23 November 1989.

35 Karen McCaffery, "London Calling," December 14-20, 1989, p. 3.

36 Jane Hegney, "Experience, Expectations Spark Law Student's 'Plea,' " *Western News*, 7 December 1989, p. 4, 6.

37 Louise Forsyth, "Says Article on Canvasser Trivialized Contribution," *Western News*, 1 February 1990.

38 Risler, "Behind the Purple Curtain."

39 Sloan, "Report on Sexism Blasted," p. 6.

40 Richard Bronaugh, "Report 'Fails as Study of Conditions at UWO,' " *Western News*, 4 January 1990.

41 Lynn E. Fleming, "Young White Males Paying for Past Prejudice," *The London Free Press*, 16 May 1991, p. A-10.

42 Robert Lannigan, "Methodology, Behaviour of Authors Criticized," *Western News*, 23 November 1989.

43 Margaret P. Moffat, "Concerned that Report Left Wrong Impression," *Western News*, 7 December 1989.

44 Sloan, "Report on Sexism Blasted."

45 Bessie Borwein, "Sexism Report at University Trivializes Real Issues," *The London Free Press*, 9 December 1989.

46 For an interesting discussion of the "cognitive dissonance" which may explain such reactions from women in a male institution, see Melissa Clark-Jones and Patricia Coyne, "Through the Back Door," *Atlantis*, 15, 2 (Spring 1990): 40. Having surveyed students who attended Bishop's, a small Canadian liberal arts university, during the first half of the twentieth century, they describe the contradictory and ambiguous responses of white female interviewees who deny discrimination while outlining detailed examples of unequal treatment: "Attendance at co-educational university implied the existence and experience of equality with men. Any experience of gender-based or other forms of inequality would create the occasion and the need to resolve the contradiction through ideological explanation or through denial. . . . Also, for them, discrimination implied total exclusion, usually on racial grounds. They were not attracted to direct identification with Blacks or Jews, though they shared a desire for inclusion and assimilation with these. When asked about 'discrimination' point blank, one woman spoke of the experience of the only Black of her time, instead of her own. Another praised Bishop's liberality in admitting Jews who, during the War, were being turned away at McGill [University]. To admit discrimination may have meant, at an emotive level, to admit inferiority. . . . Though many recall the facts of discrimination in both painful and humorous detail, they cannot call it by its name. Some repress the experience. Some displace it to other times or social groups. Some are aware of this curious break between their own experience and their collective meaning. . . . '[W]e didn't know we were having a hard time'; 'that (discrimination) is a modern concept' " (p. 45-46).

47 Sara B. Galsworthy, "Fears We May Be Alienated from 'the Real Problems,' " *Western News*, 7 December 1989, p. 4. Similar sentiments were voiced by Western law student Kathleen M. Nolan, who announced she was "sick and tired" of the "attention and hoopla" surrounding claims of pervasive sexism in the Faculty of Law. As *The Gazette*'s 14 November 1989 issue quoted her: "For Heaven's sake, there are 40,000 babies starving every day, the threat of nuclear destruction looms over our heads, thousands of people in Latin America are being

tortured each day etc. Yet it amazes me that these women have chosen as their outrage, their 'cause célèbre' gender-neutral language. Get with it" (p. 9).

48 See Louise Malette and Marie Chalouh, eds., *The Montreal Massacre* (Charlottetown: Gynergy Books, 1991). In the aftermath of the massacre, Alison Wylie gave a statement, as President of Western's Caucus on Women's Issues, on 12 December 1989, which was subsequently published in the Western's Caucus on Women's Issues *Newsletter* of January 1990. Some extracts follow: "Anything I might have written a week ago, by way of a President's Message, seems entirely beside the point now, in the aftermath of the Montreal massacre. I find the hostility of the 'backlash' as chilling as the tragedy itself. It is scarcely to be believed that anyone who followed the news — learning first that the fourteen 'students' killed were in fact all women, and then that they were systematically separated from the men and gunned down because they were women — could declare loudly and publicly that this was not a women's issue, that it was the isolated act of a madman which bears no relation to the attitudes and behaviours of 'real' men where women are concerned, and that feminists were therefore 'using' the event to promote their own 'narrow' political interests. In fact, as the reaction has deepened, the vehement hostility expressed toward women and, specifically, feminists, confirms and reconfirms the existence of exactly what it denies." "In my own case these recent events throw into particularly sharp relief all that I had found disappointing and, indeed, deeply unnerving, about the reaction of the senior administration to the *Chilly Climate Report* of which I am a co-author." "I am more deeply confirmed than ever in the conviction that things will not change without concerted, vocal, and uncompromising efforts on all our parts."

49 Alan Bass, "Grant for Video on Campus Sexism Called 'Vindication,'" *The London Free Press*, 8 May 1990.

50 Alison Uncles, "Colleges and Universities: 'Chilly Climate' Video Premiered in London," *The London Free Press*, 30 April 1991, p. B-7.

6

Reinventing Our Legacy:
The Chills Which Affect Women[1]

President's Advisory Committee
on the Status of Women
University of Saskatchewan

As is routinely emphasized in discussions of climate issues, the experiences of chilliness described by women on university and college campuses are rarely unique. Strikingly similar patterns of practice have been widely documented in the United States, for example, in the reports on "The Campus Climate" produced by the Association of American Colleges in the mid-1980s.[2] In many university and college contexts in Canada these issues have been addressed by the university task forces and committees created to develop policies on equity.

At the University of Saskatchewan, the President's Advisory Committee on the Status of Women made the workplace environment a primary focus of their 1993 report, Reinventing Our Legacy. *This document covers a wide range of issues. It begins with a section on "The Current Scenario" which includes an account of "The General Chill Which Affects Women" as well as of "Specific Chills Which Affect Women." In their discussion of the workplace environment, the authors of this report consider safety issues, sexual harassment policies, educational equity, and equity initiatives as these affect a wide range of women on the University of Saskatchewan campus: women faculty, students (graduate and undergraduate), post-doctoral fellows, technical research assistants, and staff who are members of the administrative and Supervisory Personnel Association and of the Canadian Union of Public Employees (Local 1975). Most important, the authors of* Reinventing Our Legacy *move substantially beyond a review of current conditions; they provide two final sections which describe "The Preferred Scenario" and means of "Achieving the Preferred Scenario." For present purposes, we include primarily selections from the overview of existing conditions provided in "The Current Scenario." These pro-*

vide a basis for comparison with the experiences described in other contributions to this collection.

In the excerpts from Reinventing Our Legacy *that follow, the President's Advisory Committee on the Status of Women reports the results of an extensive program of interviews and meetings with members of the university community. The authors note (in a section of the Introduction not included here) that this most recent inquiry was undertaken at the behest of President Ivany, who struck an Advisory Committee on the Status of Women at the University of Saskatchewan in 1990. The mandate he set for this committee was that it should:*

> *. . . provide information and advice on issues that affect female students, staff, and faculty on campus, in order to achieve "an improved environment for education, research and scholarly work for all students, staff and faculty on campus, and improved opportunities for women who work and study at the University of Saskatchewan."[3]*

This initiative built on the work of previous committees, the earliest mentioned having been established in 1975. Despite previous reports and some promising institutional responses, however, the authors of Reinventing Our Legacy *note that members of the current Advisory Committee on the Status of Women came to share the concerns of many that conditions had not changed as substantially in nearly 20 years as might have been hoped: "People talked about working and studying in a hostile environment where new ideas were often not welcome. They talked about harassment of a personal and sexual nature. The climate was not chilly, some said; it was frigid."[4]*

Climate issues quickly came into focus for the committee as a key area in which change would have to be made if the University of Saskatchewan was to fulfil its public commitment to employment equity and, more broadly, to creating and maintaining "a learning and working environment that is supportive of scholarship and fair treatment of all its members."[5] In addressing these issues, the President's Advisory Committee stresses that there has been change for women in Canadian universities, and that the areas in which conditions remain problematic are by no means unique to the University of Saskatchewan. They provide a summary of statistical information on the status of women in Canadian colleges and universities between 1970 and 1992 which parallels that given here in chapter 2 (above).

We are grateful to the President of the University of Saskatchewan and to the Advisory Committee on the Status of Women for permission to reprint these sections of their report. We urge any who would like to read the full text of Reinventing Our Legacy *to contact the President's Office at the University of Saskatchewan (Saskatoon, Saskatchewan   S7N 0W0).*

– Eds.

The Current Scenario

A. Introduction

Many people consider ours the most beautiful campus in Canada. Its grey-stone buildings are warm and attractive. It is well-landscaped, mugo pine intertwining with birch and dogwood. The lawns are well cared for, even in dry summers.

Amid this pastoral beauty, more than nine thousand women work and study at the University of Saskatchewan. Here is what some of them say of experiences with people who work or study alongside them:

> In the fall of 1991, as I was walking away from the Education Building, two trucks passed me. The trucks, filled with men from one of the colleges, slowed down as they passed me and one man yelled, "Hey, let's stop for a gang bang." My first reaction was one of indignation, followed immediately by fear. I was one woman and they numbered between 20 and 30. If they did actually act, what chance did I have of defending myself? With the prevalence of violence against women these days, such a threat is hardly a joke to me. (Female undergraduate)

> Less than 48 hours after announcing my intention to challenge my department's equity proceedings in the hiring of a position, I found an envelope tacked to my door. Inside was a vicious note which was read jointly by myself and a graduate student: "You fucking bitch." (Female faculty)

> One young woman was studying in the library. She began to feel very uncomfortable and noticed a male student staring at her. She tried to ignore him but finally could stand it no longer and went for coffee. She left her books and her jacket on the desk. When she returned she found him at her desk, but upon seeing her, he left. Feeling very uneasy, she packed up her books and caught a bus home. While on the bus she noticed that the man had ejaculated upon her jacket. (Female sessional)

> Male department heads need to learn how to conduct an interview. A woman applying for a clerical position was asked if she was planning to have children, her age, marital status, if she had a car and could she stay after 4:30. She wouldn't grieve because she was too afraid. (Clerk stenographer)

And here is a male voice:

> As a male on this campus I have not personally experienced any form of gender discrimination, but I have known female classmates who certainly have been discriminated against. One ... experienced a situation in which a professor referred to one of his female students as "Blondie" ... accompanied by many more derogatory remarks towards the women in the class. [When she complained to the Dean] she was informed that this was not the only complaint against this professor. [The Dean's action] consisted simply of a verbal warning. (Male undergraduate)

Those words record blatant reactions to the presence of women on the University campus, obvious reflections of the intense sexism that still pervades Saskatchewan society. There are other reactions too, sometimes more subtle, frequently unrecognized, but with an impact quite as profound as the blatant examples cited above: the systemic discrimination against women students, faculty, and staff which wastes their talents and handcuffs the University in its efforts to be all this province needs its major postsecondary institution to be.

Many examples of this kind of systemic discrimination, too, were presented to our committee hearings:

> I find it fascinating that we pay secretaries with Grade 12 education and a course from a recognized secretarial school less than we pay janitors with a Grade 10 education and the ability to do physical labour. So much for the value of an education. (Female faculty)

> Are students well served if they complete a degree without ever having a female professor? (Male faculty)

Some of the things we were told illustrate the subtle discrimination permitted and even encouraged by the processes used in this system: "Last year two of the three people on the Special Salary Increase Committee in my department voted themselves special increases. This year three of the three people voted themselves special increases."

Getting a firm grasp on the number of people who study and work at the University is difficult, but our research suggests that women make up about half of them. Few of those women hold positions of power. The senior administration is comprised of the ten-man President's Executive Committee and the Deans' Council, which includes the President's Executive Committee, the Deans, the Registrar, and the Director of Libraries. The Deans of Nursing and Graduate Studies are the only women in the 26-member senior administration. Two women and 70 men were heads of academic departments in 1992-93. There are 500 male and 17 female full professors; women make up 16% of full-time academic staff.[1]

Among undergraduates, women outnumbered men in 1991-92 for the third consecutive year, and they received 52% of undergraduate degrees in 1991. At the graduate level, 39% of students were female. They received 37% of graduate degrees in 1991, compared to 31% four years earlier.

"Though women's participation in the educational process at all levels has increased in this century, this participation remains within marked boundaries," wrote sociologist Dorothy E. Smith.[2] "Among the most important of these boundaries, I would argue, is that which reserves to men control of the policy-making and decision-making apparatus in the educational system."[3]

Women make up 42% of the members of the Administrative and Supervisory Personnel Association (ASPA); they are clustered in the lower part of the salary scale and very few of them report to women superiors. Women are 56% of the full-time membership of Canadian Union of Public Employees, local 1975 (CUPE 1975); again they are clustered in the lower part of the salary scale. About half the members of the Canadian Union of Public Employees, local 3287 (CUPE 3287) are women. No gender-based salary discrimination occurs in this union of sessional lecturers because they are paid on a per-course basis only, regardless of qualifications.

Women are the base which supports the University structure. It's not Atlas whose stout shoulders support the heavens, but his mother Clymene, his grandmother Tethys, and his many daughters — the seven Pleiades, the Hyades, and the Hesperides. At the University of Saskatchewan, their female inheritors are almost invisible.

*   *   *

B. The General Chill Which Affects Women

In gathering the information for this report, our single most crucial responsibility was to hear from people at the University of Saskatchewan about their experiences here, about the situations and conditions which affect them, and their ideas for improvement. Over the almost three years since our Committee was appointed, we have listened to a large number of people.

We held meetings to introduce ourselves to the President's Executive Committee, to the Dean's Council, to the executives of the University of Saskatchewan Student's Union, the University of Saskatchewan Faculty Association, the Canadian Union of Public Employees, local 3287 (CUPE 3287), the Canadian Union of Public Employees, local 1975 (CUPE 1975), the Administrative and Supervisory Personnel Association (ASPA), and to the Employment Equity Advisory Committee (EEAC), the Sexual Harassment Office, the Women's Centre, the Board of College Presidents, Administrative Managers Group, and the Encouraging Enrolment in Engineering group. We held ten meetings with informal groups which asked to meet with us. Although we requested such a meeting, we were unfortunately unable to meet with the Senate Executive Committee.

We broadcast our desire to receive submissions through the President's Newsletter, *The Sheaf*, and other routes on campus, and wrote specifically to the Council of Department Heads and more than 100 individuals, inviting their submissions.

These meetings and the telephone calls which poured in were valuable sources of information and guidance. Our committee was welcomed in an atmosphere of concern, but we also heard frustration about the possibility of doing anything about "the litany of horrors" surrounding women on this campus. Many people who spoke to us expressed doubt that "something will come out of this. People are tired of going through rounds of things with nothing happening," we were told. We were implored "not to do yet another study." We heard concerns about the slow rate of change, even though this is a "highly unionized campus." We received written submissions from seven organized bodies with mandates related in whole or in part to the status of women staff and/or students, such as the Status of Women Committee of the Faculty Association. We received five briefs from groups formed expressly to make submissions to our committee, and 118 briefs from one, two or three people, not only about their specific problems but frequently wide-ranging in their concern for women on this campus.

We met with 42 people to receive verbal submissions, often augmented in the form of memos or letters, with documentation of their experiences and attempts to solve problems. We received brochures from the Encouraging Enrolment in Engineering group, sharing the work it is doing to increase the number of women in that profession. Reports from this university and others were shared, and literature relevant to the field. Eighteen people asked for private meetings.

We also received 53 phone calls from people identifying problems and sharing their experiences of being female at the University of Saskatchewan. Fifteen of these calls were from people who had "exhausted all avenues" and sought advice on what to do now. Several phone calls were repeated.

A female faculty member made a telling point in her brief to our committee:

> I have also been told that women on campus have been reluctant to submit briefs to your committee in case it leads to problems in their departments. The nature of the anticipated problems is hard to specify; the fear that somehow, in some untraceable way, there would be a price to pay for such activities, is absolutely real.

A brief from a CUPE 1975 member made a similar point:

> CUPE women understand their powerless positions. They fear presenting briefs and speaking up about conditions that affect them daily.

We have to agree with the faculty member who said:

> It is a crazy situation that on a campus where the President himself has set up a special committee to work on the problems facing women at the U of S, fear of abuse of authority is making it impossible for it to do its work and for women with common interests to associate freely.

That many people raised similar points with us throughout our information-gathering process is not surprising. Those points have guided our planning and arrangement of this report. But we went beyond that. We received 130 written briefs whose content has been examined through a research technique known as content analysis; it describes the content of a particular form of communication in a quantitative fashion, so that researchers can draw inferences about the meaning of the writer's words and experiences. What that analysis showed us is that the problems women — all women: students, faculty, administration, staff — have experienced at the University of Saskatchewan fit into six broad categories:

- University culture
- University values, leadership, and initiatives
- Safety
- Workplace issues
- Curriculum issues
- Special measures germane to women's advancement.

Women told us clearly that these are the major problems they face at the University of Saskatchewan. These problems affect all groups of women on campus. In the weave of life here, these are the threads that make up the warp — the lengthwise threads in any fabric that are usually twisted harder, and through which the weft threads are woven. As we shall see later, the weft is comprised of the experiences particular to each group.

The analysis also included examination of what is not working, what is working, and what needs to be changed. Discussion of what is working is at the end of this chapter.

1. Problems with the University Culture

We should begin by defining organizational culture: in brief, it means how an organization does things. The University's culture is both its formal rules, regulations, values and norms, and the informal structures and rules about what is acceptable which have grown up alongside those formal principles. Often fine and fair-sounding formal regulations can be turned on their heads by the informal rules which define the acceptable.

This was the major category of problems described over and over in the briefs we received. The culture that has grown up at the University of Saskatchewan is not one that welcomes women, nor has it been malleable to the changes that would make it open to women, whether as students, faculty, administration, or staff.

Grouped in this category are problems identified by women about their formal and informal exclusion from the University's decision-making structure, about the lack of women in important roles, about negative attitudes from their peers, and about fear of reprisal if they should complain. On average, each brief made five references to the University culture as a problem in their daily lives on campus.

Not surprisingly, faculty women had much more to say about the University culture; on average, they made eight comments per brief about personal experience or observation of the way decisions are made around them, of negative male attitudes and the tendency of men to intimidate them in work settings, and they made calls for change. One female professor wrote:

> I had the view that committee members ought to facilitate the work of their colleagues, not put obstacles in their way — that is, I believed that rules were made to be bent, not observed without exception. This approach did not seem to go over well with some of my male colleagues, and I felt very much that my views were outside of the norm. At other times, the loathing would strike me, e.g., when I was hired into a tenure-track position and was told jokingly that the only reason I was hired was that nobody else who was a qualified ____ had applied. . . .

Another indicated that her colleague stole her research and that she is frequently ridiculed because of her beliefs or because of her gender. She said:

> My ideas have been 'stolen' — if I find something interesting and present it at a seminar, [my supervisor/colleague] gets interested and somehow gets [someone else] to take over and I get left out. How can I discuss my results when this happens! I have never felt part of our group — either I am being treated courteously or am being teased because I am a feminist or a woman.

The efforts of women on campus have contributed to awareness about equity issues and the way women have been marginalized, according to another female professor:

> . . . many initiatives [orchestrated by women] of recent years have produced an awareness that inequities do indeed exist throughout the institution. There is now a recognition of systemic factors inherent to the University's patriarchal structure, its traditions, its language, its priorities in allocating resources, the criteria it uses to measure excellence, and its various definitions of knowledge which serve to put power, resources, intellectual privilege and authority in the hands of a specific group easily defined by sex, race and class.

The briefs we received from women students contained, on average, six comments about difficulties that are caused for them by aspects of the University culture. They described the negative attitudes displayed to them by men. They referred to their informal and formal exclusion from the decision-making processes. They related incidents caused by men's tendency to intimidate them in work or study environments, and to stereotype their contributions. One student wrote:

> I had to deal with a male student who found it hard to accept that any of the three women in the lab could have more expertise/experience than he did. He had no respect for my experience, not even for my MSc degree, something which he had yet to complete. He lorded over me in areas where he had more experience and made several undermining comments such as 'What are you wrecking now?'

The insensitivity of many male professors toward women and women's issues was described by another student:

> Most of my professors have been men with little or no concern for the issues facing women. In fact, there have been a few professors whom I feel have been quite sexist and insensitive towards women. On one occasion I met with a professor because I was not clear about what he wanted for an essay assignment. He asked me why I was in university because I would probably just get married and have children.

2. *Problems with University Values, Leadership, and Initiatives*

> A university is supposed to be a place where we can explore ideas. Unfortunately the opposite is true. Many of the faculty are entrenched in tradition and will not change unless they are required to do so. (Female student)

By its values shall it be judged. Women who presented briefs to our committee judged University of Saskatchewan values and found them wanting. They reported problems with its leadership and initiatives for change. On average, each brief made four references to the University's values, leadership, and initiatives being a problem. They described a lack of commitment by senior administration, deans, or department heads to the recruitment, entry, and advancement of women in the University as a workplace or educational setting. They referred to people in senior positions who give the impression of doing something about this, but in fact do little. They pointed also to the failure to develop innovative and effective strategies for improving the status of women.

In an average five references per submission, female faculty expressed considerable frustration with the lack of priority given at the University to equity issues, and to its exploitation of women who aspire to become academics. One faculty member wrote:

> Many women, of course, never get a foot on the bottom rung of the professorial ladder. This University is guilty of appalling exploitation of women in sessional and term positions, especially when they are not in a position to take a job elsewhere because of family ties.... The recent concern of the University with equity in hiring is long overdue.

Women students agreed. Their briefs contained, on average, four references to problems caused by the culture around them, most specifically expressing disillusionment and frustration with the University's seeming inability to lead in promoting the status of women on campus, with its creation of contradictory employment practices, and with its tendency to give lip service to the need to increase the numbers of women in faculty and administration. One female graduate student wrote:

> There appears to have been little attempt in the hiring practices of our college to ensure the replacement of expertise in the feminist area of study, not to mention the much needed expansion of representation of this perspective among faculty members. Present equity hiring practices (where they do exist) of hiring any "qualified woman" are not enough. Hiring committees tend to clone themselves in their choices. Women who are chosen in such a way will most often tend to be those who most closely represent the dominant masculine perspective.

A male faculty member pointed out problems with the University's commitment to dealing efficiently with women's issues:

> ... the status of women is being handled hypocritically on this campus: on one hand, it has had, since October 1990, the President's stamp of approval; but on the other, it is being allowed to die the most demeaning death of all — death by committee.

Another brief made an interesting point about visibility:

> The relatively high visibility of women at the University serves the University very well. The names and faces of women involved in university work, disproportionate to their numbers, help to spare the University the embarrassment of hiring so few women. By doing double duty, the women permit the university community to imagine the presence of women faculty at two, three or four times their actual numbers.

One female professor spoke of the need for the University to act strongly on behalf of women, or face the accusation that it is continuing to exploit them. She wrote:

> If this serious problem is not addressed effectively, the accusation could well be made that women are serving as tokens in administrative positions and on university committees, perhaps all the better to serve the perpetuation of the status quo.

One senior woman warned, however, about the resistance to change at the University, resistance which, she said, "will seek to justify itself by affirming that the values and traditions of the University are inviolable and so cannot be examined or changed."

3. *Problems of Safety*

Women at the University of Saskatchewan experience problems with harassment of a directly sexual nature; harassment in their workplace from supervisors, peers, co-workers or colleagues; and racial harassment — all of which produce negative working conditions for them. They also fear physical attack or male hostility. On average, there were two references in each brief to safety-related matters as being a problem, but students mentioned it more often, an average of three times each. "Until our safety is guaranteed on this campus we are second-class citizens here," one said.

Students' briefs reflected experiences with sexual harassment, place of study harassment, overt discrimination, and concerns about physical safety. One graduate student told us:

> I and other women I know here have many times felt unsafe, either physically or intellectually. That is a terrible price to pay in order to share in and contribute to the life of the University.

Another woman wrote about the lack of safety in locker room areas:

> Evidently, according to a building employee as well as someone from Security on campus, there has been a continuing problem with men infiltrating women's locker rooms even prior to my experience. In spite of the evidently numerous incidents, no one thought it important to advise women that their privacy and possibly their security was at risk.

When female faculty referred to safety — an average of twice per submission — they were usually reflecting their personal experience with workplace harassment. They reported encounters with male colleagues or department heads which involved manipulation, and had overtones of hostility. They gave few references to aspects of safety that were positive, and emphasized the need to implement more stringent measures to prevent such harassment. A brief from a clerk stenographer echoed this point:

> Workplace harassment is becoming the norm in these times of economic restraint. The most innocent and powerless (usually women) are the brunt of everyone's frustration.

4. *Workplace Issues*

Briefs contained an average of one reference to workplace problems at the University of Saskatchewan. Included were references to displeasure with job/educational experiences, to problems of qualifications, to leaving one's job or educational program because of an intolerable situation, to problems of job security, dead-end jobs, salary, unclear work expectations, and what it is like to be the only woman in a work group or area.

A group of ASPA women said:

> Very few of us who report to an ASPA position report to a woman. The result for women—who tend to be junior to their male colleagues—is a sense of frustration when it comes to trying to forge a more progressive and equitable working environment. We feel excluded from participation in the decision-making process, even within our own bargaining unit. We feel isolated from one another, and many of us perceive not only that our male colleagues' priorities are different from ours but that they are given more emphasis than ours.

One sessional explained:

> Some of the women in (CUPE 3287) are as qualified as tenured or tenure-stream faculty, but their long part-time service to this University is held against them. There seems to be a prejudice operating in the form of a "glass ceiling": once a sessional, always a sessional—and no promotion. When a position becomes vacant, an outside candidate is hired.

5. Curriculum Issues

This category includes references made in the briefs to the lack of woman-centred (feminist) material in current courses at the University of Saskatchewan, and of feminist-based courses in the curriculum as a whole. It also includes reference to the absence of educational equity at the University for society's various groups, and to others' lack of understanding of the difficulties women face in educational or employment settings and of the complexity of the barriers. There was, on average, one reference to these subjects per brief.

Not surprisingly, student briefs referred more often to problems of curriculum, three times each on average. They related difficulties connected to the exclusion of women's perspective in the development of curricula, the absence of feminism in scholarly work and teaching, the male-biased content in most academic courses, and the unwillingness of some instructors to allow for change. Two students said:

> According to the University calendar, Course X is supposed to cover "recent developments, current trends and future prospects...." However, from our experience, this class is void of any recent or current concerns. Professor Y argues that "there has been no theory developed in the last 25 years." Our experiences clearly dispute this claim. Due to Professor Y's lack of familiarity with any of the theoretical trends, concerns and authors that we mentioned in class, it seems obvious to us that he is not well-versed in current [work] nor does it appear that he is making any attempt to become so.

> It has been my experience that the single most troublesome factor in the environment for education is the male gender bias which, in my opinion, pervades the curriculum with few exceptions.

Another student expressed her disillusionment about the lack of courses on women's issues:

> I came to the College excited by the fact that [it] had a feminist organization and even a feminist theory course. I leave disheartened by the knowledge that few women are willing to endure the stigma which goes hand-in-hand with belonging to such a women's organization, and discouraged by the hostility and apathy underlying the relegation of women's issues to a single class.

Many faculty briefs recognized negative aspects of curricula. Speaking of the need for change, faculty members wrote:

> There is a . . . need to examine curriculum in every academic program on campus, however removed it may at first appear to be from women's studies concerns, in order to rid courses and programs of sexist content and assumptions and to open courses and research projects to new approaches offered by feminist criticism.

> If this is an institution of higher learning, then surely what we should be monitoring are the ways we do things, our epistemological presumptions, our methods, our understanding of objects of study and their relationship to the observing subject. It is in these areas that women's studies, feminist (and other) theory have most to offer and have the capacity to change the way we do science, medicine, the humanities, social sciences, and fine arts, our pedagogy as well as our curricula. But where are the forums for such discussion?

6. Lack of Special Measures Germane to Women's Advancement

Faculty pointed three times, on average, to problems associated with accessing measures designed to enhance women's educational and employment opportunities, such as job training and development. They referred particularly to the limited availability of day care on campus, the dearth of flextime, job sharing, and maternity leave arrangements, and the difficulties of trying to manage without these structural supports. One professor wrote:

> It probably would have been better for me, career-wise, to do several post-doctoral years at a different university. This appeared unthinkable to me since I had two small children and a husband. . . . I feel that this issue is a major one that prevents women from advancing in their careers as scientists. They are judged on the same basis as men who can do several post-doctorates in a row either as single men or by dragging their family in tow. For married women, since the main duty for child-rearing remains in their domain, it is painfully difficult to follow this route.

A second female professor noted that the University has failed to provide training and mentorship programs to assist female faculty in their attempts to secure research grants.

Students referred once per brief, on average, to problems they have experienced in accessing measures designed to enhance women's opportunities for education and employment. Their problems were much like those of staff: the limited availability of child care, flextime, job sharing, and maternity leave arrangements at the University of Saskatchewan, and the consequences of trying to manage without these structural supports. One student wrote:

> Even with all of the advances that have been made for women in the past decades, the burden of child care often still falls upon women. In addition, though, there is now the extra responsibility of full-time work — it has become a necessity in many families in order for them to survive. The option of learning is only a dream — something that may only become possible after all the children have grown up. To me this amounts to a form of discrimination.... I'm tired of it always (almost always) being the woman having to ask for the different working environment so she doesn't have to be a super mom or to have to opt out of the workforce to cope.

C. Specific Chills Which Affect Women

Let us look more closely at the difficulties which face women at the University of Saskatchewan, the overt manifestations of their inequality in this, their workplace and their educational home. It will be very clear how these difficulties fit into the categories of analysis listed above.

1. A Chilly Environment for Women

Hostility from male students wears you down. (Female faculty)

Many women work and study at the University of Saskatchewan almost on sufferance. Room has been made for them, with greater or lesser willingness, but the environment remains hostile. For these women, the temperature is always −40 with a high windchill factor. But discrimination isn't always overt; it is often subtle: "It is in this subtle form that sex discrimination has been safe from scrutiny and harsh criticism. As it is hard to prove and dangerous to question, it cannot be attacked head-on," a student undergraduate told us.

There are many aspects to this inhospitable environment, this harassment based on gender, this determination to keep women at the small end of a long telescope. It is hard to give such treatment an accurate name. It is not exactly sexual harassment, because much of that has actual sexual overtones. It is closer to gender harassment, a part of sexual harassment defined as "generalized sexist remarks and behaviour not necessarily designed to elicit sexual co-operation, but to convey insulting, degrading, or sexist attitudes about women."[4] They may not be able to name it precisely, but the women who work and study at the University of Saskatchewan have no trouble describing it in all its myriad forms.

They live amidst multiple manifestations of disrespect of the sort which M. Rowe identified in post-secondary education generally.[5] She described these subtle barriers of verbal and nonverbal behaviour, unintentional and intentional discrimination as "micro-inequities." Individually, each may seem so insignificant that it is difficult to identify and protest. Piled together, however, they become formidable barriers to equal opportunities for women. They lower the quality of both educational and work experiences for women at universities.

It is true that some men, too, may suffer from the kinds of micro-inequities that Rowe identified. But experience has shown that women are the recipients of these behaviours more often, more concertedly, and with more intensity. Their treatment reflects the assumptions our society still holds about the role and abilities of women, and demonstrates that many people retain those assumptions, and act on them, perhaps unknowingly but certainly to the detriment of women.

Rowe identified the following forms of subtle discrimination against women. We had no difficulty fitting the experiences University of Saskatchewan women described to us into her categories.

i. Condescension

Many men at this University refuse to take women seriously, as either students or colleagues, and make that fact obvious through their posture, their gestures, and their tone of voice. They use what they think of as humorous images or statements that demean or trivialize people because of gender, and then insist that women who don't laugh at such jokes have no sense of humour.

> Men expect to hear women criticizing them and are prepared to dismiss them for that reason. (Female faculty member)

> When we raise questions about women's scholarship, some of the profs laugh and tell us there is "not a good body" of work in the area. (Female graduate student)

> You should be happy to have a job. Secretaries are a dime a dozen. (Male faculty to secretary)

ii. Stereotyping

Often without giving it a second thought, many men expect from women behaviour which conforms to the sex-role stereotypes implanted over many years, such as passivity and deference in demeanour, and traditional course and career choices:

> We have observed many instances where female members of a laboratory are requested to be a lab handmaid. (Group of female graduate students)

> Men have the mistaken notion that women should always be seen as a junior partner — until they are older and invisible. (Female faculty)

Members of non-dominant groups and racialised groups are often expected to speak for, control or represent their group, as if they perfectly matched the stereotype in someone's mind. Equally infuriating is to meet with the assumption that someone else knows how you think or feel (or ought to think and feel) because of your sex, race, class, age, sexual orientation, or physical condition. Women may be criticized "both for fitting stereotypes and for not fitting them."[6] "Racialised women confront both the stereotypes about women and those about the racial or ethnic group in which they are classified."[7]

iii. Sexist Comments

Expression of derogatory beliefs about women is common, giving words to such sentiments as "women are inferior," "women are not serious," "they are distracting."

> A male instructor uses females in examples of "what not to do" and males in examples of "what to do." The textbook does the same. (Female undergraduate)

iv. Hostility

> Call me fussy. I just object to someone staring at my bust all the time. (Student)

Women often experience others' feelings of hostility toward them through avoidance, expressions of annoyance, resentment, anger, and jokes and innuendos at women's expense:

> At an informal social gathering at a local bar, a female graduate student was subjected to a discussion between a male faculty member and a male graduate student. They were comparing the size of her breasts with those of other women in the bar. (Female graduate student)

> It is very difficult to capture on paper just how awful it feels to be a female student in this class. We are deeply offended by the many "jokes" the professor seems to insist upon opening each class with. These set the stage for further sexist remarks; at our expense as well as at the expense of discussion of theoretical issues. The professor bombards the students with a wide range of crude, distasteful, and sexist comments. Furthermore, he is knowingly offensive. He continues to make such remarks even after students have indicated that they are, in fact, offended. (Group of female graduate students)

In one of our classes, anger and stereotyped perceptions of "other" groups are expressed. There is blatant sexism when women speak out in class, present their ideas or become leaders of groups. We are interrupted, called stupid . . . The prof remains silent. (Female graduate students)

I have only scratched the surface of my memories. Words like the following are forever etched in my mind: "We are giving you this chance to prove yourself"; "Your lectures are unsatisfactory as you are not a dynamic lecturer"; "Your promotion was approved but the vote was not unanimous"; "The collegial system allows me to keep information from you"; "You have a very negative attitude"; "If you don't support the department head watch your back for the next three years." (Female faculty)

During a discussion on homosexuality in Lower Place Riel, some students suddenly entered, wearing military gear and carrying mock weapons. They pretended to shoot the speakers and shouted "Kill the fags!" (Female student)

v. Denial of Status and Authority

Men at all levels of the University often refuse, covertly, to acknowledge a woman's position or her scope of authority. For example, subordinates may bypass a woman staff member to go directly to her superior. Other examples occur, too. A male colleague wrote to us in support of a female colleague, documenting her excellent work and stating that "blind prejudice" had stalled her career and damaged the University:

[Her] contribution . . . ranks with the development of rust-resistant wheat and the development of the cobalt Teletherapy Unit as a University of Saskatchewan accomplishment of benefit to thousands and eventually millions of people. The failure to recognize this can only be the result of blind prejudice. (Male faculty)

My supervisor tried to publish some of my work and present it at a conference without my knowledge. He never pulled any of this on the male graduate students in the lab. The problems I had with him could fill a volume, but overall I think they resulted from the attitude on his part that it was appropriate for him to do whatever he wanted with my data, work, etc., without my involvement. (Female graduate student)

vi. Invisibility

"Women in academia, especially those who belong to one or more other non-dominant groups, find that sometimes they are treated as though they are invisible, and sometimes they are made to feel too visible."[8] An Aboriginal woman who sits on a committee with six White males will certainly feel visible, but if her ideas and suggestions are ignored, she will feel quite invisible. She is trapped whichever way she turns. Female faculty from racialised groups often find they are more tested by students; female administrative staff from non-dominant groups may be bypassed by people approaching their department for service.

Women are made invisible at universities by the failure to recognize their presence or contributions; for example, in course content. Many women at the University of Saskatchewan have been treated as invisible by faculty or superiors:

> Professor ____ has frequently ignored all of us in class, skipping over us when soliciting responses from the other (male) students. Furthermore, it appears that virtually anything we say in class is unequivocally wrong. Our experiences are definitely gender based since Professor ____ does not subject his male students to this type of disrespectful treatment. (Group of female graduate students)

> ... I came to understand why it is that women seldom speak out against and sometimes do not recognize the male gender bias in the material we study. It is because there is no room for our comments in the version of reality that we are presented with. Our words, if they occur to us, have no place, they do not fit into the discussions, and they are answers to questions that are not asked. The male point of view has in many cases become the 'objective' point of view and to protest it is to deny reality. (Female undergraduate)

> Women faculty are treated with little respect and have a low profile. Students who work with them are thought to be under a handicap. (Female graduate student)

> The "girls in the office" are incredibly undervalued within the University community. ... [It] could take a leadership role in the recognition of the importance of the work done by secretarial staff in maintaining the day-to-day functioning of departments and in setting the tone within departments. (U of S department)

> When women's history is not taught, when women's developmental psychology is not taught, when economics courses do not account for the informal economies mostly inhabited by women, when social analysis does not consider why women are not included or the particular roles women fulfil, then women's intelligence is removed. When the experience of lesbian women, Native women, women of colour, or women with disabilities is not directly addressed in the academic programs of the University, then women's interests are not being upheld. (Female faculty)

vii. Double Standards

Those who apply a double standard evaluate behaviour differently, as a function of sex attribution. They have one set of rules and standards for women, quite different from those for men. This is often seen in universities. "Research shows that regardless of academic discipline, work is rated higher when allegedly produced by a man than when allegedly produced by a woman. Other research reveals that racialised women academics are more critically evaluated by students of both sexes than are other academics."[9]

A man's non-academic experience may be regarded as enriching, a woman's as indicating lack of focus. A male instructor may be better accepted than a female one, by students of both sexes, because his voice is perceived as more authoritative:

> What I have to say doesn't have credibility. The men are listened to more and I think I have to prove myself more than a man. (Female graduate student)

> In his experience, he said, women usually don't complete a PhD because they would rather get married and have children. He also stated that it is virtually impossible to complete your studies and have children at the same time. Therefore, you should choose one or the other. Now my question is: If this is his belief, how does it affect the selections for admissions into graduate studies? (Female graduate student)

> Since I had the academic qualifications and significant work experience in the area, I applied for the position. I was told that I was too old for the position (I was just barely over 40 at the time). The employer was impressed with my excellent academic qualifications and my work and enthusiasm, but he felt a younger person would be more likely to complete studies towards a PhD and then return as full-time faculty. The person who was hired left after the term expired. I was also told I would probably not stay long in the city as my husband might be transferred. (Female faculty)

> There's an old adage that women don't need money because men are the breadwinners. This completely irrational belief must be tossed out or implemented uniformly. Should single men be paid less because they have no wife or children to support? Should single mothers be paid more because they are the breadwinner? (Clerical employee)

viii. Tokenism

The discretionary inclusion of one woman, or a few women, is not uncommon. Nor is it accidental. Tokenism occurs when someone from outside the majority — a woman, a member of a racialised group, etc. — is intentionally put in a visible position of power within a group or organization, conveying the appearance of inclusiveness though there is no real commitment to this goal. Such tokens underline rather than undermine the dominant group structure.

> Women know they are asked to be the token woman of a committee. There is no real power attached. (Female faculty)

> Women are devastated by the experience of sitting on powerful com-
> mittees and still being marginalized and silenced. (Female faculty)

A female faculty member told us of a male in an all-male faculty who
bragged: "We've done our part for gender equity. We had a female term appointment last year." And a colleague pronounced to a woman at the University of Saskatchewan: "You've got it made. You are a visible minority
and a woman."

ix. Exclusion

> There's only so much blood you can give before you're anaemic, and after
> that it's lights out and you're dead on the floor. (Female faculty)

Exclusion occurs in a variety of formal and informal ways. One female
graduate student reported that women were invited to participate in the initial stages of selecting a prospective professor for the department, but excluded from input into the final decision when two male representatives of
the student body were heard. Another remarked:

> After numerous meetings with various professors, male students are wel-
> come to remain for longer periods.
>
> Many women feel that there is less than adequate information flow to
> them. Women are not targeted for information because they are not at the
> appropriate level in the hierarchy, because the system is somewhat lax, or
> because there is not a feeling that they have a right or need to know things
> that would make them feel like "valued contributors" to the University
> community. In turn, their concerns are not addressed, and their voices are
> not heard in the policies that affect them. . . . For people in the lower levels
> of the hierarchy, there is the concern that there may be no opportunity to
> voice an opinion, that opinions voiced may be discredited, and that the
> mere act of voicing an opinion may put a person, or her job, in some jeop-
> ardy. This impacts women more severely than men, in some instances be-
> cause they are not a routine part of the "old boys network" or other means
> of indirect information flow. (U of S department)

A graduate student reported that a male student was chosen to represent her department at an important conference but no opportunities were
provided for a female to attend. Such a situation, seen as an isolated incident, can be easily justified, but the situation was reported as part of a pattern of discrimination.

x. Backlash

Women and men who support efforts to improve the status of women are
often rejected for doing so, as many at the University of Saskatchewan have
discovered.

The text used in one of my courses was extremely sexist, blaming mothers (and other women) for all that goes wrong with their children. Yet the professor did nothing to present the other side of the coin, and my comments on "mother-bashing" were met with overbearing looks from professor and students alike. (Female graduate student)

I had been discussing possible research topics with my supervisor for my thesis and grant proposal. I was interested in studying the reasons why women seemed more reluctant than men to use the services of a program. He warned me not to "get into that" because organizations would likely not allow me to do the research. He suggested that I do something more generic and less political. (Female graduate student)

The University's poor image regarding women is said to be the fault of women whose criticism tarnishes the University's reputation. (Female faculty)

The rhetoric of resistance undermines the legitimacy of efforts to alter the status of women. Words such as "personal freedom," "biological determinism," "politically correct" are used to blame women for their own situation and absolve others of responsibility for change. (Female faculty)

Backlash includes demands for authority over women by men . . . poisoned environments in which men misrepresent facts about what has occurred in conflicts they have had with women, in which anger, rage, or violence is directed toward non-compliant women, in which women are shut out of decision-making procedures that affect their lives or are deliberately blocked from movement by behind-the-scenes power plays, or in which women are intimidated into gender-stereotypic activities or treated without dignity and respect. (Female faculty)

Because of rampant homophobia and a lack of legal protection for gay and lesbian people in Saskatchewan, accusations that all feminists are lesbians silences some women and diverts attention from the fact that there is no justice for anyone until there is justice for all. (Female faculty)

xi. Divide and Conquer

The history of warfare illustrates beyond any reasonable doubt that enemies who can be divided can more easily be conquered. That tactic has been adopted with great success by those who see women, particularly feminist women, as their enemy. They quickly find ways to maximize the social distance of women from each other, for example by informing a woman that she is superior to other women or to minorities in ability or achievement. They strive particularly to separate feminists from other women, "regular women."

"The strategy of divide and rule is used again to mark out feminists as extremists who are against the interest of 'ordinary,' 'normal' women," Wise Harris quotes from the Taking Liberties Collective.[10] It is extraordinary

how often this strategy succeeds. Here at the University of Saskatchewan
we were told:

> Female students go to some effort to distance themselves from being la-
> belled feminist. Thinly-veiled derision helps. (Female undergraduate stu-
> dent)

> Those with institutional power know that if they can encourage continual
> fighting among those without power, those without power will not have
> time or energy to look at the real causes of the problems and to work to-
> gether to shift the power dynamics. If there is money for Native Studies *or*
> Women's Studies, divide and conquer strategies keep the focus on
> "either/or" rather than on the clear need for both. (Female faculty)

In the aftermath of the murders of 14 female students in Montreal, Joan
Baril wrote in an unpublished paper: "One also sees the constant attempt to
differentiate between women and feminists. According to this definition,
feminists are extremists, while women, on the other hand, are not extremist
because 'they don't make an issue of things.' The reports of violence against
women university students construct the same differentiation between
'feminists' and the 'rest of us,' polarizing popular opinion against the 'extremist' views of 'the few.'"[11]

> I'm a scholar, not a freedom fighter. (Female faculty)

"Divide and conquer" is not an unknown tactic at the University of Saskatchewan. For example, we on this committee have been called "oppor-
tunists with a political agenda" and "a committee which will encourage
women to get on the bandwagon." Added to all the other aspects of the
anti-woman environment described above, it makes life here at anything
other than the most basic, heads-down level a constant, depleting struggle.

2. Surrounded by an Old Boys' Network

Much has been said about the power of the old boys and their network in
keeping women and other 'interlopers' in the place deemed appropriate for
them by the network. It would be hard to say it better or more graphically
than one female member of the University of Saskatchewan faculty did in
her brief to our committee, a detailed, dispassionate, and analytical account
of her experience as student and faculty. "The old boys' network is self-
perpetuating and serves its members well," she said. We will quote from her
brief extensively, making only the changes needed to conceal identity.

Her description of the old boys' network, which she met first as a graduate student, is precise and understanding:

Good undergraduate students are courted to enter graduate school where they are introduced to the right people, included in social events, informed about their options for further graduate work and/or employment. Graduate students are valued because when they leave the department they are frequently employed by former graduates with the provincial government, for example. These same graduates are then often in a position to seek advice from, and/or award research contracts to, department members. Department members enjoy this relationship and are careful to send to the provincial government departments only those who will most likely become valued employees. A similar continuing relationship often develops if the students go on to other universities to continue their graduate work. In addition to service as future contacts for joint work and research contracts, they may return to be hired as faculty members in the department.... There is nothing particularly wrong with this process except that male students are considerably more valuable to the department than females as avenues for investment and sources of future pay-off.

.... For these reasons, female graduate students, even the very best, are not the valued commodity to nurture, guide, encourage, and carefully place in positions of employment. It is not the case that anyone would deliberately block a woman's career, but rather that it is much less likely that faculty will take a personal interest in the student for purposes of encouraging further education or making all the right introductions, formal and informal, to ensure career success. Once in the discipline, women are often not part of the network where decisions are made, where plans are laid, where personal contacts lead to mutually beneficial working relationships.

Things are not that much different when a woman joins the faculty, as another told us. "The 'traditions' are so deeply rooted that no one stops to think or questions what they are doing.... Male faculty members condone, support and encourage an old-fashioned and negative attitude towards women, fondly remembering the 'pranks' of their youth and upholding 'tradition.'"

3. Women Make Accommodations

How are women to respond to such an environment? How can they survive its constant attacks on so many aspects of their being?

Often they accommodate their behaviour to avoid as much of the injurious environment as they can. One female undergraduate told our committee that to avoid drawing unwanted comments from male co-workers, she went home to change clothes after classes and before going to her job on campus. Women are always taught not to be enticing or provocative in their dress. A female sessional sneaked up the back stairway to avoid walking through the area where men work, and ate lunch in a small office space to avoid comments, looks, and gestures of male co-workers in the lunch room.

One brief described to us how women respond in ways that are cultural-
ly approved for them:

- internalizing ("No one else believes this so I must be wrong"),
- minimizing ("He probably didn't mean to say that no books by feminists
  should be used because they're biased"),
- giving in,
- nurturing the oppressor ("Let me help you understand what I mean
  about women not being equal on campus"),
- or premature mutuality (letting small moves by a colleague convince you
  that he is committed to justice for women).

The situation often makes women afraid to speak out or challenge the
system because they fear losing their jobs. "It is often less frightening to live
with sexist practices than to risk losing everything," one female faculty
member suggested. They feel isolated, overwhelmed or crazy, or they find
an adequate personal solution. Some act to politicize the issues with strategies for reforming or revolutionizing the system. Some learn what to avoid.
A female faculty member reports:

> I also learned that the coffee room was the pentagon for the old boys' net-
> work. I and many other women felt nauseated upon entering the room as
> men shared inside jokes and spread gossip. I would never have gone into
> the room but had no choice since it also contained the mail slots. I finally
> would wait until evening to check the mail, hoping that everyone had gone
> home.

Fighting back can be costly:

> I became friends with a woman who was a victim of her professor's sexual
> harassment. The experience devastated her. Her life literally fell apart. She
> changed from being very active and enthusiastic with a great joy for intel-
> lectual pursuits to someone who became very introverted and afraid. She
> has since left university with no desire to return. The professor received a
> 'slap on the hand' and he continues to hold a faculty position.

The cost can be violence in which somehow the person who makes the complaint is blamed. Wise Harris explains how this transformation works:

> The mechanism is as follows: first, there is an action by some men that
> threatens and/or reinscribes women as sexual beings, or as beings limited
> by their biology; second, there is a negative reaction by women who object
> to the initial action; third, there is a frame shift that resettles the focus of
> public debate not onto the perpetrators, but onto their justified reasons for
> having behaved as they did.[12]

There is a pattern in these mechanisms which legitimizes the threats against
university women and sanction violence against feminist university women:

> First, there is a reassertion of women's 'natural' roles, made explicit by a
> reinscription in sexually vulnerable terms. . . . Then, when feminists react
> negatively, there is a violent reaction against their dissension. Those who
> dissent are threatened and deemed unnatural. The frame of the public dis-
> course then shifts away from the initial act or threat of violence, and onto
> the (in)appropriateness of the reaction by feminists.[13]

We are reminded of the violent reactions to the University of Saskatchewan's gender-neutral language policy. Those who oppose the policy use the
language of force, calling its proponents Nazis. As illustrated by a letter in
The Sheaf (March 4, 1993), some of them consider proponents of gender-
neutral language "vermin" and "a plague," and declare war on them.

4. Sexual/Gender Harassment

What could more graphically illustrate the hostile environment experienced
by women at the University of Saskatchewan than the sexual and gender
harassment which many of them undergo here?

Complaints to the University's Sexual Harassment Officer more than
doubled in the year from August 1991 to August 1992, compared to the previous year. Of the 35 complaints received in 1991-92, 19 came directly from
the complainant and 16 involved requests for consultation on situations of
harassment.[14]

i. The Policy

> The complaints cover a wide range of situations and behaviour, including
> sexist comments, humiliating jokes of a sexual nature, unwanted physical
> contact, verbal abuse, displays of obscene material, repeated, intrusive ver-
> bal or physical approaches that are directly or indirectly sexual in nature,
> and sexual assault. (Report of the Sexual Harassment Officer)

Both a sexual harassment policy and a Sexual Harassment Office were
established in 1986. The Office had a half-time Sexual Harassment Officer
until upgrading to full-time in mid-1993, responsible for education, receiving and evaluating complaints of sexual harassment, supportive counselling of complainants, policy revision, and administrative duties. She chairs
a Sexual Harassment Policy Advisory Committee which must periodically
evaluate the policy, monitor its effectiveness and recommend changes, and
assist her with education. The policy and procedures manual, revised in 1991,
is again under revision. It defines sexual harassment in the following way:

> Any form of abusive, offensive or unwelcome behaviour of a sexual nature
> constitutes sexual harassment when it may reasonably be perceived:
> 1. as a term or condition of employment or education (including availabil-
>   ity or continuation of work or study, promotion, training, or academic
>   advancement opportunities); or

2. as interfering with the use or allocation of goods, services, facilities or accommodations which are customarily available within the university; or

3. to influence decisions pertaining to employment or educational advancement, or the provision of goods and services; or

4. to interfere with job or study performance; such interference would include a negative psychological and emotional environment for work or study.

Elaboration of the definition makes clear that peer level harassment occurs, as well as harassment of persons of lower status, such as students or employees, by those of higher status, such as professors and administrators. Behaviours that might result in an allegation of sexual harassment are listed, and a distinction made between sexual harassment (". . . i.e. behaviour which may be perceived by a reasonable person to interfere with work, teaching, research, or study") and gender harassment involving behaviour which reflects a broad, negative stereotypical attitude toward a group of people because of their gender.[15] Gender harassment is not covered in the definition of sexual harassment and complaints of this nature cannot be resolved through the Sexual Harassment Office.

Complainants covered by collective agreements which contain grievance mechanisms can contact either the appropriate union representative or the Sexual Harassment Officer. Students can complain directly to the Officer or to Student Affairs officers, who should then refer them to the Sexual Harassment Officer.

Complaints are first dealt with informally, and the complainant can opt for mediation. The complainant may decide to take the next step, a formal complaint which is turned over to the appropriate University authority: the Associate Vice-President (Administration), the appropriate Dean, the Director of Libraries, the Assistant Vice-President (Student Affairs and Services), depending on the status of the complainant. This official must investigate according to specific guidelines laid out in the manual, and take appropriate action leading to resolution of the case.

ii. Problems and Issues

a. *Under-reporting of Sexual/Gender Harassment*

From 1986, when the Sexual Harassment Office and policy were established, until February 1992, 73 complaints were received. Studies at other universities indicate that only 10-20% of victims make complaints, often for fear of not being believed, fear of ridicule, or some other adverse consequence.[16] Research has shown that harassment is common, that most victims are women, and that it has deleterious effects. Twenty-three presentations made to our committee on the matter of sexual harassment do not constitute a random sample, but they do suggest that the University of Saskatchewan is no different than other universities in this respect.

Sexual/gender harassment is also under-reported because, as is well-documented, women are socialized to accept as "normal" and "a fact of life" many sexual interactions to which they do not consent, which they do not welcome, or which they find offensive. Thus, studies have reported, many women would not label such experiences as "sexual harassment."[17] This widespread acceptance of what has been called "the male sexual prerogative" must be taken into account when one defines sexual/gender harassment. It underscores the need for effective education of the campus population about the inherent sexism of such a "prerogative."

b. Historic Understaffing

The half-time Sexual Harassment Officer position which the University funded was totally inadequate, given the variety of the Officer's responsibilities and the size of the campus population. The new full-time position fits the Canadian average, according to a brief our committee received.

c. Education of the Campus Population

The Sexual Harassment Officer and Advisory Committee have engaged in several educational activities, including speaking engagements and distribution of pamphlets and other materials. Such consciousness-raising was limited by the inadequate human resources. This was unfortunate, for experience at other universities and organizations indicates that effective education programs encourage more victims to speak up and inform potential harassers of the negative sanctions for such behaviour.

d. Co-worker Sexual Harassment

This issue poses a particular challenge to any union to which the complainant belongs. There are a number of reasons for this. Although in theory the complaint is against the employer because the employer is responsible for maintaining a workplace free of sexual harassment, in practice it can be seen as a dispute between two union members — with the union caught fast in the middle. Both the complainant and the alleged harasser have certain rights, including the right to be fairly represented by the bargaining unit. This requires the union to balance the competing interests of each party.

The union must not refuse to take action because of the difficulty of its task, however. Every bargaining unit should confront this problem squarely and develop principled and effective ways to deal with it. The Resource Kit on Co-worker Sexual Harassment published by the Canadian Union of Public Employees contains a useful discussion of the issue and of possible options.[18]

e. Functions and Procedures

The Sexual Harassment Officer's responsibilities include psychological support for the victim and quasi-legal counselling. A brief presented to our committee relayed arguments against both tasks being done by the same person. The Officer must respect the client's desire for confidentiality *and* advise on possible courses of action, some of which might result in breaching that confidentiality. Further, very different sets of skills are required for emotional and quasi-legal work.

The policy manual requires that formal complaints be referred to a senior University official. These people are untrained to do such investigations, and may not be seen as capable of complete impartiality in some situations, e.g. if they have to adjudicate between the competing claims of a secretary and a department head. Intermediaries may be needed, particularly in cases involving non-academic staff whose senior University officials are in the Personnel Department. The literature suggests strongly that the redress mechanism should be separate from the Personnel Department to ensure that no biases develop among those with power to affect employment decisions.[19]

There are other problems. Appeal procedures are unclear, and the "appropriate university authority" is not required to report the investigation's outcome to the head of the administrative unit with which the respondent is affiliated, as student or employee.

f. Issues in Defining Sexual/Gender Harassment
— Problem of Definition

One of the problems in the University's definition of sexual harassment is its reliance on the concept of "reasonable perception": harassment is placed in the context of behaviour that "may reasonably be perceived" as a condition of employment or education or as interfering with the enjoyment of or access to certain goods and services. This approach fails to take into account the important point, made frequently in the literature on this subject, that many people see various forms of sexual exploitation as normal, everyday behaviour. An example is the well-documented tendency of many women to accept enforced sexualization when it comes in the guise of joking or compliments, and of many men to view such behaviour as entirely legitimate.

It is important, therefore, to use definitions which identify specific behaviours and don't depend on an assumed "reasonable perception." We suggest this definition:

> Sexual harassment consists of the sexualization of a relationship formed
> for, or in the context of, work or study. The sexualization occurs through
> the harasser's introduction or imposition of sexist or sexual remarks,

requests, or requirements, in a context where there is a formal difference in the power of the harasser and the victim (e.g. supervisor/employee relationship). Sexual harassment can also occur where no such formal differential exists, if the behaviour is unwanted by, or offensive to, the woman. Instances of harassment can be classified into the following general categories: gender harassment, sexual bribery, sexual coercion, seductive behaviour or sexual invitation which the victim identifies to the harasser as unwanted, and sexual imposition or sexual assault.[20]

This definition is based on two premises: that sexual harassment involves a confluence of authority or power relations and sexuality or sexism in a society stratified by gender; and that authority or power can be derived from a formal role (supervisor, employer, professor) and from informal power arising from the widespread acceptance of male sexual prerogative. This prerogative implies that men have the unrestricted right to initiate sexual encounters or to make a woman's sexuality salient so that it overrides her position as worker or student to sexualize an otherwise non-sexual situation. The National Advisory Council on Women's Educational Programs in the United States has defined academic sexual harassment as: "... the use of authority to emphasize the sexuality or sexual identity of the student in a manner which prevents or impairs that student's full enjoyment of educational benefits, climate, or opportunities."[21]

The general categories in Fitzgerald's definition are explained further:

Gender harassment: Generalized sexist remarks and behaviour not necessarily designed to elicit sexual cooperation, but to convey insulting, degrading or sexist attitudes about women. This would include derogatory remarks about sexual preference.
Sexual bribery: Solicitation of sexual activity or other sex-linked behaviour, such as dating, by promise of rewards.
Sexual coercion: Coercion of sexual activity or other sex-linked behaviour by threat of punishment.
Seductive behaviour or sexual invitation: Inappropriate and offensive sexual advances. There is no explicit threat or bribe attached by the harasser to the woman's negative response.
Sexual imposition or sexual assault: Attempts to fondle, touch, kiss, or grab; or sexual assault.

— University of Saskatchewan Policy
For us to recognize the sexism in our lives and confront it, we risk peer disapproval which ranges from isolation and verbal abuse to physical and sexual threats and violence. (Female undergraduate)

The current University of Saskatchewan policy distinguishes between sexual harassment — "behaviour which may be perceived by a reasonable person to interfere with work, teaching, research, and study" — and gender harassment — "behaviour reflecting a broad negative stereotypical attitude toward a group of people by virtue of gender." But, as noted earlier, the policy addresses only the former behaviour and not the latter. It adds: "Thus, sexist remarks, for example, would conform to the definition of sexual harassment provided here only if they were shown to interfere with teaching, research, job performance or study."[22]

However, sexist remarks by definition involve gender stereotyping and demeaning and insulting content, creating a poisoned environment bound to affect the emotional health of the targeted group. Such sexually-charged behaviour conveys a lack of respect which undermines the dignity of those joked about, and their sense of security. This must also be prohibited by way of University policy.

— Changes in Legal Precedents

Canadian courts and tribunals have ruled in a number of cases that the creation of an offensive environment through sexualization processes can by itself violate human rights laws. For example, the Ontario Board of Inquiry in the Cherie Bell case found that sex harassment is sex discrimination under existing laws, and that the law ought to protect employees "from the negative psychological and mental effects where adverse and gender-directed conduct... may reasonably be construed to be a condition of employment." In a later case, the chair of the Ontario Board interpreted broadly the requirement for a causal connection between harassment and tangible employment consequences, finding that harassment is discriminatory simply as a term or condition of employment.[23] In other words, the law now recognizes that a poisoned work environment is, of itself, an adverse employment consequence of sexual harassment.

The current University policy implies that the onus is on the individual to "show" that the environment created by sexual harassment has had negative effects even though the case law indicates that an employee or student subjected to such work or study environments does not need to prove additional detriment.

Other recent developments in the area of sexual harassment have firmly placed liability for the sexual harassment of workers on the employer. In *Robichaud v. Canada* (Treasury Board), the court said, "only an employer can remedy undesirable effects of [sexual harassment]; only an employer can provide the most important remedy — a healthy work environment." In addition, recent human rights decisions have included sexual orientation as a prohibited ground of discrimination. Thus, lesbophobic work conditions would be deemed harassment and could form the basis for a complaint of harassment.

The development of an internal sexual harassment policy can be beneficial in at least two ways: first, it allows for a quicker resolution of the complaint than is often available through filing a complaint with the Human Rights Commission, and second, it can improve and expand upon existing human rights legislation. The University's complaint procedure, as noted previously, is confusing, but it has proven, in some cases, to provide quicker resolutions. However, the University's definition of what behaviour constitutes sexual harassment falls short of protection already available under human rights legislation. Our proposed definition of sexual harassment will expand the present policy, fulfilling, we believe, the University's legal obligation to "provide the most important remedy — a healthy work environment." We would also add: "and place of study and work."

g. Treating Sexual Harassment as Individual and Isolated

Like other institutions with sexual harassment policies, the University's policy treats sexual harassment as an individual and isolated experience rather than seeing it as something that women frequently encounter. Removing sexual harassment from its social context isolates it from women's total experience of oppression.

This is reinforced by the use of mediation, a step included in the University's sexual harassment policy. It too treats harassment as "individualized experiences," isolating it from the rest of women's experience amidst the University's systemic discrimination.

Furthermore, mediation is problematic because it assumes that the two parties in a sexual harassment case are equal in bargaining power and ability to negotiate — despite the likelihood that one has considerably more power than the other, including power over the other's present and future.

Gender-neutral language, such as "complainant" and "respondent," should not be allowed to obscure the reality of harassment: that 95% to 99% of "complainants" are women and 95% to 99% of "respondents" are men. Using such gender-neutral language and all-encompassing terms without this recognition "denies any implication of sexual harassment in the systemic oppression of women and characterizes harassment as simply a behavioural phenomenon. The result is to marginalize harassment quantitatively (as deviant or abnormal behaviour), qualitatively (by ignoring its unique impact on women), and prescriptively (by inviting individually oriented responses)."[24]

5. Child Care — Still Largely the Woman's Job

With little social support or recognition, women in our society have primary responsibility for child care.

Geographical mobility and segmented households, combined with the ideology of family privacy, mean that women with babies get very little on-
the-job training from experienced workers. For many women, becoming a
parent is often devastating and confusing because they suddenly find
themselves in unfamiliar work situations ... [But] the care of that human
being is not defined as work: it is seen as a private, natural and essentialist
enterprise. When women complain or despair, they are frequently told,
"Well, you were the one who wanted this baby ..." But raising a baby is
not a personal hobby like raising begonias, it is an undertaking which reproduces society as well as expressing the individual need to love and
cherish children.[25]

How child care is organized, recognized, and valued contributes substantially to women's structural position in the home and the workforce.
Surveying the current 'official' status, definition, and availability of day care
in Canada shows that national policies treat the care of children as women's
work. The lack of priority or value for such care directly reflects its gendered
organization and illustrates the devalued status of women's work.

In Canada, day care falls under provincial jurisdiction. The Federal Government is involved under the Canada Assistance Plan, through child-care
expense deductions from personal income tax, and through child tax-credit
programs. Many problems have been identified with the governmental role
in providing organized child care; few of them have been alleviated, though
more and more women have joined the workforce.

i. Accessibility Issues

The structure of the university doesn't allow for recognition of single-par-
ent status. (Female student)

Lack of accessibility to licensed day-care centres has proved a consistent
problem for Canadian families. Both availability and affordability constitute access issues. A 1990 National Day Care Study calculated that the parents of more than two million children require day-care services for them.[26]
This figure does not include families in which a parent (or both parents) is
neither employed nor in school. Thus the government's own statistics endorse the idea that homemaker or household work is not "real work," that
mothering and housekeeping are appropriately fused and equally valueless
occupations, and that women do not 'require' child care unless they are
gainfully employed outside the home.

And even for the categories of parents who, according to the government, do qualify as legitimate child-care "consumers," there are not enough
spaces. The study found 320,624 child-care spaces across the country —
14.6% of what was required.[27] Rural women and those who live in smaller
communities or on reserves have even less hope of finding child care.

The supply of licensed day-care centres depends on provincial initiatives, and is uneven. Subsidies are available only for low-income families. In Saskatchewan in 1991, for example, the gross monthly income cut-off to qualify for subsidy was $1,540 plus $100 per child;[28] most whose household incomes exceed this must pay the full cost of day care. Those who do not qualify for subsidy must often look for other alternatives, since the full cost of licensed day care in Saskatchewan averages close to $400 per child per month.

Many parents opt for private arrangements, unregulated baby-sitters, 'day-care homes,' family members, neighbours, or a nightmarish and patchwork combination. Regulated, licensed day care is thus available only to the very poor and the wealthy who earn enough to benefit from the tax concessions. Those in lower- and middle-income brackets are disadvantaged in access and impaired in their decisions about study or career.[29]

ii. Child Care at the University of Saskatchewan

There is a child-care centre at the University of Saskatchewan with room for approximately 44 children. It is run by a co-operative non-profit society, and open only to children of the university community, including faculty, staff, and students. At present there are 26 children of student parents, six of staff, and 13 of faculty. (The total exceeds the enrolment because some parents fall into two categories.) Children must be at least two years old and toilet-trained. No hot lunch is served. Hours are restricted to 7:45 a.m. to 5:30 p.m. Monday to Friday, making the centre inaccessible for parents who work shifts or students taking night classes. Fees are $410 per month, which exceeds the full provincial child-care subsidy of $235 by $175. Parents who rely on being fully enrolled in an educational institution in order to qualify for the child-care subsidy often cannot afford to retain their children's space during the summer, when enrolment is traditionally lowest. This also applies to service staff in CUPE, many of whom are laid off during summer months. There may be a tendency for faculty to have greater access to available spaces because they are not dependent on seasonal income. The common perception is that there is a lengthy wait for spaces in this child-care facility.

The University of Saskatchewan Students' Union operates a child-care facility governed by a non-profit society. Membership is not restricted, but students have priority, then faculty, then the general public. The centre has approximately 60 spaces, and contains an infant child-care centre with six spaces for babies from six to 18 months. Care for babies was found to be the greatest need by the University of Saskatchewan Students' Council Daycare Advisory Board. The fees are $400 per month for children of undergraduate students, $440 for others. This is one of the highest rates in Saskatoon, if not *the* highest rate, and is contrary to the recommendations of the USSC Day-care Advisory Board's Report, *Student Childcare Need at the University of Saskatchewan* (1991), that fees be as low as possible and fully subsidized. This centre operates 7:30 a.m. to 5:30 p.m. Monday to Friday, making difficulties for students taking night classes or needing to study during weekends. The recommendation of the Daycare Advisory Board for an extensive part-time service, including drop-off service, for those who require child care outside of normal day hours was not implemented.

Although the child-care spaces on campus are considered inadequate, there are many licensed day-care centres in the residential districts surrounding the University. The main problem is access, which includes both availability and affordability. Subsidy rates have not changed in Saskatchewan for a dozen years. Although the price of day care is fairly low, and inadequate to pay decent salaries to workers at most centres, it remains a substantial financial barrier to many parents. This keeps many day-care spaces from being fully used.

Women parenting small children have diverse child-care needs and often require service outside of normal working hours. Many students attend evening classes and must have child care to do homework, study, research, and in some cases, attend meetings and rehearsals. Child-care facilities on and near the campus fail to accommodate those needs.

6. *Women's Islands Lack a Link*

Off the southern tip of Florida, a series of small islands known as the Florida Keys leads deep into the Gulf of Mexico. At one time, boats and small planes were all that linked the Keys; today, an aerial highway ties them together, passing serenely above the waves, hardly threatened even by hurricanes. Each key is unique but it is no longer alone.

At the University of Saskatchewan, there are islands where individuals and/or groups work successfully to improve the status of women: Women in Science groups, the Women's and Gender Studies program, the Employment Equity committees, the College of Education Gender Equity Committee, the Women's Centre, the Women's Studies Research Unit, and more. All are islands with energy, achievement, and diversity, able to focus a powerful intensity on women's problems. Potentially, they are a great power base for a many-fronted struggle for the status of women, but each works alone. No highway links them and lets them in on the big picture.

The structure of the University works against such a link, confining these various initiatives and activities to small compartments. There is little co-ordination or communication among them, so initiatives which might apply broadly are fragmented instead. Policies are developed, but without consultation among all who might be affected. Some activities overlap; in other cases, opportunities are missed. There is no central place which can provide help, information, and resources, or provide links with successes and warn against failures, based on local experience. As a result, energy is dissipated and potential benefits lost.

It is not necessary that all work on status of women issues be co-ordinated, of course. That could lead to an inflexibility quite as stifling and unproductive as the present situation. But the kind of compartmentaliza-tion which is occurring, abetted by the structure of the University, encour-ages the feeling that institutional commitment is lacking, even if that lack is unconscious.

The situation encourages the perception that the institutional impera-tive is to marginalize these efforts and play off one group against another, to use the existing compartmentalization as a tool to retain the *status quo*.

The islands which have been created are clearly keys to improving the status of women. Like the Florida Keys, they need a highway to bridge their separateness.

7. Lack of Statistical Information

It will never be possible to assess the gains made by women at the Universi-ty of Saskatchewan, the differences which remain between their treatment and the treatment of men, or what has still to be accomplished, without ade-quate and detailed statistical information. Unfortunately the University does not develop the type of statistical information and analysis that would provide answers to the questions that remain, or encourage the University community to ask questions about this issue.

The University has no policy requiring that compilation of statistical data include information that is gender-specific. Only with such informa-tion can quantitative analysis be done on women's current status and the gaps which still exist. Only with such analysis can plans to close those gaps be made and carried out.

The problem is also that there is not a central source for all statistical data compiled on campus. The University of Saskatchewan Statistics book con-tains data gathered by the University Studies Group (USG), some of it gender-specific. The Employment Equity Office collects or is in the process of collecting gender-specific data in certain areas. The Personnel Depart-ment does not collect statistical data in areas not contained in either the USG or the Employment Equity Office.

The only gender-specific data about students available through USG and reported in its annual Statistics volume falls into one of these categories: full- and part-time enrolment for degree programs, by college, year, and gender; full-time students by gender and college; age distribution, full- and part-time degrees; full- and part-time undergraduate degree students; full-

and part-time graduate students; admission averages (first year, first time, direct entry colleges on campus). The USG is completing an Environmental Scan which will provide demographic and economic data, but has not been required to have this information gender-specific. That the University collects no gender-specific or minority group-specific information on student withdrawals or discontinuations creates a highly significant gap in our knowledge.

Many more statistics need to be collected and widely publicized on a regular basis to tell the whole picture of male and female students at this University: the percentage of unclassified students and trends in part-time enrolments, by gender and minority status; enrolment by gender and age group, and by gender and minority status. Gender-specific and minority group statistics should be collected that enable comparisons of entry level students, retention rates by college and graduates by college, so it is possible to determine if there are differences in the retention rates each year of women and men, and of students of majority and minority status.

In the field of student aid, statistics are needed on the sources of financial support for undergraduates, by sex and type; percentage of undergraduates receiving financial aid, by sex, age, and minority status; percentage of undergraduates awarded federal financial aid, by sex, age, minority status, and type of aid; amount of federal financial aid awarded to undergraduates, by sex, age, and minority status; selected sources of support for doctoral recipients, by sex; scholarships, teaching fellowships, graduate support and undergraduate scholarships, bursaries, etc. provided by the University, by age, sex, and minority status.

Information on degrees awarded is divided by gender, but not that on certificates and diplomas. The University of Saskatchewan lacks a gender-specific and minority/majority group overview of earned degrees, and statistics should be collected on bachelor's, master's, and doctoral degrees and first professional degrees, by gender and minority group status. Also lacking is a statistical profile of doctoral recipients, by gender, age, minority group status, and college.

Statistics about the faculty include three categories of gender-specific data: distribution of full-time academic staff by age and gender, by rank and gender, and by gender, but none on part-time academic staff. Much more needs to be collected, such as the percentage of female faculty who are tenured, non-tenured, and of professorial status; tenured women as a percentage of the total faculty; percentage of tenured faculty in selected disciplines, by gender; post-doctoral and doctoral research staff, by gender. Salary comparisons are needed between female and male faculty at all levels. Some of this information is collected by Employment Equity, as we shall see, but not all of it.

The Employment Equity Office has compiled or is in the process of developing a wide range of gender-specific statistics about administrators, trustees, and staff. These include representation of women by job group (CUPE, ASPA, faculty) and by college/administration unit; representation of faculty women who receive promotions and merit increases; statistics collected as a result of the ASPA Glass Ceiling Survey; salary range analysis where designated group members (DGMs) are in the range; initial salary levels of men and women faculty to determine the differences; annual report on the hiring, promotion, and termination of DGMs and their representation in the application pool; representation of women in faculty ranks based on Statistics Canada to determine progress or the lack thereof.

Detail on the representation of women among the administrative and support staff who receive promotions and merit increases is needed, and on women administrators at the senior management level and in membership of governing bodies, by gender.

From this quick review of the information collected, it appears that the University Studies Group has been given no direction about the need to develop gender-specific and minority group status information and analyze it so the University can determine the inequities which exist between male and female, minority and majority group students, staff, and faculty. Without such complete information it is impossible to develop an effective plan to address inequities; it is hard, even, to know exactly what the inequities are.

There must be a strategic plan to drive the collection of statistical information at the University of Saskatchewan, or concerns about equity will never become a proper part of the University's overall strategic plan.

* * *

The Preferred Scenario

Examining the current situation for women at the University of Saskatchewan, listening to women's anger and bitterness — and sometimes, alas, resignation — was a daunting experience for this committee. The prospect of moving an institution as large as the University of Saskatchewan, with the inbred inertia that affects all large institutions, from that scenario to what we consider the preferred scenario is also daunting.

But in the same way that many women have determined to survive the current situation and have survived, often achieving small but valuable changes, as we have just seen, so we are determined to build an equitable University. We call on the entire University community to attend to the recommendations that follow, directing their minds and energies to implementation of them. Such attention will focus light on the importance of women's role in the University of Saskatchewan, and burn through every-thing that has demeaned that role and thwarted its fulfilment, harming the University in the process.

We move forward now with equal measures of confidence and determination to make things as they would be at the University of Saskatchewan if it were a person-centred University, a place that truly valued women. This is our preferred scenario. We believe it is both attainable and realistic. We believe that our vision of a better University will be shared by many people of both sexes on campus.

In our preferred scenario, all groups and especially those at the bottom of the hierarchy who in the past have been given the least respect will be treated humanely. They, too, receive recognition for what they do. They have input into operations and policies and are included in discussions about workload and the policies governing work, at every level, including the Board of Governors. They are treated with respect and empathy, never with inappropriate familiarity. All groups are recognized in annual reports. All employees receive genuine (i.e., authenticated, verified, properly supported) and positive feedback on their performance. The environment reinforces the employee's self-respect, and recognition of employee contributions is a key part of the University's operations.

In the preferred scenario, people see problems in their social context. At present, in many offices on this campus, there are people whose work includes solving problems on an individual model and operate in a segmented way, starting from the assumption that it is individuals who have problems and the solution is for them to adjust to the system. In the preferred scenario, looking at problems in their social context may suggest instead that the solution is to adjust the system.

It is particularly important for those who provide services to people to recognize this truth, for it represents a major change. Problems are often psychologized rather than socialized. Those who provide services need to consider the larger questions of social structure and power. Unfortunately, the University has no mechanism with which to do this, no model for combining and analyzing statistics to identify patterns of systemic problems.

The University must retain a capacity to respond to individual problems, of course. It also needs, crucially, a capacity to think about problems in a systemic way; this is especially true of offices whose mandate, in whole or in part, is the resolution of problems.

Part of the vision of the preferred scenario is that all thinking about the status of women takes special account of the needs of women who are Aboriginal and/or disabled and/or are members of other minority groups. We have learned from experience that if women are not explicitly mentioned and their needs included when policy is formed and procedures implemented, most people at this University unconsciously think in terms of the male norm. It is equally true that if Aboriginal, disabled, and minority-group women are not specifically considered when we think about how to improve the status of women, most people will unconsciously think in terms of the White female norm.

This, then, the preferred scenario, is an attainable goal. We have a foundation of solid bricks and hopeful dreams on which to build a better, fairer University. And there is energy for the building. There are people at every level of the University of Saskatchewan who recognize the ideal and are prepared to commit time, energy, and effort to achieving it. We call those people to action.

Notes

Editors' Notes

1 *Reinventing Our Legacy: Report of the President's Advisory Committee on the Status of Women* (Saskatoon: University of Saskatchewan, 1993). Selections from this report are reprinted here with the permission of President Ivany and the Advisory Committee on the Status of Women.

2 Roberta M. Hall and Bernice R. Sandler, *The Classroom Climate: A Chilly One for Women?* (Washington, DC: Project on the Status and Education of Women, Association of American Colleges, 1982); Roberta M. Hall and Bernice R. Sandler, *Out of the Classroom: A Chilly Campus Climate for Women?* (Washington, DC: Project on the Status and Education of Women, AAC, 1984); and Bernice R. Sandler, *Campus Climate Revisited: Chilly for Women Faculty, Administrators, and Graduate Students* (Washington, DC: Project on the Status and Education of Women, AAC, 1986).

3 *Reinventing Our Legacy*, p. 4.

4 Ibid., p. 5.

5 Ibid., p. 6.

Notes

1 University Studies Group, *Statistics Volume 17* (Saskatoon: University of Saskatchewan, 1992), p. 6.1.

2 Dorothy E. Smith, "A Peculiar Eclipsing: Women's Exclusion From Man's Culture," *Women's Studies International Quarterly*, 1 (1978): 287.

3 Ibid.

4 Louise F. Fitzgerald, "Sexual Harassment: The Definition and Measurement of a Construct," in M. Paludi, ed., *Ivory Power: Sexual Harassment on Campus* (Albany: State University of New York Press, 1990), p. 33-34.

5 M. Rowe, "The Saturn's Ring Phenomenon: Micro-inequities and Unequal Opportunities in the American Economy," cited in Karen Bogart, Kathleen Wells, and Mary Spence, "Improving Sex Equity in Postsecondary Education," in S. Klien, ed., *Handbook for Achieving Sex Equity through Education* (Baltimore: Johns Hopkins University Press, 1985), p. 478.

6 Paula J. Caplan, *Lifting a Ton of Feathers: A Woman's Guide to Surviving in the Academic World* (Toronto: University of Toronto Press, 1992), p. 213.

7 Ibid., p. 214

8 Ibid., p. 12.

9 Ibid.

10 Debbie Wise Harris, "Keeping Women in Our Place: Violence at Canadian Universities," *Canadian Woman Studies*, 11, 4 (1991): 40.

11 Ibid.

12 Ibid., p. 38.

13 Ibid., p. 41.

14 Carol A. Pond, *Annual Report of the Sexual Harassment Office August 1991-August 1992* (Saskatoon: University of Saskatchewan, 1992).

15 University of Saskatchewan, *Sexual Harassment Policy and Procedures Manual*, rev. ed. (Saskatoon: University of Saskatchewan, 1990).

16 Marilyn MacKenzie and Thelma Lussier, *Sexual Harassment: Report on the Results of a Survey of the University of Manitoba Community* (Winnipeg: University of Manitoba, 1988), and Carol Pritchard, *Avoiding Rape On and Off Campus* (Wenonah, NJ: State Publishing, 1985).

17 Fitzgerald, "Sexual Harassment," p. 21.

18 Canadian Union of Public Employees, *Harassment Awareness Kit* (Ottawa: Department of Equal Opportunities, Canadian Union of Public Employees, 1991).

19 A.P. Aggarwal, *Sexual Harassment in the Workplace* (Toronto: Butterworths, 1987).

20 Modified from Fitzgerald, "Sexual Harassment," and Susan A. McDaniel and Erica van Roosmalen, "Sexual Harassment in Canadian Academe: Explorations of Power and Privilege," *Atlantis*, 17, 1 (1991): 3-19

21 F. Till, *Sexual Harassment: A Report on the Sexual Harassment of Students* (Washington, DC: National Advisory Council on Women's Educational Programs, 1980), p. 7.

22 University of Saskatchewan, *Sexual Harassment Policy and Procedures Manual*, p. 4.

23 *Cox v. Jagbritte Inc.* (Ontario Board of Inquiry, 1981), 3 C.H.R.R. D/609, and *Robichaud v. Canada* (Treasury Board, 1987), 8 C.H.R.R. D/4326.

24 John Kilcoyne, *Responding to Sexual Harassment on Campus: The Seduction of Law?* (Victoria: University of Victoria, Faculty of Law, 1990), as cited in Rachel L. Osborne, "Sexual Harassment in Universities: A Critical View of the Institutional Response," *Canadian Woman Studies*, 12, 3 (1992): 72-76.

25 Harriet Rosenberg, "Motherwork, Stress and Depression: The Costs of Privatized Social Reproduction," in H.J. Maroney and M. Luxtin, eds., *Feminism and Political Economy* (Toronto: Methuen, 1987), cited in Rosanna Langer, "The Legitimization of Male Dominance in Family Law," MA thesis, University of Saskatchewan, Saskatoon, 1993.

26 Health and Welfare Canada, *Status of Day Care in Canada 1990* (Ottawa: Minister of Supply and Services Canada, 1991).

27 Ibid.

28 The Saskatchewan Childcare Association, *The Child Care Story* (Saskatoon), as cited in Langer, "The Legitimization of Male Dominance in Family Law."

29 Kathleen Mahoney, "Day Care and Equality in Canada," *Manitoba Law Journal*, 14 (1984-85): 305, 325, 326, as cited in Langer, "The Legitimization of Male Dominance in Family Law."

7

Gender Bias within the Law School: "The Memo" and Its Impact

Sheila McIntyre

As indicated in the Preface, one of the catalysts for the chilly climate projects undertaken by women faculty at the University of Western Ontario in 1988-89 was a particularly compelling account, written by Sheila McIntyre in 1986, of the chilly climate she experienced in the law school at Queen's University. The "McIntyre Memo," as it was referred to, had been widely circulated and was printed in the CAUT (Canadian Association of University Teachers) Bulletin *in 1987. During the period McIntyre describes, she confronted a range of exclusionary, devaluing, stereotyping, and revictimizing practices that closely parallel various of those reported to the authors of the* Chilly Climate Report. *Her autobiographical account of these events makes clear, in particularly graphic terms, the interplay between different forms of gender harassment, some intentionally exclusionary and devaluing, some unintentionally so, some more and others less overt in their gendered dimensions. Most important, she describes the cost exacted by a diverse range of chilly-making practices when they converge on one individual and are counter-balanced only in a limited way by other sources of support.*

We had hoped to include, as a counterpart to this widely read and influential essay, a similarly detailed autobiographical account written by a woman faculty member who worked at Western (in a faculty other than law) in the same period. The outcome for this individual was deeply disappointing to all of us who had known and worked with her. She ultimately resigned her tenure-stream position and won a settlement against the University. The terms of the settlement are confidential, but it evidently includes sufficiently stringent constraints on public discussion of the case that we could not include her essay in a collection which contains other essays about Western. When we learned that we could not publish this essay, late in the process of assembling the present collection, we confronted once

211

*again the kinds of costs that speaking out can have even when those speaking out
use official channels to seek redress — and win a favourable settlement. There is an
important sense in which our collection is misnamed. However privileged faculty
women may be, a great many cannot "break anonymity" and speak frankly, and
publicly, about the conditions under which they work.*

— Eds.

I. Introduction

In the summer of 1985, I was hired on a two year non-renewable contract to
teach law at Queen's University. A year later, I wrote the memorandum
which is reproduced as the core of this article, chronicling and analyzing incidents of sexism and anti-feminism I had observed and experienced during
my first year of teaching. I distributed the memo to the student representatives who sit on the law school's Faculty Board and to all my colleagues in
July of 1986. Over the subsequent two months, copies of the memo circulated widely from hand to hand within academic, legal, and feminist communities locally and nationally. Ultimately, someone gave a copy of the
memo to the campus newspaper at Queen's, and within a few weeks the
memo had become a national news story.

When I started to write what became the memo, I had no thought of circulating it at all. I wrote it for myself. Only with a first draft in hand did I begin to consider addressing it to my colleagues. The process of making that
decision and redrafting the text for a largely non-feminist audience which I
perceived to be resistant to recognizing, discussing, or redressing institutional gender bias was as politically significant and instructive as what happened after the memo went public.

Because I assumed the memo would have few readers outside my faculty, I originally planned to write a companion piece to the memo for a feminist readership which would reproduce the memo and elaborate upon why
I wrote it, what I learned in the process, and what happened, if anything,
following its distribution. I had no idea what to expect post-circulation. I
hoped my Faculty might finally begin to discuss purposefully the pervasiveness and damaging impact of gender bias in the law school, but it
seemed possible that my account would be disbelieved and/or met with
chilly silence. I also feared censure, further discrediting, and reprisal.

The story of what actually happened is complex, dramatic, and somewhat unaccountable. The memo continues to circulate informally. It
reached the desk of every teacher and administrator represented by the
Canadian Association of University Teachers (CAUT).[1] It generated widespread media attention, public speaking invitations, political lobbying,

letters of support, and a very small amount of hate mail. Within Queen's and at several other academic institutions, anti-sexism initiatives continue to be launched in the wake of the memo at the departmental and administrative levels, perhaps nowhere more than in my own faculty. And the consciousness of individual women and our supporters has noticeably shifted. Women across disciplines and across hierarchies are breaking their silence, fashioning new alliances, and pursuing new and old strategies to translate all this activism into permanent gains towards achieving substantive equality.

All this progress has its costs, especially for the women most visible and publicly active in pursuing our equality. Simply acknowledging the daily and systematic damage done to us as women requires courage and risks despair. Claiming and speaking of past and present abuses is painful, exhausting, and, when disbelieved, debilitating. Observing the backlash in its many forms hurts. Confronting differences among newfound allies generates self-doubt and self-judgment that sometimes lead to a new and unnerving silencing and isolation. Consciousness raising is by definition a double-edged process. The last 18 months have been no exception for the hundreds of women swept up, not necessarily by choice, in this drama. The costs being paid are as immeasurable as the real gains achieved. Examining these costs and looking to each other's needs in addition to monitoring and directing institutional responses, in my view, must attract more of women's political energy.

This article is an impressionistic and selective attempt at exploring what I consider the most interesting insights and significant political implications of the process that started when I sat down to write the chronicle of my first year of teaching. It is decidedly not one woman's story, but it is a highly subjective account. Among other things, during what I now think of as "The Memo Year," I became a symbol — protected or excluded from certain encounters and events; feared, idolized, discredited, and mythologized in ways that denied me access to the full human texture of others' experiences of the memo and its impact. Still, some patterns emerged. They seem worth sharing.

I have framed this article in five sections. The first supplies a background and specific institutional history for some of the events mentioned in the memo. In the second, I have attempted to reconstruct why and how I wrote the memo, highlighting insights that I consider potentially instructive as a matter of feminist strategy and politics. The memo itself as originally circulated is reproduced in the third section.[2] Some of the institutional consequences — positive — that followed media attention to and wide circulation of the memo are summarized and analyzed in the fourth section. Less easy to describe but perhaps the political heart of what women and other systemically oppressed individuals can learn from breaking our silences are the immeasurable shifts in consciousness and climate traceable to the memo's circulation. I have tried to identify patterns and articulate implications I see in these shifts throughout this article. Finally, the last section offers a brief epilogue: how these events have affected me, my professional agenda, my political identity.

II. Background

Due to a stable teaching complement and student enrolment as well as financial cutbacks affecting all Ontario universities, my faculty had not been in a position to do any permanent hiring since 1981. Between 1974 and 1981, 12 continuing appointments were made; only one of these openings (in 1974) went to a woman. Between 1981 and 1985, a few individuals held one-year, non-renewable contracts as visitors or sabbatical replacements. In the year prior to my arrival, two contract teachers on one-year terms had been hired: one was a feminist.

The hiring freeze resulted in predictable frustrations. Perceived substantive gaps in course offerings could not be filled; the under-representation of young scholars (in what is an aging faculty) and of women[3] could not be remedied. Some of the faculty had to teach courses they disliked; student demands for additional course offerings or for different/new teachers in certain core courses had to be tabled.

I was hired in July 1985 to replace a senior faculty member who unexpectedly accepted a position elsewhere in the University. As a term contract appointee, I was free to apply for any permanent positions which subsequently came open, but according to university policy, my contract was non-renewable. Although the hiring process was expedited because of the suddenness and mid-summer timing of the vacancy, it was otherwise routine except that the students who sit on the hiring committee were away for the summer and did not participate in interviewing any of the candidates considered for the position.

In the fall of 1985, it appeared that the Faculty would have one or more permanent openings beginning in 1986-87. As a result, hiring policies and priorities received considerable attention. The hiring committee convened two informal meetings to receive input from student representatives and the faculty. At the first meeting any and all perceived gaps and priorities were canvassed and discussed. Largely because of my input, a second meeting to discuss whether, why, and how to increase the number of women faculty was convened. Before that meeting, a past Dean and I both circulated memos arguing why hiring women should be a priority. I also proposed ways of eliminating systemic barriers against hiring women.

The second meeting was reasonably well-attended and relatively low-keyed. A variety of views for and against factoring gender into hiring decisions and giving women applicants priority were expressed. No consensus was reached; no new policy was adopted; no motions were entertained; no further meetings were scheduled. Nonetheless, rumours circulated widely among students that a new policy had been recommended or adopted to the effect that no men need apply and/or only women who were also feminists would be hired. Efforts to correct students' misinformation failed. Students demanded an open meeting with the Dean to discuss/protest the non-existent "new" policy.[4] In my view the overflow crowd was ugly, hostile, and resistant to the truth. The majority of students present did not believe the Dean, implied and remained persuaded that he, the hiring committee or the Faculty as a whole was acting in bad faith and was determined to foist unqualified (women) faculty upon them, and a few students were starkly anti-woman and anti-feminist in their remarks. Subsequent to the meeting, some letters for and against hiring women made their way to the hiring committee and other lobbying was planned but never materialized.

Ironically, no permanent positions did become available, although a few potential candidates were interviewed. Early in the new year, I was offered a job in practice at the union labour law firm with which I had had an extraordinarily rich and challenging articling experience. I weighed a number of factors and accepted the offer. With the agreement of the firm, I decided to complete the second year of my teaching contract. It is simply inaccurate to interpret that decision, as many people have, as a decision to "quit" teaching, not least because my contract at Queen's was non-renewable. Nor was my decision evidence that I believe there is less employment discrimination or systemic and personal bias against women in practice than in teaching.[5]

My actual teaching load during my first year, consistent with law school practice regarding new teachers, was reduced. I taught only two courses: a full-year small section in Torts for first-year students[6] and an upper-year seminar in advanced labour law in second term. There is no formal record appraising my teaching in either course, because my course evaluations were lost/disappeared.[7]

III. The Process of Writing the Memo

I began to write what became the memo immediately after two encounters that occurred on a single afternoon during the spring exam period. Together they underlined the degree to which students and colleagues trivialized or accepted abusive attacks and discrediting rumour campaigns against me, my feminism, and the presence of feminism in the classroom. The readiness to believe any allegations against me, however silly or contradicted by known facts; the complacency about the damage done to me and other women; the failure or refusal to acknowledge gender bias in what I took to be undisguised expressions of misogyny, or, seeing it, to care, to intervene, to be accountable; and the rationalizations for male abuse finally shook me. I was angry, exasperated, and very confused. It seemed impossible to me that so many students and colleagues should be so blind and indifferent to institutional gender bias and so ready to interpret those expressions of anti-woman or anti-feminist hostility which they did register as *my* problem, either because I provoked it ("It is not anti-feminism, Sheila; it is that you raise feminist issues in the class and in faculty meetings. Hostility is natural") or because my "bias" led me to interpret innocent/ordinary incidents as offensive/abusive/silencing toward women.

I think every feminist has experienced the undermining tension between what she knows/feels/observes to be acts of misogyny and male domination, and the external wall of denial rejecting/dismissing/reinterpreting her experience. We know we are not imagining things; and we wonder if we are imagining things. We research and teach and write about how, why, and to what ends women and our experience are devalued, silenced, and invalidated; yet such intellectual tools provide imperfect immunity from the effects of systematic invalidation of our perceptions, experience, selves. Male dominance works, on us no less than other women. It was working fairly effectively on me.

I began writing as a personal act of survival. I decided to chronicle every sexist or anti-feminist incident I could remember from my first year of teaching in order to create a "text" which I could "objectively" study. Freed from the necessity of reacting to classroom and institutional politics in an immediate ad hoc fashion, I thought I could record and then slowly and privately reflect upon the "factual" evidence to decide for myself whether my perceptions individually and in aggregate were valid. I wrote to myself for myself, and had no thought of circulating what was, in effect, an internal dialogue.

That "factual" first draft ran about 14 pages. The sheer quantity and the patterns of abuse it contained actually shocked me. It convinced me that I was not imagining or exaggerating the extent and pervasiveness of gender bias within the institution. I thought it might also convince others.[8]

The very existence of this "documentary" catalogue led me to consider going public because I thought such a presentation of facts, many of which might not be known to individual colleagues, might jog my community out of its complacency and its denial that discrimination against women students and teachers was a problem.

While considering what to do with the document, I showed it to a handful of feminist legal scholars who encouraged me to circulate it more widely. A reader familiar with the events I chronicled stated that she did not think the gendered dimensions of some of the incidents described would be apparent to male readers. I was stunned, especially given the examples she identified. As a result, I redrafted the text to make it more accessible to my male colleagues.

In the second draft, I abandoned the strictly factual approach by adding an interpretive analysis after each incident; this articulated what I saw as its gendered, misogynistic, or anti-feminist content and significance. This draft was the hardest to write because it was so subjective. Circulating a catalogue of facts felt far safer than offering feminist analysis to colleagues, many of whom are either illiterate in or unreceptive to feminist theory and critiques and many of whom had already shown a proclivity for discounting my perceptions. My uneasiness was particularly pronounced wherever I attempted to convey the violent and/or sexual dimensions of individual incidents.

The recognition/recollection that I had experienced some of the events documented as forms of sexual violence was a crucial insight for me that helped account for the fear I and other women had about going public with my story. I had originally described one of the classroom uproars to a friend as a "gang bang," and had referred to another incident as an "assault." My growing apprehension about circulating the text began to have a focus: I identified with rape victims and battered women. I expected that I would not be believed, and feared the violence would escalate either in the form of being put on trial or in the form of character assassination.[9] I also feared another year of damage caused by internalizing the hostility and invalidating conduct of students and colleagues. Finally, I experienced the nameless and disproportionate dread by which consent to hegemony is maintained — the dread which tends to make dissent literally unthinkable; the belly dread that is traceable to cultural immersion in the taken-for-granted legitimacy of an oppressive status quo.[10] Understanding my fear was determinative in the decision to go public.

There was some altruism in the decision. Having decided to leave teaching when my contract expired, it seemed likely that other women would replace me sooner or later. Burying the document might result in their facing the same hostility and discrediting I had without the fact or significance of such sexism and anti-feminism having ever been institutionally confronted. That seemed comparable to failing to report sexual assault or harassment by a known abuser and leaving him undeterred from victimizing other women.

But there was also something quite self-centred in this moment of choice. The fear of reprisal and censure I felt about informing my colleagues of my story was simply another dimension of living as a female in a woman-subordinating culture. Allowing the fear to dictate silence seemed a personal betrayal of my own struggle back to self-respect. In different ways throughout the year I had been charged with provoking the expressions of hostility to my presence and my teaching. Keeping my chronicle private for fear of "provoking" a backlash would be like saying rape victims were "asking for" violation. Women are not responsible for male violence and invalidation; men are. Telling the truth about male violations is not, by definition, justification for attack. Men have a choice. If men chose to attack me for naming past abuses, let them be accountable for that choice. All that I was responsible for was fighting and confronting my own dread.

Not coincidentally, my use of the words "abuse," "assault," and "violence," my reference to the washroom pornography, and my written identification with sexual assault victims have provoked intense reactions in women readers. For some, their shared identification with such a characterization of workplace or classroom harassment is both liberating and devastating. Other women readers resist such characterization fiercely.[11] I have heard of several women offered copies of the memo who were *afraid* to read it, afraid of its potential to upset the fragile coping strategies women use to endure hostile environments, afraid of consciously recognizing what they would prefer not to see. Perhaps because women struggle so hard for intellectual and professional acceptance and credibility in male-dominant contexts, we find it shattering to acknowledge how much we are sexualized and how much of our intellectual/professional denigration carries sexual resonance. Masculine ego gratification in putting women — especially women with (some) power — down is sexual in a culture which eroticizes the subordination of women.[12] From the front of the classroom, the sexual titillation evidently enjoyed, and the sexual swagger openly exhibited, by the usual small gang of male students who compete with each other to undercut a woman teacher's authority appear identical to that of sidewalk street oglers who by word and gesture pornograph passing women for each others' masculine approval. Even when the language of male hostility is academic rather than obscene, classroom tension is not experienced as intellectual conflict alone: women feel it physically and sexually. We feel sick, numb, bruised, molested, undressed, uglified.

Undoing the damage done by a sustained campaign of discreditation and hostility from one's peers and students is not, therefore, merely a matter of mentally identifying the gender politics of the personal and professional attacks or refuting their premises. For this reason, the process of writing successive drafts of the memo was never a purely intellectual effort. Reliving all that abuse and invalidation while writing not only caused physical pain, it released tightly contained and buried anger, grief, and fear, and forced me to realize how clenched, numb, and mute I had become. Throughout the writing I had increasing physical energy and vibrancy, so much so by contrast with my spring persona that several people remarked on it. I have seen the same vitality in dozens of women who relive and recover their own experience through reading the memo; and the same self-vacating numbness in women weighed down by internalized misogyny. It seems obvious to me now that when women repress what we know and feel of male dominance, when we mouth what men want to hear and assimilate values we do not esteem, when we embody submission to direct or indirect intimidation or denigration, it is visible physically and it is felt in our bodies. When we do not, we shine with unmuted vitality so rare that those touched by it often distrust it as manipulation or "charisma" or seduction. It is none of those things. It is no more than a glimpse of what women might look like unshackled by systemic submission to male oppression.

Three significant changes made their way into the third draft of the memo. Whereas earlier drafts contained the account of only one abusive encounter with a male colleague, this draft focused more broadly on invalidating and discrediting behaviours routinely exhibited by the majority of male faculty whenever gender bias was addressed.

Once I began to write about my colleagues' anti-feminism, my apprehension about circulating the memo increased exponentially. As a result, I decided to introduce the section on my colleagues with a preface that articulated why I feared giving them the memo and writing critically of their conduct.

It is no revelation to feminists to remark that the power to name one's world carries with it some power of control over it. Naming my fears up front diminished a kind of amorphous dread about going public. I did not actually believe that articulating the range of negative responses I feared would preclude their occurrence, though I hoped readers whose reactions conformed to my apprehensions might think twice about the fairness or appropriateness of some of these reactions before encountering me. The struggle to name my fears simply supplied a concrete base from which I could address how I would react if and when particular reprisals began. A few days before the memo circulated, I met with three other women faculty members and we shared our individual and collective fears about the potential fallout. That discussion helped banish some of our personal nightmares and generated some practical and appealing proposals for coping with or building on the kinds of negative consequences we considered most probable.

The final addition to the third draft was the last long paragraph. It is the only section of the memo written exclusively for women readers and, partly for that reason, seemed risky in the extreme. It is intensely personal and made me feel completely naked to readers, a good number of whom already saw me as "Woman," as over-sensitive/emotional/unprofessional and given to exaggeration. I feared it might give unsympathetic male readers an excuse to dismiss the entire preceding text. I also think, in retrospect, that I feared women readers' reactions. In my view, most women struggling to survive in hostile environments often go dead in a variety of ways. Mostly, we make little compromises with our selves: we go silent, withhold our selves, and disengage in situations we care deeply about so that we trade self-respect for what we hope to secure by invisibility and male acceptance. I was certain that most women would recognize the despair of knowingly cooperating in our own deaths; and I feared they might hate me for reminding them, for signalling that we have a choice — constrained, costly, not always resurrecting — but a choice.

Prior to distributing the fourth and final draft of the memo, I circulated it in whole or in part to almost everyone referred to specifically in ways which might identify them.[13] I gave a copy to the unnamed colleague whose threatening behaviour I detailed at some length in the memo and invited him to put in writing any comments or perceived inaccuracies in my account so that I could make any necessary changes prior to distribution. I also indicated that if he wished to write his own version of the incident to be appended to the memo — with or without his name on it — I would distribute the appendix with the memo. He did write to me but he did not write his own version either for inclusion with the memo or later.

The personal process of writing chronicles like the memo has, I believe, much to recommend itself to all women. Excavating and reflecting on one's own experiences of misogyny can be a largely unmediated[14] confrontation with one's self — the self that internalized contempt for women, the self that answers male hostility with appeasement, the self that chooses to deny the pervasiveness of male domination for fear of being unable to function otherwise.

Women's equality cannot be secured if women continue to embody and personify all that male culture has projected on and into "woman." Nor can women be role models to anyone when we operate with self-contempt, self-effacement, or self-deceit. If we do male oppression's work for men, devaluing our selves, then men — with reason — disregard us all the more, and, to the extent we are tokens, views us as discountable proxies for other women. When we settle for scraps, why should the women who look to us as precedents imagine themselves qualified for more. Relative to most of the women watching us with hope and envy, we are privileged. We already have academic/professional training, hierarchical platforms from which to speak, (qualified) social status. If we sell our integrity in any form — our dignity; our right to freedom from physical, intellectual or emotional violation; our principles; our womanhood — in the search for external (male) acceptance or reward, at best we secure empty, fraudulent stature at all women's expense. Institutional acceptance on such terms ought to be unthinkable.

When you swallow poison, you have to purge it from your system or die. You cannot pretend that it is not there or imagine yourself immune or assume an antidote will materialize if you just hang on long enough. The unavoidable first step in resisting the male version of womanhood is to resist self-deceit by struggling to tell the truth to our selves. As if it matters to our selves to want self-respect, to have integrity. As if what we know, see, feel and believe should be worth knowing, seeing, feeling and believing personally, subjectively.

In face of the near totality of systemic male domination, claiming our personal integrity and the faith that it matters is, by definition, empowering. I have come to believe that embodied, voiced, lived out integrity is unmistakable in the moment of its expression and nearly unmediated by gender, race, class and other distorting filters. Its expression pierces one's own and others' defences, self-deceit and despair. However reinterpreted after the fact, in the still moment of her expression, a woman centred in her simple assertion of authentic self-respect occupies a space that cannot be penetrated, thingified, devalued or trivialized.[15] That space, even momentarily, causes internalized (self) hatred to falter, makes the habit of self-deceit more difficult, suggests that resigned acquiescence is no more than an option.

I am saying, of course, that our individual and collective histories must be voiced unapologetically, unmediated, and so often that they do not make the national news. When women break our silence, our voices resonate in other women's muted selves and something permanent shifts. New voices emerge. Many retreat in a panic to the old lies. A few do not. Those few, mobilized, touch other women. But this is to get ahead of the story.

IV. The Memo[16]

Now that my first year of teaching is over, I want to circulate an extensive addendum to my October memo ("Faculty Recruitment Policy: Women Faculty")[17] addressing, again, the impact of the gender imbalance within the law school on women students and faculty.

I have three aims in addressing this issue again. First, I hope to generate more individual and collective attention to gender bias here. Second, I hope that by chronicling some of my personal experiences as a woman teacher who was the object of fairly sustained anti-feminist abuse this year, what I wrote about last fall might become more concrete and accessible to those who do not perceive gender bias to be a problem we need to confront as a community. Finally, I hope we will stop interpreting individual incidents of sexism and anti-feminism as anomalies or as proxies for other institutional problems. I do not deny that we have other institutional problems or that these problems were often tangled into anti-woman or anti-feminist events. However, I have become exasperated and angered by the consistency with which gender has been so regularly factored out of our interpretations of these events, not least because I was so often the woman/feminist under attack.

There is not one woman who observed or heard about the incidents I will chronicle who did not immediately grasp the explicit gender bias they demonstrated.[18] But there are many men — students and faculty alike — who observed or heard about them who routinely dismissed, discounted, or (re)interpreted them as evidence of something else, anything else, but gender bias, let alone bias which is pervasive.

When I wrote that first memo, I was committed to teaching as my legal career. I have always wanted to teach. In particular I wanted to teach here. And I wanted to teach as a feminist. In my application to teach at Queen's, I explained at some length the way my feminism informs why, what, and how I want to teach. My October memo also conveys some of the value I personally attach to the difference women who identify as women can bring to what have been historically and remain disproportionately male-defined and male-centred models of legal discourse, thought, doctrine, process, professionalism, and education. My view was and is that as long as what is male-defined and male-centred about law remains unacknowledged, unexplored, and unexpressed, women's interests, experiences, and perspectives will be excluded, devalued, and subverted in the classroom and the profession, and in the larger society shaped by current law and legal institutions.

There are many strains of feminism. What they have in common are two very simple premises: within and by means of male-dominated social institutions in our culture, women are unequal to men; and such inequality is both unjust and changeable. Feminism is not simply an intellectual perspective embracing equality as an idea; it is a full-hearted commitment to pursue women's full, substantive equality and to oppose women's inequality. Or as a friend of mine has said, "Feminism springs from the impulse to self-respect in every woman." It is not something one puts aside when entering the classroom or one's professional life, especially in an institution focused on principles of justice.

As a teacher, my ambition has been as modest as it is radical: to help create a space in my classroom and in this institution where women's interests, experiences and views — including my own — can be voiced as legitimately, seriously, and safely as men's, and can be perceived and accepted as contributions which are relevant, valid, and indispensible to the study and practice of law. This has been my working model of a pedagogy of equality.

In September I had a lot of faith in the potential difference such a feminist commitment might bring to the classroom, to individual students' perceptions of law and of women, and to the faculty as a whole. Although I expected some hostility and opposition, I believed nonetheless that in academic work and life I would enjoy more freedom, support, and scope than in practice to express and develop my personal and professional interests. I thought that what I consider the male "tilt" of law was largely unreflective and was rarely grounded in intentional bias or overt anti-feminism. Each of these views has been deeply shaken.

Some of my experiences this year were very moving, energizing, rewarding, and cause for pride. But I was also the target of a lot of abuse, and I suffered the worst and most sustained alienation I have ever endured.

Although I am ambivalent about drawing conclusions from a single year on faculty, my experiences were similar to those of other feminist faculty I have consulted[19] and similar to those I lived through as a woman law student. My preliminary conclusion is that it is emotionally destructive and intellectually disabling for me — and I believe for most feminists — to try to exist on a law school faculty. Even though next year I expect I will have more support and credibility, I am not really comforted. My expectations would be much different and far grimmer were I teaching more overtly feminist material.

So. I want to outline some of the major events which have led me to these conclusions. It seems to me that if we confront what happened to me, we may begin to deal more effectively with why we have problems attracting women faculty, why feminists are under-represented among women applicants, and why women students as well as women teachers are so disadvantaged and damaged by the gender imbalance here. What few colleagues appreciate is that students as a group observed much more of the opposition to my presence, my values (real or imagined) and my academic freedom than anyone on the teaching staff. We should ask ourselves some hard questions about what they learned in the process.

V. The Classroom

Despite what some of you may have heard or inferred, there were actually only two explosive confrontations in my classrooms all year that turned on my feminism.

1. In October, shortly before our informal meeting on hiring policy, there was a mutiny in my Torts class staged by several men students who pre-arranged, in their words, "to take a run at Sheila." There were three triggers. They were angered by my use of gender neutral ("individuals," "person") and gender-inclusive ("women and men," "he or she") language in lieu of the generic male idiom ("men," "he"). They construed my linguistic usage to be "shoving my politics down students' throats." As well, I had

used two gender-loaded hypotheticals during the first six weeks of classes to refine the students' definitions of intentional torts. (We had also used hypotheticals based on age, disability, class, race, etc.). But the crucial catalyst was my introduction to some cases I wanted them to read on battery; specifically *Fillipowich*.[20]

Fillipowich stands for the propositions that fist-fights are a "weakness" to which "manly flesh" is heir; that so long as civilization exists, "men" will resolve disputes with their fists; and that the injuries suffered from punches are *de minimis*, and would cause "amused discussion in a pub but no litigation." I had asked students to prepare for class by considering whether the *ratio* applied to "men" or "people," and whether the trial outcome would or should have been any different if any of the parties had been a woman. When students arrived in class two days later, the male mutiny occurred.

The details of what happened in class are difficult to describe. About six men were deliberately disruptive, uncooperative, interruptive, and angry.[21] To my surprise, they endorsed the propositions outlined above and belligerently tried to prevent students who disagreed with their position from speaking, by a combination of insult, interruption, hostile gestures, and increasingly voluble but untenable argument. When I tried to legitimize the contributions of other students, they were equally abusive to me. Their bottom line, albeit only indirectly conveyed, was: we do not want to talk about gender; and we will not; and we will not let anyone else talk either. When their muscle-flexing failed to force me to move onto another case, one mutineer began shouting at me, insisting that the questions I had asked were irrelevant and a waste of time. He demanded that we move to another case.

Afterwards, I asked a senior male colleague how he taught the case and what happened. He spent three classes on the case during which the obvious gender issue was raised but there was no uproar. Rather than endorsing the *Fillipowich dicta*, most of his men students considered the *dicta* insulting of men. Although we undoubtedly handled the case differently, I think it's safe to say that I did not raise gender inappropriately. I believe the difference between the two classes' reactions can be explained largely by male students' greater tolerance toward discussions of gender bias in law when a man who is not labelled a feminist introduces the topic.

After the mutiny I saw a parade of individual students. Two feminists disclosed the same distress. Both had felt mine was the only class in which they could raise feminist issues or in which women's perspectives were addressed. (I know other colleagues have raised gender issues since; maybe they had already. This was not how these two students felt.) Both women felt attacked, shocked, and silenced by the *Fillipowich* class. They no longer felt it safe to speak, and they feared that even if they did raise feminist concerns and I validated their viewpoint, I would be targeted for more male student abuse. The more distressed of the two wanted to quit law school.

A couple of other women in the class appeared and presented a mixed message. On the one hand, they wanted me to know they supported my raising of gender issues and were interested in discussing them; on the other hand, they urged me not to do it again because they were afraid of what might happen (to me or to them was not clear).

I saw two students who were not in my class, but who had heard about the uproar. Both complained that gender was never raised in their Torts classes or in other classes, even when they considered gender a relevant issue. The woman student wanted advice on how to raise gender issues without being mocked or censured. We discussed some strategies. She tried one in her next class and was trivialized. The male student, rather than trying to find ways to raise topics he felt were not being addressed, wanted to audit my class. I refused.

The most shocking encounter was the visit of a male student in my class who claimed to be the delegate of the men who had decided to "take a run at" me. Although their mutiny had failed to control class discussion, he told me not only how they wanted material taught and discussed in future, but he warned me also that if I did not want to be attacked again, I had better not raise gender again.

Frankly I cannot imagine any male professor being so brazenly attacked in class, being told how to teach law, or being threatened by first year students particularly so early in term when students are usually so unsure of themselves. The more usual pattern is for students to complain among themselves and/or to another teacher, or even to the Dean, but not to criticize (and threaten) their evaluators directly, for fear of personal or academic reprisal. Hierarchy works that way.

In my case, hierarchy did not operate typically for several reasons. First, I am junior and it is safer to attack me than, say, a senior male colleague. Second, I consciously conduct my classes in a (relatively) non-hierarchical and non-authoritarian way, which makes it safer, I believe, for students to challenge me. They knew enough about my rejection of abuse of authority to trust I would probably not punish them. Third, I am a woman. These men students believed they commanded sufficient power and legitimacy — albeit as a gang — to force me to do what they wanted through in-class and extra-class coercion. In a conflict between one woman teacher and six men, they expected direct threats would silence me. Finally, I am a feminist. In taking a run at me for addressing gender bias, these men felt confident they were in the right. They assumed unquestioningly that because the most vocal males in the class did not wish to discuss gender and because none of their other (male) teachers addressed gender, I or women students should not raise the topic. My informant made it quite clear that he and his allies believed that when women did raise the topic, we were raising "personal" or "political" issues irrelevant to "law." This encounter and its themes constitute classic instances of a male viewpoint being seen quite unreflectively as the only viewpoint, which viewpoint men consider self-evidently valid, legal and neutral. It is also a rather stark example of how women's minority voice can be intimidated, silenced, and invalidated.

There was never another incident of this type in my Torts class, nor was I threatened again. In fact, we studied other gender-loaded cases without disruption, and sometimes men raised the issue. A few students adopted gender-neutral language; three students opted to write papers on the patriarchal dimensions of legal education (one was male); and the class chose to work on pornography for Integrated Forum,[22] devoting a substantial portion of its time to feminist analysis.

However, the impact of that single class lingered. I was never unmindful of it in preparing for class or in mediating class discussion. Nor, I believe, were the women students in my class ever again unconscious of the potential costs of raising gender on their own or of expressing views contrary to those taken by the men who had organized the mutiny.

As well, the incident became legendary. That single class in October was (ab)used for the remainder of the year by upper-year students to fuel opposition to my presence and to the hiring of more women. They cited my Torts class to illustrate their claim to at least one colleague and to the Principal of Queen's that our current hiring policies are undermining academic excellence in the law school. Their position was/is that I am neither qualified nor competent to teach. They continued to cite a (non-existent) mass discontent in my Torts class as late as the end of March as evidence of my unsuitability. I am informed that they did so without my students' knowledge. I have a lot of trouble with the logic that because six male students staged an anti-feminist mutiny, I am unqualified to teach.

2. The second explosion occurred in my Labour seminar quite unexpectedly. I had begun the class by expressing concern that some students rarely participated in class discussions, and invited suggestions on what we could do to make it easier for everyone to speak. We agreed that each speaker would select the next speaker instead of having me recognize hands. We also agreed people should not interrupt each other or speak until their hands had been recognized by the previous speaker.

Mid-way through the discussion, a woman who rarely spoke raised her hand and was recognized. She explained that she had trouble entering the discussion in this class as in its predecessors because she found the discourse and its underlying assumptions too adversarial, too uncritical of the value of conflict, too quick to view power as the efficacy of unions. Another quiet woman raised her hand and was recognized. She concurred, but went further. She labelled what she found exclusionary the "maleness" of both the discourse and our working model of labour law and labour relations.

Before the second woman finished, a left-wing male interrupted her and started shouting, telling her she was "wrong" and insisting that power struggle is essential to liberation, including women's. She responded by saying they simply disagreed. Everyone then turned to me to see what I would do. I said nothing. A second man changed the subject and embarked on a fairly elaborate speech on how management could use first contract legislation to defeat unions. His emphasis was on power and conflict underlined by extremely combative language ("kick the hell out of the union," etc.). A third man followed and expressed both confusion and exasperation, asking if we could get back to discussing "law," because we were getting off track.

At that point, I entered the discussion and asked the class to reflect on what had just happened. Two usually silent women had spoken and explained why they had trouble participating. One was interrupted and called "wrong;" then the subject was changed; then their contribution was characterized as non-law. I suggested their contributions introduced an alternative model of law and labour relations which we might try to explore. Again there was an uproar. I was shouted down by the left-wing male and denounced as a "bourgeois feminist." The original woman speaker suggested we might try to discuss contract bargaining in terms of codetermination and human relations. She was called a collaborator and dismissed as proposing a cooptive model. No one pursued her suggestion. I proposed we draw up two models for a first contract: one under the working model premised on conflict, power, inequality, and private property; the other premised on codetermination, communal interests, and equality.

About five male students put down their pens, pulled back their chairs, and glared at me, refusing to participate. No one invited the two women who had advanced an alternative model to articulate what their vision might include. They became silent. A few men ventured some possibilities, but were met with open anger from other men who interrupted, laughed, or talked over them, insisting that conflict is unavoidable in law as in life, and that because alternatives are legally unimaginable, we should not talk of alternatives. For the last 15 minutes of class, I was the only woman who spoke at all. So noisy did the intra-male arguments become that a teacher from the adjacent classroom came by to ask us to be quiet.

To be fair, there were other heated arguments in class based on union vs. management perspectives. They were different in three respects. First, unlike the ideological labour divide, the gender explosion was never explored again. Some students did begin to introduce the concept of the "conflict model" into discussions and to suggest possible weaknesses with it. They were all men. And they did it as an aside. The five women students avoided the topic except in written work for my eyes only. Second, there was a disturbing lingering effect. Two women students who had been quiet all term (not the two who had criticized the conflict model) came to me to say they were too intimidated to speak in class, especially after the gender explosion. One asked if she could substitute an extra paper for that portion of her grade based on class participation. Finally, students knew I was on the union side of the labour divide and the feminist side of the gender divide. Yet, although pro-management students directly asked me whether my pro-union background would result in their being penalized for seminar or written work advancing pro-management views, no one asked me whether s/he would be penalized for anti-feminist views. As I understand this, gender politics, unlike labour politics, were seen to have no academic relevance even though both politics had been part of classroom discussion.

As with the Torts uproar, I have trouble imagining a similar scene in a male colleague's class. My sense is that the two women who challenged the "maleness" of classroom discussion were less likely to have done so in those terms without a feminist at the front of the class. I am fairly certain a male colleague would not have pursued their vision as seriously as I did or been denounced as a "bourgeois feminist" for doing so. Finally, when a professor backs a topic as a legitimate line of enquiry — especially if s/he is known to have some expertise in that field — students do not often explode and furiously argue that the topic is legally impermissible.

3. There were many other occasions when my perspective (real or imagined) caused tension and/or hostility.

- I was told in the fall that one of my Torts students had complained to a woman friend that he objected to my "feminist" method, which he defined as my showing openly that I *cared* about what I was teaching and about the outcome of cases.
- Two of my Torts students asked a colleague whether he did not think my use of gender-neutral language was silly/ inappropriate. I am relieved my colleague both endorsed my practice and indicated he is revising a textbook to eliminate the generic male idiom. I am distressed that gender-*neutral* usage is so rare that students consider it biased or unorthodox. If, in fact, I am not the only first-year teacher using neutral or inclusive language, then the question becomes: why is it problematic when a woman uses it but not when a man does? A colleague recently argued that gender-neutral language can be "militant" depending on the "context." Meaning what?
- In my first Labour seminar we had a go-around to introduce ourselves. I did so by outlining my labour-related background. Immediately a male law student challenged, "Is that all?" Initially perplexed, I realized he

was referring to my "politics." I added that I am a feminist and that M.I.R. students[23] would be unaware that I had been the centre of some controversy in the fall for proposing we take active measures to hire more women. I asked him if that covered his concern. He smiled and said yes. (It has since occurred to me that his question might really have been about what many students then deemed the "inadequacy" of my academic credentials.)

- At the end of term, I received a cheeky note from a student attached to his final paper explaining mockingly why he preferred to use the male pronoun in his essay. (I had never suggested otherwise to anyone.)
- In May, a feminist student who had been in my Torts class and who had successfully balloted for my Collective Agreement course next fall was told she had made a "mistake" because I taught my students "feminist Torts" and I am unqualified to teach. My critic is a woman. She also considered my former student's balloting successfully for two other courses taught by women "mistakes" because we are variously unqualified. When asked whether she knew what these three teachers' credentials were, she replied in the negative.

    4. I was also visited by a number of women students who reported sexist or anti-feminist incidents in their classes and in the school.

- I was told a woman student was whistled at by a male professor when she walked into class one day.
- The Women and the Law notice board was trashed at least twice with graffiti equating feminism with lesbianism. This also occurred here when I was a student; and it occurred at U of T as well.
- I was visited in the fall by two senior students who wanted advice about how to make the Women and the Law caucus less ostracized. Their fear? Everyone thought they were man-hating lesbians.
- I had at least two dozen visits from women students who found remarks (including dirty jokes) made in class by their professors to be sexist and offensive and/or who had been trivialized for raising gender issues. A total of nine colleagues were involved.
- Several students have reported they find the handling of sexual assault law in class and in practice and in final exams insensitive.
- I was told of more than one occasion when feminist students who sit together were addressed by their professors as a lump. These professors would point to the group and ask what they thought, identifying them interchangeably as a politics rather than as individuals.

I heard of these incidents on a regular basis, which adds a dimension, I think, to the content of students' need for "role models." More than half of these women were not in my classes. They came to me quite simply because I am a woman and a feminist and would understand their distress.

Almost invariably, the exchange took the form of questions: did I think what had happened was sexist/offensive/anti-feminist? did I think the point she had raised which was trivialized was invalid? did I think she was unreasonable to be offended and upset? do I think it is better to challenge sexist remarks in class or to let them pass? Or the big question: do I think this institution and/or this profession is so systemically biased against women that she will always be the victim of gender bias?

What I find so troubling about these encounters, aside from their frequency and the amount of gender bias they disclose, is how desperate these students are for validation. It is bad enough women should so often witness or be the butt of sexism here. It is far worse they should be so undermined by student and professorial obliviousness to its offensiveness that they feel "unreasonable" for being upset. Often these encounters begin with the student reporting what awful things are being said about me as a way of leading into what awful thing just happened to her. Meaning: if it happened to me, then maybe I'll believe it is not her fault and she is not imagining things. It is unpardonable that women should be so fearful of having their struggle for respect discounted, so grateful simply for being listened to seriously and believed.

It has been painful to watch the acclimatization of these students. Although the overt sexism, anti-feminism, and homophobia they reported shocked them, they were initially galvanized by it. They trusted that by naming and challenging prejudice, they could enlighten their peers and teachers, mobilize support for egalitarian change, and disarm their critics. They began boldly and full of optimism. From visit to visit they changed. One was labelled a lesbian, marginalized, shunned, and discredited. At least three were so trivialized or silenced by their teachers (by feminist-baiting jokes, by having their questions left unanswered and dropped as if they had never spoken, by having their hands ignored, by having the questions they would likely raise pre-empted by professorial direction that there would be no time in class to discuss the "policy implications" of a sexist rule) that they stopped challenging remarks or reasoning which they found sexist. Two began to skip classes. The most energetic reformist became seriously depressed. Though she continued to dissent, her voice was muted: she stopped talking in class and occasionally spoke to her teachers in private about remarks she had found offensive, but she did so jokingly and appeasingly. Without exception, students who initially consulted with me about positive strategies to promote equality now consult me about survival strategies for enduring law school. I know of three publicly feminist students who are currently deliberating about whether to quit law school.

Because my presence this year took on a symbolic dimension for both my detractors and my supporters, my decision to leave teaching has also become symbolic. Pro-feminist and other non-mainstream students feel I have let them down. They also feel my departure signifies that there is no room for non-mainstream people or expression within this institution.

VI. The Hiring Issue

Contrary to general perception, the mass student protest meeting triggered by false rumours of our "change" in hiring policy was not a one-shot explosion. It festered for months.

Those who were there will have observed (or should have) that not one student among the 180 present had the courage to endorse without qualifying backsteps that we should hire more women. No one at all suggested that we hire more feminists. In fact, six members of the Women and the Law Caucus had met the night before to prepare what they wanted to say in favour of hiring women, especially feminists. They were all too intimidated to speak at the meeting, and later they punished themselves for their silence.

At least one student at the protest meeting raised what I took to be the underbelly issue. He was the first to make a statement rather than to question the Dean. He stated that he opposed the "new" policy because it meant by definition lowering our academic standards. Active measures to recruit more women, he said, would result in hiring less qualified teachers. His equation of women with incompetence was so bald that several students hissed.

Another student demanded that the Dean guarantee students would have meaningful influence in all future hiring decisions. When the Dean explained the existing mechanism for student input, another student challenged him and asked if it were not true that at least one recent appointment had been made without any students present. I took that as a veiled criticism of my appointment. I also inferred that some students believed that if they had been present last summer, I would not have been hired.

Whether or not that was the import of the question, students did believe I should not have been hired. A few weeks after the mob meeting, the student president visited my office ostensibly to get permission to circulate my October memo beyond the students who sit on Faculty Board. In the course of our exchange, he volunteered that "as I knew" much of the student protest was "personal": they believed I was/am unqualified and incompetent. Some of these students also believed I would not have been hired had students been on campus during the interviewing process, and a few believed they had been deliberately excluded. (I have just heard a variant of this, propagated by a non-right-wing woman. She thinks the hiring committee snuck me into the faculty in bad faith by doing an end-run around "normal" hiring standards.)

I asked him whether any of these students were taught by me, whether they had seen my credentials, whether they knew who else had been interviewed or what the other candidates' credentials were. He answered no to all these questions. (The woman referred to above also has no knowledge of my credentials although she asserted I have only one degree. I have three.)

The conspiracy theory turns on three things. A feminist on a one-year contract was my "predecessor" (the other contract appointments of the last two years do not count because, as the student President told me, they were not feminists); a senior feminist ("Z") sits on the hiring committee; and the Dean lives with "Z." Q.E.D.

I also discussed the allegedly "new" hiring policy with the student president. I asked him if he was aware that there is no new policy, and if he was aware we made no decision to hire more women, to alter our hiring criteria or to hire only women or only feminists. Yes, he said, he knew, but it did not matter because the hiring process was "stacked." I asked him if he was aware that at the informal meeting addressing what, if anything, to do about hiring women, no one agreed with what I had written in my October memo except "Z," and many people spoke against parts of it. Yes, but the hiring process was stacked.

When he indicated students wanted my memo in order to prepare submissions to the hiring committee to oppose my proposals, I asked if I'd be circulated a copy. He thought not. I invited him to arrange a meeting with any students who wanted to question me about my memo or simply to pursue the hiring issue more openly. He declined, saying if I showed up it would be a "slug-out." He suggested some of the opposition to my presence might be diminished if I made my credentials available to students. I declined, arguing I would not defend myself against nameless attackers or unsubstantiated charges unless they made their allegations public, and I would not circulate my credentials unless all new faculty — men as well as women, feminists as well as non-feminists — were required to do so to justify their presence to students.

That was in late November. In February a male student came to me in some distress to ask how I could be so friendly to students knowing they were discrediting my credentials and competence openly. I told him such attacks had been a phenomenon of the late fall only, tied to the hiring issue, and had not resurfaced. He contradicted me, indicating he had heard this line of talk often in the basement and the General Office area in second term. I have since heard this from others of all political stripes, so I take it the audience was not select.

His real source of distress was that I had shown up as pornography on the men students' bathroom walls. I actually surveyed the washroom walls one night. There are hundreds of entries (there are none in the women's), many of them law-related witticisms or standard excremental humour. What is significant to me is that although about 10 male professors are described in insulting ways, they are denigrated for their teaching or their lack of intelligence. Conversely, three women professors are insulted, but only in sexual terms. We are named and cartooned naked, portrayed as sexually repugnant; or we are the object of speculation about our sexual activities or orientation. Two men receive similar treatment: a staff member considered homosexual and the Dean. But the Dean is only sexualized where "Z" also appears sexualized.

Nor was the pornographic objectifying of women faculty buried in the context of dozens of other sexual entries about women. Aside from the three women professors, only three other women appear in perhaps 400-600 entries. A woman staff member was the object of a non-sexual joke. A woman (first name only) is the object of several heterosexual fantasies. And a woman student (full name stated) who is openly feminist is described as a castrator who collects penises. I show up as Z's wife and as a lesbian: "Sheila McIntyre sucks clits and tits." You try walking into a classroom feeling human when you know 60% of the student population may have read such entries, may find them amusing or the ultimate insult, and the words stay on the walls. I find it curious that when I am publicly denigrated for my academic incompetence, that does not show up once on the bathroom walls even though male colleagues' deemed incompetence does. But when the attack is for male eyes only, I am pornography.

In early May, I was again visited by the outgoing student president. He expressed surprise that I was leaving teaching. I expressed surprise he might have thought it had been a pleasant year for me. He laughed and assured me my problems are over because I have "proved" myself, and I'll like my course evaluations. (I had asked him to get me the evaluation forms and distributed them in my Torts and Labour classes. I haven't seen them yet, but as he was in the Labour seminar and collected the evaluations, he probably has seen their contents.)[24]

We had a long — and quite bizarre — conversation about the hiring issue. I was quite candid about what I had found so offensive about the student rumour campaign against me, and he did not find fault with my version. He conceded that my academic freedom had been undermined — it was my feminism that had generated and/or justified such hostility in his view; that is why students did not attack the other new women teachers. He agreed I had been condemned by rumours known to be unsubstantiated; that I had been deprived of a right to any public hearing, to know my accusers, and to any right of reply. (My fault in his view: I should have submitted my credentials to these nameless detractors for their approval.) He admitted that the students who continued to discredit my credentials had not been in my classes. He volunteered that one of the main mischiefmakers was a grad student who wanted my job. And he predicted there will be no such unrest in future once there is a new Dean who, among other things, is not living with a faculty feminist. When I remarked that I had found the rumour campaign both cowardly and appalling given the degree of bad faith, dishonesty, and injustice involved, his parting shot was a cheery: "Well, no real harm was done."

When I spoke to a colleague about this encounter, I learned he had had a visit in late March from four graduating students (all male) who aired a number of their concerns about the "decline" in academic standards in the Faculty. Though none of them had been my students, they cited my lack of credentials/competence as an illustration of the decline. Their reference point was my Torts class. They indicated they had gone to the Principal of Queen's with their complaints.

VII. My Colleagues

I do not feel optimistic that the preceding pages will be read tolerantly — meaning with an open mind and giving me any benefit of any doubt. It has been that kind of year. More to the point, whenever I have discussed these incidents, my listeners have reacted in one or more of the following ways. They feel accused, so they become defensive and unable to listen; they remember or interpret isolated details differently, and so discount the pattern of the totality and/or they recall a single analogous event attacking another colleague (which may not be analogous at all), and so discount the pattern of the totality; and/or they become hostile because they do not want to believe this occurred so they refuse to believe it, and blame me for reporting what happened and/or for not reporting it earlier. (Sort of like rape evidence rules: a recent complaint is more credible than a delayed one; and a victim's testimony is inherently suspect, possibly vindictive, and not probative where it conflicts with the assailant's or the adjudicator's interpretation.)

My response is this. Most of you were aware of some of these events, but not of all of them; and I think you should know all that I know. Some of you know of events I was not told about, and my pieces may help reveal the pattern. The lived impacted of the pattern which is both anti-woman and antifeminist had enormous consequences for me and for students. I believe those consequences matter enough that we should all be pushed to confront a difficult and painful reality within this institution.

One painful reality is that feminism simply defined is a commitment to equality. Not to man-hating, not to women's superiority. Just to equality. And feminism was a bad word this year, an illegitimate value system, an invitation to or justification for attack.

Another painful reality is that a number of my colleagues have shown an easy complacency in believing and even repeating student disparagement of my qualifications and competence without inquiring whether my detractors had ever been in my classrooms, not to mention what might lie behind the rumour campaign. This Faculty hired me having screened and interviewed several other candidates according to existing hiring procedures. Some of you taught me. None of you sat in my classes. You should have, at least, questioned what was going on in defence of your own hiring decision. For the record, I am a good teacher.

So another painful reality is that I am afraid to circulate this memo. A colleague recently told me that the problem with feminists, including me, is that we are too "defensive" and we should just "do it." My reaction is that whenever I have done "it" — meaning take a feminist position or report the anti-feminist sequelae — I have paid dearly. Without exception. So "defensive," aside from carrying a blame-the-victim load, does not quite capture my learned reaction. Realistically apprehensive gets it better.

The most painful reality is that I am particularly afraid to write this section on my colleagues. My sense is that although the chronicle of student anti-feminism may not be believed or reflected upon seriously, what I write about colleagues is simply impermissible, so will be treated like a declaration of war, justifying direct reprisal. One friend expects that the mildest response will be insulting dismissal: "she just could not take it; she's too sensitive." Most women I have consulted expect far worse. The expectation is that to document factual events will be seen to violate collegiality standards and to provoke non-collegial personal attack. That the events documented report violations of collegiality will get lost.

Here's my justification. 1) These events did happen. They are true. 2) Women in general tend not to report male violence or harassment for fear of making things worse (viz. the under-reporting of rape, domestic violence, and sexual harassment). Our fear of reprisal leads us to prefer to cut our losses. Our fearful silence leaves the fact and extent of our abuse invisible and obviates recognizing that a problem exists, which in turn precludes institutional redress.

1. Shortly after I circulated my October memo, I was both publicly and privately attacked by a male colleague. He sneered at me in a faculty-wide memo, dressed me down publicly in the halls, and then rebuked, insulted, and threatened me in my office for about 45 minutes. Before the office bar-

rage, another colleague forewarned me that the confrontation was about to take place, by which I deduce I was also being attacked behind my back.

The office encounter was devastating. He said, "look, lady, you're coming on too strong around here," and then cited my voicing feminist concerns as my offence. He called me "non-collegial" for having expressed views which differed from his on a committee and for my hiring memo. I was faulted for not being sufficiently "deferential" as a junior faculty member. (Imagine a White male saying that to a Black colleague.) And I was warned explicitly that as a junior teacher on a short contract, I had better alter my conduct (i.e., stop advancing women's rights issues) if I hoped to be rehired. I may misremember, but I think he also stated explicitly (he certainly implied) he could take steps to jeopardize my being rehired.

What began as a recriminatory lecture became uglier when I neither accepted his criticism and denigration of my motives nor undertook to be silent if we ever disagree in future or if an institutional issue raises feminist concerns.

After attacking my conduct and character, he assailed my memo on hiring. He objected to my elaboration of what I believe it means to be a role model. His view? He "and those he'd talked to" did not believe I see as many students as I claimed on women-centred or on counselling issues (I am a liar); even if I do this much student advising, it is "unprofessional" and will harm students because "nurturing" them will prevent them from developing the independence and self-sufficiency they need to be lawyers; and even if I disagree with that view, if I continue to make myself available to students, I will never be rehired because I will fail to do enough research and writing to be competitive.

Finally, although he'd begun by warning me that continuing to speak as a feminist would subvert the likelihood of my being rehired, he also claimed that he "and others he'd talked to" agreed my memo and its proposal that we consider expanding our criteria of merit to embrace women's difference was a self-serving tactic to make the faculty alter its hiring standards in order to get myself rehired.

When I did not concur with his critique, he labelled my conduct "tough." I asked what "toughness" had to do with the fact that we disagree on many things. He became furious and retorted, "Look, lady, if you keep taking that attitude" the risk to your teaching career is "your problem." He then stormed out of my office and slammed my door. He later returned and quasi-apologized, and we agreed to disagree.

There are three things that continue to outrage me about this attack. The first is that a few colleagues heard about it and dismissed it because it has happened before. Basically their attitude was, "Oh, that is just 'X.' He usually attacks junior faculty at least once and he usually does it in private, so nothing can be done. It is nothing personal."

My view is that this should have been stopped long ago, because if it's happened to other new or junior faculty and if that is common knowledge, it is not private. Perhaps nothing can ensure it stops, but at least we could name this pattern of conduct for what it is — bullying, rank-pulling, cowardly abuse of hierarchy, and intimidation — and take an institutional and public stand that such conduct is unacceptable. I think it is inadequate to re-assure his victims privately that they are not alone, and to choose to mop up the damage after the fact rather than to try to prevent its recurrence. My guess is we all have remained silent because we are all somewhat intimidat-ed and we fear an ugly encounter will follow if we censure such conduct. This means we are complicit in its continuation, allowing each new teacher to suffer abuse alone as a kind of inevitable though regrettable rite of pas-sage.

Second, I am angry because gender gets factored out of the attack I expe-rienced. My being junior is relevant to some of his rage at my disagreeing with him in public forums and my refusal to cave to his threats. That is the bullying dimension common to the attack on me and on prior rookies.

What is not common is the particular content and tone of the abuse. My "coming on too strong," my "toughness," and my "non-collegiality" were all directly charged to particular feminist positions I had taken on, e.g., in-viting more women speakers and on hiring more women. My "unprofes-sionality" lay in being responsive to women-centred student concerns in a womanish way. Twice in the barrage his riposte was, "Look, lady. . . ." He used his wife's opinion to corroborate one of his attacks on my motives, and cited women students he had consulted as authority for denouncing other aspects of my conduct. My sin was twofold: being a *junior woman* who had not been sufficiently deferential to a *senior man*.

Finally, I am angry still because I am frightened of him. I consider his verbal assault to have been unwarranted, irrational, and quite violent. When I thought back over the abusive incidents which have shaped my ex-perience this year, this one stands out most vividly and unforgettably. Yet I have debated for at least a month about whether to include it because I feel so certain that to report these facts will trigger another personal attack. Maybe in public, probably not. Maybe to my face, maybe behind my back. It outrages me that to report male violence here, as elsewhere in society, will leave me as victim of that violence vulnerable to retaliation. And it worries me that publicizing male violence will be seen to be an act of violence on my part. The polite thing to do, the collegial thing to do, the safe thing to do, is suffer abuse privately rather than to urge recognition of its existence.

One more thing. I would have welcomed face to face dialogue with col-leagues who disagree with my October memo. My recollection is that only three colleagues did seek me out for such conversations. But there is a difference between dialogue and diatribe, mutual exchange of views with both sides listening to the other, and one-sided imposition of a viewpoint punctuated by threats, insults, and allegations of *mala fides*. On any view, this encounter crossed the line between a difference of ideas and ugly personal attack.

2. No other colleague has been intentionally abusive to me, and no other colleague frightens me like this. But I would not say my views are generally respected or supported. Tensions have been relatively civilized: more than a few jovial put-downs; a certain "there-she-goes-again" attitude if I raise gender in informal or formal faculty exchanges; a few occasions of barely suppressed anger when male colleagues become defensive for being reminded, however indirectly, of the unconscious maleness of their stances; several occasions when my views have been grossly mis-stated (invariably to my disadvantage) and those mis-statements offered as justifications for anti-feminist fall-out; a repeated pattern of being *told* by male colleagues how I should react to abusive incidents rather than being *asked* how I did react, how I interpret them or why I interpret them as I do; and an almost total refusal to take reports of sexism and anti-feminism within this institution seriously as a matter of significance to us all.

As I understand the inattention to women's inequality here, one causal factor is that "Z" and I tend to be the only voices identifying or raising questions about such inequality. Because we are women and feminists, we are both seen to be "biased" rather than, say, qualified, and our views are discredited. Because male colleagues so rarely recognize gender bias and so rarely raise women's issues, "Z" and I are seen to be obsessed and, hence, prone to misinterpret "neutral" events as problematic for woman. That we may see what we do and see it differently from men precisely because we are women and because we carry the burden of representing women's interests on faculty seems to be discounted. That our perspective so rarely generates interest in exploring the possibility that gender might account for the disjunction between our observations, experiences and analysis and those of male colleagues suggests to me that unconscious gender bias is operating. Paradigmatically, our views (women's views) are considered biased while men's are considered neutral; our views are discredited and the "neutral" view is authoritative.

3. My experiences have been repeatedly reinterpreted for me by male colleagues who fail to see or do not want to see gender bias here. At best, if I relate an experience of overt anti-feminism which a colleague witnessed or heard about, he will ultimately admit that it never occurred to him but, yes, he guesses that might have to do with gender. Far more often, another interpretation prevails: that's not sexism or anti-feminism, that is just students' typical resistance to professors with a theoretical approach; or that is just the

discrimination (gender-neutral) experienced by all junior faculty; or that is just first year teaching; or that is just the proxy for students' discontent that we did not hire someone to buttress our offerings in X area; or that is just another example of the swing to the Right in this generation of students. My position is rarely that these other causal factors are not operating at all; it is that gender is operating too. But I am routinely misheard to say that gender alone explains the particular incident. And, too often, in a fairly patronizing way I am discounted because I am too new here to appreciate that the other gender-neutral factors provide full explanation for what's going on. The question consistently begged is: why do I see gender as a factor where non-feminists do not; and why do non-feminists deny gender is at least a factor when I perceive that it is? Put another way, why do male and female interpretations so differ?

There is a lot of student discontent and there are many unpleasant moments in and outside the classroom which we all find unnerving or disheartening. No teacher is universally esteemed by students, and no teacher, especially a new teacher, is entitled to automatic respect. But my experience, I think, was out of the ordinary.

I was not given a chance to earn respect, especially by people who were not my students. I was assumed to be incompetent, credentials unseen, actual student testimony to the contrary. And those who latched onto the incompetency allegation did so only after the issue of hiring more women was raised, and only after my October memo was circulated. One episode in a year-long Torts class was made to stand for the whole, and that episode focused on gender.

The mob gathering, to a large degree, was organized by students who, I believe, deliberately miscommunicated what they heard at the informal meeting about hiring more women. At least one student who had attended the informal meeting tried to correct the false rumours. No one wanted to listen to him. After the mass protest meeting, the student opponents of hiring more women did not care that their facts were wrong, and did not have the courage to make their allegations institutionally public. For them it was self-evident that to hire a women means to lower our academic standards of excellence — especially if the woman in question is a feminist, especially if a feminist sits on the hiring committee, especially if the Dean lives with that feminist. That I had so recently been a student here was certainly a factor in the rumour-mongering. But hardly the whole story; 180 students did not mount their protest because we were thinking of hiring other young faculty.

I was never real, never a person in all this. I was "Woman." I was "Feminist." And I was discredited *per se*. I was misquoted in preposterous ways quite routinely and no one either came to me to question or challenge these preposterous views or to double check the accuracy of the hearsay. "Feminism" was deemed "radical" and the attribution of outlandish and discreditable views to a radical didn't breed scepticism or suspicions of bad faith. I believe that part of what made me so easy a target was precisely that I was so "thingified." Being abusive is easier when you don't see your victim as a person.

I was thingified by colleagues as well as students, in face to face encounters as well as beyond my presence. Most commonly I was told about myself, presented with someone else's authoritative version of me as if I were a character in a story, as if we were discussing some third person who was not present in the room. Not infrequently, I was casually presented with an insulting version of myself in a matter-of-fact fashion by a speaker who was clearly not only unaware of being hurtful but who did not expect me to *feel* insulted. As if a "feminist" is a perspective, and so without feelings. Typically the insults caricature me as a fist-shaking, strident militant or propagate the view that I am an incompetent teacher. A classic example was a colleague waiting until the summer to tell me — in the presence of three colleagues including the Dean — that he had heard "so many complaints about me" from one student that he'd become tired of talking to him. This revelation was offered to prove that my "problem" was that "I had let a few students get to me."

Another form of depersonalization is having the acts or views of another woman colleague attributed to me or *vice versa*. The telling point is that even if we disclaim authorship, the speaker continues as if authorship is irrelevant because we are all interchangeable. Similarly, the views of other feminists are often projected onto me as if the prior question of whether I hold such views is insignificant to the conversation.

Finally, I want to describe the cumulative personal cost of all this. My basic coping strategy beginning in late fall was to withdraw from almost all informal and extra-curricular contacts with colleagues and students; to disengage when I found collegial interactions offensive or exclusionary; to accept abuse as the price for any feminist stance; and to share my research interests only with women, mostly outside the faculty. In sum, I worked largely in isolation not because I am non-collegial, but because I was so alienated. I also gave up reporting particular anti-feminist events to individual male colleagues and stopped seeking advice because my account of what had happened was so often disbelieved or invalidated.

I had increasing difficulty feeling anything — even anger — so often was I thingified, assumed to have opinions only on women's issues with those opinions assumed to be predictable. Typically, I was lobbed "woman" questions not because the questioner was interested in hearing or discussing my views, but because he wanted to see how I'd react or to use me as a prop for manufacturing controversy. With each unpleasant encounter I withdrew more. On several occasions I had trouble seeing colleagues as people. I'd perceive them as "types" just as they did me.

After the informal hiring meeting, I told two colleagues I would not apply if a teaching position came open. I internalized the various castigations of my motives, the constant denigration of my abilities, and decided I would concentrate on research and writing so that I would be more competitive in the next round of hiring.[25] Ultimately I accepted my being hired was a fluke. When deciding whether to accept the job I was offered in practice, I jettisoned my idea(l)s about what teaching means to me, and looked instead at my actual experience. The picture was pretty bleak.

Then I consulted the only two feminists I know who have both taught and practised law. One, a prominent Toronto litigator for a large corporate firm, said she had enjoyed far more freedom of expression and freedom to pursue feminist issues in practice than in teaching. She claimed she has never felt silenced in practice; often felt silenced in teaching. A year ago I would not have believed her.

The other is an internationally renowned lawyer and scholar whose teaching has always focused on and developed feminist jurisprudence. She considered teaching her calling, a career to which she had a deep personal commitment. She began with my belief that bringing a feminist perspective to the law school classroom could matter to women's equality in the profession and in our society. She is no longer committed to teaching because "what had been a calling became an ordeal." She urged me to take the job in practice.

She catalogued similar, but more and uglier, instances of abuse as a law teacher which escalated the more credentialed she became[26] and the more famous she became for her successful feminist achievements in the non-academic world. She, too, has been the victim of vicious rumour campaigns; she, too, has been the target of pre-arranged classroom disruption by male students and then had their violence used against her as evidence of her deemed inadequacy as a teacher; she, too, has been turned into pornography in the law school; and she, too, has had her opinions and her written work grotesquely misrepresented and then had the misrepresentation used to justify the discrediting of her scholarship. The difference is that she has an outstanding publishing, teaching, and litigation record. However, the most prestigious institutions at which she has taught have not offered her a permanent teaching position. Among other things, she has been considered "non-collegial."

Neither of these women had unremittingly negative experiences in academia. Nor have I. We have each had some faculty support, much support from our own students, and moments when we felt our presence changed for the better our students' lives and the future of women in this culture. None of us feels, however, that these rewarding moments make the bad ones worth the personal cost. Or that no real harm was done. A lot of harm was done, and not just to ourselves.

In addition to teaching my students law this year, I had one political goal which deeply matters to me personally: to lend the hierarchical authority of my position and to use my presence to validate women's voices in the classroom and in institutional life in order to help women feel it is both safe and legitimate to speak from their own perspective and their own experience when studying or practising law. What has most devastated me in looking back over the last year is that I am undecided about whether my presence actually made participating in law school life harder or easier for woman students. I am unsure exactly what role model I became.

I believe it is plausible that for every woman who gained some strength to speak from her own perspective and experience by my example, another learned it pays to remain silent or to pretend to fit a male model of lawyering; and that for every student who came to believe in the validity or even the possibility of working with law and from within legal institutions to advance woman's equality, another came to despair. And I know of students who suffered a particularly female form of vicarious liability: they paid when I paid; they were faulted when I was faulted; they felt silenced when I was or appeared to be silenced. And I know of others who tried to put distance between themselves as women and me lest they be the object of guilt by association.

I am also apprehensive about what men students learned of their own power and women's relative powerlessness participating in or watching efforts to discredit and disempower me, especially by use of force. What can it possibly mean when a spokesman for my detractors tells me, believing it, that "no harm was done?" And have we made progress or lost ground when he assures me the harm will stop because I have "proved" myself by male-defined terms?

I still believe the law school would be far less damaging to women if more women faculty were hired. And I believe legal education will reinforce the inequality of women until more feminists are hired. But until women — especially feminists — represent more than a visibly isolated minority perceived to be aberrant, we will continue to be easy targets for abuse by those who will not acknowledge personally or publicly the sexism and anti-feminism which fuel their hostility to and discrediting of women's perspectives and interests. And so long as feminists are so isolated, our serial victimization can be personalized as our own problem caused by our personal views, rather than as an institutional problem caused by institutional opposition to and devaluation of the class of which we are individual members. In the result, a blame-the-victim, she-was-asking-for-it rationalization prevails. When this pattern works effectively, the victim will internalize all this publicly denied male hostility, and doubt, then fault, then hate her self.

As a friend of mine once said, "They wanted me to cooperate in my own death." This spring, a part of me, the part I take to be my best self, went dead. I was silenced and came to believe that finding my voice again does not matter; in fact, that nothing I care deeply about matters within these walls. My continued silence amounts to cooperating in my own death. The process of writing this document, by externalizing the abuse, and by speaking from my experience in my own words and in my own way, has been a process of reclaiming that lost self and affirming "I am." That is: I care about what happened; and I really believe it matters within these walls.

My position has changed since the October memo. I believe we should make hiring *feminists* a priority. And we should hire them in twos or threes.[27]

VIII. The Measurable Impact of the Memo

The Lull before the Storm

In the first days after the memo's distribution, I had several visits from individual colleagues and support staff. All were shocked, genuinely dismayed, sympathetic and, in a few cases, ashamed. Male colleagues tended to discuss ways of taking action to remedy the problem; women readers tended to express identification with my story, often needing to share their own comparable experiences, usually faulting themselves for having remained silent in the face of offensive or denigrating treatment. Women also talked of remedies, but the focus was on how to struggle personally in oppressive situations or environments.

By the end of the first week three developments took place. Some men began to reveal their anger, albeit mutedly. They focused on the "unfairness" of my going public when they had been unaware of much (but not all) of what I had reported, or on my "failure" to have spoken up earlier or to have asked for their help. As well, discussion started to become gender-neutralized. Colleagues would ask, "whatever happened to our old collegiality?" or "what are the implications of an aging faculty to all this?" or "how can we better promote individual academic freedom?" Earlier talk of convening formal or informal meetings to discuss either the memo or institutional gender bias ceased. Finally, I was approached to see if I were willing to participate in "conciliation" with the unnamed colleague whose abusive conduct I had reported and analyzed at some length in the memo.[28] The object of such conciliation was to "de-escalate" the polarizing tensions created by the memo, to facilitate a "return to collegiality" and to see if the unnamed colleague and I could "mediate" our differences.

This last encounter was strategically significant. To begin with, whatever polarization of opinion existed in the Faculty, I had been entirely excluded from access to or contact with those critical of my views or conduct. To a large extent, this pattern has continued. Few of my critics oppose me, my circulating the memo, or my views openly. The discrediting continues, but usually behind my back or in forums providing me no right of reply. Commonly, men (and occasionally, women) criticize me to another woman; often the woman urges the critic to speak to me directly; rarely does he follow through. Not uncommonly such exchanges serve as tests of the political allegiances of the woman listener. I personally find such male conduct cowardly and repugnant.

As for the specific invitation to conciliate and de-escalate conflict within my faculty, I demurred. Smoothing over the gender divide itself could be achieved only by my publicly recanting. Mediating a reported conflict between my account of a colleague's intimidation tactics and his own required at a minimum that he make his account public. So long as he aired his account only to other male colleagues, they and only they bore the burden of de-escalating tension. If he were contemplating reprisals (a lawsuit was mentioned by the colleague exploring my willingness to conciliate), colleagues could abstain from comment, encourage, or discourage him. Because I was telling the truth and I believe my colleagues knew it, approaching me to be peacemaker while they were ducking struck me as unsavoury and, again, cowardly. I found particularly insulting the appeal to collegiality that would enlist me to restore it, when so little had been extended to me during the previous year.

This conciliation initiative I also take to reflect a pattern. Woman report misogyny and then are asked to take the initiative to kiss and make up by placating wounded male egos or by forgiving the wrongs done themselves prior to male admission of wrongdoing or by undertaking to start fresh as if no wrong were done. Such appeals to our womanly beneficence or Gilliganesque[29] relational skills and caring instincts are tempting, but should be resisted. So, too, should tugs at female guilt. Since post-memo discussions began, women have been routinely urged to show less "intolerance" toward others' (i.e., men's) imperfections (i.e., sexism, anti-feminism, and misogyny). We have been rebuked for being "insensitive" to men's insecurity about discussing gender bias in case they inadvertently betray sexism. The memo has been described frequently in violent language — "slamming" or "striking a blow" or "hitting out at" or "hard-hitting," etc. — and these terms are intended as pejoratives signalling unfeminine conduct. Feminists have also been charged with abusing our "power" and exercising "hegemony" in controlling university policies.[30]

Smoothing over the rifts which become visible when male dominance is exposed, or caving before such guilt-inducers amounts to a retreat, obscuring the very real disparities of power constructing gender intolerance, insensitivity, and violence, and pre-empting the painful, awkward, and necessary discussions without which oppression cannot be identified or altered. Naming misogyny what it is does not amount to intolerance towards individual men but towards intolerable conduct. Men's security in their unchallenged authority[31] born of women's individual and collective subordination is precisely what must be threatened and eliminated by feminist struggle. Confronting male bias and dominance is unfeminine, does empower women, and could be revolutionary.[32] But breaking our silence is not violent, merely an articulate claim to personal integrity. Conciliatory stances have tactical worth only if they achieve concrete substantive gains for women. They are backsliding appeasement moves when we are asked to lie about our lived experience of real oppression or to endorse measures that betray other women or relinquish the little women have secured.

The Press (The Storm)

For two months after the memo first circulated, very little happened at the faculty or institutional level,[33] although the memo circulated widely among returning students, feminist scholars, other academics, and the Kingston women's community. Through September, I received about 10 to 15 letters, calls, or personal visits each week, increasingly from strangers. Most of those who contacted me were supportive, most were women and many of them had similar stories to tell.

In early October, I received two phone calls within two days of each other asking me about my press strategy. As it had never occurred to me that the memo would circulate so widely, it had also never crossed my mind that the press might become involved. A day later a journalist from the campus newspaper, the *Queen's Journal*, called me for an interview. She had her facts wrong and had not read the memo. I declined to be interviewed until she had read it and until I had delivered two major public lectures that week. She persisted, sensing a scoop in a document that had been "public" for two months. I urged her to sit on her story for two days because getting the facts right and the presentation of the story would matter so much to women throughout the University. She published the story anyway, getting some facts wrong, giving the erroneous impression she had interviewed me, adopting misleading and sensational headlines (the front page headline used violent language to characterize the memo; the second page highlighted the washroom pornography). The paper's editor, relying on her flawed account, wrote an editorial that redoubled the damage, grossly overstating the case I had made, presenting as fact pure speculation about my motives, aspirations, and state of mind, paraphrasing one part of the memo with quasi-libellous results, and trashing the law school's stance on the basis of unsubstantiated assumptions.[34]

To put it mildly, no one was happy with them or with me. Former students were outraged at being turned into sensational copy through excerpts which made discreditable behaviour look worse; some students and colleagues attributed the overstatements and inaccuracies to me, not knowing I had not even been interviewed; classrooms were abuzz. Students rallied to defend the law school's good name, drafting letters to the editor dissociating themselves either from the handful of "bad apples" I had described or from me and my teaching goals or my views on the pervasiveness of gender bias in the law school.

By day's end, the Kingston paper (*The Whig-Standard*) was on the story. I and the law school were blessed by the fact that a feminist wrote the story. She did her homework, sought suggestions on how to avoid the damage done by the student paper, read the entire final draft to me for an accuracy check, and produced two sensitive and balanced feature articles. I was also fortunate in my Dean. He had been one of the most consistently supportive male colleagues I had; he backed me publicly to the press; and his remarks were carried in the national wire service summary of the two Kingston features. My good fortune held when *The Whig Standard* ran an editorial written by another feminist that supported my writing and circulating the memo, located institutional gender bias in faculties other than the law school, spoke eloquently of the reasons women tend to remain silent about sexism and to abandon struggles for change, and urged more women to find voice.[35]

It is impossible to guess what might have happened had the Kingston and, hence, national press coverage not been so well-written and pro-feminist.[36] Nor is it clear to me whether *any* substantive institutional change within the law school or the University would have occurred without the pressures brought by media attention. Similarly, had my Dean not backed me publicly to what became a national audience, it is difficult to tell how the University would have responded. My guess is that without such a combination of positive supports, I would have been crucified and the topic of gender bias would have been buried.

As it was, women had to mobilize quickly to prevent the university administration from adopting the easiest fix possible, which was being urged by friendly and hostile forces alike: a formal investigation of the law school and/or my "allegations." This would have contained or suppressed public debate, isolated me, and suspended much of the spontaneous activism triggered by the media coverage. In the week after the first press stories, an ad hoc coalition that included students, law school support staff,[37] University administrators, and faculty from several departments was formed. Its first agenda was to generate a letter campaign opposing any investigation and asserting that gender bias existed cross-campus.[38] Whether formal investigation was ever likely, it did not happen. As well, the message that gender bias was pervasive throughout the University registered, and spawned unprecedented institutional attention to the status of women on campus.

Institutional Responses

Within a few weeks of the press attention,[39] virtually every level of the University administration was addressing gender bias on site. Consultations occurred among some constituencies although autonomous discussions were the norm. The Principal announced he would report to the Senate on the topic, and discussions began in earnest. Parties involved included: the Deans, the Faculty Association, Faculty Boards, the Association of Women Teaching at Queen's, the Women's Studies Group, individual departments and the law school faculty.

After the Principal requested a report from the Dean of the law school, faculty members convened for the first time to discuss the memo, nearly three full months after the memo first circulated. Before the meeting, a group of women faculty met twice to swap information on male colleagues' stances about the meeting,[40] to anticipate the best and worst scenarios, and plan tactics for responding to each and, most importantly, to discuss our individual and collective fears about the meeting. Airing our fears and devising ways of accommodating or overcoming them, in my view, accounts for what was successful about the meeting.

We feared, variously: admitting to each other our real differences in perception and experience of male bias; revealing such differences publicly with the risk that lack of unanimity might be (ab)used to isolate and discredit some of us; losing emotional control either by crying or getting angry; being too defensive or too mutually protective such that necessary discussion, conflict, or confrontation might be suppressed; allowing attention to be focused unduly on me. Through our conversations, some of our differences and our fears diminished. We also devised a number of strategies for resisting their exploitation or misinterpretation. We discovered that our common agenda was to ensure that colleagues finally started talking and that we all thought that unexpressed sexism or anti-feminism would be worse than hearing offensive or hurtful remarks. Accordingly, we agreed not to rush to each other's aid unless signalled. (We never succeeded in selecting a rescue gesture.) We planned ways of preventing any one woman from being called on to speak for all women and agreed not to accept such a role if pressured.

We designated the woman who felt most "different" from the collective to chair the meeting, thereby alleviating her own fears of being used to divide and conquer the group and tapping her superior facilitating skills. Once again, naming fear gave us more control over an unpredictable situation, and reduced individual anxiety levels, not least because in our fear we had something fundamental in common.

The meeting itself was indescribably complex. Four women who had, in my experience, never attended a faculty meeting and whose unjustly low status made them vulnerable, showed up. The first 12 speakers were men (which was helpful in determining the lay of the land), and they divided into two camps. Four men proposed we conduct an "investigation" whose object, variously, was to judge the merits of my "allegations," to determine *if* gender bias was really a problem or, at least, a problem of sufficient scope to warrant institutional attention/redress, or to reconcile some women's claims that they had never experienced any discrimination within the law school with those of women who affirmed male bias was systemic and destructive. This camp was opposed by the majority of male faculty on several grounds: an investigation would achieve little constructive good and might be destructive to those most at risk; there is no single correct version of the realities of gender bias, though no reason to believe the law school is exempt from discrimination endemic elsewhere in our society, so the task becomes addressing how feminist/women faculty and students can enjoy academic freedom to express their views; pluralism is a good thing, and attempting to reconcile different views and values is misguided.

Each of these themes has been repeated in subsequent formal and informal discussions on this topic which I have attended. Women planning or plunged into similar mixed-sex discussions of institutional male bias should expect such approaches, and be ready to respond in ways which might further women's interests.

Ultimately, in what stretched into a nearly four hour meeting, all eight women present spoke. In itself, this was a remarkable breakthrough. Seven spoke in solidarity as women, affirming that institutional male bias exists and is damaging to women, rebutting or critically analyzing some speakers' "evidence" that the problem is minor or non-existent or of concern to only a small minority of feminists and, with one exception, drawing on their own experience to authenticate the destructiveness to women's personal and professional lives of maintaining the status quo. Two of these women's voices were stunningly courageous, moving, and effective in bringing the damage of male norms and male bias home to the room instead of keeping it conceptual, abstract, and benign. I felt as if my community was transformed when they spoke.[41] If the memo had had no other impact, those two moments of women speaking from painful personal experience and claiming their own self-respect by risking hard truths would be permanently incandescent, cause for collective pride.

The Responses of Women Faculty

Not all the women called upon to respond to the memo's disclosures and their wake enjoyed the solidarity or opportunity for collective strategizing that some of the law school women did. The campus-wide spotlight on gender bias exposed all university women as women, subjecting them to questioning about their politics, their experience of sex discrimination, their opinions on the egalitarian credentials of male coworkers or superiors and their views about me/the memo. Such women are vulnerable on several levels. When asked if they have ever experienced or witnessed male bias on site they are in a double bind. If they say no, they are at risk of being used to pre-empt discussions of sexism in their own workplace and/or to discredit women who have reported sex discrimination. If they say yes, they risk being discredited as I have been and/or of being faulted for their prior silence and/or of being suddenly recruited to be the official voice of women/feminism in their office or department. Once designated such an official voice, they are called on to educate their coworkers, to bear responsibility for proposing and implementing reforms, and to comment on demand to each new campus development on the issue. Not infrequently, they are expected to disclose personal traumas or indignities for curious spectators eager to understand the nature of women's oppression. Worse, some departments have struck "balanced" committees to study if there is any problem locally, recruiting the lone feminist — often a woman on a non-continuing appointment — to sit side by side with an overtly anti-feminist woman and a few liberal men.

By sheer good luck, two existing organizations of women faculty[42] had previously scheduled meetings that took place immediately following the press blitz. This allowed many faculty women to develop strategies for coping with this exposure and its demands. As an immediate goal, we undertook to use every public forum we could — letters, media interviews, and meetings with departmental or university administrators — to emphasize the disparate burden institutional discussions of male bias place on women, especially women isolated in their departments and/or lacking job security. This message has registered on women reporters, interviewers and officials far more than on men, largely because women know what women have to fear from voicing woman-centred or feminist views in male-dominated environments, and men, who tend to conceive of male domination as an abstraction whose existence or harm is debatable, have enormous difficulty grasping that women fear them, not some abstraction.

The mixed-sex discussions and male-authored responses to institutional gender bias I have seen reveal that men commonly de-gender the problem by construing it as an issue of "academic freedom" whose solution lies in fostering pluralist tolerance of different views.[43] This is usually code for male tolerance of, rather than serious engagement with, the expression of women's views, and female tolerance of men's denial that male dominance is a problem. Even those few men who genuinely accept that traditional disciplinary content and pedagogy are not objective and that feminist scholarship is not biased, man-hating propaganda, often resist recognizing that their traditionalist perspective is privileged by and implicated in male domination which secures for them and their views credibility and status that unorthodox "perspectives" do not enjoy. As a result, whereas anti-feminist male scholars consider the denigration of feminists appropriate,[44] liberal male scholars who are pluralists about feminism consider the denigration of feminists aberrant, and therefore discount women's fears about naming or "debating"[45] the nature and impact of male bias in male company. They tend to see the novel initiative of placing gender bias on the departmental, faculty, or university agenda for academic debate sufficient encouragement to elicit honest input from women.

In virtually all institutional forums where the existence and significance of gender bias are debated, women as a group are outnumbered and outranked by men — men on whom these women likely depend for professional credit and advancement. Women, therefore, tend to remain silent. To generate substantive discussion, one or more women must resort to first-person testimony about personal experiences of sexism and its costs. This violates established (male) norms of academic discourse and risks undermining the speaker's professional credibility by being subjective, emotional, and anything but abstract.

Some subjective testimonials, however, win credibility almost by definition. Women who deny their own and other women's oppression to their male peers and superiors are *believed*. And they are cited. Constantly. Usually in their absence. They are cited by men to women as "proof" that either there is no gender problem or that the existence and magnitude of the problem are debatable. I know such women exist; but they rarely appear in person to refute other women's testimony of local male bias, and in my view their numbers are inflated by the men who believe them. That it is safer and more professionally rewarding for women to remain silent or to offer assurances that they have never experienced local sexism and anti-feminism rarely seems to register on men in power. One can understand men's interest in believing such women; but it is the interest of the oppressor — at best, complacent and naively credulous; at worst, cynical and disingenuous.

It is not clear to me that the timing or framing of institutional discussions of male bias will ever be in women's control or on our terms. Constructing such discussions as a matter of women's "academic freedom," however, is not a little ironic if women are forced to speak in order for men to believe there is any problem at all, pressured to take sides against other women and heard without any acknowledgement that they are disproportionately at risk in identifying as women when their job security, professional credibility and personal popularity turn on conforming to male standards, administered by male authorities in a male-dominated profession.

Two other strategies emerged from meetings of women faculty organizations. We opted not to propose any specific institutional reforms, not to endorse as our own any specific remedies proposed by other constituencies, and not to reduce the number of initiatives being developed by consolidating our efforts with any administrative organizations to generate a single plank of responses to campus gender bias. We were worried about two possibilities: being landed with the primary burden for solving the problems faced by women across disciplines and across hierarchies; and being seen to endorse the types of modest, finite, and bureaucratic remedies likely to gain common support across different interest groups. Our public stance was that both short-and long-term strategies from as many sources as possible needed exploration, development, and implementation through broad consultation. It is premature to assess whether this strategy has been effective. To date, the only University-wide initiative launched with the Principal's backing has been the requirement that all seven faculties[46] submit reports to the University Senate on gender bias within their community.

The second strategy adopted by feminist faculty was a loosely designed boycott of taken-for-granted demands on our time and expertise by colleagues who expect us to tutor them and their students in state-of-the-art feminist theory and scholarship which we have spent years acquiring and get little or no credit for knowing. We decided to insist our colleagues begin to take responsibility for familiarizing themselves and their students with the basic feminist texts in their fields. How we do this remains a matter of personal choice. To this end some women have circulated feminist bibliographies throughout their departments; some have given colleagues articles to read, refusing to discuss the topic further until the reading has been done; others have referred colleagues to resident feminist experts on a topic rather than sacrificing their own time to précis it for unserious listeners; others have simply announced that the existing division of labour must stop and male colleagues should begin doing what they are paid to do: read, study, and think about all recent literature in their field, including feminist research.

If nothing else, this move has made many colleagues aware of how many of their own students rely on feminist colleagues to teach them and of the sheer volume of feminist scholarly output. This approach also reveals that feminists do not speak with one voice. In my faculty, the circulation of feminist articles is unprecedented and some non-feminists are doing the reading. As well, several colleagues have approached feminist students and faculty for suggestions on ways that feminist perspectives, materials, and legal theory might be incorporated into their courses. In other law schools where I have criticized the existing division of labour and argued non-feminist scholars should familiarize themselves with the basic literature, a few academics (usually women) have pledged to do so. Given that we want to encourage student research on feminist topics, I see no way of sending students away just because they are not in our classrooms. However, I think all feminists should begin to log such demands on their time and expertise and ensure colleagues both discover and credit the work involved.

Responses in the Law School

When I wrote the memo I was deeply ambivalent about whether my presence had made law school life more or less bearable for women students. There is no question that observing what happened to me, hearing the rumours, and paying for supporting me demoralized and frightened many women. Some men gained stature for putting me down publicly, and that, too, unnerved many women. News, not always accurate, of hostility to my presence had spread to other law schools long before I wrote the memo, with unknowable chilling effect. If to be a feminist at the front of the classroom generated professional discreditation, women students may be excused for accepting that it pays to remain silent, to endure sexist treatment, and to assimilate malestream thinking and conduct.

Without diminishing the emotional costs, the heightened vulnerability, and the exhausting amount of political, educational, and feminist support work triggered by the memo's publicity and borne disproportionately by small pockets of committed feminists, I believe the destructive cycle I lived and observed last year has been altered. Throughout the law school, consciousness of male bias and its damage has been elevated. Feminist discourse and critique are more common, more publicly voiced, and more expected. In some quarters it is silently tolerated where once it was disparaged; in others it is legitimated both by students and teachers. When criticized for thoughtlessly sexist attitudes or reasoning, many individuals are now less ready to deny their fault and less defensive. So many new voices have adopted gender-inclusive language or name male bias when it appears that publicly feminist students are no longer lumped together interchangeably.

In at least a dozen courses during the 1986-87 academic year, full classes were devoted to discussing gender bias in the law school and the law. Reports are that students were more insightful and candid than colleagues expected. Visiting feminist speakers[47] helped legitimize feminist legal research. But, by their report, audience reactions were more receptive, enlightened, and engaging than in other law schools they had visited. Members of the Women and the Law Collective, though visibly weary, seem less garrisoned than during my first year of teaching. In the spring of 1986, they sponsored a pub (as do most student organizations periodically during the year) and debated how to hide their sponsorship so that it would not be boycotted. A year later, their openly sponsored pub drew record attendance and profits. The Collective has also undertaken several projects designed to improve women's lives outside the walls of the law school: they have launched a complaint against the frequently racist, sexist, and homophobic Engineering newspaper using the new sexual harassment procedure; they conducted a survey of Ontario law firms aimed at documenting the employment and promotional status of women and visible minority lawyers; they organized and administered a large conference for January 1988 ("Ideals and Realities: Feminism in the Study and Practice of Law") which featured some 40 panelists and drew an audience of approximately 300.

During 1986-87, an ad hoc group of women and men students mobilized and secured Faculty Board approval of a "Commitment of Principle Relating to Gender Issues," which now appears in the calendar. This statement includes commitment to ameliorate "the historic and *current* inequalities between women and men" by: urging use of gender-inclusive language in all law school publications, materials, and exams and in the classroom; production of in-house casebooks and selection of commercial textbooks to include non-stereotypical roles for women, inclusion of legal issues "relevant to the historic and current inequality of women," and presentation of women's interests; use of supplementary materials and resources where textbooks have perceived inadequacies in their treatment of women or sex inequality; and faculty *encouragement* of students "who attempt to develop thought and theories concerning the relationship between sex discrimination and the law."[48]

In addition to attending campus lobbies on sexism and lectures and seminars within the law school by feminist scholars, support staff have begun to mobilize around gender issues specific to their own needs and concerns such as opportunities for job-sharing. As well, they have sought representation on Faculty Board, which is currently composed only of faculty members and student representatives. Support staff are also routinely included for the first time on the mailing list for Women and the Law Collective events, and in certain faculty gatherings. In the spring of 1987, the Faculty Board approved a new lecture course ("Law, Gender and Equality")[49] to serve as an introduction to the law of sex (in)equality and as a foundation of the existing seminar in Feminist Jurisprudence. The new course was staffed and offered in the fall of 1987. Staffing was possible because, after the six-year freeze on hiring, three continuing appointments were made in early 1987. All three positions have been filled by women. Each is also a committed feminist legal scholar. I am one of the three.[50]

These appointments have increased exponentially the amount of feminist and women-friendly teaching and research on site. Feminist content is being integrated into so-called "core" courses like labour law, tax, family and criminal law as well as into perspective and theory courses. All this activity has generated a broader pro-woman and pro-feminist student base. It has also triggered a backlash evident in petitions against a woman-centred Advocacy seminar and an Advanced Tax course; in homophobic washroom graffiti; in the student input into the interviewing of prospective faculty. There have also been tension-filled silences when specifically gender-based issues come to institutional bodies. Nonetheless, by contrast with most Canadian law schools, Queen's now houses exceptional feminist activity. Nowhere are there more feminist and pro-feminist women legal scholars; nowhere a more gender-conscious student body (although the graduation of the class admitted the same year I arrived may alter this consciousness).

IX. Epilogue

Eighteen months ago I distributed the first 45 copies of the memo within my faculty. The intervening period has been unforgettable: exhausting, healing, angering, heartwarming, galvanizing, painful, intellectually fertile, and overwhelmingly busy. I have never learned so much so rapidly; never been so opportunely placed to translate my learning to the audience I most wished to reach. I learned the generosity of women's community, and the numbing hurt we can cause each other by our differences over matters of survival. I had a crash course in academic and institutional politics. Without any forewarning, I experienced the costs and the gratifications of celebrity and the (temporary) power along with depersonalizing distance it brings.

For nine months, I lost my privacy while experiencing increasing isolation as an object of intense scrutiny, curiosity, speculation, hostility, and fantasy. As a symbol upon whom others projected their fears, angers, and desires, I had enormous difficulty feeling real. And as a symbol, I often forgot to be human: to admit my limits, express my needs, confess hurt. My sense of my self was never more in flux; ultimately never more open to reconsideration.

Following the teaching year that made me question whether my presence harmed women more than it empowered them, the memo year gradu-
ally restored my personal, professional, and intellectual confidence and affirmed my commitment to teaching. It was not the celebrity that achieved
these results, but the contacts my celebrity generated. My work was credited and supported by those for whom I remain in this profession; women
and non-mainstream students. But the memo, the struggle it records, and
the act of naming misogyny also led literally hundreds of people —
overwhelmingly women — to write or phone or drop by my office or introduce themselves on the street. Most supported me and most disclosed comparable experiences from their own lives. Women faculty from some 30
American and Canadian universities and virtually every academic discipline wrote offering support or corroboration. I heard also from depart-
ment-store saleswomen, my students' parents, prison guards, clergy, colleagues' wives, journalists, homemakers, therapists, artisans — in short
women whose lives connected with mine through the sharing of the daily
lived experience of sexism.

These contacts were emotionally demanding and sometimes devastating as I heard again and again of the damage women endure under male
domination. Many of the stories I heard reduced my chronicle to a modest
case of injury. I think now that I was partly addicted to these exchanges because they made me feel needed and worthwhile after a year of feeling my
abilities constantly denigrated and perceiving my ambitions to be futile.
Partly, though, these contacts offered a rare gift worth receiving: the opportunity to witness the work to which I am committed esteemed by others.

Between October 1986 and June 1987, I delivered 25 public addresses to
a variety of audiences: other law schools, colleagues' classes, conferences,
and community groups. At the time, the pace and emotional overload of
these appearances seemed both unbearable and exhilarating. Looking back,
I wonder what drove me to keep accepting invitations. I enjoyed talking
feminism in a context where doing so was expected and scheduled rather
than resisted and faulted. I relished the opportunity to articulate what I was
learning from the post-memo dramas. The publicity which brought me
speaking invitations also brought me a kind of immunity from public attack
in forums where feminists are often silenced or baited. My critics, I suspect,
feared I would turn them into headlines. But, as well, substantial sections of
my audiences were intensely engaged and openly supportive. The hostile
listeners had probably never been so outnumbered.

The immunity and the passion to speak of what has been so long unnamed in its concrete, subjective detail, allowed me to express unmuted
what I know through experience and observation of misogyny, male violence, the law's maleness, and its destructive impact on women. Wherever I

spoke, women's faces gripped me: faces hungry for validation, faces devastated to acknowledge the privatized damage normally kept buried. It was these faces I locked onto when I spoke, not those of the sceptics or the hostile. After each address, women of the hungry, devastated faces would approach me privately and ask me, nearly inaudibly, "You mean I am not crazy?" dreading I would not take them seriously. I think I needed them as much as they needed me. The contact allowed us all to excorcise and externalize the damage we are done by male legal institutions.

Finally, the memo year taught me how much I, like other feminists I know, are hooked on and burdened by being cast in the role as "The Strong One." This is "Superwoman" with a vengeance. In addition to combining a demanding career with politics and with private life, without a map and with little institutional (and in many cases, domestic) support, we also undertake to be brave and wise and otherwise exemplary for the women watching us as role models. In my experience, this includes being endlessly accessible, publicly and privately supportive of all women seeking support, emotionally engaged, and a model of uncompromising resistance. Our limited numbers and the urgency of the feminist project drive us to meet these impossible standards. But also, I believe, being "The Strong One" without whose energy and political acumen the job will not get done (or get done right) is self-aggrandizing and ultimately self-destructive. It also is isolating: those who consult "Strong Women" seeking support, counsel, comfort and purpose easily become dependents whose relation to their role models turns on and is constrained by a mutually alienating hierarchy.

When I wrote the memo, I concluded that part of me had gone dead in my first year of teaching. The process of externalizing that year's experience only revived some of the clenched and numb surfaces. The extraordinarily intense academic year that followed circulation of the memo within my Faculty revitalized the teacher I am. But it is also true that I have learned enormous amounts and grown in directions I know to be promising since I chose to decline most invitations placing me and the memo in the spotlight. I am in this struggle for the long run, and I have relinquished my grip on being "The Strong One." I now perceive the wisdom of accepting my limits, providing for my personal needs, and creating space for other women to stretch their most vital selves. Despite the many larger than life dramatics of "The Memo Year," experiencing that drama and reflecting upon it have completed the process of self-affirmation that began when I sat down to write.

Acknowledgements

During my first year of teaching and during the year that followed the circulation of the memo, hundreds of women of all occupations and political identities offered me timely support. To each of them who may read this, understand: it mattered. Among these women were a few whose contact and example and courage have kept me in the legal profession and in legal education (a dubious commendation in some feminists' eyes), and who helped me grow. Their presence and community remains crucial. My thanks to: Beverley Baines for keeping the faith over a decade and for listening tirelessly; Virginia Bartley for human insight; Sharon Cohen for generosity and determined activism; Susan Cole for her reach; Mary Crnkovich for balance; Mary Eaton for courage; Catharine MacKinnon for truth-telling; Judy Parrack for listening; Toni Pickard for honesty and facing-the-dread; Kathleen Rockhill for sharing the hope and pain; Bette Solomon for caring to help me own my self; and Carol Zavitz for constancy and friendship. They have all been my teachers. I am trying to be a good student.

Notes

1 The memo was printed in the *CAUT Bulletin*, 34, 1 (1987): 7; the circulation of the *Bulletin* is 28,000. This essay, which frames the discussion of how Sheila McIntyre came to write the memo and of reactions to it, was originally published in the *Canadian Journal of Women and the Law*, 2, 1 (1987-88): 362.

2 The only changes I have made in the original memo are the deletion of the few names that appeared in it and very minor editorial corrections.

3 I am often asked how many women teach in the Queen's Faculty of Law. The answer is that it depends how you count. There were three tenured women when I arrived; one taught full time, one taught part time but was on sick leave, and the Chief Librarian taught one course. I and another woman on contract appointment each taught two courses and the Registrar taught a single course. Another way of counting is to distinguish permanent from impermanent faculty. The ratio was 26 permanent and 6 non-permanent men to 3 permanent and 3 non-permanent women. Finally, one can count the total courses taught by men and women. When all faculty, both permanent and impermanent, are considered, 18% of all courses were taught by women. When only permanent faculty are considered, only 8% of courses are taught by women. This latter ratio is perhaps most accurate as a way of assessing how many women are "on faculty" for several reasons: it indicates the level of commitment to including women permanently in the teaching roster; it signals how accessible women are to students for non-classroom interactions like counselling, mentoring, assisting in students' research needs, etc.; it conveys imperfectly what influence women faculty have in the administrative and collegial work of the Faculty (only full-time contract appointees and part-time permanent faculty serve on committees; special lecturers and sessional/adjunct appointees do not and, in addition, rarely attend Faculty Board meetings).

4 In the memo I refer to this open meeting as the "protest" meeting. It was not a discussion meeting, but consisted of preliminary remarks by the Dean followed by questions whose content presupposed hiring policy had changed or was about to change in a way that was discriminatory and would result in hiring less than qualified teachers and/or propagandists.

5 I do believe, however, that the political stakes, and therefore the personal costs, of being a feminist in the law school are higher than in practice.

6 At Queen's, the first-year class is divided into six "small sections" of 24-25 students in which one of the core courses is taught. The professor is also assigned an extra hour per week in which to teach legal research and writing skills. Students do two or three written assignments in their small section as well as a final exam. During the spring term, first-year classes are cancelled for a week, and each small section designs a schedule of activities around one or two legal issues to integrate what they are learning through use of films, experts, background reading, and practical skills (interviewing, negotiating, preparing submissions for boards of inquiry, mooting, etc.). This event is called "Integrated Forum" week. The small-section instructor is the primary facilitator for the project.

7 The course evaluation process at Queen's is administered exclusively by students. For unknown reasons, the student government failed to organize the distribution and collection of evaluations in the spring term of 1986. I approached the student president and asked for evaluation forms and arranged that student reps distribute them in both my classes because, as a rookie teacher, I wanted the feedback. To my knowledge no other faculty member took such initiative. As a result, the forms collected in my classes may have been lost because there was no central collection point for them, although I understand they were at some point in the office of the student government. In any event, when I asked that they be collated in the fall of 1986, they had disappeared.

8 Convincing the disbelievers served personal as well as political needs: I wanted to be believed. I was hurt and rattled by being so systematically discounted. My personal needs were, of course, political, too. Isolating and undermining women *individually* and making them feel personally deviant, inadequate, and worthless is a *systemic* practice and outcome of male domination.

9 Most of my fears proved justified. When the media attention peaked, there was wide rumour that the University administration was being pressured to conduct a formal investigation of the law school and/or my "allegations." There was also a small faction within the law school pressing for an investigation of what I had written. Both moves were blocked. But there is no question that many proponents of the investigation route as well as other individuals consider my account untrue, vindictive, biased, or exaggerated. The object of the investigation was to discredit me and/or my account, precisely the defence tactic of a rape trial.

As for character assassination, it became worse and far more public and widespread once the memo went public. Originally, my detractors rumoured that I was not the *most* qualified of the candidates interviewed when I was hired; in the fall of 1986, the charge was that I was one of or the *least* qualified. I have since heard that repetition of both versions has circulated nationwide, generally as proof that the abuses I documented were justified [!] or as critique for my going public (I have falsely alleged sexism to excuse legitimate criticism of my incompetence). The most bizarre version is that I adopted a feminist stance and then publicized anti-feminist fall-out in order to get myself rehired. Some critics voice this view with grudging admiration: if I am smart enough to have pulled this manoeuvre off, I must not be as incompetent as alleged.

Similarly, the sexualized discrediting became worse with the circulation of the memo. During my first year of teaching, lesbian labelling was quasi-private, limited to casual conversation and to the men's bathroom walls. Following media attention, many classrooms devoted discussion time to gender bias. In one classroom a student aired a new rumour about me: I had slept with one of my women students. Ironically, articulating the rumour was intended to affirm that I was the target of discrediting stories just as I claimed in the memo. In my view, this remains the most vicious libel yet expressed against me. Other feminist scholars consider such libels commonplace against feminist teachers. Leaving aside that most feminists deplore all professor/student affairs, whether or not the student is subject to the professor's grading authority, what outrages me about the lie is that such rumours may inhibit women students from associating with faculty feminists for fear of being targets of similar rumours or of having their good grades discredited.

There is a pattern in these rumours. Reporting and opposing male bias evokes three misogynist stereotypes: I am uncreditworthy (like other female victims of sexual assault); I am unprofessional/unqualified/incompetent (I do not conform to male-imposed standards of either professionality or female assimilation); I am sexually "deviant" and/or predatory (I do not conform to male-imposed standards of female attractiveness/sexual subordination).

10 I am grateful to Toni Pickard for this insight. She refers to counter-hegemonic activity as "moving against the dread"; the measure of how subversive a particular act is with reference to a given individual's socialization is the degree of dread attached.

11 After I delivered a public lecture on the maleness of law at another law school, a senior woman scholar dissociated herself from my views and my experiences. She was told by a student that she is also denigrated on the student washroom walls. Initially disbelieving and then shocked, she finally asserted, "I'm sure it's not personal." She is correct, of course, that the pornography targeting her individually is grounded in unindividuated vilification of "Woman" or "Lesbian" or whatever. But the porn had her name on it, was directed specifically against her in her professional community (though in an all-male space only), and put her down individually and personally.

12 See Catharine A. MacKinnon, *Feminism Unmodified: Discourses on Life and Law* (Cambridge and London: Harvard University Press, 1987), p. 6-7, 15.

13 There were a few exceptions. I did not pre-circulate the memo to the outgoing student president or to a male colleague I named in a context which was to his credit. I did not circulate an advanced copy or excerpts to any readers who might recognize themselves in an anecdote but who would not be recognizable to anyone else.

14 Unmediated by external disapproval, disbelief, or revisionism, and unmediated by the problem of translating female experience for male or anti-feminist listeners.

15 I am *not* saying such moments pose no risk. It is common for women's detractors to attempt to explain away or reinterpret these moments in a discrediting way and not uncommon for misogynists to desire nothing more deeply than to snuff the moment or the woman who created it.

16 I circulated the memo with a covering note explaining that I hoped the memo would generate discussion before classes began and indicating that the memo would appear as part of the text of an article I was writing for a feminist journal. I specifically welcomed feedback "whether critical or supportive."

17 A copy of the "October memo" is on file with *CJWL*.

18 When I wrote this sentence it was true. Once the memo became public, there were women readers — teachers and students — who did not see the gender bias in the incidents I described. I heard from some colleagues that they had heard from women students who claimed they had never witnessed any sexism in the law school or experienced any sex discrimination. I also received letters, visits, and phone calls from literally hundreds of women who neither dissent from my analysis of the incidents described nor deny that they have witnessed and experienced quite comparable events in their own academic or professional lives. Some Queen's law students stated they have personally never experienced what I describe but believe totally in the accuracy of what I report.

One of the most interesting phenomena is women who tell me that before they read the memo or even after reading it they would have said they had never experienced discriminatory treatment like that I described, but two days later "it happened to them, too." My interpretation of this is that "it" was happening all along, but the memo gave them a vocabulary to interpret it and/or a different way of perceiving their environment.

19 See, e.g., Christine Boyle's "Teaching Law as if Women Really Mattered: or What about the Washrooms?" a paper presented at the 1986 annual meeting of the Canadian Association of Law Teachers. [Subsequently published in *Canadian Journal of Women and Law*, 2 (1986): 96.]

20 *Fillipowich v. Nahachewsky* (1969), 3 D.L.R. (3d) 544 (Sask. Q.B.).

21 Because there were only 24 students in the class, the intensity and impact of this disruption was substantial.

22 For a description of Integrated Forum, see n. 6.

23 Students pursuing a Master's degree in Industrial Relations (M.I.R.) may enrol in law school courses. They pursue the bulk of their coursework and research in a building far removed from the law school. The five M.I.R. students in my class in the spring term were unaware of the agitation around the hiring issue in the fall.

24 For details about the course evaluation process, see n. 7.

25 My decision not to apply for any 1986-87 opening was neither a decision against teaching nor evidence that I then believed I was unqualified/incompetent. Looking back, I think what undermined my confidence as early as that hiring meeting in early November was the discussion of traits considered priorities in potential candiates. I perceived the sundry portraits of the perfect candidate, combined with the tepid to non-existent commitment to hire more women, as exclusionary. I concluded I would never be rehired unless I met what many of my colleagues viewed as genderless and what I view as male standards of worth.

26 I wish to underline this point. In my view, it is being gendered female which grounds the widely accepted presumption of incompetence. And it is being feminist and female which triggers the abuse. Credentials are ultimately irrelevant, though the assumption that women and feminists have none, or few, or have slept their way to success or were-hired-only-because-they-are-women is about the equation of womanhood with lack of competence. Men — and only men — have rationalized abuse of junior women as normal. Students (gender neutral) it is said always go for blood when they smell weakness. One of my colleagues insisted, for instance, that when students perceive such weaknesses as "the professor being unprepared for class, or being a woman, or not knowing one's subject," they go for blood. In my experience, only *some* students, and only male students, go for the blood. The crucial question is why womanhood should be seen as a "weakness" that provokes violence. The same colleague also saw nothing unobjectionable about the male washroom pornography of women faculty. One of the targets, he asserted, was a bad teacher. (Incompetence again.) This does not account for the form of the denigration and why pornographing of faculty is reserved for women (or allegedly gay men).

27 My original hiring memo proposed that at a minimum we should adopt a tie-breaker model of hiring where a woman candidate considered relatively equal to any male candidate(s) would be hired. I also proposed active recruiting of women that would indicate that this Faculty is committed to "hiring women as women," and is sensitive to and prepared to validate the difference women bring to law. Finally, I proposed we review our hiring criteria to identify those which disadvantage women and to expand the criteria to credit the difference(s) women bring to legal education. I went on to suggest qualities characteristic of women scholars with whom I feel community. Nowhere did I use the word feminist, though the scholars whose work I cited and the qualities I listed are all feminists. (I was heard and reported to have proposed we hire only women and only feminists.) I did, however, refer to the value of hiring women who identify as women.

28 See text at pages 236-38 of this book.

29 Carol Gilligan, *In a Different Voice: Psychological Theory and Women's Development* (Cambridge and London: Harvard University Press, 1982). It is problematic enough when skills/ethical qualities such as caring, giving primacy to sustaining relationship, nurturing, integrating, and so on are distinctively female virtues, given that such qualities are a product of socialization in the interests of male dominance. It is extremely suspect when men, reacting to disclosures of sexism, anti-feminism, and misogyny, pressure women to use our female virtues to smooth over discord caused by such disclosures.

30 See, e.g., letter to the editor by Professor David Toogood, *Queen's Journal*, January 30, 1987, and the "Viewpoint" column in the February 1987 issue of the *CAUT Bulletin* by Jeanne Phelps-Wilson.

31 By the term "authority" I wish to convey the socio-cultural pre-eminence born of women's subordination; the hegemonically enforced authoritativeness of men's perspective; the stature of men's self-referential merit criteria; the presumed universality of men's pronouncements on topics about which they know little or nothing, chief among which is women's experience of sexual inequality; and the deportmental confidence which accompanies the expectation that such authority is one's right and one's dues.

32 I am reminded of a passage from Nawal El Saadawi, *Woman at Point Zero*, trans. Sherif Hetata (London: Zed Publishers, 1983): "They said, 'You are a savage and dangerous woman.' (I said,) 'I am speaking the truth. And the truth is savage and dangerous' "; cited in MacKinnon, *Feminism Unmodified*, p. 5.

33 The only institutional response took the form of a question to the Dean of the law school in the first Faculty Board meeting in the fall of 1986. A colleague asked what the Dean was doing to pursue the institutional issues raised by the memo. The Dean indicated he was in the Faculty's hands and would take action if asked. Dead silence. The original questioner then proposed the Dean explore ways of responding to the institutional issues. There was no mention of the issue at the next Faculty Board meeting. By the third fall meeting, the press attention had begun and the Principal had requested a report from the Dean.

34 These articles can be found in the *Queen's Journal*, October 10, 1986.

35 The two journalists involved were Anne Kershaw (*The Whig-Standard* [Kingston], October 17 and 18, 1986) and Brenda Large (ibid., October 21, 1986).

36 There is no question in my mind that the articles written by Ms. Kershaw and the editorial by Ms. Large positively contributed to women's struggles at Queen's. Basically, we were believed by the press, and our struggle was seen to be part of women's broader social struggles for equality, which struggles were taken seriously. We were just plain lucky. In future, I would not leave such matters to chance. Feminists must cultivate media contacts who are also pro-feminist or, at least, not anti-feminist.

37 The participation of the support staff at the law school in activities traceable to the memo has been remarkable. Several women spoke to me individually immediately after the memo circulated, one offering to testify in my support should there be any investigation of specific "allegations" made in the memo. Six support staff left work early to attend a public lecture I gave on the maleness of law; nine support staff left work early to attend the first meeting of the ad hoc coalition. Their personal support to me through the media blitz was timely, extensive, and invaluable.

38 Later, the coalition solicited other women's stories of sexism and anti-feminism, publishing several in its first newsletter. Mid-winter, the coalition arranged a "Sexism Awareness Day" and co-ordinated a variety of informal events and displays highlighting pro-woman activities on campus.

39 Anne Kershaw's stories were condensed and carried by Canadian press in daily newspapers nationally. The story also generated local and provincial radio coverage and, later, coverage in several university newspapers and at least one national magazine.

40 A minority of men on faculty were opposed to an all-faculty meeting. They wanted student representatives present. All women on faculty opposed the inclusion of students until: (a) faculty had attempted to talk with each other at least once; and (b) student representatives had met with students to have views to represent. The women's position was not that faculty should never meet with students to discuss institutional gender bias and/or the memo, but that we should break the silence among ourselves first and schedule joint faculty-student meetings later. As a formal matter, there has never been a follow-up meeting with faculty and students, or with faculty and support staff, or with all three communities.

41 Not everyone was moved by these women's voices. After the second woman spoke, a male colleague was so crudely insensitive he took my breath away. On the other hand, another male colleague contrasted that callousness with the "authenticity" of the woman's contribution. Something shifted.

42 These organizations are: The Association of Women Teaching at Queen's (which provides a community and, sometimes, lobbying ground for all full-time, part-time, and adjunct women teaching at the University) and The Women's Studies Group (which is a fluid, unstructured caucus of women currently teaching in or administratively supporting or hoping to teach in the Women's Studies degree program). There is, of course, considerable overlap in membership, though the priorities and politics of the two groups do not necessarily coincide.

43 The silencing and denigration of scholars who bring a feminist perspective to their teaching and research or who speak from their experience as women in the classroom and their publications do raise an issue of academic freedom. However, to construe gender bias in the university exclusively as a problem of academic freedom is to obscure the sexism, misogyny, and homophobia fuelling student and collegial hostility to the presence and the voice of women/feminists. It is also to ignore the very concrete experience of being the target of sexist and misogynist comments, rumours, contempt, sexual harassment, and discreditation. More, violation of my academic freedom was the least of what was violated in my first year of teaching.

I think universities will have made progress when they genuinely accept that feminist scholarship *is* scholarship and therefore entitled to the protection of academic freedom. When the majority of male scholars accept that their gender shapes what and how they teach and research, what they count as scholarship, what they recognize as knowable, women and feminist scholars will be closer to enjoying conditions under which discussions about academic freedom and gender can be non-coercive and non-threatening to women's professional status. But only when the mind/body split isolating violence against women from academic (and other) ideology and distinguishing the delegitimization of feminist ideas for the devaluation of women generally is rejected will systemic institutional discrimination against women and feminists be fully addressed.

The same analysis applies to racism in the universities. Student and collegial hostility to race-conscious teaching by Asian, Aboriginal, Black, Middle Eastern, or Hispanic scholars is never simply hostility to their ideas; nor is it experienced as such. As with gender, competence is aligned with membership in the dominant elite: allegations of incompetence against a visible minority scholar are frequent, unsubstantiated, and readily accepted. The violation of minority scholars is never just to their ideas or because of their ideas: it is racist, experienced as an assault on their identity, and grounded in their mere presence on the turf of the dominant with teacher power over the domination. See Derrick Bell, "The Price and Pain of Racial Perspective," *Stanford Law School Journal* (May 1986).

44 Professor Toogood, n. 30, wrote with reference to my memo: "hostility is the only intelligent response to an organization [feminism] bent on the intellectual violation of the professoriate..." and "we cannot now or in the future offer a cloak of respectability to individuals or organizations wishing to have an exclusive, unchallenged right to give their version of current and historical events in our schools and universities, especially where these views attempt to vilify identifiable sections of the community with conspiracy and oppression myths. We take this to be a self-evident truth regardless of whether those involved are fascists or feminists." His letter compares feminist teachers to James Keegstra.

45 That university administrators hope to raise awareness of the academic freedom issues involved in anti-feminism by fostering departmental "debate" suggests much of the problem women face. If we must "debate" whether male dominance exists or is oppressive before we can address appropriate remedial strategies, the talk is doomed. I believe women would be much more willing to participate and speak honestly if conversations began with the rec-

ognition that male dominance exists systemically, that presumptively it also exists in our own workplaces such that women have much to risk in discussing its manifestations with their male peers and superiors and that "debate," if any, should centre on how to compensate for and eliminate it.

46 The seven Faculties are: Arts and Science, Business, Education, Engineering, Law, Medicine, and Nursing. The School of Graduate Studies also submitted a report.

47 In the 1986-87 academic year, the visitors committee elected to remedy the near-total absence of women speakers visiting the Faculty in the previous year by inviting several feminist legal scholars to deliver faculty seminars and public lectures. The timing was nearly perfect: the speakers were not just well received, but part of a dynamic political drama. It helped that they delivered interesting and impressive original research.

48 The full text may be found in the 1987-88 Faculty of Law calendar for Queen's University. Italics mine.

49 This course is modelled on the one pioneered by Professor Mary Jane Mossman at Osgoode Hall Law School and discussed in " 'Otherness' and the Law School: A Comment on Teaching Gender Equality," *Canadian Journal of Women and the Law*, 1, 1 (1985): 213.

50 The other two are Kathleen Lahey and Sheila Noonan. Professor Lahey began teaching at Queen's in the fall of 1987. Professor Noonan did not join the Faculty until July 1988. Additionally, in the fall of 1987, Charlene Mandell was appointed Director of the Correctional Law Project. She is the first woman to hold that position at Queen's. In the summer of 1987, Pat Olson, Legal Aid Review Counsel, became a pernament member of the Faculty rather than a renewable-term contract appointee.

8

Ka-Nin-Geh-Heh-Gah-E-
Sa-Nonh-Yah-Gah

Patricia A. Monture

*In this essay, Patricia Monture-OKanee describes the experience of attending a con-
ference held in the summer of 1987; she was, at the time, a law student at Queen's
University.[1] She provides, in rich and compelling detail, a personal account of the
impact of chilly-making practices and attitudes that are substantially racist, as well
as sexist. As was noted in the prefatory remarks published with her essay when it
appeared in the* Canadian Journal of Women and the Law,[2] *she "deals with
theories of racism and disavantage, coping with racism, and conflicts between Native women and their feminist sisters, making connections between racism and sexism that are rarely made."[3] In this she "follows the oral tradition of her nation,"[4]
exemplifying again, and commenting further upon, the importance of grounding
discussion experientially, which figures so centrally in her Introduction to this volume.*

– Eds.

I have come to realize the importance of the experiential because without
human experience we will never achieve a true form of equality. In order to
understand equality, people must understand caring. Without understanding caring, we cannot understand "peoplehood," be it in a community as
small as a gathering of a few people to something as large as the global community. Each person must be respected for whom and what they are. Only
when we all understand caring will we have reached equality.

Native[1] history is oral history. It is probably fortunate for Native people
today that so many of our histories are oral histories. Information that was
kept in peoples' heads was not available to Europeans; could not be
changed and moulded into pictures of "savagery" and "paganism." Tradition, or oral history as a method of sharing the lessons of life with children

and young people also had the advantage that the Elders told us stories. They did not tell us what to do or how to do it or figure out the world for us — they told us a story about their experience, about their life or their grandfather's or grandmother's or auntie's or uncle's lives. It is in this manner that Indian people are taught independence as well as taught respect because you have to do your own figuring for yourself.

Following this tradition or oral history and storytelling, I want to share one of my experiences with you. Like most other academics, I spend at least a little bit of time going to conferences, listening to other people, and learning and sharing what we are thinking. This is a story about a conference I attended, a legal conference, that I want to tell you. It is also a story about anger. My anger is not unique to this conference; it is paralleled at many other conferences I have been to and the classes I have been to, most other days in my life, so it is an important story.

I arrived at the conference at supper time. That was no mistake. I wanted people to be busy doing something else when I arrived. You see, when you know you are going to be the only Indian in the place, it is not exactly a comfortable feeling. Although the drive from my home to the lodge where the conference was being held was only 45 minutes, it seemed much longer.

I was scared. I was scared because I was going to be the only Indian person in pretty much a room full of White people. And it just was not any old bunch of White people; this was a gathering of university professors — law professors from elite and non-elite schools all across the continent; the kind of people I had held in awe and respect through these last eight years of university; people who are published and doing the things now that I am still dreaming of doing and working toward.

I was scared too because I know that those people do not think the same as I do. White people do not line up reality in the same way that I do. They do not understand life and creation the same as I do. They do not know things in the same way that I do. I guess what I am not saying, because I am trying to be polite, is that I know that racism exists in Canada. I know that, because I have lived it.

I planned well; everybody was busy when I arrived at the conference. I checked in and got unpacked and settled without incident and decided that I would go for a walk to stretch my legs. I was happy and relieved to be out in the woods again, near the water. As the earth is my mother, being close to her is always calming. As soon as I got outside of my room, I bumped into a couple of women friends, women that I went to school with at Queen's. They are students, too, so that lessened the burden of feeling a little out of my element as a student in with all these professors. I started to unwind and feel much more comfortable.

It was not very long before it was time to go to the evening session. It was a large group session. It had been explained to me earlier that we would be breaking down into four small working groups first thing the next morning. In order to set the stage for that, the entire group (approximately 50 people) was meeting for a discussion that evening. The discussion was down the road and around the bend in a community hall in this small village where the lodge was located. It was kind of nostalgic and rustic and I had managed to shake most of my fears before I got there.

I think the topic of discussion that evening was racism. I am finding that my memory is a little bit foggy after the events to follow. I know that I sat and listened. I wanted to know where people were coming from. I was not going to jump with both feet into a situation and gathering I knew very little about.

I know that I was not entirely happy about what I heard, that it did not sit well and I lost the comfortable feeling that I had carried with me into the room. I know that because I spoke, and if I remember right, I spoke about understanding and respect. I spoke about how it is that the position of Native people is so frequently described as a position of disadvantage. This is not true simply for Native people, but also for Black people and Chinese people and Chicano people and Mexican people and anybody else who does not fit into the norm of White and middle class. Generically, I am speaking about racism and sexism and classism and all the other "ism's" and of how the individuals who fit those stereotypical classifications get qualified as disadvantaged. We are only disadvantaged if you are using a White, middle-class yardstick. I quite frequently find that White, middle-class yardstick is a yardstick of materialism. We will see how valued you are by the size of your bank account or the number of degrees you can write after your name.

I explained how I just could not understand how Native people are disadvantaged. Looking only at the materialistic yardstick, just about everybody in the country knows that we have less education and less income and more kids and less life expectancy than the majority of the other people in this country, but I still do not see, I said, how we are truly disadvantaged. You see, when non-Indian people are not satisfied with the world they see around them, and it seems to me that more and more of the people that I meet are in this position, well, those people do not have anywhere to turn. They have nowhere to run to. I have an entire community, or rather, pockets of community all over this land. Wherever you find Native people, things are done in a different way, against a different value system. And the measure is not materialism. It is not what you are that counts, it is who you are. So when the world of the dominant culture hurts me and I cannot take it anymore, I have a place to go where things are different. I simply do not understand how that is disadvantaged.

I also do not understand that by having the teachings of the Elders avail-able to me — different ways of learning, different ways of knowing, the ways of traditional spirituality — that I am more disadvantaged than White people. I have had the opportunity to learn Native teachings, to learn about body, mind, and spirit; to learn about balance. Most of the time I am a happy and complete individual, but when I look around me at the people at uni-versity, this is not by and large what I see. I see a lot of people who are hurt, a lot of people who know how to live in their heads and do not know that anything else even exists. I have a hard time understanding again how my experience is an experience of disadvantage. Disadvantage is a nice, soft, comfortable word to describe dispossession, to describe a situation of force whereby our very existence, our histories, are erased continuously right be-fore our eyes. Words like disadvantage conceal racism.

When I left the gathering, I remember I felt a little bewildered. Why was it my professor friend had so insisted that I go to this conference? I had spo-ken, but I did not feel like many people had listened. I know they did not lis-ten. It did not seem that people wanted to hear what I was saying, it did not seem like most of the people in that room wanted to understand how it was that we are different. This bewildered me, but it did not surprise me. This re-fusal, this inability to accept difference and respect difference and rejoice in difference is the point at which my anger grows. Equality is really a celebra-tion of difference.

There was a reception after the gathering back at another room at the lodge and I went to that. I really did not talk to anybody except for the two students that I had met earlier, and looking back I think that was because I was looking for a safe place to be. A safe place to stand, one that was not threatening. My experience of the first evening at the conference set the stage for the following day. I did not stay at that reception for very long. I did not feel comfortable. Why should I stay? I was tired, so I went to sleep.

The next morning I got up and went over to breakfast. What a breakfast we had! The food was so good. Again, I stayed pretty close to the women I knew from Queen's. I had decided through breakfast that I just wanted to watch again for a while because I definitely was not feeling like I was in a safe place. This is pretty typical of an Indian person who is not feeling com-fortable. We are taught that inaction is a better course than action because it is in that manner that we learn where it is we are and how to participate.

During breakfast, the professor friend who had invited me and who was involved in organizing the conference came over to me and asked me if I would mind changing small section groups because one group only had one "person of colour" in it. My friend did not want to leave that person all by themselves. On one hand I was really pleased that this professor was conscious enough to know that when you leave a minority person alone in a gathering of non-minority people, you are leaving that person in a vulnerable spot. But at the same time, the conscious shuffling of bodies from one group to another made me uneasy. Was I no more than a coloured face? This shuffling of bodies contrasts against the Indian way, in which things are allowed to happen as they should. This belief reflects the recognition that we cannot control our natural environment. We cannot master the universe. I have not been able to unpack the feeling of discomfort that the move from one group to another group caused. But it did serve to intensify the fact that I really just wanted to watch and that I really was not trusting the people that were around me. This should be understood as my fear and my difficulty and my problem. It has to be my problem as it is my daily reality. If what I am saying is going to be understood, it must be understood as what I, as one particular person, am feeling and am experiencing and what I think of it. I think it is of value in that experience is the experience of a member of a dispossessed group within this society.

The morning session and lunch were rather uneventful for me. We had a good intellectual talk in my small section and a good effort at getting to know one another. For the most part, I sat back and listened and did not have a whole lot to say. My friends will tell you that is somewhat unusual. I was starting to feel probably a little bit comfortable again. After lunch, we went back to our small session.

I should probably tell you a little bit about the woman who stepped forward as chair at this particular small section meeting. She was not the group facilitator. She is a White woman, I guess from a fairly privileged background. She teaches at an elite United States law school. She conveys herself in a caring manner.

She started the afternoon session by telling a story. That story was about a 67-year-old Black woman, whose name I forget, who lived in the Bronx or some place like that. She was poor. She was a month behind in her rent. Because she was a month behind in her rent, her landlord wanted to evict her. She was old and arthritic and had no place to move to, so she just decided that she was not going to go. The landlord contacted the police and the police came to her apartment door and told her she had to move, I guess. Well, if I remember right, they kicked in her door and found her with a knife — she was not going to leave her home. So the policeman, another Black man, shot her hand off. I am not too sure how or why or the details, I have lost them. Then he shot her in the head, dead. The police officer was eventually charged with murder or manslaughter, the point being that there were criminal charges laid. He was not convicted, I do not know if that means we are supposed to believe that this 67-year-old Black arthritic woman was a danger to society or what, but she is dead.

In the manner of good lawyering, we began to pick at this hypothetical. What if she had been a White woman and he had been a Black man, would he have been convicted? What if he had been a White man, would he have been convicted? And on and on and on in the method of legalism we went. I started squirming in my chair. I did not miss the fact that the Black woman in the room was not missing the fact that I was squirming in my chair. I could not identify why, but the conversation we were having hurt.

I suppose I sat and listened for about half an hour. I am not sure how much I really listened. I was thinking quite intensely on why is this hurting me. Why is this experience so brutal. Why do I want to get up and leave the room. I do not want to hear anymore of this.

By the time I spoke I was almost in tears. What it was that I had identified was that we were talking about my life. I do not know when I am going to pick up the phone and hear about the friend who committed suicide, the acquaintance that got shot by the police, the Native prison inmate that was killed in an alleged hostage taking, ironically two days after two Indian inmates in Stoney Mountain had killed a White prison guard. This is my life. I do not have any control over the pain and brutality of living the life of a dispossessed person. I cannot control when that pain is going to enter into my life. I had gone away for this conference quite settled with having to deal with racism, pure and simple. But, I was not ready to have my pain appropriated. I am pretty possessive about my pain. I worked hard for it. Some days it is all I have. Some days it is the only thing I can feel. Do not try to take that away from too. That was happening to me in that discussion. My pain was being taken away from me and put on the table and poked and prodded with these sticks, these hypotheticals. "Let's see what happened next?" I felt very, very much under a microscope, even if it was not my own personal experience that was being examined.

I explained this to the group and I know I cried a little bit, I do not hide my emotions and I guess that is difficult for some people to handle. I probably talked for five or so minutes trying to explain what it was that was troubling me, upsetting me. I put it all on the table. When I was done, like so many times before, everybody just kind of sat there and looked at me. I watched the Black woman in the room quite carefully. She seemed relieved, so I guessed what I had done was alright and I waited.

The woman who was facilitating the conversation said essentially, "What do we do next? I think what Trisha said is important and what do we do from here? Does this mean that we cannot discuss issues of racism because we are causing more hurt when we do?"

I did not like the sound of that idea too much because I do not think until racism is understood we are ever going to be rid of racism, that is the kind of beast that it is. I thought about my criminal law class in first year. When we had to deal with the issue of rape, or whenever the issue of rape had to be dealt with, be it in the rules of evidence or whatever, people took great pains to make sure that they are not inflicting any harm on any of the women in the room. "You never know when one of the women in the room in the class that you are teaching has been a victim of rape." But as an Indian woman, I have never had the same courtesy extended to me.

In my first-year criminal law, for example, I remember taking a case, a case about an Indian man. I think he was charged with breaking and entering. He was under the influence at the time of the offence. I do not remember the point of the case or the legal issue at stake, but at sentencing the judge was describing this Indian man and it kind of went like this: "He is Indian and he is drunk and he is illiterate" and all of that belongs in one mouthful, so it is not a problem if we send him to jail for X number of years. "After all, he can go and see the rest of the Indians in jail." This case was only about 10 or 15 years old at the time I studied it, which was four years ago. The Professor certainly made no more note than in passing, if he did that much, that this was a stereotype of Indian people that was being portrayed and conveyed by the judge. I was hurt. I had felt very exposed at having my personhood and my reality laid bare on the table in front of the people in class without my consent. In that very same course the very same professor, at some length and with great caution, dealt with the issue of rape, explaining that he did not want to inflict any harm on any women in the class. He certainly hoped that this would not be the case. Yet, when we deal with the issue of racism, very much so do we allow ourselves to be blind to the further pain that we are inflicting.

So I felt strong, although quite exhausted, at having put on the table the way I had been feeling as we talked in hypothetical terms about the murder of this Black woman in the United States by the police officer. I felt that — and maybe this is self-congratulatory — my tears and my pain had brought us to a really good place. The rest of the discussion that afternoon focused on racism and how to deal with racism in a classroom. How do we talk about racism? When do we talk about racism? In what manner do we talk about racism? Several of the men brought up how they would identify with feeling invisible, as I had earlier mentioned, when the issue of gender was discussed. Men are seen as the perpetrator and never the victims of the social reality that we live in. I thought that was a good point and all in all we had a good discussion that afternoon.

I left and went back to my room to have a little bit of a rest before dinner and did not stay for the wine and cheese or before dinner drinks that was going on after our small section. I needed some time and some space to be alone to let the rawness subside. At six o'clock I went to supper, I sat beside a law professor from California, a Chicano man, I believe. We had an animated chat. During our conversation, I remember noticing that a very heated discussion was occurring at the dinner table behind me. It involved the woman who had headed up my small section that afternoon and the two women friends from Queen's who were attending the conference as students. It also involved at least several other White men. At the time, I had the feeling that something important was going on in that discussion, but I did not pay any attention to it. After supper there were no activities scheduled for the evening. It was just a rest and socializing time. I socialized a bit and chatted and then went back and crawled into my bed, still feeling quite exhausted.

The following morning, all the small sections were to meet to discuss what had gone on the previous day. I found it very, very difficult to get out of bed that morning. I was feeling very exposed and raw. I just did not feel up to walking into breakfast where I could possibly have to carry on a conversation, especially a conversation about yesterday's discussions. So I waited around for the general store to open so I could go in and get myself a cup of coffee. The plenary started before I got my coffee.

I arrived at the plenary to hear the woman who had introduced the story of the Black woman's murder in our small section quite emphatically, and almost to the point of being defensive, insist that the issue she was talking about was not an issue of gender. This puzzled me greatly, because the woman in question is a White woman, and by her own admission she does not know very much about racism. I sat through a lot of that conversation not knowing quite what to think, knowing I did not understand what I heard. The conversation kept returning to the woman's insistence that this is not a gender issue.

At some point during that conversation, I finally figured out what everyone was talking about when one of the women there described what had taken place at the dinner table behind me the night before. During this discussion of the dinner table incident, a Hawaiian law professor, also a minority woman, offered this story. She was having dinner with a group of her legal colleagues. The topic of the conversation at that dinner was sports. As she told the story, the conversation began to centre around specific athletes, I believe football players, and what the people at the table thought of each of these superstar athletes. The woman who was telling the story was asked to comment on a certain individual and she said something like, "I used to really like him. I used to think this man was a great, great athlete. Then I saw him advertising beer or underwear or some such thing on television and I do not believe he is really interested in sports for the sake of sports. With all these endorsements that he has been doing, I think he is interested in sports only for money." The unfortunate part of that comment, and the woman did definitely confess that she simply did not know what else to say and did not know an awful lot about football or sports, was that the athlete in question was Jewish. There was a Jewish man sitting at the table at the dinner, and he took offence at the woman's comments. To him it sounded like very much "those money grubbing Jews" stereotype again. This was definitely not the intent of the woman. Her point in telling this story was that intent does not excuse somebody from racism. Racism is racism, and racism stings. All the good intentions in the world do not take away the sting and do not take away the pain.

Shortly after the story was told, the session got very interesting. One of the men who had eaten dinner the night before with the woman who told that story identified himself. He was quite defensive. He took great pains to explain that he did not intend to harm anyone, but that he was seriously questioning whether the conference was accomplishing anything. I do not remember all that he said. What I do remember was getting angry. I said to one of the Queen's students next to me that I was getting very, very tired of hearing White men speaking for me, especially when I am in the room. I am quite capable of speaking for myself.

At this point, I began to notice that my friends were definitely uncomfortable. They were more uncomfortable than I was, and I could not quite figure out why. The whole morning I got the feeling that everybody else had a secret that excluded me. Something very important and very definite was going on here and I was somehow being excluded from it, and I could not quite grasp what it was. I was very shortly to find out.

After the man had finished speaking, the woman who had initiated the conversation that morning and he got into a definite back and forth — very argumentative, very quick, with each attacking each other's position. Each stating how important the issue of racism was, both stating that racism had very much been dealt with. The man insisted that with all this experiential stuff we were definitely going overboard, and that it was certainly time for us to begin dealing with important things like "mega-theory." "Let's make this academic and stop feeling for a while." He also took great pains to explain all he had done to help minority people and how long he had been there for minority people. I think he was questioned about how he knew he was helping if he did not know what minority people actually felt.

Anyway, this arguing match went back and forth and back and forth, with emotions getting higher and higher on both sides of it. All through it, the woman insisted, "No, we are talking about racism, not gender. The fact that I am a White woman and that two other women there were White women and that the three men that were there were White men did not make it an issue of gender. Yes, there were issues of gender involved in it, but that was not the important issue." I was getting very bewildered about how this was not an issue of gender. I mean, we were talking about White people, all White people.

Everything clicked into place when I realized why it was not an issue of gender: the comment that had gotten the entire conversation going the evening before had been made when one of the men and the woman were talking about whether this conference was too experiential. The woman from my small section had said, "No, it is not experiential. Let me show you the good stuff that can come out of the experiential, let me show you the good stuff that came out of the pain." When she finished telling the story about the pain that I had laid on the table the previous afternoon, the man had said "The pain of minority people is like television, we can turn it on and off as we want to." The woman who had brought this conversation to the meeting and put it on the table that morning had finally let that comment slip into the conversation.

I was stunned. I was standing up speaking before I knew it. I cannot find the words to describe how brutalized I felt when those words came out. That was me that was being discussed all morning. Did the man intend to belittle my pain and my life? Did he know how deeply he had clawed into my essence? Did that woman intend to appropriate my pain for her own use, stealing my very existence, as so many other White, well-meaning, middle- and upper-class feminists have done?

It is difficult for me to remember what it was that I said. I know I cried. In many ways it was an emotional outburst and I was aware, I think, that the people there might discount my words on this ground. But, I said what I thought needed to be thought about. It has been too long, I said, that we have not been listened to. Whenever something like this happens in discussion of gender and race, I cannot separate them. I do not know, when something like this happens to me, when it is happening to me because I am a woman, when it is happening to me because I am an Indian, or when it is happening to me because I am an Indian woman. The forum has not been set yet in which those issues can be discussed. There are a lot of teachings that Indian people have about balance and harmony and tranquillity, about well-being. The modern education system is not aware of these things. They have not listened, they have not understood, they still believe that they are going to help us. Well, I do not want to be a White person. You cannot make me be a White person. You cannot help me be a White person. Look at this world, look at what is around you. The earth is my mother. She is being raped. She is being destroyed. There will not be anything left soon if we do not start taking care of the earth. And you, as a White man, and you, as a White woman, stand there and tell me that I do not know, I do not understand — because I feel. I cannot know?

I was angry all right, and I was hurt, I do not know how long I stood and spoke before exhaustion and numbness set in. I responded to what had been said that day as violence, for what had been done to me that day was violence. The White people there had already decided that I was not supposed to hear about that comment. That comment was what had been making the friend next to me so uncomfortable: she was afraid that that comment would slip out and I would be hurt. Well, I am glad that it did slip out, even thought I was hurt. I do not deserve to have those things kept from me. As I said before, my pain is all I have got some days. Do not take it away from me. It is mine. Understand it, understand where the pain comes from and why: I have to struggle with that. If we cannot understand this pain that women, that Indian women, that Black women, that Hawaiian women, that Chicana women go through, we are never going to understand anything. All that mega-theory will not get us anywhere because without that understanding, mega-theory does not mean anything, does not reflect reality, does not reflect people's experience.

I remember speaking again about being labeled disadvantaged. Sure, Native people in this country are disadvantaged, everybody knows that. Everybody knows the statistics. But those are all social and economic variables. You cannot go out and measure how happy people are. You cannot count happiness. You cannot turn happiness into nice neat tidy statistics. Native people are only disadvantaged if you use that materialistic yardstick. If you accept those kinds of measures about who is good and who is not, Indian people are not "good." But if you want to go to a community where you are cared about as an individual who is important, go to a traditional Indian community. That is not disadvantaged. What I have had is a real and an important advantage. When that world out there has hurt me, when I grew up and I did not like what I found and did not like what I saw out there in the city, I had some place to run to. I had another alternative. Most people do not walk into another alternative lifestyle, another alternative value structure. They do not have the same kind of access to those things because they are not people of a minority culture. I do not want to be called disadvantaged anymore. Call me economically poor, call me uneducated, call me all of those things. The education I have got does not mean anything. Do not call me disadvantaged anymore.

I think I talked a long time. I do not know. I think I was in shock. I felt brutalized, violated, victimized — all of those things — but I was not silent. I knew I had to respond, I knew I could not sit there and let it continue. I could not consent to my own disappearance and my own death. I could not watch anymore, so I spoke. I was standing up speaking before I even realized that I was standing up speaking, at least 30 seconds went by before I realized I was on my feet addressing this group, I am saying something, again. When are those of you who inflict racism, who appropriate pain, who speak with no knowledge or respect when you ought to know to listen and accept, going to take hard looks at yourself instead of at me. How can you

continue to look to me to carry what is your responsibility? And when I
speak and the brutality of my experience hurts you, you hide behind your
hurt. You point the finger at me and you claim I hurt you. I will not carry
your responsibility any more. Your pain is unfortunate. But do not look to
me to soften it. Look to yourself.

I wanted to sit down but I could not. I kept talking and trying to explain
until I could not talk anymore. The words were all there in my head, my
mind was fine, it was going 90 miles a minute and I wanted to keep on talking. Then I just shut down, there was nothing left, no strength left to keep
trying to explain. I have explained this same thing so many times that I get
exhausted. But, if one person in that room understood what I had to say, understood what it is that so many Indian people I have listened to and spoken
to have said, heard what the Elders have taught me, if one person understood it, it was worth that last ounce of energy. If I had to speak again to-
morrow and the day after and the day after, it will be worth speaking again.

I reached a point where I just could not talk anymore, but I did not know
how to stop. Everybody else just sat there. I looked at them and they looked
and looked and looked at me and I felt as if I had been caught under a microscope: "What is she going to do next. Let's watch." I could not think how to
sit down. I could not think how to finish what I had started saying. I did not
know what to do. Finally, I looked some more and they looked back some
more and I ended my talk the only way I knew how. That was in an Indian
way, and that was to say: "Megwetch, I am glad you listened. I am glad that
I stood up and talked, let these words I have spoken be good words." Then I
sat down. After I sat down, I looked at them some more and they looked at
me. My friend put her hand on my knee and gave it a squeeze. I wiped some
more tears away and I felt at least as though I had a little bit of energy. A
woman across the room very much wanted to break the silence. That is another difference between Indians and non-Indians. Indians understand that
silence is not a bad thing and silence can mean a lot of things. A lot of things
can be said without opening your mouth. The silence itself did not make me
uncomfortable, but the fact that everybody else in the room was uncomfortable with the silence made me uncomfortable.

Eventually, this woman spoke and she said: "What can I do to help?"
Well, that pulled the rug right out from under my feet again, because I do
not need you to help me. Helping is offensive; it buys into the "I am better
than you are" routine. I know the woman who spoke did not intend to inflict that fresh pain; I know she did not understand that, but all I could think
of were some unpleasant things to say to her. I was to the point where I was
defensive and I knew I could not speak in that manner because I knew she
had spoken from a kind and sincere place, the only words that she knew
how to speak. I was very grateful when one of the other minority women,

the one who had earlier told the story of how intent does not excuse racism, spoke very eloquently indeed and addressed the issue in a good way. I was very grateful for that and it made me smile. It made me smile because when we women — we Indian women and Black women and Chinese women and Hispanic women — are together we take care of each other. She took care of me and she spoke when I could not speak anymore. She carried the ball for awhile, which is something you see all too rarely in this individualistic world that we live in. When will all peoples, all nations, all colours, respect the circle of life?

After that, the session got wrapped up and there was a lot of nervous energy in that air. People did not know what to do. Before I knew what happened, I was surrounded by the men and women of colour who sat in that room. In their physical proximity to me I felt safeness. I knew they understood, I knew they had been there too and they stayed there with me and it was good.

Another good thing happened. We went to lunch together and we did something we oh so rarely do at a racism conference: we sat together and we talked about what racism means to us. What it means to go to a conference like this and never get a chance to be with each other and we do not get a chance to hear each other. We do not know what the differences are between a Black woman's experience and an Indian woman's experience because we have never had the chance to talk about it. This is one of the ways that racism and oppression are perpetuated. But we need to talk about it, so that is what we did. We talked about our need to talk about it and it was a start and it was a good lunch. The reason that we all went to lunch together was because we wanted to demonstrate to the White people there that we do stand together, that there is solidarity amongst us. You cannot attack the only Indian woman at a conference and think that the Black women are not going to be there standing beside her, because they will be there standing beside her.

This story does not have an end. It goes on and on and on. When I am done telling this one, I can tell you another one and another one and another one and another one. I want to know and I want to believe that it makes a difference. That what I have struggled with will make a difference to my son and to his children and to those who come after. We have an obligation to those children to see that there is something here for them, but I am scared that that is not happening and it is not happening fast enough and that it is not happening quick enough. How many hundreds and hundreds of years have we been doing this? And when is it going to stop?

Tonight these questions are just too big and too hard and I am too alone.

Notes

Editors' Notes

1 This esssay originally appeared as "Ka-Nin-Geh-Heh-Gah-E-Sa-Nonh-Yah-Gah," *Canadian Journal of Women and the Law*, 2 (1986): 159-70.
2 Ibid., p. 159.
3 Ibid.
4 Ibid.

Note

1 This is the language, Native or Indian, that appeared in the original text. Although in recent years I have adopted institutional language, Aboriginal Peoples, I did not feel it was appropriate to change the name I use to call myself in this paper.

9

The Gender Wars: "Where the Boys Are"[1]

Bruce Feldthusen

This essay, first published in 1990, reflects upon the response of male faculty to the inclusion of women and women's concerns within the academy. In its focus on (White) male academics, the essay departs in some respects from the rest of this volume. But it adds a centrally important dimension to the understanding of the chilly climate as it attempts to analyze the role of men in creating and sustaining an environment which so many women find unsettling and inhospitable.

The author, a full professor at a faculty of law, takes as his point of departure a series of public events which occurred over the past several years at a number of university law schools. Faculties of law have become sites of particularly vociferous struggle over the legitimacy of feminist research and feminist political principles (especially where these affect the recruitment, hiring, and promotion of faculty members, teaching methodologies and the design of curriculum). In some faculties of law, sufficiently large numbers of female faculty were hired during the 1980s to create a definable presence, even to establish "a critical mass" of women. The women in some law faculties were able to work jointly and collaboratively to seek to improve the situation for female students and faculty. In keeping with their growing numbers and collective strength, the demands they made upon their professional faculties escalated. So did the response of their male colleagues. This essay attempts to make sense of the different patterns exhibited by male faculty members as they react to feminist organizing within the academy. Although the analysis is centred upon faculties of law, much of it appears to be applicable across disciplines and even to faculties which contain fewer, and less visibly feminist, female faculty.

– Eds.

1. Introduction

Tension over gender issues is manifest in Ontario law schools. In many cases, the term "gender wars" might be appropriate.[1] This tension is well recognized by most legal academics, members of the bar, and the general public that reads the Ontario newspapers. In this article I attempt to explain the role of male law professors in this war.[2]

There is probably nothing unique about the gender wars within law schools. Law schools are merely one forum in which the battles are being waged in a particular way at a particular time. If there is anything unusual, it is that notoriously conservative faculties supplying a notoriously conservative profession find themselves at the vanguard of social change. This role is not one for which most law faculties have been well prepared.[3]

This tension, even the war, is not new, but two things have changed in recent years. First, the number of feminists in legal education has increased to the point that they are no longer willing to suffer in silence.[4] They are demanding that gender issues be addressed, and that they be addressed as gender issues. Second, the media have taken an interest in what feminists have to say. This media interest is no coincidence. The public funds legal education. Law schools train people who will shape the public agenda. Law schools are not the private preserve of professors, students, and the profession they service, let alone a select group thereof. The public has a legitimate concern with how lawyers are educated and a right to know that many male law professors are indifferent or hostile to the nation's equality laws. The public has a right and a duty to demand that legal education change.

The gender wars in Canadian law schools first surfaced publicly and dramatically in 1986, when a copy of the now famous "McIntyre Memo" was leaked to the press. This internal faculty memo detailed the sexist and anti-feminist treatment received by a junior feminist law professor at Queen's law school.[5] This event probably marks the beginning of the most significant change in gender relations ever experienced in Ontario law schools. What women in legal education had been saying privately and in their own networks became Canada-wide news. Sheila McIntyre's experience encouraged others to break public silence.

In 1987, York University chose as the new Dean for Osgoode Hall Law School an external male candidate over an internal feminist candidate, Mary Jane Mossman. The decision did not sit well with many students who saw it as gender discrimination. At graduation, many wore buttons stating "Dare to Dream of a Feminist Dean," and showered Mossman with pink carnations as she sat on the platform. Significantly, many women law professors, graduates, and students across the province agreed. Media interest increased when more than 100 of them filed a complaint of sex discrimination with the Ontario Human Rights Commission, alleging both discrimination against Mossman and systemic discrimination throughout the law school. The issues raised continue to provoke debate, sometimes hostile, within Osgoode Hall. The ongoing settlement process holds the media's attention.[6] Meanwhile, media exchanges that pit students against faculty and against one another proliferate.[7]

In December 1989, the Associate Dean of the law school at the University of Western Ontario, Craig Brown, also a member of the Appointments Committee, released a memo on hiring policy to the faculty. The thrust of it was the need for long-term commitment to junior faculty. His proposal was supportive of three people seeking renewal of one-year contracts, two of whom were women. One was a visible feminist scholar, and both were active on issues affecting women in the law school. The next day Brown acknowledged and criticized sexism within his Faculty in an interview with the local newspaper. Two days later he was fired unceremoniously from his position as Associate Dean and removed from the Appointments Committee by the Dean, ostensibly for breaching the confidentiality of the Appointments Committee. He brought suit for wrongful dismissal. The media followed the story closely. The battle was joined irrevocably when half the faculty published an Open Letter supporting his dismissal. Another third of the faculty revolted in response to what they perceived as blunt power gender politics. The faculty remain at loggerheads, with the majority refusing to acknowledge any connection to gender issues at all.[8]

Much of what follows is based on personal observation at the Faculty of Law at the University of Western Ontario, where I took my LLB degree, and where I have been on faculty since 1977. Some of it may not be applicable to other law schools, but it is supplemented with reference to the few written records which exist of women's experience at other Canadian common law and civil law schools.[9] The patterns, often the particular episodes, seem to occur with remarkable similarity whenever they are reported.

Gender issues at most Canadian law schools have yet to make the headlines or the law reviews. It is tempting, but implausible, to suppose that this signifies the absence of gender tension. It is more likely that the tension exists everywhere in legal education, but has yet to be recognized as gender tension by male law professors. It would be refreshing to think some law schools have succeeded in integrating women's issues without serious opposition.[10] There are, however, other possible explanations. The apparent quiet may signify only that the catalytic event that will release the tensions has yet to occur. It may signify that feminists at those schools are not yet sufficiently empowered to take an active public stance. Indeed, some Canadian law schools lack even a single scholar engaged in explicit feminist teaching or scholarship. However much criticism may be fairly made of the particu-

lar schools referred to herein, still stronger criticism deserves to be made of
those schools that have silenced women completely.

There are a number of things that I do not purport to do in this article. I
do not attempt to be impersonal; my personal views affect much of the analysis. I do not attempt to be neutral or unbiased; I am openly supportive of an
expanded feminist presence within legal education, and supportive of the
fundamental changes which their meaningful presence entails. I am ap-
palled by the indifference and outright hostility to feminism demonstrated
by many of my colleagues on both institutional and personal levels. The role
of the law students is not considered; they are more than foot soldiers.[11] I
say virtually nothing about other forms of discrimination, such as that undoubtedly experienced by people of the First Nations, people of colour, and
people with disabilities. This omission does not suggest that I regard gender
discrimination as the most pressing issue of discrimination in legal education. Rather, it speaks to my own ignorance and to the relative absence of
visible minorities in legal education which inhibits all of us from learning
more about the full force of discrimination. Finally, I attempt no analysis of
the role of women, feminist or not, in the law school gender wars. I readily
concede that such an analysis might have more explanatory power than
what follows.

The most obvious reason why men in the law schools remain ignorant of
feminism in the legal context, and indifferent or hostile to a meaningful feminist presence within the law schools, is simply that they are men. Feminism
as a critique of male and male-dominated culture is not naturally appealing
to a male audience. I explore this point briefly in the first part of the article.

While simply being men may prove to be the ultimate explanation for
male hostility to feminism within the law schools, it is the wrong place to begin. It assumes that male professors have a reasoned idea of what a meaningful feminist presence within the law schools would entail, and that they
have rejected it as hostile to their interests as men.[12] The truth is that most
male law professors do not engage with the feminist critique at all. Mostly,
male law professors experience feminism superficially, as a nuisance.[13] Policies requiring gender sensitivity in law school activities inconvenience
men.[14] Beyond these superficial levels of familiarity, men exercise their ultimate tool of oppression, their "right not to know."[15] Men and women perceive and experience reality differently. The right not to know enables men
to ignore this, and if forced to confront it, to deny it. Men assume that their
perception of reality *is* reality. This assumption is the critical focus of my
analysis. Only when the right not to know is exposed, only when men acknowledge and abandon it, does a consideration of whether feminism is
truly antithetical to the interests of men become relevant. In the second part

of my article, I illustrate how the right not to know provokes, shapes, and prolongs manifest gender warfare within the law schools.

In the third part, I pursue the "right not to know" theme somewhat differently. Men rarely experience feminism as threatening to their interests as men. The exercise of the right not to know enables men to deny the significance of gender for men as much as it enables men to deny its significance for women. Instead, men experience feminism as threatening to their more narrowly defined interests, interests which they assume are gender-neutral. Furthermore, they experience feminism as threatening to themselves individually. I analyze this point by dividing male law professors into analytical interest groups and considering the significance of gender in what men perceive as gender-neutral encounters.

2. What if Men Knew?

> Who can doubt . . . that it is the old [White male] guard which has the most to lose in giving up a world view that locates it at the very hub of the universe, protected by those "universal" laws which operate for its comfort and advantage?[16]

That equal treatment without discrimination on the basis of sex, or any other basis, might mean a better society for all of us is an abstraction that is not easily grasped. If grasped, it is not necessarily one that appeals to the privileged male. In legal education, as elsewhere, feminists attack basic assumptions that men take for granted, and the privileges accruing to men as a result.

When a man abandons his right not to know, he has little or no idea where this will take him,[17] which is perhaps a good thing in the short run. When men begin to recognize the existence and import of realities other than their own, they may well balk. It entails both a loss of male privilege and an apparent loss of male self. As Clare Dalton says:

> It is not simply a matter of filling, finally, some previously identified and oddly persistent gaps in one's understanding. It involves recognizing that the entire perceptual and conceptual apparatus one has previously relied on for knowledge about the world may be faulty. It involves remaking the map of the world one carries about in one's head so that the gaps appear, generating the recognition that they need to be filled. And since it is in relation to this interior map that one locates and identifies oneself, it involves being ready to meet some unfamiliar and sometimes unwelcome images of oneself.[18]

Dalton suggests that men will balk at the guilt and shame they will experience over their own past conduct. More likely, it is the present and future implications for the individual male who abandons his right not to know which may stop him in his tracks. The individual male would have to consider the reality of power, thereby undermining the conception of formal equality that justifies so much substantive inequality from which he benefits.[19] False parallelism ("the same thing happens to me") would be exposed. The individual male would have to acknowledge that his many accomplishments in life were not earned solely as just rewards for his exceptional talent. He would have to evaluate feminist demands for women's space as an issue of distributive justice, rather than as an issue of corrective or retributive justice where he feels he is on solid ground. This shift is personally threatening, threatening in a way that matters to men.

It is impossible at this stage to determine whether most men can ever accept a meaningful feminist presence within the law schools. Their constant exercise of the right not to know prevents us from testing such a hypothesis. It may be that the right not to know is a self-serving technique employed by men who have resolved to perpetuate their self-centred universe. Or, it may be that men are also victims of their own male culture. It is difficult for men to abandon their tendency to define social reality, including the reality of legal education, solely on their own terms. The male culture is dominant, and arrogance and paternalism are deeply engrained in it.[20]

On one level it does not matter why men exercise the right not to know, because it is no excuse for discrimination. The distinction between conscious and unconscious discrimination only matters if one assumes there exists a male audience to which the feminist critique is alien, but nevertheless an audience which could be "prepared to make space for it in their minds and hearts."[21] If one wishes to reach this audience, one must first overcome their exercise of the right not to know.[22] To this issue I now turn.

3. The Right Not to Know

The test of strength of any ideology is the extent to which its basic presuppositions remain not merely unquestioned but literally unrecognized.[23]

Change comes with learning to see and understand the world through new perspectives, understanding the feelings of those who see it differently, and learning to accord equal respect to those differences, those realities, and the people whose lives they reflect.[24]

Most men do not reflect on or analyze feminism at all. They tend to be woefully ignorant about feminism. There is something in the male culture or psyche which inhibits men from even considering seriously feminist theory. This inhibition makes it very difficult for feminists in the law school to engage their male colleagues in meaningful debate, let alone to elicit their support.

Obviously this tendency is self-serving and perpetuates male power, but it is probably not a conscious strategic choice for most men. Rather it comes from an inability or unwillingness to perceive the world through the eyes of others. "Men hold *their* truths to be self-evident."[25] The feminist critique is so foreign to the way in which most individual males perceive social reality that it strikes them as irrational and incoherent. The typical male response is to dismiss the critique entirely. This response is not merely a rejection of feminist theory and its implications for legal education. It is also a rejection of men's responsibility to inform themselves about and then to join the debate. Feminists are asking men to see the world from a perspective other than their own, and in addition, to make room for women and others who can. At this stage it is unclear how many men can comprehend the demand, let alone attempt to comply.

Attempting to confront the male right not to know is like peeling an onion layer by layer. There are many layers. One cries. One wonders whether the core holds anything different from the outer layers.

In 1989 a group of 26 male and female law students at Western encountered the right not to know layer by layer. They posted a petition on the student notice board calling for an institutional response to sexism and sexual harassment. The petitions gave non-identifying examples of sexual harassment of students, and of sexism in the classroom. The students sought no trial or punishment. They wanted the school to acknowledge that it had an institutional problem, and to respond to it as an institution. This petition marked the beginning of open gender warfare at Western.

At the first layer, men ignore problems experienced by women. Most of the examples listed in the petition were generally, if unofficially, known to members of faculty, and had been ignored. The petition was provocative because it challenged a derivative of the right not to know, the male right to ignore women's problems. It requires a great deal of perseverance to peel back this layer, as well as a willingness to be branded as non-collegial for having done so. The students who signed the petition peeled back this layer and paid the price.[26]

When confronted with problems raised by women, the second layer of the right not to know is often denial of the significance of gender. At my Faculty, those who raise the issue of sexism are accused of having "genderitis," a phenomenon explored in the next section. The student petitioners were spared this difficulty. No one could deny the significance of gender to the outrageous incidents of sexual harassment alleged in their petition.

In stressing institutional responsibility, the petition expressed the perspective of women. "[W]omen see themselves as essentially connected to others and as members of a community while men see themselves as essentially autonomous and independent of others."[27] The difference is especially pronounced when dealing with gender issues. Feminists focus on patterns of discrimination and privilege which are explicable in the aggregate on the basis of sex. They relate individual episodes to social patterns, seeing discrimination as systemic.[28] They see progress as requiring changes to the gendered patterns, not merely or mainly to the behaviour and attitudes of individual men. In contrast, men tend more than women to see events as isolated, individual episodes, and are reluctant to see patterns of behaviour explicable on the basis of sex. By this exercise of the right not to know, men distance themselves from the conduct of their brothers.

Consider, for example, the different reactions to the Montreal massacre of 14 women — 12 engineering students, one nursing student, and a staff member. The assailant walked into a classroom shouting: "You're all a bunch of feminists" and opened fire. Many feminists argued that all men bear some responsibility for the shooting. Most men denied this allegation vehemently.[29] So pronounced was the anti-feminist backlash that followed that some feminists felt compelled to deny that feminists were responsible for the massacre.[30] The debate was examined thoroughly by the media, especially in Kingston where tension over the incident surfaced within Queen's law school.[31]

To members of a male culture that focuses on the individual actor, it seems profoundly unjust that men in general might be expected to take some responsibility for the Montreal killings. Men see the responsibility for the murders solely as the individual responsibility of the assailant. They see themselves as totally divorced from the event. They were not in Montreal. They did not pull the trigger. They see the event as gender neutral. It is purely contingent that the assailant was a male who targeted women assuming that they were feminists. Many men cannot conceive that women as a group might view the event as an episode within a broader pattern of violence against women. They object to the politicizing of an obvious act of individual deviance.

So it is in the law schools.[32] Women see and experience episode after episode of sexism and they say: "We have a problem of sexism within the law school." Men see less of this phenomenon and experience none of it in the way women do. A male professor suggests at faculty council that the "Women and the Law" course ought to be "excreted" from the calendar.[33] Other men say nothing. Later they say: "That was just Professor A. He is rude to everyone." A male professor circulates a memo ridiculing a feminist colleague's academic work.[34] Again male colleagues say nothing in public. Later men say: "That was just Professor B." Complaints surface about the trivialization of rape in the classroom.[35] "That was just Professor C." A male professor suggests at a faculty meeting that "capital punishment" would be appropriate discipline for women who complain about sexism in the law school. "That is just Professor D." A male professor confronts a woman in her office to harangue her about her gender politics with such force she is left physically intimidated.[36] At Western, it is dismissed as just Professor E. At Queen's, ". . . that is just 'X.' "[37] At Osgoode it may be ". . . rare, an unfortunate outcome of the chance confrontation of a sensitive individual with an insensitive faculty member. . . ."[38]

On my faculty there have been more of such episodes committed by more different men than there are women on faculty. Most of my male colleagues continue to view them as nothing more than a list of individual episodes. The suggestion in the petition that Western had an institutional problem of sexism fell on ears that will not hear. The petition failed to peel back this layer of the right not to know. "It's just so and so."[39]

When forced to confront women's problems, men deny women's definitions of problems. Not only is it just so and so, but "He (I) did not mean it." Men deny that sexism has significance unless the male signifies it by his malicious intent. The Supreme Court of Canada becomes invisible to many male law professors when it rules on gender discrimination.[40]

In cases of unequivocally inappropriate conduct (i.e., recognized even by men), men insist on redefining women's problems in their own terms and then grafting on male solutions. The petitioners wanted a change in the law school culture.[41] Most men perceived the petition as gratuitous nastiness. How, male professors asked, can the institution respond if the women will not make formal complaints? Again the right not to know allows them to overlook the obvious reasons why women law students do not make formal complaints.[42] But beyond that, men want formal complaints, adversarial adjudication (by men), and sanction of individual actors. They seek retribution based on individual moral wrongdoing. Their right not to know about the dynamics of discrimination becomes their excuse for failing to address it.

The other general male response to the petition was defensiveness, personal and institutional.[43] When women describe conduct as sexist they generally mean that the conduct is experienced by women as demeaning. Men only hear their own definitions. Bring a sexist remark to the attention of the typical male law professor and he hears an accusation that he is a moral reprobate.[44] Many of my colleagues felt that the anonymous accounts in the petition had branded them individually as harassers.[45] From the right not to know derives the right to take offence. A woman's experience of sexual harassment pales in comparison to the indignity the male inflicts on himself. As one of my male colleagues summed it up in a letter of response to the student petition, "I am deeply hurt."

Finally, those who object to discrimination at Western have been met with the damning accusation: "They meet in groups!" Male professors, on the other hand, meet behind closed doors with faculty and students they assume are supportive to discuss the "feminist conspiracy" to "take over the law school."[46] They fail to realize that the notion of takeover implies that they control the school and that it will have to be taken from them; that sharing, not takeover, is the agenda of equality. They legitimize their hostility as a defence against a "conspiracy" they have constructed in their own minds.

We are thus embroiled in a gender conflict which is perceived entirely differently by the two sides. For most women it is a struggle against oppression; for most men, it is a war between two equally empowered camps of extremists.

On the one hand, we have a group of people seeking to address sexual harassment, abusive misogyny, and thoughtless discrimination.[47] Their "attacks" generally consist of benign references to generic "male" behaviour. They encounter indifference, accusations of "gender-itis," "It's just so and so," "He (I) didn't mean it," demands for formal complaints, defensive hurt feelings, attacks on their right to meet in groups, and invocation of a conspiratorial plot. These "counter-attacks" are usually personal.[48]

On the other hand, most male law professors see themselves as innocent neutrals involved unfairly in a war between two warring factions — the feminists and the male "so and so's." Even left-leaning men claim a similar middle ground, although they are more prone to describe themselves as sympathetic to women, or even as feminists themselves, rather than as neutral. They simply redefine the factions, and distance themselves from the feminists on faculty by describing them as "right wing"[49] or "bourgeois"[50] feminists. Only the social conservatives,[51] as a group, would eschew the neutrality claim.

This impasse is not a sad case of miscommunication between two well-meaning groups. It is another example of "a male viewpoint being seen quite unreflectively as the only viewpoint, which viewpoint men consider self-evidently valid, legal and neutral."[52] It results in any number of different male positions on the role of women and feminism in legal education, each of which is regarded as correct, neutral, and reasonable by the male expounding it. These self-proclaimed neutrals include a number of men whose conduct is among the most overtly hostile to the interests of women. Seldom is the position of any self-proclaimed neutral rationally grounded, or informed by research or consultation with women. Nor is it likely to be shaken if these faults are pointed out. This arrogance is possible only in a male culture in which an individual male's opinion is the legitimate standard for his views and conduct. It is paternalistic in form and conduct, the very object of the feminist critique.

There also exists a smaller group of men within a law school who might make a more credible claim of neutrality. They neither sexually harass nor ridicule women's proposals at faculty meetings, or in the classroom, or in the press. They try to use gender-neutral language and gender-inclusive examples. They tend to be polite to everyone and are not easily identified with any factions within the school. If they have strong views on gender issues, they keep them to themselves. They may be conservatives, liberals, or left-leaning, and often appear apolitical on most issues. They see their personal conduct as appropriate and therefore as neutral. They see the gender wars as unpleasant external events. They were not in Montreal. They did not pull the trigger.

For feminists, this claim to neutrality is also false. Feminists may distinguish between those who actively attack the interests of women and those who sit passively and observe the attacks. But they do not regard those who stand silent in the face of hostility to women as neutral.

On my faculty, I have seen women's courses ridiculed at faculty meetings by their male colleagues. I have seen feminist writing by my colleagues ridiculed in public by their male colleagues. I have seen women faculty members insulted viciously in the public press. I have heard sexual harassment, even rape, trivialized in public by male colleagues. I have seen women colleagues intimidated physically by male colleagues. Inevitably, I have also seen the vast majority of my male colleagues stand silent in observation of this hostile behaviour. I have been guilty of this silence myself.

Why do men, especially potentially supportive men, stand silent? One possibility is that some are no more supportive of women in the law schools than any other men. They may be simply more polite, and more prudent. Or, they may be the type of person disinclined to take a public stance on any controversial issue. This approach would be exacerbated by the risk of sanction from other men. Women report frequent private visits from men in this group expressing their outrage over conduct which they left unchallenged in public. Ultimately, however, it all comes down to a more benign exercise of the right not to know. These men have defined gender discrimination in terms of individual conduct. They have addressed the problem as they perceive it, as individuals. Their right not to know allows them to go no further. They are the "enablers," a critical force on the side of anti-feminist men in the gender wars.

Of all the barriers to mutual respect and tolerance, to meaningful equality within the law schools, the exercise of the male right not to know is the most immediately pressing. It renders any further civil progress impossible. It goes beyond a trivialization of women's experience to the point of denying the existence of women's experience. So gendered is this tendency that it is impossible to illustrate with a concrete example of how women might similarly dismiss men.

The right not to know outrages women, and so it should. It also frustrates women because there is so little they can do to overcome it. Men must bear the entire responsibility for the refusal to consider seriously the well-

articulated and intensely personal perspectives of women in legal education. Men who choose to confront feminism in legal education with the right
not to know must accept responsibility for the declaration of gender warfare. It is they who have determined the hostile path.

4. Gender-itis

Although we are not perfect, it is not sexism that is rampant, but what I call
"gender-itis." This is the placing of gender at the centre of the universe
with the assumption that all issues revolve around it. . . . Life has its share
of disappointments for both sexes.[53]

So far, I have discussed gender warfare in a manifestly gendered context.
Much, perhaps most, gender warfare in the law schools occurs over what
men perceive as gender-neutral issues. When allegations of sexism deal
with conduct more subtle than physical harassment or abusive language,
complainants are described as mentally ill. They have "gender-itis" says
one of my colleagues.

For example, the Craig Brown memo and its aftermath did not arise in a
gender-neutral vacuum. The appointments process at Western has been a
gender issue for several years. Many of us at Western had observed an overt
anti-feminist campaign mounted by several male colleagues in an effort to
discredit a feminist colleague. Others on faculty help by circulating their in-
dictments, and others passively acquiesce. The Brown memo was supportive of this woman and the other who had also taken an active stand against
sexism in the law school. But 16 members of our faculty denied any connection between the memo and gender issues. In their Open Letter response to
the Brown firing, they said: "Professor Brown's dismissal had nothing to do
with his opinions concerning the treatment of women in the Faculty of Law.
His memorandum did not mention and did not even allude to this issue."

As the issues become more subtle, the problem becomes more intractable. I believe that many contentious issues within law schools contain a significant gender component, but men do not experience them this way. Most
men do not see "men" as a significant reference group for any purpose. Our
culture nurtures men as a group "automatically." When men experience
feminism as threatening, they experience it as threatening to their more narrowly defined interests, or to themselves as individuals.

Below, I consider more narrowly defined male interest groups within
the law schools, and how these specific interests mesh or clash with feminism in legal education. I discuss three different types of conservatives: the
social, the professional, and the institutional conservatives. I also discuss
leftists.[54] These are analytical categories only, and do not necessarily exist as
recognizable functioning groups within the schools. The categories are not

all mutually exclusive, so any given male might be associated with one or several categories.

From the male point of view, the analysis reveals specific interests within each group which provide additional reasons why men would oppose, or at least refuse to support feminism within law schools.[55] Men perceive their opposition to the goals of feminism as gender neutral, not anti-feminist. For that reason, many male law professors will object not only to the details of what follows, but to the very assertion that it has anything to do with gender. They will see the conflicts I describe as gender-neutral differences of political, institutional, or personal philosophy. And they will resent what they see as the pervasive force of feminism attacking their political, institutional, and personal freedom.

From the perspective of women, the narrower or personal interests of their male colleagues are strongly related to their status as men. When any predominantly male group clashes with any predominantly female group, neither the substance of the debate, nor the manner in which it is carried out, will be gender neutral.

5. The Social Conservatives

The social conservatives are the easiest to identify, because they reject feminism openly. Their background ideology is one which stresses inherent difference on the basis of sex, and holds that this difference entails different social roles for men and women. "Conservatives either claim that the female role is not inferior to that of the male, or they argue that women are inherently better adapted than men to the traditional female sex role. All feminists reject the first claim (but) some modern feminists have revived the latter claim."[56] Most social conservatives, by now, have accepted that women have a legitimate role in the legal professoriate, but they do not accept that women should have a legitimate right to shape that role from a woman's perspective. Obviously, the debate between social conservatives and feminists is not gender neutral.

Conservatives are not necessarily or always the most vociferous objectors to women's presence in the law schools. Like anyone else, conservatives may be polite or hostile, active, or passive, but they do tend to be more openly intolerant of feminism on an intellectual level.[57] Feminism is experienced by conservative men as a concrete threat to their fundamental beliefs. There is little hope that conservatives will ever accept a feminist perspective as a legitimate contribution to legal education. One can predict with relative ease where a conservative will stand on any issue with manifest feminist content. The most one can reasonably expect is that they will resign themselves to the inroads which feminism has made in the law schools and confine their attacks to legitimate means. However, one cannot expect the conservative to acknowledge or to address the imbalance of power which permeates such a debate, an imbalance which exists in differential access to senior academic positions, and access to print, for example.

6. Professional Conservatives[58]

Every law school experiences tension between those who emphasize the professional training aspect of legal education and those who emphasize legal education as a university discipline. That very statement could provoke endless and probably hostile debate. There is no reason why concrete professional training cannot achieve the highest academic standards say some. The very best professional training is a purely theoretical education grounded in the humanities and social sciences say others.

As an ideal type, the professional model accepts that the overwhelmingly dominant purpose of legal education is to prepare students for the practice of law. It describes the practice of law primarily by subject matter. Lawyers draw wills, so Wills is a professional course, and so on. Its newest version includes skills training. Lawyers negotiate, so Negotiations is a professional course, and so on. The professional model is conservative in that it tends to take the practice of law as given, and to respond to practice rather than to attempt to shape it. The professional model perceives of the law professor as a teacher of these professional data and skills. Research is directed primarily to the practising bar and judiciary as a contribution to the professional enterprise.

There is no reason to suppose that professional conservatives are necessarily, or even mainly, social conservatives. Most professional conservatives on law faculties are men, perhaps simply because most professors are men, particularly at the senior level. The Canadian law schools' gradual shift away from a purely professional model is relatively recent,[59] so many men were themselves educated in a purely professional training environment.

For the most part, feminist perspectives on legal education do not fit within the professional model. The practice of law taken as a given excludes many issues and perspectives affecting women. One of the goals of feminists is to have the legal system recognize issues affecting women. Another is to have the profession recognize a different women's perspective on traditional legal issues. In this sense, feminist perspectives are diametrically opposed to the conservative professional model of legal education. This is also true of others such as those who seek to bring First Nations' cultural perspectives to legal education.

Feminists also tend to look well beyond the practice of law as the justification for legal education. They see law as part of the power structure which shapes social reality for women and men. In this sense, feminist perspectives are more in keeping with a university academic model than a professional training model. Since feminists object to the power structures of society, including law, they reject a conservative approach to the study of law.

For men who are professional conservatives, this is a gender-neutral debate over what is law, and then over what and how law should be taught. Lawyers do not practise feminist legal theory, so there is a limit to how much theory, let alone feminist theory, should be taught in a law school. Lawyers practise criminal law, not perspectives on criminal law. If a woman's perspective on family law should be taught, why not a man's? Law is law and feminism is feminism. The role of a law school is to teach law, not feminism (or marxism or anti-racism . . .). A feminist perspective is "personal" or "political," not "law."[60] Professional conservatives experience women's complaints as irrational, even incoherent. Feminists experience this debate in which they are always outnumbered as a fundamental denial of the right of women to participate in the shaping of legal education.

Now that the Charter of Rights and Freedoms[61] and human rights legislation, for example, have moved equality discourse into the professional arena, one would think that the professional conservative might accept some feminist content in legal education on his own terms. Yet, a common response is to treat gender equality issues as a gender-neutral topic.[62] A feminist perspective is a biased perspective: "our [women's] views are discredited and the 'neutral' view is authoritative."[63] But is the professional conservative's conception of legal practice as it exists either neutral or accurate? One student at Osgoode Hall challenged this conception directly: "What is really being taught in first year courses? Is it how to function effectively as a lawyer, or is it a 19th century liberal view of how society should be?"[64]

In addition, male colleagues continue to excuse inappropriate sexist conduct of themselves and others because it was not deliberate. They do this despite definitive legal rulings from the Supreme Court of Canada which hold that the legal concept of discrimination pertains to the impact on the victims, not to the intent or motive of the perpetrators. It is difficult to imagine that law professors are completely unaware of Supreme Court rulings; perhaps they regard them as irrelevant to their own personal actions.[65]

The significance of gender in the professional conservative vs. feminist debate is not always subtle. Standard professional qualifications of feminists are often discredited or ignored because they are feminists.[66] An appointments candidate at our faculty once delivered a talk on the Human Rights complaint being brought against Osgoode Hall Law School by more than 100 women. Her talk was dismissed by many male faculty members because it was "not law," a dismissal that may or may not have been questioned when the action culminated in a settlement of nearly $1 million.[67]

On the initiative of students, our faculty decided to add an anti-discrimination statement to the faculty calendar. The first proposal to faculty council, prepared in consultation with some faculty members, was completely unsatisfactory. I doubt whether any women were consulted. I know that no persons of colour and no feminists were consulted, although two feminists on faculty have specific expertise in this area. Perhaps they were considered biased. Perhaps they were not considered at all. Overall, then, while feminist content in legal education encounters the same hostility from professional conservatives that any "non-professional" perspective does, it encounters additional hostility because it is feminist.[68]

Every law school also experiences tension over the amount of outside work done by members of its faculty.[69] Some law professors maintain private consulting or adjudication businesses in addition to their teaching and research tasks within the law school. One of the main justifications for extensive outside work of a transactional nature is that it contributes to professors' ability to provide professional education and scholarship. Extensive and lucrative labour arbitration practices, law firm consulting practices, and even part-time legal practices are thereby rationalized as part of the professorial role.

It is not surprising that most professors engaged in extensive outside transactional legal work are male professional conservatives,[70] many of whom feel particularly threatened by anyone who advocates the university model.[71] Supporters of the university model deny the professional conservatives' claims that extensive outside income is necessary to attract and retain the "best" legal academics, and that extensive outside work is a desirable complement to the professorial role. Feminists and others attempting to secure some legitimate space within the law schools also resent being treated as serfs by absentee landlords.

In some cases, the connection between outside work and anti-feminism is explicit and deliberate. At one Western faculty meeting, a professor delivered an unusually lengthy, bizarre, and hostile speech, overtly and frighteningly anti-feminist in content. As usual, the remarks went unchallenged. Later, the professor indicated to a member of faculty that he regretted the incident, explaining that he had decided to address the issue as he did in order to deflect attention away from an anticipated discussion about outside work. One must wonder whether gender issues are raised to disguise other issues as often as other issues are emphasized in order to deny the significance of gender.

If the debate were simply one between mostly male professional conservatives and university model supporters, including most women, it would still contribute to the gender wars. Once outside transactional work is taken into account, the financial and personal stakes for the professional conservative are much higher. Tension over the independently problematic issue of outside work then manifests itself as a battle in the gender wars.

7. Institutional Conservatives

Institutional conservatives are committed to maintaining the law school as it was, or at least as they perceive it to have been, in the past. They rely heavily on the symbols of law school tradition, and display and demand fierce loyalty to that abstraction.[72] Differences of opinion about legal education are characterized as disloyalty to the school.[73] Because the history of most Canadian law schools is relatively short, this group may include early graduates of the school and some of the earliest professors, as well as their subsequent converts. Institutional conservatives are not necessarily social conservatives, but tend to be professional conservatives because the tradition they revere was one where professional education dominated.

The number of institutional conservatives within a law school and their relative power is likely to differ from school to school. At Western, they are numerous and effectively have controlled the school for much of at least the last two decades.[74] For example, in 1989, a formal dinner was held to honour a number of retiring professors, and the end of a decanal term. A senior member of faculty spoke from the podium in honour of the outgoing Dean, reminiscing about the night the two of them got together to decide which one of them would become Dean. Ostensibly, a Dean is selected by a university committee, with input from all members of faculty, but it is not so surprising that the speaker thought two men could get together and make that decision. He had ample evidence to support that view. It is more surprising that he thought it perfectly appropriate to acknowledge this in public. It is a fact of Western law school's culture that relatively few noticed or cared that he did.

I emphasize this culture because it may distort the analysis of institutional conservatism which follows. I have only experienced and can only discuss institutional conservatism in combination with monopoly of power within the law school. It may well be that the monopoly of power by any group of men has far more significant implications for feminism within a law school than whether that power group consists of social conservatives, professional conservatives, institutional conservatives, or whatever. I must leave it to readers from institutions controlled by men other than institutional conservatives to complete the analysis.

Every law school undoubtedly has some institutional conservatives. It is also likely that the law school tradition which they seek to uphold is more than 20 years old, when there were virtually no women teaching in Canadian law schools. The ideal against which institutional conservatives measure their faculties has no female presence. There are no "old girls," which explains why one will find female social conservatives, female professional conservatives, left-leaning women, and others in the law schools, but few, if any, female institutional conservatives.

Despite the fact that women began to join faculties of law approximately 15 years ago, there is little evidence they are yet being integrated into the traditional myths of the law schools. For example, the most senior woman at Western was hired 15 years ago, and she managed to survive in isolation by fitting in for many years. Now that she has chosen to speak on issues affecting women in the law school, she finds herself criticized for fracturing long-standing friendships with her colleagues. She is regarded as a traitor to the Western myth. I have heard myself described the same way. Institutional conservatives value loyalty to their image of the faculty above all else and sincerely believe it to be an equal opportunity image.

Sports figure prominently in male culture, often to the exclusion of women, and are perhaps unusually prominent in the institutional conservative culture at Western. For example, male members of Faculty have been playing touch football competitively and successfully against students for almost 20 years. I have played for 12 years myself. Hardly a post-game beer drinking session goes by without several team members reminiscing about the good old games, all played before my time. I have seen and heard more important issues of faculty policy resolved over post-game beers than at any faculty meeting. Golf is another major male-bonding activity. A university President and former Dean of Law recently published a law journal article based on golf as a judicial metaphor for concerted labour activity.[75] For the indoor season, the faculty lounge is dominated by a pool table. Some men and women have objected to this. Women have claimed that they avoid the lounge because of it. I have never seen a more animated response from our faculty on any issue than that which emerged in response to the challenge to the right to play pool in the lounge.[76]

A senior faculty member at Western's Faculty of Law once described it proudly as "The Oakland Raiders" of legal education, an interesting example on several fronts. First, the analogy is meaningless to someone who is not a professional football fan, that is, to the majority of women. Second, I am not sure that it is an image most women would wish to claim for their school. The Oakland Raiders were at the time a highly successful professional football team, but were also notorious in football circles as a renegade franchise. They were not cooperative with other teams or the league, and were well known as a team that played hard and dirty, took their penalties, and prevailed in spite of them.[77] Winning at the expense of cooperation and in spite of the rules is not revered by all as a model for legal education. This image thus conveys to most women, unintentionally I am sure, that our faculty is something they do not comprehend, and would not aspire to if they could. Western's fascination with the Raiders is not unique. In a speech honouring Law Dean Robert Prichard's appointment as President of the University of Toronto in 1989, a male professor from the University of Toronto compared Prichard favourably to Ken Stabler, a famous former Raider quarterback.[78] At the time, I thought the anecdote amusing and very effective. In retrospect I realize, and I am sure the speaker would agree, it was meaningless to roughly one half of the audience.

As between the phenomenon of sexism and complaints about sexism, the latter is the greater evil for the institutional conservative. There arises a "repeated pattern of being *told* by male colleagues how I should react. . . ."[79] "The polite thing to do, the collegial thing to do, the safe thing to do, is to suffer abuse privately rather than to urge recognition of its existence."[80] Complaints challenge the institutional vision and challenge the authority of the ruling institutional conservatives.

A good example is found in the eventual official response to the student petition discussed earlier,[81] issued in the form of an Open Letter, signed and widely distributed by the outgoing and incoming Deans. It exhibited the three key elements to the institutional conservative approach to gender issues:

1. The Assertion of Credentials: "We are both graduates of this Law School. We both chose to return here after cutting our professional teeth elsewhere."

2. The Vision of Traditional Western: "We affirm, with conviction born of experience, that one of the great strengths of this faculty . . . has been the remarkable extent to which students, staff and faculty have lived and worked in harmony and with affection."[82]

3. Shoot the Messenger: "[R]umour, vague allegations and innuendo are not positive. They are destructive and inherently unfair. . . . Whatever goal is sought, the end is not always justification for the means."

If complaints are a problem for institutional conservatives, public complaints are an outrage. Institutional conservatives perceive issues within the school as purely internal "private" matters. To air problems about the school externally is to breach one of the strongest taboos. To speak to the press, however cautiously, is the ultimate act of disloyalty.

On the surface, this taboo is gender neutral.[83] Institutional conservatives perhaps fail to appreciate that their definition of what is private shields power-monopolizing men from criticism. It silences those who would challenge that power monopoly, including feminists. In claiming the exclusive right to resolve disputes within the school internally, they fail to recognize a fundamental principle of natural justice, that one should not judge in one's own cause. They fail to recognize another when they refuse to recognize the rights of others to be heard. They also ignore that the taboo is enforced differently when broken by people who raise gender issues in public. Women faculty members have been chastised privately and at faculty meetings, and have been called to account by the Dean for raising gender concerns about the law school with outsiders. I have been quoted a number of times in the press about general and specific gender issues within the law school. I do not imagine that this media exposure has been appreciated by most of my male colleagues, but none has challenged directly my right to do so. Their own "Open Letters" and letters to the editor denying gender issues, or newspaper columns attacking feminists in the law schools, do not seem to be as problematic for institutional conservatives. Dissidents are denied the benefits of the institutional conservative's own rules, but given a disproportionate penalty when they breach them.

It seems inevitable that feminists will continue to raise gender issues, and other excluded groups other basic issues, in the public realm. This phenomenon is not unique to the law schools.[84] If one cannot join the club, why obey its rules? A consensus-based institutional contract theory of law school governance is meaningless when men fail to hold up their end of the bargain. However hostile the press may be on occasion, both the press and the general public seem far more supportive of women's issues in the law schools than do most male law professors. Beyond that, the debate belongs to the public, which is precisely why the press is interested. The battle to keep the gender wars "private" has already been lost. If institutional conservatives wish to keep their dirty laundry out of the public eye, they had better do their laundry.

As the controlling force in law school hiring, institutional conservatives were often responsible for the initial inroads made by women in law schools. They have allowed courses on issues affecting women into the curriculum and have hired women.[85] If aggregate hiring or salary data reveal preferential treatment of men, they have individual explanations.[86] One man was the "superior" candidate that year; another man filled a curriculum "need" the next; and another man had more "relevant" experience the year after that. The notion that the concepts of superiority, need, or relevance are subjective and gender biased strikes most men as incoherent. Observations of this sort are experienced by men as attacks on their personal integrity.

The supportive institutional conservative believes he has given a great deal to the feminists, and in some individual cases, the feminists would be the first to agree. But feminists perceive that they have been "given" less than they are entitled to, in principle and in law. Faced with continuing feminist demands for more, the supportive male becomes puzzled and eventually angry by the ingratitude shown by the women. The feminist critique is experienced as disloyal and personal, not political, rendering the rational discourse virtually useless. When women ask for a meaningful role in the formal and informal decision-making processes within a law school dominated by institutional conservatives, eventually they will ask for more than the vision can accommodate. At that point the women are seen as uncollegial and disruptive.

When institutional conservatives are forced to face allegations of sexism or claims for women's space, they resist on grounds they truly believe are gender neutral. Institutional loyalty to their self-constructed image justifies this resistance in their minds. It is not perceived as sexist, because truly the claims of women have never entered their minds.

The prospect for any meaningful change in legal education is poor when any one group perceives itself as the legitimate and exclusive authority within an institution. All change must come on its terms or not at all, and the terms of institutional conservatives seldom take into account the interests of women and/or minority groups. They have constructed a value hierarchy which permits them to ignore social, legal, and academic developments in equality theory. What makes the problem so intractable is that this group is not composed mainly of men who are deliberately hostile to the interests of women. On the contrary, many are sincerely concerned about discrimination as they see it. The problem is that they do not and will not see it.

8. The Leftists

Leftist men do not pose much of a numerical threat to feminists or to anyone else in the law schools.[87] Many law schools have more radical feminists on faculty than men of the radical left. Superficial observation would suggest that leftist men would be natural allies of feminists, but the evidence is mixed.[88] Some leftist men are tolerant or supportive, but leftist men have been among the most active opponents of feminism in more than one Canadian law school.

Leftist men and feminists should have much in common. At the core, both emphasize the exercise of power by the relatively powerful over the relatively powerless. Both understand, at least at an intellectual level, the politics of oppression. They object for similar reasons to the anti-egalitarian philosophy of conservatism and the formal egalitarianism of liberalism. They study patterns, not isolated episodes. They are both outsiders in the mainstream culture of law and legal education. Indeed, most feminists seem quite sympathetic to the issues raised by the left. The feminist critique of Marxism is directed to what it excludes, not to what it includes.[89] Virtually all leftist men proclaim support for feminism. Some feminists, no doubt, fail to appreciate the significance of social class in their analysis, but I know of no feminist in Canadian legal education who attacks either the leftist perspective, or leftists personally. Some leftist men in legal education cannot make the same claim with respect to feminism.

The fundamental philosophical difference is that for the leftist, the basis of oppression is class, whereas for the radical feminist, it is sex. Even this difference is relatively small between leftist men and socialist feminists; it is sufficiently small that it should not wipe out all the common ground. This political difference therefore fails to account for the animosity which many leftist men exhibit towards feminists in their midst.

Part of the explanation must be that leftist men are men. No man teaching in a law school can claim to be a member of the lower class. Leftist men, like any other man teaching in university, benefit from being male. Feminism attacks their right to do so. Women benefit from their class, but they retain their personal identification with the sexual core of their philosophy regardless of their social class. Interaction between the two is interaction between someone experiencing discrimination personally because of her sex, and someone analyzing discrimination which is no longer experienced personally, if it ever was. When leftist men attack feminists they attack them personally in a manner in which feminists do not and could not attack them.

Jealousy, political and personal, is probably also relevant. Leftist men are no longer the "lone rebels" in legal education. The doors of the law schools opened just a crack for leftist men shortly before they opened a crack for women. The force of the political left in North American society began to wane in the 1970s just as the force of the feminist movement began to grow. The law schools were not likely to double the size of the crack in the doorway to admit both leftist men and feminists, so they have been forced to compete for limited access to legal education. Feminists seem to have come out ahead, in law, policy, and actual hiring. It is quite understandable that leftist men would find this unfair.

Individual leftist men may also believe themselves to be doubly damned. On the one hand, as men, they experience all the unfairness that so many men perceive as the result of feminism. The feminist critique of male behaviour seldom excludes them, and sometimes singles them out for particular criticism.[90] It is difficult enough for a leftist theorist to find a place in law teaching without also having to contend with perceived preferential hiring policies on the basis of sex.[91] On the other hand, they are not part of the mainstream law school culture. Some had achieved a comfortable niche, the social activist tolerated or even appreciated as a symbol of tolerance and diversity by the various conservative factions. Unlike feminists in some law schools, radical leftists never achieved the critical mass which might have made them a threat. Today, leftist men find themselves being eclipsed in numbers and influence by feminists. It is not really surprising that this small, vulnerable group finds it expeditious to side in conduct, if not rhetoric, with other men who have the power to protect them, rather than with another vulnerable group that threatens them. As long as leftist men remain so isolated in legal education, some will find siding with the controlling power at the law schools their best survival strategy. As long as they remain too few to threaten the conservative culture, they will be welcome to do so. Only an alteration of the balance of power away from the dominant conservative culture will benefit both people of the left and feminists.

9. Conclusions

Le Féminisme est une perspective politique qui vient des femmes mais "droit devenir la politique des hommes." [Feminism is a political perspective that comes from women but "must become the politics of men."][92]

What is most needed in this world, where our understandings are not as shared as we would wish — or as would be convenient — is for all of us to listen to each other and to *listen especially* to those who speak from the margins, in whatever way.... Of course, for any of that to happen, they must speak. *We* must speak.[93] (Emphasis in original.)

This article began as a purely experiential account which I later attempted to integrate with what others had written. Often, I write first and research afterwards. One risk in this method is that one discovers that it has all been said before, which is what I discovered about this article. Few of my observations and factual accounts have not been made before by women who teach in Canadian law schools. I conclude that we are dealing not with isolated incidents, but with patterns of behaviour which repeat in every law school where they are documented. The common strand in all these patterns is the exercise of the male right not to know; men are responsible for the gender wars in the law schools.

Men, especially White middle-class men, must take responsibility to discover social reality as it is experienced by others. This process has two stages. First, men must abandon their right not to know. Then, they must come to grips with knowing. In my opinion, the first stage is more difficult than the second.

It does not matter to victims of discrimination whether the right not to know is an unreflective exercise of male arrogance, or a self-serving, power-perpetuating technique. The right not to know excuses nothing. Any man who is committed to equal treatment of women and others must take this first step.

Moreover, men must take this responsibility themselves. Men have more power to end the gender wars than do women. There is little more that women can do to entice them to exercise it. The message is there for men who want to hear it. Some women may be willing to help, but it is not their responsibility to do so.

It should concern the men who sit on university boards and in university administration that some universities appear to be more reactionary than the general public they are supposed to serve. In the 1990s it is inexcusable that one can become a senior university administrator without having abandoned one's right not to know. It is inexcusable that any man who has not abandoned his right not to know should be deemed fit to become Dean of a university faculty. No Dean or faculty who cares about the future of education can afford to hire any male who has not abandoned his right not to know. It is not only a matter of legal and moral obligation, but also a matter of sound university management. A great deal of important and exciting scholarship is being produced by feminists and by members of minority groups. Men who control universities who fail to recognize this fact will find their universities on the verge of becoming socially obsolete.[94]

It is embarrassing to all of us in legal education that so many law schools have to be dragged kicking and screaming in the wake of progressive equality legislation and crystal-clear pronouncements on the law of discrimination by the Supreme Court of Canada. Law schools are sitting in a time warp while their own discipline passes them by. If the men who control law schools care about legal education, they must catch up with the law and with the society it serves. Otherwise, as is happening in engineering, members of the profession may take the initiative to stamp out sexism in the law schools.[95]

Here are a few suggestions for men who wish to make a difference. Men ought to educate themselves by reading the exceptional feminist writing which is available. We might then discuss with women what we can do.[96] We must attempt to refrain from the natural male tendency to tell the women why they are wrong.

We must break our own silence. Some men are incurable misogynists. Their outrageous sexist conduct can and must be stopped. If other men took responsibility for stopping this conduct, the burden resting upon victims of it would be eased. Tenured male professors must abandon their cocoons of self-defined neutrality and fight publicly the abuse of their women colleagues, students, and staff. Deans and university administrators must also take responsibility. If they will not, they must be challenged through every possible avenue.

A meaningful feminist presence in law schools entails a great deal more than silencing "so and so," no matter how many "so and so's" there may be.

Again, men who profess a belief in equality and who wish an end to the gender wars must take responsibility. Equal treatment of women requires more than gender-neutral language, gender-inclusive examples, and guest lecturers to give a woman's perspective. Men who profess to be supportive must acknowledge and abandon their right not to know, layer by layer. We must listen to and hear women. Then we must construct a gender-inclusive reality and reflect it in our conduct, our scholarship, and our teaching. Otherwise, we are as responsible for the gender wars as is "so and so." We should be, and should expect to be, treated as such.

Tenured male professors who are beginning to abandon their right not to know have a special duty. It is not so much that women need, or for that matter necessarily want, the support of men because they are men. In equal numbers, with equal power, the women would hold their own quite nicely. They need support of tenured men because they are badly outnumbered and under-powered in legal education.[97] The main contribution men can make is to shift the imbalance of power which makes the unequal treatment of women and others possible. White middle-class men must share the right to shape legal education with others.

The prospect of trying to treat people equally is frightening to most men because it is entirely new to them.[98] Actually trying to treat people equally is far less frightening. Male law professors are used to succeeding at what they do, but learning to fail is part of learning about the world as others experience it. If legal academics truly enjoy to learn, as they should, this process may be the ultimate learning experience. Listening is often more enlightening than speaking. Cooperation is often more exhilarating than exercising power.[99] Difference is more stimulating than sameness.[100] Trying to treat people equally has a utilitarian appeal as well as a moral one.

Meanwhile, while we await a widespread transformation in male culture, what can women and supportive men do? What we can do is what we have been doing and more of it. We must respect the power of breaking silence. We must expose sexist misconduct. We must challenge recalcitrant administrators. Write to them. Call them out at public meetings. Use faculty grievance procedures. Expose misconduct and administrative inaction in law journals and the public press. Work together. If one is untenured and isolated on faculty, reach out to other groups on campus. Call colleagues at other law schools. Speak to your students. I do not suggest organizing students, which is inappropriate, impossible, and unnecessary.[101] Just educate and inform them. Good scholarship and good teaching are powerful tools. All of us at Western who care about these issues owe a great deal to the many supportive female and male students who have courageously stood up to sexism in an environment where even tenured faculty are nervous to do the same.

Let me end on a sober note. The gender wars as they are being fought today are largely wars between White middle-class males and White middle-class females. I hope that feminists can learn from the experience of tension between the left and feminism, and not repeat it. There are few visible-minority law professors, let alone a critical mass, in legal education. The invisible minorities wisely remain invisible. There are far too few Francophones educated in Québec working in the common law schools, a fact which cannot and will not continue. Perhaps optimistically, I foresee the 1990s as a decade where visible minorities including people of colour and members of the First Nations will begin to make modest inroads into legal education.[102] They do and will experience the same difficulties experienced by leftist men, women, and feminists, and they do and will experience unique difficulties. They do and will experience the White middle-class right not to know. They have probably experienced it while reading this article.

Acknowledgements

Writing this paper has been a uniquely nerve-wracking experience. Thanks to the help and support of colleagues across the country, it has also been uniquely rewarding. Constance Backhouse, Jamie Cassels, Diana Majury, Sheila McIntyre, and Michael Peirce offered insightful criticisms of earlier drafts, some of which saved me from making serious errors. Most of my female colleagues and several of my male colleagues supported the enterprise throughout. The efforts of many of my students to combat gender discrimination in law schools has been an inspiration. The Women and the Law section of the Canadian Association of Law Teachers was kind enough to allow me to present this paper at the annual meeting in Victoria in June 1990, where Lorenne Clark and Janet Baldwin provided supportive comment. As a result of that exposure, I have received constructive criticism and encouragement from men and women across the country. The paper would not have been possible without the written record of gender discrimination at Canadian law schools provided by the women authors cited throughout the text. I thank you all.

Notes

Editors' Note
1 This chapter originally appeared in the *Canadian Journal of Women and the Law*, 4 (1990): 66-95. It is reprinted here with permission of the author and the editors of *CJWL*.

Notes

1 There is a serious shortcoming with the "war" metaphor, which Sheila McIntyre was kind enough to bring to my attention. The metaphor suggests symmetry in the interaction, "attack" and "counter-attack," which does not exist. There is no symmetry between the breaking of silence to name the abuse and discrimination experienced by women, and the aggressively hostile responses that are documented in this paper. There is no symmetry between "No Means No" and "No Means Harder." See Katherine Govier, "A Time to Be Just," *Queen's Alumni Review*, 64, 2 (1990): 12. Perhaps part of the problem is that men too readily see this as a war, too readily perceive the exposition of women's concerns as an attack, and too readily respond in an attacking mode. I believe this paper supports the conclusion that it would be more apt to describe the women as engaged in a struggle against oppression than as engaged in a war.

2 I am a male law professor. This article is full of generalizations about men and male law professors. Most of them apply, as generalizations, to me. There is depressingly little criticism in the paper which does not, or did not once, apply to me. Unless it is clear otherwise from the text, I make no claim to having distanced myself from the male culture which I criticize.

3 Law schools have been ill prepared to function as academic faculties. Legal education has a relatively short history as an academic discipline. The break from purely conservative professional training occurred around 1948-49, and it proceeds slowly today. See the Consultative Group on Research and Education in Law, *Law and Learning: Report to the Social Sciences and Humanities Research Council of Canada* (Ottawa: Minister of Supply and Services, 1983) (chaired by Harry W. Arthurs), p. 13 and generally.

   Law schools have been also ill prepared to cope with the sudden and significant presence of women which has occurred during the last 15 years or so. Law schools are often better funded than other university departments and there is more turnover in a professional faculty. Thus, law schools have probably been able to do relatively more entry-level hiring. In the 1980s, this has meant hiring more women and more feminists. A critical mass of feminists (two?) is probably necessary for a sustained gender war. Interestingly, the growing presence of women in legal education received scant attention in *Law and Learning*.

   Law schools have been ill prepared for the rapid changes which have occurred in the law affecting women. The Charter in particular has moved the traditionally conservative practice of law into an active and overt policy-shaping role. Women's concerns are reflected in many new legislative initiatives. The law has become a high-profile avenue for addressing gender discrimination. Academics literate in the feminist analysis of law find an increasingly receptive audience in other disciplines and in the general public. Finally, it may be that the general hostility or indifference to feminism exhibited by male law professors is greater than that exhibited by males elsewhere, and this is what has brought the gender wars to the forefront in legal education.

4 "There are many strains of feminism. What they have in common are two very simple premises: within and by means of male-dominated social institutions in our culture, women are unequal to men; and such inequality is both unjust and changeable" (Sheila McIntyre, "Gender Bias Within the Law School: 'The Memo' and Its Impact," *Canadian Journal of Women and the Law*, 2, 2 [1987-88]: 362, 374; included here as chapter 7).

5 See ibid. See also Jennifer K. Bankier, "Women and the Law School: Problems and Potential," *Chitty's Law Journal*, 22 (1974): 171, which appears to have been one of the first efforts at breaking the silence.

6 The most detailed public report of the "settlement" appears in "Sex Discrimination Complaint at York Resolved," *OCUFA Forum*, 6, 15 (1990): 4. It is now rumoured that the "settlement" is dissolving. Formal minutes of settlement have yet to be signed. Two written reports have emerged as a result of the litigation. *The Report of the Gender Equality Committee*

(Brenda Cossman and Bruce Ryder, Co-chairs, 1990), on reserve at the Osgoode Hall Law Library, is the report of an internal committee at the law school. Although not identified as a draft, it is reportedly being revised. The second, a report of a private employment equity consultant to the Gender Equality Committee, is marked "Confidential," although its contents have been summarized in the press. In "Osgoode Cited for Discrimination against Women and Minorities," *The Globe and Mail* (National), 8 February 1990, p. A19, the Report is quoted as saying: "Cumulative adverse impact on women faculty due to working conditions, current employment systems and unresolved equity issues is severe." The article reports that faculty voted against adopting the consultant's report. See also Paula Todd, "Feminists Targets at Osgoode Hall Law Students Say," *The Toronto Star*, 30 March 1990, p. B13.

7 See, for example, Todd, "Feminists Targets." In another letter to the editor, the Dean and Associate Dean of Osgoode Hall described a frightened female student's complaint about administrative inaction in response to complaints of sexism as "Mean-spirited assertions...," *The Toronto Star*, 7 April 1990, p. D3. Law students objecting to the attention given to gender issues replied in a letter to the editor, "Osgoode's Silent Majority Speaks Out," *The Toronto Star*, 7 May 1990, p. A16.

8 I will return to this aspect of the controversy. The general tendency to deny the relevance of gender will be emphasized throughout the paper. See also McIntyre, "Gender Bias," p. 373, 388-89.

9 See Ann Robinson, "Thémis retrouve l'usage de la vue" (roughly translated as: The Goddess of Justice Recovers Her Sight), *Canadian Journal of Women and the Law*, 3, 1 (1989): 211. This article surveys the number of feminists employed and active in the civil schools. A similar survey should be conducted, published, and addressed in the common law schools.

10 I do not deny that some law schools may have done better and are doing better than others on some fronts.

11 Primarily, students are the direct and indirect victims of gender discrimination in the law schools. See, generally, Bankier, "Women and the Law School." The hostility of male law students to women professors and students and to feminism has been well documented. See, for example, McIntyre, "Gender Bias." I could document it easily at Western. However, I prefer to emphasize the courageous and active support in the battle against sexism which has come from a large number of male and female students at Western and elsewhere. These students deserve a great deal more credit than they have received.

12 So distant is that goal that I doubt whether many feminists have yet had the opportunity to develop a full appreciation of what a meaningful feminist presence would entail. Nadya Aisenberg and Mona Harrington express the general idea in *Women of Academe: Outsiders in the Sacred Grove* (Amherst: University of Massachusetts Press, 1988), p. 136, 139, as follows: "what women want is a radically different system of professional organization — indeed of social organization... one that opposes excessive hierarchy and exclusivity in the holding of authority, one that incorporates diversity, spreads authority through processes of cooperation, resists centrality both in the holding of political and intellectual authority and in the defining of truth and value.... One can scarcely imagine a more radical shift in power, in the placement of social authority, than the actual inclusion of women in professional life in numbers and on terms equal to those of men. It would not be a matter of retaining the status quo with fuller lives for women *added on*." In "Liberty, Equality, Fraternity — and Sorority," in Anne Bayefsky, ed., *Legal Theory Meets Legal Practice* (Edmonton: Academic Printing and Publishing, 1988), p. 261, 274, Lorenne M.G. Clark says: "What women want is the equal right with men to be represented in that decision-making.... In the end, what women want is as much 'liberty' as men. This, however, by no means entails that they want the same 'liberties' as men." In "'Otherness' and the Law School: A Comment on Teaching Gender Equality," *Canadian Journal of Women and the*

Law, 1, 1 (1985): 213, 218, Mary Jane Mossman says: "The challenge for feminism in law schools is to transform the normative tradition of law so that what law now recognizes as "Otherness" is seen as central to an understanding of law and society." See also Susan B. Boyd and Elizabeth A. Sheehy, "Feminist Perspectives on Law: Canadian Theory and Practice," *Canadian Journal of Women and the Law*, 2, 1 (1986): 36-38, and Elizabeth A. Sheehy and Susan B. Boyd, *Canadian Feminist Perspectives on Law: An Annotated Bibliography of Interdisciplinary Writings* (Toronto: Resources for Feminist Research, 1989), for a summary of relevant literature and a comprehensive bibliography.

13 "Many male professors now appear so afraid of offending female students that their lectures are often stifled and unimaginative, disrupted by their urgency to ensure that 'he' or 'she' was utilized, form to the detriment of substance sometimes being emphasized." Taken from a letter to the editor of *The London Free Press* written by a third-year female law student, 11 November 1989, p. F3.

14 Not all faculties have such mandatory policies. At Western, a resolution of Faculty Council introduced by students resolves that faculty "consider employing" *inter alia* non-sexist language and non-stereotyped examples.

15 Maude Barlow, external consultant on sexual harassment, speaking to the Law Faculty at Western, 7 March 1990. See also Govier, "A Time to Be Just," p. 16, quoting Dean Whyte of Queen's law school: "There is a failure in Queen's people to understand how vital feminists are to the struggle for justice. They think they can be just on their own, without listening to feminists."

16 Clare Dalton, "The Faithful Liberal and the Question of Diversity," *Harvard Women's Law Journal*, 12 (1989): 1.

17 For example, the general failure of men to speak out in the face of outrageous treatment experienced by women may in part be explained by the absence of cultural norms to govern the situation. Ordinarily, men experience far less difficulty in taking public stances than do women. Ordinarily, when the issue is inappropriate treatment of women, traditional male culture would suggest a chivalrous response. But male culture has yet to develop norms for dealing with feminists. Otherwise sensitive men may fail to appreciate that feminists, like any other person, appreciate non-paternalistic support. They may find their helpful inclinations inconsistent with feminism as they perceive it. If feminists object to doors being held for them, might they also object to support from men?

18 Dalton, "The Faithful Liberal," p. 1-2.

19 Clark, "Liberty, Equality, Fraternity," p. 272.

20 I believe that some men use the right not to know deliberately and others unreflectively. As to the relative number of men within the second category, and as to how many of them would be more supportive if they acknowledged their right not to know, I have no idea.

21 Dalton, "The Faithful Liberal," p. 1.

22 I do not intend to criticize women who regard the idea that women must make the effort to understand men as part of the problem rather than its solution. I hope this analysis assists women in whatever course they choose to pursue.

23 Lorenne M.G. Clark, "Politics and Law: The Theory and Practice of the Ideology of Male Supremacy or, It Wasn't God Who Made Honky Tonk Angels," in David N. Weisstub, ed., *Law and Policy* (Toronto: Osgoode Hall Annual Lecture Series, 1976), p. 35.

24 Clark, "Liberty, Equality, Fraternity," p. 261.

25 Ann Scales, "Militarism, Male Dominance and Law: Feminist Jurisprudence as Oxymoron," *Harvard Women's Law Journal*, 12 (1989): 25, 36. Catharine MacKinnon refers to this as male "point-of-viewlessness." See "Feminism, Marxism, Method, and the State: Toward Feminist Jurisprudence," *Signs*, 8 (1983): 635, 639.

26 See the discussion of the institutional response below.

27 Madame Justice Bertha Wilson, "Will Women Judges Really Make A Difference?," Fourth Annual Barbara Betcherman Memorial Lecture, Osgoode Hall Law School, 8 February

1990, p. 19, paraphrasing Carol Gilligan, *In a Different Voice: Psychological Theory and Women's Development* (Cambridge, MA: Harvard University Press, 1982). In Alan Bass, "Women More Caring and It's Hurting Them," *The London Free Press*, 9 May 1990, p. A1, a co-author of a sociological study describes the study's findings as follows: "Women tend to focus on caring about others more than men do.... Men ... either failed to notice or quickly forgot about other people's problems, including their wives'."

28 *Action Travail des Femmes v. Canadian National Railway*, [1987] 1 S.C.R. 1114, 1139: "[S]ystemic discrimination in an employment context is discrimination which results from the simple operation of established procedures of recruitment, hiring and promotion, none of which is necessarily designed to promote discrimination. The discrimination is then reinforced by the very exclusion of the disadvantaged group because the exclusion fosters the belief, both within and outside the group, that the exclusion is the result of 'natural' forces, for example, that women 'just can't do the job.'" See Rosalie S. Abella, *Equity in Employment: A Royal Commission Report* [Ottawa: Minister of Supply and Services, 1984], p. 9-10. For a concrete example in the law school setting, see Robinson, "Thémis retrouve."

29 Only 30% of males surveyed said the act said anything about the problems of male violence towards females; 65% denied this. Forty-three percent of women, 47% of those between 18 and 34, saw the connection. "Fifty Nine Per Cent Call Massacre Only Random Act, Poll Finds," *The Toronto Star* (Southam News), 29 December 1989, p. A1, A4, reporting the results of an Angus Reid poll.

30 "Feminism Is Not to Blame," *The Whig-Standard* (Kingston; CP), 14 December 1989, p. 12, quoting Ginette Busque of the Canadian Advisory Council on the Status of Women.

31 The general issues and comments were covered extensively in *The Whig-Standard* (Kingston) throughout the month of December 1989. Two male law students at Queen's were alleged to have entered a law class and fired imaginary machine-gun fire at female students (*The Whig-Standard*, 8 December 1989). The story was later declared false and exaggerated. One witness confirmed that a male student had run across the class, pretending to duck bullets (*The Whig-Standard*, 9 December 1989, p. 1). A feminist law professor who was misquoted was blamed for the false story. Dean John Whyte was criticized for his reaction to the initial report, and graffiti saying "Whyte lies" is reported to have appeared on campus. See also Govier, "A Time to Be Just," p. 13, where some refreshingly candid and helpful remarks of Dean Whyte are quoted. See also *The Report of the Gender Equality Committee*, p. 63-67, where a student commented on similar Montreal-related tension at Osgoode Hall.

32 Unless otherwise noted, the incidents described in this paragraph have occurred at Western's law school. Comparable episodes at other law schools are footnoted. This is not "just Western," "just Queen's," and "just Osgoode Hall." At every law school where public documentation has occurred the patterns are similar.

33 For examples of more polite comments to the same effect, see Robinson, "Thémis retrouve," p. 222, 229, 230.

34 Similar events have happened at Queen's. See McIntyre, "Gender Bias," p. 386, 391.

35 See also McIntyre, "Gender Bias," p. 381, and *The Report of the Gender Equality Committee*, p. 16.

36 McIntyre, "Gender Bias," p. 386-88, reports a virtually identical incident. For other reports of physically threatening conduct see Robinson, "Thémis retrouve," p. 228, 230, 231. See also Todd, "Feminists Targets." Foot-high swastikas juxtaposed against the women's symbol appeared on desks at Osgoode Hall. A female student reports being the target of physical threats and verbal abuse. "Several law professors expressed outrage at the graffiti but said they could not speak publicly because of fear for their jobs or criticism from other staff members." See, generally, Govier, "A Time to Be Just," p. 16.

37 McIntyre, "Gender Bias," p. 387.

38 *The Report of the Gender Equality Committee*, p. 18. It is unclear in the *Report* whether the authors accepted this explanation; they did not reject it explicitly.

39 As to the importance of breaking through this barrier, see Sheila McIntyre, "Promethea Unbound: A Feminist Perspective on Law in the University," *University of New Brunswick Law Journal*, 38 (1988): 157, 160, 173.

40 *Action Travail*, [1987] 1 S.C.R. 1114. Similar treatment or worse is extended to Supreme Court judges who take a women's perspective. See Robinson, "Thémis retrouve," p. 227.

41 A good example of this may be found in the Open Letter signed by the Western Deans, discussed below. Note also the emphasis on formal complaint mechanisms in *The Report of the Gender Equality Committee*. The significance of the difference between the two approaches for the victims of discrimination is well outlined in *Action Travail*, [1987] 1 S.C.R. 1114.

42 As if fear of academic and professional repercussions were not enough, some male professors actively discourage students from making complaints. See Robinson, "Thémis retrouve," p. 231-32.

43 See below where the Deans' Open Letter response to the student petition is discussed.

44 Again, for the identical observation, see McIntyre, "Promethea Unbound," p. 171.

45 It strikes me as strange that two or three examples of harassment would lead so many individual men in a group of 30 to believe they had been accused personally. In contrast, the Gender Equality Committee at Osgoode Hall deliberately solicited anonymous critiques on gender issues from its student body in its effort to examine systemic discrimination (*The Report of the Gender Equality Committee*, p. 16).

46 Again, exactly the same phenomenon is described by McIntyre, "Promethea Unbound," p. 168, where she uses the expression "takeover conspiracy."

47 We are a long way from a meaningful feminist presence, philosophical debate, and subtle problems of gender and other inclusiveness.

48 See my comments in n. 1 on the "war" metaphor.

49 Rob Martin, "A New Power in Law: Right-wing Feminism," *Lawyers Weekly*, 9, 24 (1989): 7, and Rob Martin, "More on Right-wing Feminism: Folly in the Law School," *Lawyers Weekly*, 9, 26 (1989): 7.

50 McIntyre, "Gender Bias," p. 378-79.

51 See my discussion of social conservatives below.

52 McIntyre, "Gender Bias," p. 377.

53 "Law School Dismissal Not an Issue of Sexism," letter by male law professor at Western to *The London Free Press*, 16 December 1989, p. F3. Much of the letter consisted of criticism of a named third-year female law student who had dared to suggest the significance of gender. The insensitivity of male law professors and deans to the power imbalance which exists between them and their students, especially their female students, is remarkable. In another letter to the editor, the Dean and Associate Dean of Osgoode Hall described a frightened female student's complaint about administrative inaction in response to complaints of sexism as "Mean-spirited Assertions..." (in *The Toronto Star*, 7 April 1990, p. D3). See also the Open Letter response to the student petition, discussed below.

54 The absence of liberals in my analysis has puzzled me as much as it has puzzled others who have commented on the paper. The best explanation I can offer was provided by Jamie Cassels, who suggested: "[L]iberalism may not be so much an independent category as an overarching ideology that unites most of the others. The blindness to the facts of disadvantage supported by a reliance on formal equality, the separation of law and politics, the denial of personal knowledge, the separation of public and private, and appeals to academic freedom, neutrality, and objectivity are themes that pop up throughout your paper" (letter dated 20 June 1990; on file with the author).

55 It does not purport to correlate to particularly offensive conduct. For example, I observe no correlation between association with a particular group and a tendency to harass students

or otherwise actively abuse women faculty personally or professionally. Personality variables probably have more explanatory power for particularly egregious conduct.

56 Alison Jaggar, "Political Philosophies of Women's Liberation," in Sharon Bishop and Marjorie Weinzweig, eds., *Philosophy and Women* (Belmont, CA: Wadsworth, 1979), p. 258.

57 Religion figures prominently in the views of many conservatives, which sometimes makes accommodation with feminism more difficult, if not impossible. For example, if feminism is described as "the work of the Devil," as it has been by one of my conservative colleagues, further dialogue will not be conducive to accommodation.

58 At some Canadian law schools, it might be necessary to broaden this analysis to include a discussion of "academic conservatives," men who defend a particular theoretical model of legitimate legal academic discourse and who deny other models including the feminist perspective. On this issue, see Dalton, "The Faithful Liberal," criticizing Owen M. Fiss, "The Death of the Law," *Cornell Law Review*, 72 (1986-87): 1. At many Canadian law schools, feminists carry a large part of the burden of making space for the general academic model as well as for the feminist version.

59 See, generally, Arthurs, *Law and Learning*, especially p. 136-40, for a more gentle analysis of the issues discussed below.

60 McIntyre, "Gender Bias," p. 377.

61 The Canadian Charter of Rights and Freedoms, *Constitution Act*, 1982, as enacted by *Canada Act (U.K.)*, c. 11, Sched. B.

62 Once equality is the law, it is assumed that equality exists and that therefore a feminist perspective is unnecessary. See Robinson, "Thémis retrouve," p. 227.

63 McIntyre, "Gender Bias," p. 388. See also Robinson, "Thémis retrouve," p. 227, for a comment on the treatment of women judges at the Supreme Court of Canada.

64 *The Report of the Gender Equality Committee*, p. 17. Some of the more interesting comments from the Gender Equality Committee at Osgoode Hall pertain to the incongruence between the curriculum which exists and the reality of law school and the legal profession today. "Canadian society is no longer the sole preserve of white males" (ibid., p. 32).

65 *Action Travail*, [1987] 1 S.C.R. 1114. See also McIntyre, "Promethea Unbound," p. 157.

66 This is one theme in the McIntyre memo, "Gender Bias," summarized at p. 385. At Western the fact that a feminist was one of the very few members of faculty to obtain a SSHRCC grant, having been judged worthy by *her* peers, is treated as evidence of a feminist conspiracy rather than as an accomplishment. See, generally, McIntyre, "Promethea Unbound."

67 See the information contained in n. 6. It is interesting to contrast the attitude of members of the bar who practise in this area. Many have approached this woman, anxious to learn as much as they can about the complaint. Professionals use different criteria than professional conservatives in the law schools to define what is practical.

68 For a detailed analysis of the means employed to devalue feminist scholarship, see, generally, McIntyre, "Promethea Unbound," especially n. 56.

69 At Western, no formal policy governs the extent or nature of outside work, and no reporting is required, so it is difficult to measure precisely the scope of the problem. Several years ago, the Dean imposed a requirement that each member of faculty must have scheduled classes at least three days of the week, in an effort to increase faculty presence within the school during teaching hours. A senior member of faculty with an extensive arbitration practice resigned in protest over interference with his "academic freedom."

70 More men than women teach in the law schools. Most women were hired recently, during the period where the university model was growing. There is no great demand for a feminist presence in transactional legal work. The legal profession undoubtedly discriminates systemically against women who might otherwise care to do extensive transactional work. Child care is the "outside" work of necessity for many female professors. Feminists work outside the law school, but often in the community on a volunteer basis.

71 I should note that those who are promoting a feminist presence at Western have received support from some men who are engaged in extensive outside work. At least in the minds of some, the outside work problem need not be engaged on the backs of women.

72 The fascination with tradition at Queen's University is noted by Govier, "A Time to Be Just," p. 13-14. President Smith, in his article, "Values at Queen's," *Queen's Alumni Review*, 64, 2 (1990): 29, provides ample evidence for Govier's observation. He uses the word "tradition" in three successive sentences to justify administrative inaction during the "No Means Yes" episode at Queen's in the fall of 1989.

73 The themes of collegiality and loyalty dominate discourse at Western. Again, the identical observation has been made by McIntyre, "Promethea Unbound," p. 169, 171.

74 I do not wish to suggest that the Deans have all been institutional conservatives. For example, from 1974-79 the Dean was David Johnston, now Principal of McGill University. I would not associate him with any of the categories used in this paper, and most certainly not with the institutional conservatives. Significantly, it was he who hired the first identifiable feminist to teach at Western's law school.

75 Harry Arthurs, "The Right to Golf: Reflections on the Future of Workers Unions and the Rest of Us Under the Charter," *Queen's Law Journal*, 13, 2 (1988): 17. The source of the metaphor is *Reference Re Public Service Employee Relations Act*, [1987] 1 S.C.R. 313, 408 per McIntyre J.

76 Coincidentally, after this article was written, the Dean announced that the pool table would be auctioned off. He pointed out that the table dominated the lounge and that few people used it.

77 Incidentally, since that time the team's fortunes have declined markedly. The now-Los Angeles Raiders have been a mediocre and nondescript franchise for most of the 1980s. Perhaps in quest for its own lost tradition, the franchise announced in March 1990 that it would be returning to Oakland. Thereafter, in the face of active opposition by citizens' groups in Oakland, the city indicated that the Raiders would not be welcome.

78 The speaker discovered the anecdote in Alvin B. Rubin, "Does Law Matter? A Judge's Response to the Critical Legal Studies Movement," *Journal of Legal Education*, 37 (1987): 307.

79 McIntyre, "Gender Bias," p. 388.

80 Ibid.

81 The general reaction to the petition, including the official Open Letter response, was summed up by a female law student in "UWO Reacted with Hostility to Students' Sexism Memo," letter to the editor of *The London Free Press*, 16 December 1989, p. F3: "The reaction to this memo was mostly one of wounded outrage. There was a general refusal to admit that any problem existed at all within the faculty, and even if it did, it was so trivial as not to warrant either complaint or any attempt at solving it."

82 There is little objective evidence for such a mythical past. I doubt this view is shared by many women students and faculty, or by men and women from visible minority groups. One could staff a first-class law school with White male professors, formerly at Western and now working elsewhere in Canada, who would disagree.

83 It is perceived as such in much the same way as the distinction between public and private law is perceived as gender neutral. See Clark, "Liberty, Equality, Fraternity," p. 278-81.

84 Claire Bernstein, "Outspoken Judges Help Credibility," *The London Free Press*, 13 March 1990, p. A9: "[A]s women have moved into positions of power and respect within the judicial establishment, they are perhaps less restricted than their male counterparts to throw off the rules of conformity to outdated limitations, because they're not shackled with membership in the 'old boys' club that imposes subtle pressure on male jurists to stay within the 'rules.'"

85 Only two women on Western's faculty could have been identified as visible feminists at the time of hiring. It is significant that the first was hired by an external Dean. The second was hired by an institutional conservative Dean with a good grasp of feminist issues and a

sincere commitment to increasing the feminist presence. She began and remains, however, on precarious one-year, limited-term contracts, under constant siege from male faculty.

86 For some revealing information about salary differentials between men and women in one Ontario law school, see Emily Carasco, "A Case of Double Jeopardy: Race and Gender," *Canadian Journal of Women and the Law*, 6 (1993): 142, and *The University of Windsor and the Faculty Association of the University of Windsor, In the Matter of the Grievance of Emily Carasco* (Arbitrator Gail Brent, 29 March 1990, unreported). On file at the University of Ottawa Law Library.

87 I speak here of the radical left, those who openly identify with socialism or marxism. I exclude the left-leaning or ethical liberal who retains the individualistic emphasis of liberalism, albeit tempered by a concern for less fortunate individuals. When I use the term "left-leaning," I intend to group these liberals with the radical left.

88 See Dalton, "The Faithful Liberal," p. 9, where the role of the critical legal studies movement receives comment.

89 See, for example, Clark, "Honky Tonk," p. 42-52; Mary O'Brien and Sheila McIntyre, "Patriarchal Hegemony and Legal Education," *Canadian Journal of Women and the Law*, 2, 1 (1986): 69; and MacKinnon, "Feminism, Marxism."

90 See, for example, Andrea Dworkin, "Why So-called Radical Men Love and Need Pornography," in Laura Lederer, ed., *Take Back the Night: Women on Pornography* (New York: W. Morrow, 1980), p. 148.

91 I emphasize "perceived." Not all law schools have policies that purport to favour women, and not all of these actually favour women. For example, many have "other things being equal, hire women" policies, but the feminist critique is that the men who make the decisions do not perceive other things as equal. Queen's did hire three visible feminists in one year. Five of Western's last eight limited-term appointments have been women, which might suggest a preference. However, two of the women are gone, and the positions of two others are in jeopardy. All the men began on two- or three-year contracts, whereas two of the women received one-year contracts. No one, male or female, can make a meaningful contribution to legal education operating under the uncertainty of a one-year contract. An observation to this effect in Craig Brown's memo, discussed above, led to his firing.

92 Robinson, "Thémis retrouve," p. 223-24, citing Charlotte Bunch from A. Michel, "Le complexe militaro-industriel et la violence a l'egard des femmes," *Nouvelles questions feministes* (1985), p. 62.

93 Toni Pickard, "Is Real Life Finally Happening?" *Canadian Journal of Women and the Law*, 2, 2 (1986): 432, 439.

94 Govier, "A Time to Be Just," quoting Jessica Slights, Chair of the AMS Gender Issues Committee: "If Queen's doesn't change quickly enough it will find itself relegated to a very minor position on the scales of universities." Even the business community is beginning to express concern about the state of gender relations in the universities. See Tom Kierans, "Where Were the Guardians?" *The Globe & Mail Report on Business*, May 1990, p. 47.

95 A newly formed committee of the Association of Professional Engineers of Ontario was given the power to recommend "public sanctions" against universities that do not control sexist behaviour ("Engineers' Watchdog Vows Clampdown on Sexism," *The Toronto Star*, 7 April 1990, p. A3).

96 This suggestion has provoked more response from women who have criticized the draft than most others. I do not wish to suggest that men are entitled to a primer course from feminists as an alternative to taking the time to inform themselves, nor that it is the responsibility of women to educate men. I do believe that women who choose to do so can make an important contribution through voluntary interaction with sincere and reasonably well-informed men.

97 Women in the law schools experience fear when they speak out, real fear experienced in every dimension of their lives. See Christine Boyle, "Teaching Law as if Women Really

Mattered, or, What About the Washrooms," *Canadian Journal of Women and the Law*, 2, 1 (1986): 96, 109-11. The employment equity consultant's report to Osgoode Hall, described in n. 6, deals with women's fear in detail. See also McIntyre, "Gender Bias," p. 386-88; Todd, "Feminist Targets"; and Govier, "A Time to Be Just," p. 16. I suppose I shall now discover whether a man who speaks out will experience some of the same fear.

98 I emphasize "try." White males have a longer way to go than most, but we all have a long way to go before we can claim that we do treat people equally. In the interim, the legendary male ego helps. Many men can cope with the assumption, however true or false, that they would have been just as successful in a non-discriminatory world. The male propensity to individualize allows him to isolate other, less-talented men as the beneficiaries of discrimination.

99 As feminists well know, the support of others really matters here. Men who abandon their right not to know can help one another a great deal. They can benefit from the process of cooperation as much as from the outcome. Women can and do help immensely. It is incredible how supportive my feminist colleagues and women students have been as I stumble through feminism like a bull (*sic*) in a china shop.

100 For a provocative discussion of difference, see Audre Lorde, "Age, Race, Class, and Sex: Women Redefining Difference," in Audre Lorde, *Sister Outsider* (Freedom, CA: Crossing Press, 1984), p. 114.

101 Students have taken a number of initiatives against gender discrimination at Western. Inevitably, it is assumed that they were put up to it by faculty members as part of the feminist plot. There is no appreciation of how insulting this assumption is to the students.

102 For example, Dalhousie Law School has hired two First Nations women on faculty, Patricia Monture and Aki-Kwe (Mary Ellen Turpel), and introduced the "Law Program for Indigenous Blacks and Micmacs: Access to Law." See also "Harvard Law Professor Quits Until Black Woman Is Named," *New York Times*, 24 April 1990, p. A1.

10

"Race Relations" Policy Brought to Life: A Case Study of One Anti-Harassment Protocol

Leela MadhavaRau

During the 1980s, many universities developed "sexual harassment policies," proclaiming that all members of the university had the right to study and work in an environment free of discrimination. By 1990, some universities had expanded these policies, or designed parallel policies, to cover "racial harassment" as well. The connections between gender and race discrimination are increasingly raised, particularly by women of colour, who find their experience of both intertwined, often inseparably.[1] It is critically important that White women learn to shift their focus from an overly generalized perspective of gender as a universal construct to reflect upon the power dimensions of White racial privilege.[2] To the extent that we fail fully to integrate race and gender analyses, we pursue strategies and goals which replicate oppressive racial structures and behaviour.

This essay provides a case study of the response within one university to the Race Relations Policy it adopted in 1990. The author, a university-based Race Relations Officer, describes her experience in attempting to implement the policy within an institutional climate that is obviously as chilly, if not chillier, for women and men of diverse races as it is for White women.

Two things are striking about this case and relevant to discussions of the chilly climate for women in colleges and universities. First, this is the story not just of one particularly painful and controversial anti-harassment case but of the public debate sparked by this case and of the process of review through which the Race Relations Policy was subsequently revised. In the eyes of many this was a process by which the Race Relations Policy was effectively gutted; ironically, this was the view both of those who upheld the original policy (or, indeed, found it already disturbingly weak) as well as of critics who were pleased to report that the revised policy was acceptable because it was so weakened it would be unlikely to do anyone any harm.[3]

The public debate over this policy was dominated by the voices of those who see themselves as the potential target of frivolous or otherwise unjustified complaints.[4] Not surprisingly, little was heard from or about the standpoint of those who might have justifiable complaints and now even less support than ever for pursuing them. Leela MadhavaRau's discussion raises a series of questions that were noticeably absent from the public debate. For example, what are the implications of this debate for those who confront racist attitudes and practices, and who might have occasion to turn to the Race Relations Officer and policy for support and redress? We fear that the events described here cannot but have undermined any confidence they may have had in institutional mechanisms for safeguarding their right to learn and work and teach in a non-racist environment. While protections against unfair accusations are crucially important, there was noticeably little discussion of how counterbalancing protections might be built into the new Race Relations Policy for those who are already at a disadvantage, not just as potential targets of racism but also, disproportionately, as students, staff, and junior faculty who continue to occupy the most vulnerable positions in the university community and employment structures. Many who have worked to improve the climate of their workplace will see in this account powerful evidence of the fragility of our gains in recent years.

A second striking feature of this case is the illustration it provides of ways in which extant power structures circumscribe speech. Of necessity, MadhavaRau's account calls into question the title of this volume as misleadingly optimistic; the extent to which she can speak out on the issues she addresses here is necessarily limited by the conditions of her appointment as a Race Relations Officer. All harassment prevention offices afford confidentiality to both parties in any complaint which, while necessary, reduces the ability of an officer to respond to rumour or innuendo circulating about a specific complaint. Those who experience harassment often find themselves even more sharply, if informally, constrained in what they can say by the conditions under which they speak — by the fear that, at best, they will not be heard or, at worst, that the objections they raise will be disbelieved, will deepen the chilliness they hope to change, or will bring reprisals they cannot afford to risk. Those who criticize the policy and MadhavaRau's handling of the case in question evidently felt less constrained, either by institutional restrictions or by a more general concern for the implications of their speech. Thus, while her critics decry the power she and other equity officers are alleged to have to "administrative[ly] harass" members of the university community,[5] the irony is that MadhavaRau can tell the story she tells only through the published record, which is dominated by the voices of critics who, in many cases, call into question the very idea of a race relations policy. Whatever the merits of the case in question, the public debate described here illustrates the very real asymmetries that persist in the capacity to exercise rights of speech, even in a context where institutional mechanisms exist to protect those who are most vulnerable against the infringement of these rights, and most vulnerable to the harms that can be done by those who have disproportionate power to exercise them.

While there are many points of resonance with women's experiences of being silenced (or remaining silent, by judicious and sometimes fearful choice), MadhavaRau describes events in which racism is in the foreground and is, in some ways, strategically dissociated from sexism despite close linkages between the institutional policies governing sexual and racial harassment. To the extent that women in the academy reinforce this dissociation and continue to fight for equity along gender lines without engaging issues of racism — and of homophobia and ablism and ageism, among other forms of systemic oppression that are constitutive of gender structures and identities — we contribute, actively or by complicity, to an environment in which one oppression can be played off against another and the voices of those whose privilege is challenged can continue to dominate debate. MadhavaRau's essay makes clear how urgent is the task of redirecting feminist analysis and activism to make anti-racism a central and defining commitment of the women's movement.

– Eds.

I. Introduction

This is, for the most part, a personal account of the implementation of a "race relations" policy at the University of Western Ontario. In this chapter I recount the chronology of events in the investigation, hearing, and aftermath of one particularly controversial complaint that was heard under this policy. In order to move beyond a clinical detailing of my time as Race Relations Officer, I would have liked to have introduced a sub-text through which the reader could recognize the pain, anger, frustration, and disbelief that permeated my working life. Yet, in a book focused on women and their experiences of the chilly climate, I found that interweaving to be too difficult. The only words which do not follow the more detached academic gaze have been relegated to the Afterword.

When I first began my work as Race Relations Officer in 1991, I was optimistic, if slightly wary. After all, most of what I knew about the University and issues of "race" revolved around the aftermath of Philippe Rushton's 1989 presentation at the American Association for the Advancement of Science (AAAS) conference in San Francisco of the now infamous "Evolutionary Biology and Heritable Traits (with Reference to Oriental-White-Black Differences)" paper. That incident should have warned me because it was not long before I began to question my ability to effect real change. When individuals reacted in fear to the use of the terminology of "anti-racism education," and refused point-blank to include the words "anti-racism" in my office title, my wariness began to turn to a deep frustration. It appeared that, for many individuals "racism" is recognizable only in its most explicit and extreme forms, as associated with images of the Ku Klux Klan marching onto campus in full regalia, burning crosses and consigning Jews and Blacks to the flames.

The Race Relations Policy

I had been hired to administer a Race Relations Policy that had its roots in a collaboration between the University Chaplains, the London Urban Alliance on Race Relations, and what is now the Ontario Anti-Racism Secretariat, all of whom approached the President of the University in 1986 to "suggest that an examination of race relations at Western be undertaken."[1] The President created an Advisory Committee on Race Relations which began its work in 1987. The Committee undertook a survey to determine the "race relations climate" among the student population (both graduate and undergraduate). Altogether 9.1% of the students who were surveyed reported that they had been the object of at least one actual or perceived racist incident in the previous year. Public hearings convened by the Committee found that, "the Western campus was not seen as a 'cosmopolitan' place. Evidence of this could be found frequently in and out of the classroom, in assumptions accepted as true by individuals, both faculty and students, who were often unaware that stereotyping of minority communities underlay those assumptions."[2] Following this data-gathering exercise, the Committee made several recommendations to the President, including the development of a race relations policy and procedures. It must be noted that these recommendations were made in June 1989, several months after Philippe Rushton gave his controversial AAAS paper in San Francisco.

A committee began to write draft versions of what was to become Western's Race Relations Policy, and on 20 September 1990, this policy was passed by Western's Senate. It stated that "every member of the university has the right to study and work in an environment free of discrimination and harassment on the basis of race." "Racial discrimination" was defined as:

> differential treatment of an individual or group that is not based on individual or group performance, but arises only from racial-group membership.

"Racial harassment" was defined as:

> unwelcome attention of a racially oriented nature, including remarks, jokes, gestures, slurs, innuendoes, or other behaviour, verbal or physical, which is directed at an individual or group by another person or group who knows, or ought reasonably to know, that this attention is unwarranted.

The policy further noted that:

> racial discrimination or harassment on the basis of:
>
> (a) doctrines or practices which declare inherent superiority due to race, or
> (b) claims that human abilities are determined by race
> (c) or on any other grounds
>
> *is hereby condemned and will not be tolerated.*[3]

Dissatisfaction about the policy was expressed by a number of individuals on campus, but most vocal were the members of the Academic Coalition for Equality (ACE), a group which was established following Rushton's presentation in San Francisco. ACE believed the Race Relations Policy was too weak and would prove ineffectual in dealing with situations such as that of Rushton. The University hired its first Race Relations Officer, myself, in June 1991.

Combining Theory with Practice

Few people today seem interested in addressing systemic issues to do with racism; indeed, few seem prepared to address any but the most blatant and individualized forms of racism. Certainly, few seem willing to look inside themselves and perform self-analysis on issues of "race." It continues to amaze me what powerful effects can follow from the few words, "all of us have the potential to be racist, to some extent." Among anti-racism practitioners and many people of colour words such as these would simply be taken for granted, but in a university community already riven by racial and gender tensions, they can become the focal point for a campaign against race relations policies and anti-racism education and activism. At a university at which the term "race" was being used primarily to refer to biologically determined categories of difference, my attempts to redefine "race" and "racism" as a social construct were wholly unsuccessful.

Many have been unable to understand another common element of anti-racist thought. As Essed puts this point,

> The concept of "power" (the oppression of other racial/ethnic groups based on one's own position of power) is fundamental to understanding the meaning and function of racism. Without access to the power to actually harm the "other" as a group, one may be guilty of pre-judgement — believing wrong or negative information about that group — and of individual discrimination but not of racism.[4]

In this discussion Essed not only characterizes cultural, institutional, and individual racism but also, and more importantly, she describes the notion of "everyday racism." By this she means, "the various types and expressions of racism experienced by ethnic groups in everyday contact with members of the more powerful (white) group. Everyday racism is, thus, racism from the point of view of people of colour, defined by those who experience it."[5] Essed makes several further points vital to a deeper understanding of the dynamics at work in racist environments:

> Covert racism does not necessarily imply that the underlying racist feelings are being concealed intentionally. In a racist society, public morality and the accepted norms may actually condemn racism. But the concepts of white superiority and the rejection of blacks will already have established themselves to such an extent that instead of being exceptional, they become "normal." From the point of view of people of colour, it is possible to sense the presence of racism, and, through various observations and insights, to make it almost intangible. But even then it may be difficult to make any concrete accusations because the racism is usually denied. "I didn't mean it that way" is a standard response, reflecting this denial.
>
> A variety of studies have shown that those who are discriminated against appear to have more insight into discrimination mechanisms than those who discriminate. This rather broad conclusion confirms the notion that blacks have a certain amount of expertise about racism through extensive experience with whites. The latter, conversely, are often hardly aware of the racism in their own attitudes and behaviour.[6]

I have never been naive enough to believe that universities are truly bastions of "free" thought, but it was at the University of Western Ontario that I came to understand, first hand, the operation of what may be termed "selective academic freedom." Haideh Moghissi draws on her experiences at another Canadian university to describe what she refers to as "racism and sexism in academic practice."[7] Her analysis is incisive:

> It is usually harder to reveal the subtle, unconscious racism of intellectuals and the incredible tolerance of racism in academic institutions than to expose a man in the street who commits overt racism. Most academics disguise their racist attitudes and practices more competently, and hide and suppress challenges to such beliefs more effectively, by resorting to more benign notions and seemingly neutral criteria, such as academic freedom and academic excellence. This is also true for sexist and misogynist attitudes and practices. It is also the case that most intellectuals suffer from a "cognitive incapacity," to borrow from Anthony Appiah's term, to recognize racism, particularly their own racism. Underlying the notion of "excellence" in such cases is the belief that being qualified and being coloured and/or female are mutually exclusive. . . .
>
> Almost no one likes to be considered racist. In fact often people who inflict racism are not even aware of the harm done and are surprised, even offended, when individuals who are the object of the harm understand their actions as racist. This is particularly the case in those institutions and communities which present and preserve an idealized imagery of liberalism,

openness and diversity, such as universities, for most liberal and left educators tend to understand racism only in terms of overt words and actions
deriving from malicious intentions and fail to recognize that highly educated and otherwise gentle and civil individuals can also be guilty of preju-
dicial perceptions and practices.

The racist and sexist behaviours and practices in academia typically do
not include hard and convincing-beyond-doubt evidence, such as bodily
harm or explicit derogatory statement. This, however, does not make racism and sexism in academia more benign — far from it. Academic institutions produce knowledge and reproduce the ideological make-up of every
society. Through educating and training the future elite of every society
their intellectual produce has far-reaching impacts on the whole society.
Moreover, one always finds the racism of intellectuals more harmful. This
is not only because it takes one off-guard. It is also because intellectual racism requires that we put our energies into a battle that need not and should
not exist, blocking the way for communication and cooperation in other social and political battlegrounds.[8]

With this outline of the practice of racism in the academy in hand, it
might be appropriate to describe something of my background. I am the
daughter of a "mixed marriage," father born in Bangalore, India, and White
mother born in England. I was born in London, England, and moved to
Canada when I was seven years old. I didn't realize that I was of "ambiguous ethnicity" until I was nine years old, and children began following me
home from school, in Welland, Ontario, chanting "Paki, Paki." I couldn't
understand it. I had never been to Pakistan. I told my mother and she started crying, telling me that one reason our family had immigrated to Canada
had been to escape racism in Britain. That event opened up new vistas for
me. I wanted to understand my Indian heritage but I knew that I would
probably always live in "the West." When I first went to university at
McGill, I became more active in anti-racism work and began to meet members of the Indian community. I felt more comfortable in the identity which I
was slowly constructing for myself, but I was not entirely content. I undertook graduate studies in social anthropology at the University of Cambridge and met more members of the Indian community who accepted me
without the continual questioning of my ethnicity I found in the broader society. Then I went to India for four months, staying initially with my family
but later travelling on my own around the country. I began planting roots in
Bangalore, securing a stronger place in my immediate family. I later selected
a PhD topic which would allow me to explore in more depth the position of
young, second-generation Asian women in Britain. I know I could not have
applied for the Race Relations Officer's job if I had not begun the search for
my own ethnic identity.

II. Implementing a Race Relations Policy: A Case Study

On 6 December 1991, a Western student lodged an informal complaint with the University's Race Relations Office, alleging racial harassment on the part of a tenured female professor (hereafter "Professor X"). Most of the subsequent proceedings were shielded from public scrutiny under policies of confidentiality maintained by the University throughout the investigation and adjudication of the complaint. Professor X, her lawyer, and the University of Western Ontario Faculty Association (UWOFA) chose to make public certain information and documents relating to the case. While they were certainly within their rights to do so, subsequent discussion has necessarily been based on information about the case that has been selectively disclosed by the respondent and her representatives. It has been the position of the Race Relations Office, throughout the proceedings and their aftermath, to refuse to release publicly any material relating to the case. While this imbalance makes a full analysis extremely difficult, it is possible to piece together a partial description of the proceedings based on the information made public by the respondent and her advocates.

The complaint centred on a statement made by Professor X during a class in December 1991. A local newspaper columnist for *The London Free Press* described the incident as follows: "According to [Professor X's] lawyer . . . the essence of the case against her is that she upset the feelings of [a] student [of Y background] by suggesting that he ought to know the [language translation] for "condemnation" inasmuch as he had told the class about how officials in [the student's country of origin] condemned almost everyone."[9] A more detailed article on the case appearing in the same paper on 20 March 1993 described the incident that sparked the complaint more fully:

> During the class discussion, an ethnic student told the class about persecution by officials against people in his country. About six weeks later, during a similar discussion [Professor X] noted the student's repeated misuse of [a] verb . . . that means "to condemn." According to [Professor X], she attempted to correct him by way of analogy, repeating a phrase he had used earlier "as you (the student) said, in (your country) they condemn everyone."[10]

Professor X described the incident in her own words in a letter to Western's President, 28 January 1993, which she later published in the UWO Faculty Association newsletter.

> His allegation of racism was based on one statement: I corrected his repeated misuse of the verb . . . (to condemn) to translate each of the words convert, consisting, conversion and consider in a translation class. Rather than provide the direct English equivalent, I proceeded by analogy and ex-

ample, saying . . ."As you said [student's name]: 'In [student's country of origin] they condemn everyone.' " This referred to an earlier statement *he* had volunteered in class concerning his country of origin when we were discussing problems arising when translating for refugees who have suffered persecution in their countries. The phrase was his, not mine.[11]

The student concerned came to the Race Relations Office, seeking a letter of apology. Professor X says "she was put under pressure to write a letter of apology, or at least one suggesting that she had been insensitive."[12] Attempts at informal mediation failed,[13] and the case was sent to a hearing before an external adjudicator, the first (and to date, only) such hearing ever held under Western's Race Relations Policy. A professor of law at another Ontario university was appointed and held this hearing on 27 April 1992. Her full decision, released to the parties six weeks later, on 9 June 1992, has never been made public. Western's President subsequently wrote to the adjudicator requesting clarification of her ruling and, after receiving the required clarification, announced that "the complaint did not establish a case of racial harassment and that the case was dismissed."[14] The UWO Faculty Association reported in January 1993 that "the report says that a 'letter regretting pain caused to' the complainant would have been helpful, but that there was 'no evidence that Professor [X] violated the letter of the [policy on the] prohibition of racial harassment."[15] *The London Free Press* reported that "[Professor X] was cleared of the harassment charge," although the adjudicator had accused Professor X of lacking "the hallmark of a caring and sensitive member of the teaching profession."[16]

At a meeting of the Faculty Association on 13 October 1992, approximately 50 faculty members called for the Race Relations Policy to be "scrapped and replaced with a new one."[17] Their call followed a public statement by the respondent expressing her dissatisfaction with the judgment, claiming she was a "victim" of the race relations policy and "zealously persecuted" during the course of events by the Race Relations Officer. Professor X demanded "a full apology on behalf of the University," payment for "all legal costs and other related expenses," and "compensation in the amount of one year's salary." Professor X stated that her case raised "serious questions concerning human rights, academic freedom, and educational standards."[18] In a letter she wrote to the President she stated: "Because I find racism so abhorrent, I have fought this accusation. It would have been much easier for me to go along with the attitude that 'it's no big deal, just apologize and get it over with.' Racism is serious and must be dealt with seriously. To accept a trivial accusation is to trivialize racism."[19]

The furore over this case led the President to request a review of the procedural aspects of the case by an acknowledged authority on administrative law at yet a third Ontario university. Following the report of this external expert, a university press release concluded that, "the review and all existing documentation support the appropriateness, legality and proper conduct of the proceedings. In particular, they indicate that the University's Race Relations Officer behaved responsibly and with integrity and propriety in discharging her mandate under the Race Relations Policy."[20]

The London Free Press ran a full-page feature about this single case, discussing the "shrinking middle ground between those who see some recent policy initiatives as dangerous experiments in social engineering and those who see them as vital steps toward creating a more inclusive, less discriminatory environment." The article continued:

> the Professor [X] affair was not your ordinary, garden-variety, controversy-of-the-week at Western. It was a whopper of a tempest in this ivory-towered teapot. . . . At the heart of the reaction to the [X] case is a growing unease about the direction Western has taken on many issues of social equity. . . . Despite the fact that it's not popular, or even wise given the political climate on campuses, to speak out against these policies, there's an increasingly vocal opposition growing. Provincial and national groups have sprung up, linked loosely by their concern over "academic freedom."[21]

One inevitable source of imbalance in the reporting of harassment cases is the inability of practitioners to respond in the media, as all cases are held in confidence. Most officers will not reveal details under any circumstances, leading frequently to personalized attacks based on inaccurate information promulgated by the alleged harasser. Several misconceptions became increasingly entrenched in the public discussion of the case I describe here, in part because the Race Relations Office continued to refuse to reveal details about the case. It is possible at this point to correct some of the misconceptions by drawing upon documents which ultimately became part of the public record. For example, much was said in public debate about the involvement of the Race Relations Office in drafting the actual letter of complaint. Professor X asserted in the letter described above that the student "lodged a further accusation in a letter written by Ms. MadhavaRau."[22] My "authorship" of the letter was picked up by faculty and media alike and eventually led to a call for my dismissal, published in Western's student newspaper, *The Gazette*, 11 November 1992: "Rau was partisan because she composed a letter of attack on professor [X] and had a student sign it. . . ."[23] *The Gazette*, 25 November 1992: "In a letter [Professor X] wrote that was obtained by *The Gazette*, she stated . . . that Rau wrote a letter of accusation on behalf of the complainant and made him sign it. Rau later admitted to that action during the tribunal."[24] *The Gazette*, 13 November 1992:

> Leela MadhavaRau allegedly wrote a letter of complaint on behalf of the complainant, having the student ultimately sign a letter written by someone else.... If Leela Rau is found to have perjured herself by essentially forging a letter of complaint, she should be dismissed.[25]

The truth is, of course, far more prosaic. The Race Relations and Sexual Harassment offices have produced a leaflet entitled *A Letter May Help*, which is provided freely to members of the University. The officers always offer their services in reading over a letter and offering suggestions which may lead to a resolution of the complaint. This service is available equally to respondents and complainants. The external reviewer commented on the authorship of the letter of complaint at some length in his report:

> More specifically, I should say that Professor [X] overstates the issue of the authorship of the letter that was sent to her after the mediation session over the signature of The Complainant. The impression given by Professor [X] is one of initial perjured testimony by Ms. MadhavaRau as to who actually "wrote" the letter followed by a grudging concession that the Race Relations Officer, not The Complainant had "written" it. In fact, as it came out in testimony, the only real issue was over the extent of the influence of Ms. MadhavaRau in the writing of that letter. Did she do so much in terms of its contents and language that it should be regarded as her letter, not The Complainant's? The fact that she participated in some measure was never denied. Moreover, at the end of all this, this issue was never pursued to a conclusion in his cross-examination by [the respondent's representative], presumably because of its marginal relevance in terms of the way he was presenting the case at the hearing.[26]

Another example of overt exaggeration and distortion of fact comes in Professor X's assertion that I "began" my sworn statement at the hearing "by declaring: 'We are all racists.'"[27] This comment was picked up by a number of faculty members and used to imply a degree of bias which would render me incapable of performing my role. A recent example comes from a Professor of the English Department, in a letter of 14 April 1994, to *Western News*:

> It is becoming increasingly fashionable to see racism and sexism as evils that pervade our unconscious minds. During the now notorious ... tribunal, Western's Race Relations Officer dismissed Professor [X]'s insistence on her innocence with the counter-claim that "we are all, to some extent, racists." ... On the Race Relations Officer's own admission, she is herself a "racist" (albeit only "to some extent"), so how can she claim the moral authority to prosecute anybody else?[28]

I intend to address the notion of inherent racism later in this chapter, but wish to clarify at this point the misconstruction of my actual testimony. The external reviewer spoke to this matter specifically in his report:

Finally, and perhaps most importantly, Professor [X]'s statement that Ms. MadhavaRau "began her sworn statement . . . by declaring: 'We are all racists'" is simply not true. Midway through her cross-examination . . . after she had given her evidence in chief, Ms. MadhavaRau in a matter of fact manner said the following: "No, I think that people who are thinking about issues of racism on a constant basis have a knowledge and understanding that all of us are racist to some extent." In the context, it was not a gratuitous statement but a response that was invited by the question that was asked.[29]

Finally, there were misconceptions about the mediation process initiated under the Race Relations Policy. The Faculty Association did not discuss why the attempted mediation failed, but made allusion to the fact that further sessions should have been conducted.[30] This position is rooted in a misinterpretation of the mediation process, the belief that if one party wishes to continue that it is sufficient to convene a mediation session. The reality, of course, is that mediation requires two (or more) parties who agree voluntarily to an attempt to "talk the problem out."

The promulgation of inaccurate information is exacerbated, on occasion, by members of the campus media at a number of Canadian universities who question the credentials of anti-racism practitioners and sexual harassment officers. Some have insinuated that jobs are granted on the basis of "race" and gender rather than qualifications. Our inability to provide details about complaints or to reveal information such as name and status in the university has also led a number of correspondents to accuse equity officers of inventing cases to keep themselves in work. The oft-reiterated statement that equity officers would be only too happy to work themselves out of a job is met with incredulity and disbelief. A Professor of the Sociology Department provides one example of this tactic in a letter of 14 October 1993 to *Western News*:

> Now we have in this university a structure in which the Race Relations Officer is highly motivated to maximize the number of "convictions," or "findings" of professorial improper conduct. First, the present Race Relations Officer is on record concerning the severe state of racism here, and seems to be personally committed to that position. Further, the position itself is a very well-compensated post, with no history to lend it security, in a time of great financial constraint. A Race Relations Officer who minimized the severity of racial problems on campus might find the position itself eliminated.[31]

Another common theme in the pages of the local press involved references to the Race Relations and Sexual Harassment Officers as instruments of totalitarian regimes, the tired "thought police" argument. In a 22 October 1992 letter to the *Western News*, a Professor of the Department of History wrote:

The notion of imposing ideological conformity on a society is no longer confined to Latin America. It is also active in North America. Indeed, it is on this campus. My colleague, Professor [X], has some understanding of what Isabella's Spain was like beyond her professional competence. An individual reported her to the Race Relations office where apparently she was considered guilty until she proved her innocence before a tribunal. . . . In this case a university policy and its administration proved akin to Isabella's inquisition.[32]

A Professor of the Department of French echoed these sentiments in a letter of 6 April 1993:

Sexual harassment is an ugly thing and should be stamped out with the utmost energy, but not in a manner reminiscent of the one advocated by members of a movement of budding French Fascists of the not too distant past who, in order to fight the real or imaginary evils they perceived in society, were prepared to use all means available to them, *even legal ones* [emphasis in original].[33]

In a similar vein a regular columnist with *The London Free Press* wrote:

Had [Professor X] been found guilty, she could have been forced to apologise to the student and take a re-education course in racial sensitivity — punishments worthy of Maoist China, not a free university . . . It should go without saying that if any racist engages in *physical* [my emphasis] intimidation or violence on campus, if any sexist so much as touches a female student inappropriately, the long arm of the law should reach out and prosecute the offender. Abusive words are entirely different. Perhaps, a sensitive campus mediator could play a useful role in resolving disputes over allegedly racist and sexist remarks. On no account, though, should any agency of the university undertake to punish freedom of speech.[34]

It is curious to note the distinction made explicitly between verbal and physical harassment; freedom of speech rhetoric is reiterated with no understanding or acknowledgment of the consequences of verbal racial harassment.

Paddy Stamp, the Sexual Harassment Advisor at the University of Toronto, wrote succinctly about the perception of anti-racism and sexual harassment offices on Canadian campuses, in the context of a controversy on her own campus:

At some point this debate collided with the recent media hysteria about the supposed "political correctness movement" on university campuses, and this gave rise to a veritable mass-production industry of hypothesis and speculation about — at its more volatile end — how a revised sexual harassment policy would become a weapon in the hands of a lunatic fringe of politically correct totalitarian thought police, hell bent on destroying any vestige of academic freedom on Canadian campuses.[35]

For many working in the anti-harassment field, the idea that we are powerful thought police marching to a Fascist-Maoist beat is at best ridiculous but at worst sadly ironic. In some universities in Canada, there is a single individual responsible for all "human rights issues," at others there is one person with responsibility for sexual harassment, another for anti-racism work and perhaps one working on issues of disability or sexual identity. In a few rare cases, another person has responsibility for Aboriginal issues on campus. All are woefully underfunded and bear responsibility for university communities with populations of tens of thousands. Few, if any, officers have top-level administrative status and most work with little institutional support. The scenario would be risible if it were not gaining currency.

But it is this image of the "language" or "thought police" which now dominates the everyday perception of anti-racism and sexual harassment policies; indeed, a W5 television documentary focusing on Western was entitled "Harassment Police." When the conversation turns to a discussion of these policies, it is common to hear, "But what can we say these days without being reported? Why can't I say that my female colleague looks good in red? Why can't I teach my course on sexuality? If I can't call them Orientals, what am I supposed to call them?" It is all too easy for the mythology to develop that anti-harassment policies are being written to stop all casual conversations and prevent professors from teaching their courses. This mythology becomes entrenched as the flames are fanned by groups such as the Society for Academic Freedom and Scholarship (SAFS). SAFS was established in London, Ontario in March 1992. The goals of SAFS, as specified in their newsletter, are to resist the ideological misuse of teaching and scholarship; to support rigorous standards in research and teaching in university hiring practices; and to preserve academic freedom and the free exchange of ideas, regardless of popular doctrine.[36]

The "academic freedom" supporters rely on a few key texts for their information on this issue. A Professor of the Department of History cited one in a letter to the *Western News* of 25 November 1993:

> According to an article entitled "The Textbook Wars," published in the September 20 issue of *National Review*, California's "Standing Committee to Review Textbooks from a Multicultural Perspective" once detected "racism" in all the following statements: 1. "The afternoon turned black." 2. "It's going to be a black winter." 3. "The deputy's face darkened." No kidding.[37]

This Professor then goes on to quote that icon and spokesperson for the "academic freedom" movement, Dinesh D'Souza. It was D'Souza who was invited to give the keynote address to a conference sponsored by SAFS and the Fraser Institute in March 1993 entitled, "The University in Jeopardy." He asked the audience: "Do colleges and universities fight discrimination by institutionalizing new forms of it? As professors, the challenge is to stand and thwart the tide."[38]

Such exaggerations serve to bring those wary of anti-racism policies into the "academic freedom" camp, as well as perpetuating the mythology of the all-powerful equity police against whose superior weaponry (so to speak) professors must battle.

While anti-harassment policies do receive approval from different corners of the university community, few supporters respond to the proponents of academic freedom in the pages of their university newspapers. They recognize the futility of trying to sway the other side, and for students there is the spectre of criticizing a movement which may be supported by their professors. Until anti-racism and sexual harassment offices have proven themselves to be more than lightning rods that protect the administration, they are unlikely to find supporters who will respond to their critics, especially in a climate where the media is dominated by well-established anti-equity groups. These concerns emerge clearly in a recent report on "Anti-Racism Student Organizing in Canadian Universities." The authors of this Report quote members of the Academic Coalition for Equality (ACE) who commented on the post-Rushton environment at Western:

> The administration's response to pressure by ACE was the creation of a race relations policy and a race relations officer. ACE was initially sceptical about the motives of the policy and effectiveness of the race relations officer. ACE decided to work with the officer after she demonstrated an interest in the community and a support for the issues. Since ACE has been able to communicate positively with this person, it is reported that the person is now "under attack" by the administration.[39]

When harassment cases become news, negative feedback can also come from unexpected sources, including student representatives. One such example is found in a November 1992 editorial in *The Gazette*, the University's student newspaper:

> There is very little in the policy to prevent an active witchhunt of anyone who might be innocent. Societal paranoia surrounding racial discrimination has victimized [Professor X]. The Race Relations Policy as it stands does far more to promote and encourage racial hysteria than to encourage and nurture healthy relations between the races. [Professor X] has given up close to a year of her life to protect her reputation in this community and has made an extensive financial and psychological commitment to do so.[40]

A convocation address at Simon Fraser University given by a Professor in the Psychology Department and founding President of the Society for Academic Freedom and Scholarship received wide media attention, including radio coverage on CBC's *As It Happens*. Yet the speech was nothing more than a reiteration of the rhetoric outlined above:

> ... totalitarian regimes typically begin with the suppression of free speech. Can we honestly claim there is any fundamental difference between the Communist and fascist control of academia of the past and the suppression of ideas which is spreading throughout our campuses today? ... Thought police have no place in free society, much less in a university.[41]

It was heartening to read the single response to this convocation speech. The writer is a student who spent her final year working on a draft anti-racism policy at the University of Guelph:

> I would question how free academe has been in the past. ... Essentially, the university community has held in place a power structure or institution that has censored the voices of marginalized peoples since the European invasion of Turtle Island (the aboriginal name for North America) and the subsequent invention of the Canadian university. ... It is so easy to cry academic freedom, to haul out the old thought police and drum up visions of *Nineteen Eighty-Four* in the minds of white Canadians.[42]

Nonetheless, the image of the all-powerful anti-harassment officer is further entrenched by faculty members who commented on the Race Relations Officer's "harass[ment]" of Professor X. A letter published in *Western News* in October 1992 by a Professor of English illustrates this well:

> The racial harassment office's harassing of Professor [X] raises serious concerns for everyone on this campus. ... [W]hat is the role of the race relations office? Is it a purely advisory body or does it have the coercive force of law? If the latter, why is it needed when there are already laws prohibiting the incitement of racial hatred in Canada? I know of no UWO policy that states that members of this university have less freedom of speech than other Canadians.[43]

Thus, the allegation of using racially insensitive language is not seen as harassment but when someone is charged under a Race Relations Policy with "racial harassment," the Race Relations Officer is considered a harasser for fulfilling her mandate.

The letter raises another objection to race relations policies and offices frequently invoked by the supporters of "academic freedom": that the services of institutionally based anti-harassment offices are redundant given that harassment and discrimination are prohibited by federal and/or provincial law. For example, the Ontario Human Rights Code makes it unlawful to discriminate on the basis of race or sex, including a number of other grounds such as ancestry, place of origin, colour, ethnic origin, citizenship, creed, or religion, and provides various enforcement mechanisms for investigating violations of its provisions.[44] For those who support in-house policies, it is clear that provincial and federal human rights codes are too slow and cumbersome to deal with situations which can often be resolved by sitting down and discussing the problem. The majority of harassment cases still go unreported, and returning to a reliance on "outside" legislation will ensure that the reporting rates drop even lower.

It is ironic, given the nature of this book, that the graphic picture of universities as institutions with a "chilly climate," a phrase first used in Bernice Sandler's ground-breaking report on sexual harassment of women in post-secondary education, is now being appropriated by those who invoke "academic freedom" arguments in an effort to discredit equity policies. A Professor of History made such charges in a letter to *Western News* of 22 October 1992:

> The R[ace] R[elations] O[fficer], if money is to be spent on having one at all, should be a person of both judicial temperament and unquestioned credibility. . . . The Race Relations Policy threatens to create a chilly climate for anybody who may wish to express opinions about (for example) the quality of government in post-colonial Africa, or the sources of crime in multiracial cities.[45]

Those responsible for equity policies have made it clear that they value the *principle* of academic freedom but do not believe that academic freedom is absolute. Academic freedom brings with it academic responsibility. When that responsibility is ignored, absolute academic freedom cannot exist. It must be conceded that academic freedom frequently enhances the power and privilege of those who already possess those advantages. For these individuals to talk of the creation of a chilly climate is analogous to a dictatorship saying it is unfair for its citizens to challenge the status quo. To restrict racist, sexist, homophobic, and all harassing speech is, pardon the cliché, to "level the playing field" for all.

Increasingly, the language of harassment is also becoming institutionalized. Glossaries are now de rigueur at the end of all policy documents. In many cases, the definitions provided therein differ minutely with regard to explanations of the concepts of "race," "racism," and "anti-racism." In the literature provided by the Race Relations office, I utilized material to show the clear distinction between "race relations" and "anti-racism":

> The goal of "race relations" is to remove discriminatory barriers and ensure equal opportunity for all people without discrimination based on culture, religion or race. The term may apply, as it does at the University of Western Ontario, to policies designed to promote "harmonious inter-racial and cross-cultural communication." Such policies may also encourage the elimination of racial intolerance and the reduction of racial tension and conflict that are caused by prejudicial attitudes.
>
> Anti-racism goes one step further in recognizing and documenting the fact that racism exists in society and, therefore, institutions are affected by

racism. Anti-racism education provides the analytical tools to critically acknowledge, recognize and examine the origins of racist ideas and practice, and to understand the implications of our own race and actions in the promotion of, or struggle against, racism.

The two concepts are linked by the desire to eliminate racial prejudice. However, in order to effect real change there must be an acceptance that racism does exist within the institution and all members of the University community must play a role in working toward an "anti-racist" environment for work and study.

Such a statement became necessary when I began monitoring the reactions to the term "anti-racist" ("Why are you people always so negative?"). I recommended that Western's policy be re-named a "Race Relations and Anti-Racism Education Policy." The response to this suggestion was that this was an antagonistic move designed to irritate and also that it implied racism was systemic. This, of course, is the very point that anti-racism practitioners are making and is summed up by Richard Willey: "Multi-cultural" policies have invariably been couched in the bland and safe language of tolerance, harmony and mutual understanding, not in the contentious realities of prejudice and discrimination.[46]

One example of a consummate counter-argument to the "language is not important" claim is Robert Moore's piece, "A Short Play on Black and White Words":

> Some may blackly (angrily) accuse me of trying to blacken (defame) the English language, to give it a black eye (mark of shame) by writing such black words (hostile). They may denigrate (to cast aspersions; to darken) me by accusing me of being blackhearted (malevolent), of having a black outlook (pessimistic; dismal) on life, of being a blackguard (scoundrel) — which would certainly be a black mark (detrimental fact) against me. Some may black-brow (scowl at) me and hope that a black cat crosses in front of me because of this black deed. I may become a black sheep (one who causes shame or embarrassment because of deviation from the accepted standards), who will be black-balled (ostracized) by being placed on a blacklist (list of undesirables) in an attempt to blackmail (to force or coerce into a particular action) me to retract my words. But attempts to blackjack (to compel by threat) me will have a Chinaman's chance of success, for I am not a yellow-bellied Indian-giver of words, who will whitewash (cover up or gloss over vices or crimes) a black lie (harmful, inexcusable). I challenge the purity and innocence (white) of the English language. I don't see things in black and white (entirely bad or entirely good) terms, for I am a white man (marked by upright firmness) if there ever was one. However, it would be a black day when I would not "call a spade a spade," even though some will suggest a white man calling the English language racist is like the pot calling the kettle black. While many may be niggardly

(grudging, scanty) in their support, others will be honest and decent — and to them I say, that's very white of you (honest, decent).

The preceding is of course a white lie (not intended to cause harm), meant only to illustrate some examples of racist terminology in the English language.[47]

The effect of institutionalization on harassment policies is becoming an issue as anti-harassment work within the places of work and study becomes more common. Frequently these policies are presumed, by those who support the "rights" approach, to prevent one individual infringing on the rights of another individual. Where there has been a violation of these individual rights, the state (in this case, the University) should intervene. For those who take a "responsibility" stance, the presumptions are very different. It is the well-being of the collectivity which is to be examined, making all responsible for ensuring "fairness."

This distinction extends to the very titles that anti-harassment policies bear. For the many practitioners who understand the category of "race" itself to be socially constructed, all racial terminology is fraught with ambiguities. However, the term "race relations policy" reflects a "rights" position, while "anti-racism policy" places the onus on the collectivity and reinforces the need for community responsibility. Jewson and Mason make a similar observation in their discussion of equal opportunity policies in Britain where they draw a distinction between "liberal" and "radical" principles.[48]

"Liberal" policies define equality of opportunity as existing when all individuals are enabled freely and equally to compete for social rewards. "Radical" policy seeks to intervene directly in workplace practices in order to achieve a fair distribution of rewards among employees, and is concerned, primarily, with the outcome of the contest rather than the rules of the game, with the fairness of the distribution of rewards rather than the fairness of procedures. In my view this explains why "liberal" race relations policies lead to a ranking of forms of harassment and discrimination whereby physical violence is seen as "real racism" while the more insidious aspects of systemic racism are disregarded.

III. The Larger Context

Responses in the Academy

Opinions about both racial and sexual harassment now receive distinctive and political treatment within the academy. These terms themselves are part of the war between those who favour "academic equality" and those who use "academic freedom" as their rallying cry. One person's notion of harassment is, for another, an exercise of "academic freedom." Terminology such as "racial harassment" seems to be leading anti-racist practitioners into a debate over whether racism is an issue requiring the development of specific policy. The definition of "racial harassment" with which I work (the full text of which is quoted above) contains elements similar to many other policies in Canada. In particular, the reference to knowledge that the attention is unwanted is common. But how should an individual "know" an action is racist, and what onus is placed on the "victim" to inform the individual that they find the behaviour offensive? As millions watched the Anita Hill/Clarence Thomas debacle on television, one question that recurred was, "Why didn't she tell anyone? Why wouldn't she complain if she didn't like it?" With such questions the very real possibility that a complainant might fear a harasser is casually dismissed, and the end result is that the responsibility for ending harassment reverts to the complainant. In the university setting there is little acknowledgment of the power relations (between professor and student, supervisor and employee, man and woman) that usually structure harassment cases. It is this that raises the question of whose academic freedom is being curtailed by racist teachings and comments or by anti-racism policies.

Paramount in the debate over terminology such as "racial harassment" and "anti-racism" policies are the implications of using the term "racist." If one is alleged to have committed racial harassment, does one de facto become a racist? This possibility has incensed many "liberal" members of the university who have long seen themselves as opposing racism because they are against apartheid and White supremacy movements. Reactions to the case of Professor X provide a clear example of this concern. Perhaps anti-racism practitioners exacerbate matters by their blunt suggestion that everyone has the potential to be racist, regardless of ethnocultural origins. But not all of us are in such positions of power that imputing racism in these general (systemic) terms can lead to differential treatment which may be (and is) seen as harassment. In an editorial in *The Toronto Star* it was stated: "Racist. Used as an epithet, it evokes a strong, ugly reaction. Understanding its power, its sting and its implications, one might expect that its use would be exercised judiciously and with care. Not always so."[49] The presumption here seems to be that unless someone is a card-carrying member of a White supremacist organization, the term "racist" cannot be used; the appeal to judicious use becomes a technique for rendering anti-racism policies ineffective. I find it ironic that, when the question is asked, "Are you ever racist?," it is often only I and other "people of colour" who respond, "Yes, on occasion I am insensitive in a way that can be construed as racism." It would appear that it is now more hurtful to call someone a "racist" than a "Paki," "Nigger," or "Chink."

The case of Professor X and the subsequent backlash from the "academic freedom" camp raise the question of whether anti-racism philosophy is negotiable, and if so, to what extent. While entering into a debate over policy and procedures is necessary and often productive, should practition-ers simply begin from a baseline that systemic discrimination is extant in "Western" society and refuse to concede to the requests for specific ex-amples? I have found that the media does not want to hear of the systemic bias present in curriculum, university admissions procedures, and general administrative structure, but persists in the belief that racism consists of iso-lated incidents of verbal abuse or physical violence. Nor are reporters the only ones refuting suggestions of systemic discrimination. When an article profiling the Race Relations Office appeared in *The London Free Press* in August 1992, the President wrote a letter to the editor commenting upon a correction I had made in a letter to the editor printed some days earlier:

> [T]he specific examples which introduced and set the tone of the original article were fabricated by the author, Dave Miller of *The Free Press*, presum-ably to add "punch" to the story — as were cloudy and generalized sug-gestions that the classroom environment, most specifically the grading sys-tem, is pervasively tainted with an atmosphere of bias, as are the univer-sity's admissions procedures. This is simply not the case.[50]

Most anti-harassment workers understand that this is a new legal (mine)-field and that race relations policies will need continual review and revision. Yet it appears that opponents will see changes to policy as admissions of past procedural irregularities and mishandling of earlier complaints.

In my role as an "officer" enforcing an anti-harassment policy, I often feel that I act as the conscience of the University, there to remind the com-munity that the University of Western Ontario is now ready to accept differ-ence. Yet this is always a very careful process of negotiation, walking a tight-rope between many factions who can be easily irritated by the efforts of anti-harassment offices. At a meeting of a committee which dealt with "women's issues" on campus, I made the point that men of colour are also placed in vulnerable situations and women of colour even more so. I was told that this was not relevant. This struck me as a clear attempt to reject the link between generalized racism and violence. A few meetings later, a (White) committee member stated that this particular committee had to be-gin looking at women who were in a double or triple jeopardy situation, for example, women of colour. I was astonished and observed that when I had made the same point previously, I had been shut down. The response was that the committee needed "community input," that contemporary art of gathering together those chosen by the "mainstream" to represent the "community" and asking questions. I found the response ironic. Clearly, I am not representative of all women of colour in the university community. Who did this committee consider to be an appropriate representative? Why was the idea of focusing special attention on women of colour paid little heed until put forward by a White woman? Do the White women on the committee represent all White women on campus or was my representativeness an issue because I am different in some way? By such methods others draw distinctions within the racial minority community, determining how that community is represented in the University and rendering the Anti-Racism Officer powerless and ineffectual.

I have been monitoring the reactions of individuals when a case of racial discrimination or harassment comes forward. In many instances, just as with sexual harassment cases, the complainant is described by the respondent as mentally ill and unbalanced, as using "race" to obtain special considerations, or as a "poor student who wants higher grades." To cope with this lack of understanding of racial harassment and discrimination, I often resort to "pop anthropology" to explain the situation to a respondent. On the one hand, I should be discussing the facts of racism but on the other, I am driven into the trap of explaining behaviour in a broad "cross-cultural context" as a gentle way of making a point. So, while people rarely want to hear about racism, I am seen as the source of all types of "cross-cultural" information — religion, dress, food, or specific queries such as etiquette if you are invited to a Somali employee's house for dinner. I find myself saying well, in my family or community or religion we do this. This appropriation is not something with which I am entirely comfortable, but experience, whether from my own family or that acquired through my anthropological work, appears to be the best way to answer a question or respond to a comment. I often think of Westwood and Bhachu's point that, "Ethnography is ... a positive tool in our struggle against the racism of British society and a means whereby insiders' accounts can construct both the detail and the parameters in which minority cultures and lives will be understood, academically and more generally."[51] The means to use ethnography in such a meaningful way presumes an interest and time frame far beyond that with which an anti-harassment officer will be provided in a university setting. Thus, as an anthropologist, I am left feeling that the use of cross-cultural material has resulted in a dilution of the issues surrounding racism and anti-racism.

Government Intervention

In 1993, the Ontario government put forward a number of initiatives to promote "Aboriginal, racial and ethnocultural equity in Ontario schools, colleges and universities." The proposals suggested that all educational establishments, be they primary schools or universities, would be required to develop and implement anti-racism policies. They included a written *Framework Regarding Prevention of Harassment and Discrimination in Ontario Universities*. It remains to be seen what will result from this move towards the institutionalization of policy, especially as the *Framework* prescribes certain elements which should be contained in all policies. The possibility of what would be a province-wide policy for all universities leads back to the argument of "academic freedom" supporters who object that in-house policies are a duplication of provincial and federal laws, laws which they have grudgingly accepted. However, this *Framework* caused a furore rarely seen on Canadian campuses. The negative response focused on two areas: the concerns that this *Framework* might be an attempt to remove universities' traditional autonomy and, more obviously, that it represents an infringement on academic freedom.[52]

A petition was circulated through Ontario universities. At Western, a number of faculty members were centrally involved in the campaign against the *Framework*.[53] At the time of writing, no one was pacified by the Ontario government's *Framework*. Unhappy anti-racism practitioners have not been consulted, although the "academic freedom" supporters believe we back the policy. The "academic freedom" camp believes this is a "government Diktat," which "would make every fascist government proud."[54]

IV. Conclusion

The particular case that I describe here has now moved well beyond the gates of the University and into the realm of legend as an example of abuse caused by equity policies. When Robert Fulford spoke at Western in March 1994, Professor X had supplied him with her side of the story. Fulford spoke about how Western had "bungled its handling of a recent racial harassment charge":

> Under [Western's Race Relations] policy the good sense and good faith of the university officials have been tested and have been found sadly inadequate, with extremely unhappy results. I'm talking, of course, about the case involving [Professor X]. . . . The obvious point is that good sense did not prevail here, and on the basis of a silly and groundless accusation she was put to needless trouble. We should always bear her case in mind when we imagine that these rules will be administered sensibly and with restraint. They will not be.[55]

Clearly, someone had also passed along some documentation of this case to Alan Borovoy, general counsel to the Canadian Civil Liberties Association, who made it part of his newspaper column in *The Toronto Star* on 30 March 1994: "At the University of Western Ontario in the early 1990s, a . . . professor was subjected to a racial harassment complaint because, in the course of explaining the correct use of the word "condemn," she reportedly referred to the experiences of condemnation suffered by the people of [a foreign country]. This offended a student who comes from [this country]."[56]

At the same time, it was announced in the *Western News* on 24 February 1994, that a "settlement" had been reached between the University and Professor X. The settlement, according to the President, met with the approval of "all parties." Presumably, he meant by this Professor X, himself, and the Faculty Association. The Race Relations Office had not been consulted, nor we assume, had the student who brought the initial complaint. Professor X was quoted as follows: "I'm totally satisfied with the agreement. It's only unfortunate that it's taken two years."[57] She described the terms of the agreement as including a year's leave of absence with pay in lieu of a cash settlement, payment of her legal fees, a statement of regret already issued by the University, and review of the University's race relations policy.[58]

It is interesting to note that the next week, a "clarification" appeared in *Western News*:

> [Professor X] . . . wishes to clarify two matters reported in a story published in the February 24 issue of *Western News* about her recent settlement with the University.

> [Professor X] did not receive any statement of regret for pain and suffering. "In fact, I publicly rejected that offer precisely because it addressed the effects and not the cause of the accusation against me," she said. "What I did receive from the University was a public statement absolving me of the accusation of racial harassment." . . . [T]he "study leave which has been approved by the President's Office . . . is part of the Alternate Career Opportunities, Retention and Development of Faculty agreement."[59]

The Race Relations Policy referred to throughout this chapter was sent into review in March 1993. Members of the Review Committee were apparently selected on the basis of their neutrality on issues of racism. I question how anyone can be "neutral" on issues such as racism and sexism. Furthermore, the President informed me that, due to my lack of neutrality, I was not to be part of the review process.[60] I think this is a telling point on which to conclude: that knowledge of racism and anti-racism in both an innate and theoretical sense renders one biased. This point was expressed in a letter to the *Western News* written by a group of faculty and staff members on 14 April 1994:

> In our view, a not surprising view in an academic setting, social change is knowledge-based and knowledge-driven. There is a body of knowledge about race, race relations, racism, systemic discrimination, harassment, human rights, and so on. The assumption seems to be that knowledge about racism will be a barrier to fair resolution of complaints. Is knowledge of history a barrier to fair grading of history essays?[61]

The revised Race Relations Policy was debated at Senate on 22 September 1994. The Student Senate Caucus attempted to make a number of substantial amendments, all but two of which were defeated. In the course of debate it was suggested that if the Senate were to defeat this policy there was the possibility that faculty could no longer teach about sickle-cell anaemia, a type of nasal carcinoma in South Chinese populations, and safe sex and AIDS as someone might find the topic "irritating" and therefore file a complaint under the 1990 Race Relations Policy. Presumably swayed by this incredible illogic, the new policy was passed by Senate. The following week, on 29 September 1994, the revised Race Relations Policy was passed by the Board of Governors, with no debate.

Afterword: The Personal Cost

For some time I have been trying to think of an analogy which would convey graphically my feelings during these years. When the image first came, I rejected it in disbelief but the feelings engendered in me at Western have been a part of my life only once before, following a sexual assault on a deserted Montreal street in 1985. I do not make this comparison lightly; it has taken me some courage and time to write these words. They may not be popular — the trial by media of a Race Relations Officer will be seen by some as reducing the tragedy of sexual assault on women. However, *for me* the two experiences were alike. In both instances, there was a sense of loss of control, whether it is being dragged across a street, screams stifled by an unknown attacker or waiting day after day for letters and editorials of hatred, intimidation, and vitriol. The sense of being wrong, although intellectually you know you did the right thing, was very similar. But perhaps what remains with me from both instances is the fear and violation. In one case the violation was physical, in the other, a more subtle form of mental or intellectual attack. But in both instances, I was exposed and there seemed to be no escape.

The only event which prevented the last two years from becoming unbearable was the birth of my son in April 1993. However, the time before his birth was an unremitting nightmare. Through the worst moments on campus, with the denunciations and calls for my dismissal, what saved me was protecting and nurturing this being. Try to eat, try to relax, don't just sit there and weep, think of the child — these injunctions from friends, family, and midwives kept me going and gave me the courage to continue. Yet at the same time, this led to the development of a public persona (that persona reflected in the previous pages). I knew people didn't really want to hear that I felt I was balancing on the edge of an abyss so I strove to make others comfortable. What is surprising, on reflection, is that so many people did not delve deeper, despite their innate knowledge that my life must be hellish. So I fought to maintain my composure, never knowing what might be thrown at me from one day to the next, worried that at some time the armour would crack, and my anger and pain revealed to a university which had rendered me guilty without trial. During these bleak days I was told, on more than one occasion, "You should expect this, it is a part of your job," as if nearly a year's worth of persecution based on misinformation should be a minor irritant. As the level of disinformation increased, I worried increasingly about the impact this was having on the child. If something was wrong, it would be my fault for not managing to divorce myself from "work." But working for a more equitable world can never be just "work"; the commitment has to be that much deeper, a fact never understood by those who were seeking to destroy me. When we discovered that our son was born with a birth defect that would require surgery, I felt immense guilt. However, slowly I am beginning to realize that no work environment should have the right to make anyone feel that guilt. "All members of the university have the right *to study and work in an environment free of discrimination and harassment.*"[62] I quoted that phrase to so many people knowing that my own workplace was characterized by harassment and intimidation.

What allowed much of the feeding frenzy to occur was the demonization of Leela MadhavaRau, woman. After a while, I doubt that those spreading their slanderous letters around the campus ever thought about me as a human being. It is so much easier to condemn someone to "death" if you can forget that they are, in any way, like you. It is even easier to undertake this process if the individual in question is 30 or under, a woman, and "of colour" because to the many writers of letters I am even less like them. What happened in this case has taken on a life of its own, fuelled no doubt by those who would prefer that anti-harassment policies be removed from all universities and colleges. Yet the particular political characterization which is given to the case and the lack of acknowledgement of the confidentiality afforded to both sides in all cases has led to a downward spiral in "race relations" at the University, particularly at the faculty level. Those same faculty members who pride themselves on analytical skills have never made the simple deduction that they are hearing only one side of a complex story. The stifling of anti-harassment officers through the preservation of confidentiality is a notion that cannot be repeated too often. We are condemned because we cannot respond to the campaigns waged by others. Yet few of us would change the necessity of maintaining confidentiality if people are to have the right to speak of harassment and discrimination.

On 3 October 1994, I tendered my resignation from my position as Race Relations Officer at the University of Western Ontario. Two paragraphs from my letter summarize what lay behind my resignation:

I realize that I will not be able to change . . . attitudes, behaviour and minds . . . by resigning from my position. I am certain that a collective sigh of relief will go up that another "troublemaker" will be leaving. What a pity that so many of us are women, people of colour, people with disabilities and members of the First Nations. I wish that some of the naysayers could experience the following: After the Senate debate, as I sat crying on a bench on Alumni Circle, members of the Black Students Association came up to try and comfort me. They said that they didn't have tears because they really didn't expect anything more. And as they looked at my young son, they added, "They don't care because they don't have to care." And maybe, it will only be when the impact of that message hits . . . the University community that true equity will come to the campus.

I regret being obliged to resign from my position because I believe I have discharged my responsibilities to the very best of my abilities; given the constraints under which I operate, I have done a good job. . . . I regret giving victory to those who will sing paeans to my departure but there is no gainsaying the reality of my utter powerlessness in this situation. There will be many people who will be very disappointed in my departure. Their disappointment will not be with me but with an university which forces employees who are also women of colour into such circumstances.

I had made my resignation effective 30 May 1995. On 12 October 1994, I received a response to my letter, the essence of which was that the University did not want me to report for work after 15 December 1994.

I have met head-on the forces of "backlash." I am fully prepared to speak out about what this experience has done to my commitment to the establishment of a truly inclusive university: it has strengthened my determination in a way that would not have happened in the natural course of events. Everywhere I work, there goes with me a card my grandfather gave to me:

Our dearest possession is life and since it is given to us to live but once we must live as to feel no torturing regrets for years without purpose; so live as not to be seared with the shame of a cowardly and trivial past; so live, that dying we can say: "All our lives and all our strength were given to the finest cause in the world — the liberation of humanity."[63]

I write this chapter in the hope that the endurance Sanjay showed in utero will not be required in order for him to receive equitable treatment as he travels through life. I also write for my colleagues whose support makes a dream of equity appear possible.

Notes

Editors' Notes

1 See, for example, discussions by Patricia A. Monture, "Ka-Nin-Geh-Heh-Gah-E-Sa-Nonh-Yah-Gah" ("Flint Woman"), *Canadian Journal of Women and the Law*, 2 (1986): 159 (included here as chapter 8); Mary Ellen Turpel (Aki-Kwe), "Patriarchy and Paternalism: The Legacy of the Canadian State for First Nations Women," *Canadian Journal of Women and the Law*, 6 (1993): 174; and Nitya Duclos, "Disappearing Women: Racial Minority Women in Human Rights Cases," *Canadian Journal of Women and the Law*, 6 (1993): 25.

2 For a more detailed discussion of the dangers of making generalizations based on gender, see Audre Lorde, *Sister Outsider: Essays and Speeches* (Trumansburg, NY: Crossing Press, 1984); Esmeralda M.A. Thornhill, "Focus on Black Women," *Canadian Journal of Women and the Law*, 1 (1985): 153; Esmeralda M.A. Thornhill, "Black Women's Studies in Teaching Related to Women: Help or Hindrance to Universal Sisterhood?" *The Issue is ISM: Women of Colour Speak Out*, Fireweed's Issue 16 (Toronto: Sister Vision, Black Women and Women of Colour Press, 1989); and Elizabeth V. Spelman, *Inessential Woman: Problems of Exclusion in Feminist Thought* (Boston: Beacon Press, 1988).

3 See, for example, further discussion in the Conclusion (chapter 12) of Kenneth Hilborn's assessment, "Probably Will Do No Harm if Honestly Interpreted," *Western News*, 21 April 1994.

4 Leela MadhavaRau mentions several critical responses to the process that were published in *Western News* in the course of the debate. One which focuses specifically on the question raised here was Bruce Feldthusen's letter to the editor, "Question: Is Something Wrong with This Picture?" *Western News*, 14 October 1993, p. 13. For the text of this letter, see chapter 12, n. 100.

5 See, for example, H.-J. Klatt, "What's Wrong with Racial and Sexual Harassment?," *Western News*, 28 October 1993, p. 16.

Notes

1 "Report of the (First) President's Advisory Committee on Race Relations," University of Western Ontario, June 1989, p. 2.

2 Ibid., Appendix E, p. 2.

3 The University of Western Ontario, "Race Relations Policies and Procedures" (London, ON: Race Relations Office, University of Western Ontario, 1994), emphasis in the original.

4 Philomena Essed, *Everyday Racism* (Alameda, CA: Hunter House, 1990), p. 11.

5 Ibid., p. 31.

6 Ibid., p. 34.

7 Haideh Moghissi, "Racism and Sexism in Academic Practice: A Case Study," in Haleh Afshar and Mary Maynard, eds., *The Dynamics of Race and Gender* (London: Taylor and Francis, 1994), p. 222-34.

8 Ibid., p. 223.

9 Rory Leishman, "Race Policy Threatens Free Speech," *The London Free Press*, November 1992, p. 3.

10 Stephen Northfield, "No Middle Ground," *The London Free Press*, 20 March 1993, p. E1.

11 "Race Relations Issues: A Statement to UWOFA Members," *UWOFA Review*, 25, 2 (January 1993): 20.

12 Northfield, "No Middle Ground," p. E1.

13 Ibid.

14 "Race Relations Issues," p. 5.

15 Ibid.

16 Leishman, "Race Policy Threatens Free Speech," p. E1.

17 Jim Anderson, "Race Relations Policy Draws Faculty Fire," *Western News*, 15 October 1992, p. 1.
18 Letter of respondent to UWO President, 31 July 1992, as discussed in "Race Relations Issues," p. 6. The letter itself was not reprinted in the *UWOFA Review*, but the portions of this letter quoted here appeared in Kleri Venizelos, "Prof Criticizes Race Officer," *The Gazette*, 11 November 1992, p. 1; James McCarten, "Race Relations Policy to Receive More Review," *The Gazette*, 24 November 1992; and "The Truth Is What Needs Reviewing," *The Gazette*, 25 November 1992, editorial column. The letter was sent to numerous faculty members, as noted by Kenneth Hilborn: "Prof. [X]'s letter to [UWO President], dated July 31, has been widely read on campus. I received a copy from the Society for Academic Freedom and Scholarship" (see Kenneth Hilborn, "Finds Disturbing Aspects to Race Relations Policy," *Western News*, 22 October 1992, p. 13). In the President's letter to Professor X of 20 November 1992, he states: "Your letter to me of July 31, 1992, was circulated throughout the University, and similar representation was evidently made to the Faculty Association, and, presumably, to the Canadian Association of University Teachers" (see "Race Relations Issues," p. 16). A copy of the letter was delivered anonymously to the Race Relations office.
19 Letter of respondent to UWO President, 28 January 1993, reprinted in "Race Relations Issues," p. 23.
20 "Race Relations Policy to Be Reviewed," UWO Media Release, Department of University Relations, 23 November 1992.
21 Northfield, "No Middle Ground," p. E1.
22 Letter from respondent to UWO President, 28 January 1993, reprinted in "Race Relations Issues," p. 20.
23 Venizelos, "Prof Criticizes Race Officer," p. 3.
24 Editorial, "The Truth Is What Needs Reviewing."
25 Editorial, "Time to Bail a Sinking Ship," *The Gazette*, 13 November 1992.
26 "Report of Professor D. Mullan, Faculty of Law, Queen's University, 16 November 1992," *UWOFA Review*, 25, 2 (January 1993): 12.
27 Ibid.
28 John Leonard, "Issue Is Not Academic Freedom, but Freedom," *Western News*, 14 April 1994, p. 13.
29 "Report of Professor D. Mullan," p. 12.
30 The position of the Faculty Association was set out in "Race Relations Issues," p. 2: "The informal mediation legislated by the policy and intended, so far as is possible, to find a mutually agreeable solution was, in this instance, limited to a single session, even though Professor [X] specifically requested additional attempts at mediation."
31 Richard Henshel, " 'Overwhelming Deficiency' Seen in Committee Report," *Western News*, 14 October 1993.
32 J.C.M. Ogelsby, "The Problem of Imposing Ideological Conformity," *Western News*, 22 October 1992.
33 F.R. Atance, "Adherence to the Letter, Spirit of the Law Urged," *Western News*, 15 April 1993, p. 11.
34 Leishman, "Race Policy Threatens Free Speech."
35 Paddy Stamp, Sexual Harassment Officer, University of Toronto, "Policy Development at the University of Toronto," *CAASHE Newsletter*, 4, 1 (March 1992): 3.
36 Society for Academic Freedom and Scholarship, *Newsletter*, 2 (November 1992): 1.
37 Kenneth H.W. Hilborn, "Urges that Definition Be 'Clarified and Restricted,' " *Western News*, 25 November 1993.
38 "Bogus Multiculturalism Affects U.S. Universities," *Western News*, 18 March 1993, p. 7.
39 Steve Hick and Ron Santos, "Anti-Racism Student Organizing in Canadian Universities" (Ottawa: School of Social Work, Carleton University, 1993), p. 26.
40 Editorial, "Time to Bail a Sinking Ship."

41 Doreen Kimura, "Universities and the Thought Police," *The Globe and Mail*, 28 May 1993.

42 Leanne Simpson, "When Racism Gets Swept under the Mat of Freedom," *The Globe and Mail*, 16 July 1993.

43 John Leonard, "No Room in Democracy for 'Kangaroo Courts,'" *Western News*, 29 October 1992.

44 See *Human Rights Code*, R.S.O. 1990, c. H.19.

45 Hilborn, "Finds Disturbing Aspects to Race Relations Policy."

46 Richard Willey, *Race, Equality and Schools* (London and New York: Methuen, 1984), p. 2.

47 Robert B. Moore, "Racist Stereotyping in the English Language," in Margaret L. Andersen and Patricia Hill Collins, eds., *Race, Class and Gender* (Belmont, CA: Wadsworth Publishing, 1992), p. 318.

48 Nick Jewson and David Mason, "The Theory and Practice of Equal Opportunity Policies: Liberal and Radical Approaches," in Peter Braham, Ali Rattansi, and Richard Skellington, eds., *Racism and Antiracism* (London: Sage Publications, 1992), p. 221-22.

49 Editorial, "Dealing with Word 'Racist,'" *The Toronto Star*, 1 November 1992, p. B2.

50 K. George Pedersen, "Dramatizing University Racism Story Irresponsible," *The London Free Press*, 15 September 1992, p. B6.

51 Sallie Westwood and Parminder Bhachu, eds., *Enterprising Women* (London: Routledge, 1988), p. 13.

52 Mary-Jane Egan, "Noted Author Says Policy Paper Threat to Freedom," *The London Free Press*, 24 March 1994.

53 For local (Western) press commentary on the petition opposing the *Framework*, see "Petition Reflection of Anger," *Western News*, 24 March 1994, p. 3-4; Kleri Venizelos, "Profs Protest Guidelines," *The Gazette*, 16 February 1994; and Editorial, "Ailing Policies Need Expert Assistance," *The Gazette*, 16 February 1994.

54 H.-J. Klatt, "Universities Urged to Oppose Government Diktat," *Western News*, 10 February 1994, p. 13.

55 Robert Fulford, "Zero Tolerance for Freedom of Speech on Campus," notes for speech delivered at the University of Western Ontario, 23 March 1994, p. 6-7. See also press coverage of this speech in Egan, "Noted Author Says Policy Paper Threat to Freedom."

56 A. Alan Borovoy, "Academia Already Has Muzzles Out," *The Toronto Star*, 30 March 1994, p. A19.

57 "University, [Professor X] Settle," *Western News*, 24 February 1994.

58 Ibid.

59 "Clarification on Settlement," *Western News*, 10 March 1994, p. 4.

60 Questioned about why the composition of the review panel was made up of "non-experts" in the field of race relations, the President stated that he "deliberately didn't place an expert on the panel," and that he "put a lot of thought into the selection of the panel and [felt] confident that they [would] do a thorough and unbiased review." Minutes of the President's Advisory Committee on Race Relations, UWO, 15 February 1993, p. 1-2.

61 Frances Bauer et al., "Grave Concerns Regarding Proposed Race Relations Policy," *Western News*, 14 April 1994, p. 11.

62 University of Western Ontario, "Race Relations Policy and Procedures," emphasis in the original.

63 I have never felt it important to investigate the source of this quotation but did decide to update the pronouns.

11

Lesbian Perspectives

Claire Young and Diana Majury

The essays written by Claire Young and Diana Majury begin the critique of recent chilly climate reports and discussions from a lesbian perspective. The authors review the reports written at Western in the late 1980s (chapters 3, 4, and 5 in this volume) and comment upon the marginalization of lesbians within the academy. They document some of the individual, institutional, and governmental practices that contribute to a homophobic, anti-lesbian environment and they describe how the assumption of heterosexuality which underlies much feminist analysis and activism contributes in fundamental ways to poisoning the workplace for lesbians. These papers provide a provocative and rich understanding of why it is critically important that the experiences and needs of lesbians be central to chilly climate research if this work is not to marginalize lesbians further within post-secondary institutions.

– Eds.

Lesbian Absence in Chilly Climate Studies — Claire Young

Introduction

I approach the writing of this chapter with great trepidation. I taught at the University of Western Ontario from the mid-1980s to the early 1990s, the last three years as a tenured Associate Professor. In late 1991, I spoke in the University for the first time as a lesbian, although I had self-identified as a lesbian for many years prior to that time. It was no coincidence that my "coming out"[1] coincided with my return to Western after a sabbatical which had followed the approval of my tenure and promotion to Associate Professor. When originally asked by the editors (my friends and ex-colleagues) if I would contribute a chapter to this book that looked at the issues from a lesbian perspective, I said no. My reasons were many. My first thought was that lesbians were conspicuously absent and virtually undiscernible in the book; why should I participate in redressing this situation? Surely it is up to the authors to recognize this and acknowledge their complicity in this omission. But then I began to think hard about why lesbians are missing from this picture and I began to realize that the tale is much more complicated than I had originally thought.

This book is an historical document and I/we are part of that history. I cannot single out any particular individual associated with this book for condemnation when I think about the silence surrounding lesbians at Western. Yes, no-one asked me how I experienced the chilly climate as a lesbian, but the reasons for that have a lot to do with the fact that I was not "out" as a lesbian at Western at that time.[2]

So we had those who were nervous about asking "the questions," or raising the issues for fear of intruding into a private space, and those of us who were so used to not being asked that it never occurred to us that we had a voice which it might have been safe to exercise. I remember well being interviewed for the *Chilly Climate Report* (included here as chapter 3) and speaking about my experiences as a woman and as a feminist, but quite deliberately not speaking as a lesbian. Now when I read that chapter and see my "contribution" it seems as if that was another person. In fact it was another time. But this is not meant to be absolution for those connected with this book or the work on the chilly climate that went on in the late 1980s.

What I want to do is to explore this omission and in so doing think about how we as women who experienced the chilly climate with all its frigidity experienced it differently from our heterosexual sisters, and in so doing restore our voice to this story. That is not an easy task. But it is a critical exercise (in more ways than one!), and while some may be concerned that it draws divisions among us and presents a disunited front to those we challenge in our struggle to eradicate the chilly climate, I believe that we cannot delude ourselves (and others) into believing that we are a monolithic group. We must recognize and respect the differences between us whether they be by reason of race, ability, class, or sexual identity. Only then can we collectively struggle towards our common goals. The lesbian experience of the chilly climate is one that must be part of any enterprise for change. What we intend to do in this chapter is explore the apparent absence of lesbians in this book, try to redress the omission by describing our chilly climate, and consider how the *Chilly Climate Report* would have been different had we been included.

Lesbian Absence

The *Chilly Climate Report,* and the related reports and discussions that appear in this book, are about how women who are mostly White, middle-class, able-bodied, and heterosexual experienced gender bias at the University of Western Ontario. This is so, even though we know that these are not the only women who experienced that gender bias and the chilly climate. The missing women include not only lesbians but also women of colour, women with disabilities, Jewish women, and so on. These women are missing in two ways. First, they are missing by reason of their absence from the institution itself, because they have not been hired in any significant numbers. Or, if hired, many have not been retained. Secondly, lesbians who are working at the University are missing from the *Chilly Climate Report* by reason of their lack of distinctiveness to the writers of the *Report*. It is this second aspect of lesbian absence that we focus on in this chapter.

Any exploration of how these women could have been so imperceptible in an examination of the chilly climate at a university has to be placed in the context of the time. Prior to the 1980s, much feminist work tended to suppress and ignore the differences between us. Many feminists searched for a collective and united challenge to the patriarchy and the misogyny we all experienced. But that "collective" action rendered many of us submerged and unacknowledged. It spoke only about the experiences of a homogeneous group of women. Consequently, much of the writing on lesbian issues was left to lesbian feminists, that on racism to feminists of colour, and so on. Slowly this changed. Feminists who had not been doing this writing began to realize how inadequate their work was when it spoke as though women were a monolithic group. The *Chilly Climate Report* was released in 1989, a time when much of this work was being done and therefore our absence is, at first blush, startling. This chapter will attempt to put us back in the picture by first exploring where we are especially excluded, and then attempting to determine why we were not included and what the consequences of our absence are. Our intention is to introduce lesbians into the picture, to fill in the gaps where possible. In so doing we believe this book will be enriched. We are deeply appreciative of the authors' desire to remedy the "glaring omissions" and to make this work "fully inclusive of the experience of oppression, in all its diversity"[3] by inviting us and others to contribute chapters. Our focus is on chapters 3, 4, and 5 ("An Historical Perspective" [the *Backhouse Report*], "The Chilly Climate for Faculty Women at Western" [the *Chilly Climate Report*], and "Epilogue").

We are all familiar with the *caveats* that accompany our work. We use them to raise those issues that we feel are beyond the scope of our inquiry, apologize for our inability to explore them, and flag them for future work. Chapter 3, "An Historical Perspective," opens with such a *caveat*, and this is where one first experiences lesbian absence. This is not, as one might expect, because the *caveat* apologizes for the omission of lesbians from the analysis. Rather it is because the *caveat* apologizes for the non-examination of discrimination on the basis of race, disability or class.[4]

It is silent with respect to lesbians. We do not even exist in the "list" of those who suffer additional forms of oppression. We are undiscernible to the author of this piece. Why? One reason is that, as noted in the concluding chapter, we are not included for employment equity purposes in the Federal Contractors Program.[5] On a broader level, lesbian marginalization has a lot to do with the fact that many of us (but not all) visually appear to be no different than heterosexual women.[6]

We thereby become undetectable as lesbians and are subsumed under the category "woman." Consequently we are not recognized as differently or additionally oppressed than other women. Heterosexuality is presumed, and that presumption requires us constantly to affirm our lesbian identity in order to make ourselves recognized as lesbians. On a personal level, what we find particularly disturbing about our omission from this work is that the author knew many lesbians at Western and yet even this personal knowledge did not prompt her to, at the very least, include lesbians on the list of women she chose to exclude. Again, we speculate that the reason was primarily that we were believed to be just the same as other women.

The *Chilly Climate Report* also opens with a *caveat*. This time it is "the very serious problems of discrimination against women and men of diverse races, persons with disabilities, Native people, and other disadvantaged groups" that are not dealt with.[7] This list is more extensive than that in the previous chapter, but again there is no direct mention of lesbians, although presumably we are included in the non-specific reference to disadvantaged groups.

One part of the *Chilly Climate Report* particularly troubles us. We have discussed the absence of lesbians in the *Report*, but the word "lesbian" is used once, although that is by a respondent and not by the authors. The paragraph entitled "At Least We Know She's Straight" details the experience of a female faculty member who included material on "homosexuality and lesbianism" in her courses.[8] She describes how this led to students complaining she was gay, and said "It was amazingly upsetting. I don't have biases against people who are gay, but to be labelled something you're not. . . ."[9] We appreciate that the comments made by the respondents are not those of the authors of the *Report*. Nevertheless, we feel strongly that this section is highly problematic and at best can be described as not affirming of lesbians and at worst as lesbian hating. First, the title given to the paragraph is inappropriate, especially given the fact that this is the first mention of lesbians in the *Report*. We note that the previous paragraph is titled "Isolation" and the succeeding paragraph "Safety and Sexual Harassment," both head-ings that flag issues of concern to women on campus. For us this leaves one with the impression that being seen as "straight" is also an issue of concern for women on campus. While this may be true for some heterosexual women, it contributes to the oppression of lesbians by implying that lesbian identity is undesirable. Secondly, we question why, given that this was the first mention in the *Report* of lesbianism, the authors did not attempt to contextualize these comments or indeed point out the extreme hatred of lesbians within the institution that contributed to the feeling by this respondent that she had to assert her heterosexuality. The statement by the respondent also deserved editorial comment with respect to her assertion that the issue for her was being labelled something she was not. Again, that line reinforces our oppression and to include it without comment is to further reinforce it. This section of the *Report*, which also includes the comments of another respondent who described how a candidate for appointment was not hired because it was suspected that she was a lesbian, stands alone.[10] The issues it raises are never referred to again, even though the *Report* has a conclusion that draws some of its themes together. Somehow this is even more problematic than just omitting lesbians all together.

The assumption of heterosexuality as the norm underlies this entire collection of work. Nowhere is this more apparent than in the discussion of "partner" hiring and benefits.[11] The problems of women being viewed as hired only because a department wished to hire their husband or male partner is discussed with no reference at all to lesbian couples and their experience. Again, the material on benefits and maternity leave assumes that those requiring maternity leave are heterosexual women.[12] All these examples highlight for us the absence of the lesbian voice and thereby contribute to our marginalization by exclusion.

We find it quite ironic that one of the criticisms of the *Chilly Climate Report* made by the administration was that it was "not representative of women's experiences at Western considered either collectively or individually, and that therefore any conclusions ... drawn are false generalizations."[13] Of course this critique on the basis of representativeness is not because lesbians, women of colour, women with disabilities, and other marginalized women are not present in the account of the chilly climate. Rather the critique is that the women interviewed are not representative because they do not include those who are content with the state of affairs at the University. The author responds by stating that "the experiences we describe are not, in any of the senses identified, 'unrepresentative' of the kinds of difficulties that at least 35 women currently face at Western."[14] We agree with the author that the work is representative in terms of describing 35 very different experiences of the chilly climate, but we note that the difficulties the respondents raised did not adequately reflect the difficulties faced by many

other women, including lesbians, who are doubly oppressed both by reason
of their gender and their sexual identity. Even though lesbians were interviewed, their experience of the chilly climate as lesbians did not emerge.
That leads us to the difficult question of why lesbians are largely absent in
this tale.

As Diana Majury and I indicate in our introductory statements, we recognize that we also have to take responsibility for our complicity here. I was
interviewed for the *Chilly Climate Report* and, as mentioned in my introduction, did not speak as a lesbian. The reasons for that were several. I was not
"out" at the University and that in and of itself is enough to cause the interviewer (who probably knew that I was a lesbian) to not ask me to speak as a
lesbian. So then the question is why I could not, in this private and anonymous space, speak as a lesbian, and that is a harder question to answer.
Clearly, my own internalized homophobia had a lot to do with it. I worked
hard to keep my work life separate from my personal life, fully believing
that such was appropriate and indeed possible. This in turn allowed me to
delude myself into believing that my sexual identity was irrelevant in the
work context. As I am sometimes asked by well-meaning heterosexual
friends, "what's one's sexual preference got to do with one's work?" In fact,
the answer is a lot. Sexual identity is not merely about who one sleeps with
in private, it is about how one lives one's life in public. Life in the public
work place is a constant reminder that the assumption is one of a heterosexual world. Not to be able to speak up and refute that assumption is to perpetuate the myth and contribute to the oppression of lesbians.[15] Furthermore, living in the "closet" in the work environment had a lot to do with my
own inability fully to understand or recognize the extent of lesbian oppression at the University. In hindsight, I now realize how vitally important it is
to be out in the University, if that is possible. By remaining closeted for as
long as I did, I contributed to and perpetuated the marginalization of lesbians.

But complicity by lesbians is only one reason for this marginalization.
The *Chilly Climate Report* has to be seen as the radical document that it was.
The authors took the unbelievably brave course of calling the institution
where they were all employed sexist and the perpetrator of the most mas-
sive gender discrimination. And they did so not simply in an academic paper buried in an academic journal, but in a report circulated widely within
the institution ensuring that their findings were thereby accessible to all.
While they clearly did not anticipate the furore that followed the release of
the *Report*,[16] there is no doubt that they had to make calculated decisions
about how to maximize the effectiveness of the *Report*. For all kinds of reasons that cannot be discussed in detail due to space constraints, it is quite
clear to us that raising "lesbian issues" (or using the L word) often engen-

ders the most vehement reactions. The issue of one's sexuality seems to be particularly threatening to some. The authors may well have felt that the University (and others) would use the stories of oppression of a marginalized group (lesbians) to marginalize the *Report* and its recommendations. But if this is so, it is to us a bit of a cop-out. While the inclusion of lesbian experiences of the chilly climate might have provoked a different response from the administration, it must have been clear to the authors that a report of this nature would never be fully accepted by the administration. It was always going to be challenged and devalued. So any attempt to make the *Report* more acceptable by leaving out the experiences of lesbians and other oppressed women was not only misguided but also reinforced the discrimination against those women. The inclusion of our experiences would have meant a great deal in terms of support and solidarity.

The *caveat* at the beginning of "An Historical Perspective" (chapter 3) and the related chapters also gives us a clue as to why lesbians were left out. That *caveat* refers to the lack of data on race and disability, because the federal programs did not begin to require the collection and reporting of such data until 1988. If statistics on women of colour and women with disabilities were not available, then they certainly were not available for lesbians. As mentioned earlier, lesbians have never been included in the Federal Contractors Program for the purposes of employment equity, an omission which we condemn. But lack of available statistics is not a justifiable reason for our omission from work that looks at the chilly climate. While no formal surveys may have been carried out, there are statistics from informal surveys available. Furthermore, why are such statistics necessary in this context? The chapters of this book are primarily anecdotal; the *Chilly Climate Report* is based on interviews, not statistics.

What are the consequences of the apparent absence of lesbians in this collection? Unfortunately, because this is such an important contribution to the literature on discrimination against women in the academy, the consequences are serious. By giving an incomplete picture, the authors participate in reinforcing the assumption of heterosexuality. Lesbians do not exist in the story, although we know they do in reality. It is especially problematic given that the perpetuation of lesbian marginalization is pervasive but something we do not expect to see in work by our feminist colleagues. Feminist work has become increasingly more cognizant of and inclusive with respect to our issues. But as we said at the outset, this is a work of its time. It has to be judged in that context.

If there is one thing I am sure of after thinking about these issues, it is how important it is to be out in the University. Lesbian absence has been our main critique of this book and yet, as mentioned, lesbians are perceived as an "invisible minority," and many of them are able to remain closeted. It is imperative as we struggle collectively as women on issues such as the chilly climate that we speak out along with women of colour and women with disabilities, as lesbians, and that means we have to be publicly identifiable.

Lesbian Experiences of the Chilly Climate — Diana Majury

Introduction

Lesbian marginalization — it is so much a part of our existence, even for those of us who consider ourselves "out," even when we are with our feminist colleagues, sometimes even when we are with other lesbians. The primary question that reading the manuscript for this book has raised for me is that of my own participation in lesbian marginalization, in my own marginalization. That participation takes many forms and comes from many places: my own failure at times even to notice the absence of lesbians and lesbian issues; a fear and uncertainty about how to challenge fellow feminists, friends, allies for their omissions, omissions I might well have made myself; a concern that I will fail to integrate issues of race, disability, and class in my discussions of lesbianism; my fears of competition among the omitted groups. In this particular project, my hesitance is in part about discussing lesbian marginalization in work by and about a group of women that I know to include lesbians; am I outing them, trashing them, further isolating them?

It is particularly hard, and probably particularly important, to respond to, add to, critique, the work of people whom you admire and love and to whom you owe a huge debt for the risks they have taken for you and for others. I greatly respect the authors for asking us to respond to some of the omissions in their work.

I started teaching full time in the law faculty at Western during the fall of 1989 when the *Chilly Climate Report* was released. Although I was not interviewed for the *Report*, many of my stories are there, told by other women from other departments. Reading the manuscript was very affirming — there was so much I could relate to, so many shared experiences, so much support. But many of my stories are not there and some of the ways in which the stories are related in the reports made me feel more isolated and marginalized. So, for me, this is what this chapter is about — lesbian marginalization, lesbian oppression — and more importantly — lesbian affirmation, lesbian pride.

Lesbian Experiences of the Chilly Climate

In this chapter, we wanted to include some experiences and issues that make the climate specifically chilly for lesbians. In so doing, we are not trying to talk about some generalizable "lesbian experience"; there are individual differences, as well as systemic differences in how lesbians experience the chill. Claire Young and I are both white, non-disabled, middle-class, Christian lesbians; we have both spent some portion of our adult lives as active heterosexuals. The experiences of lesbians of colour, Aboriginal lesbians, working-class lesbians, Jewish lesbians, lesbians with disabilities are no doubt very different from ours. And the climate is differently chilly depending on whether or not you are "out" and how "out" you are. The climate is different depending upon how publicly identifiable you are as a lesbian, that is, how much you look like a dyke.

We speak here from our own experiences, from what we have seen and observed, and from reading and talking to other lesbians. We have not done any "research" on the chilly climate for lesbians at Western. As far as we know, this work has not yet been done. Given that neither of us is still at Western,[17] we have not been able to canvass other lesbians there in any systematic way. But we didn't think it was appropriate simply to point out the absence of lesbians and the heterosexism in the reports on chilly climate issues at Western included in this book. In the spirit of these reports, we wanted to try to give some concreteness to our marginalization. In what follows, there are a few of our "stories" set in italics to provide some specific examples among our otherwise general comments.

Much of the chilliness of the climate described in this book does apply to us — as women, as feminists, and as lesbians. The sexism and sex discrimination experienced by women are often exacerbated for lesbians, who may be seen by the climate-setters as the most not-like women and, at the same time, the most threatening women. Virtually all of the forms of chilliness described in this book have a lesbian take or spin to them. The "host of subtle personal and social barriers" that Alison Wylie describes in chapter 2 as functioning on an institutional level operate in many of the same ways for lesbians as for other women.[18] But the barriers also operate on different levels and in different ways. Stereotyping, devaluation, exclusion, and revictimization are very much part of our experiences as lesbians. Given the marginalization of lesbians and lesbian issues, these informal anti-lesbian practices and policies tend to be even further "below the level of awareness" and more easily dismissed as trivial and isolated incidents. These issues are discussed below under the heading "Institutional Chills."

However, it would be misleading for us to discuss these practices only in terms of the "institution" in the context of this book in which "women" are not really seen as part of that institution. The chilly climate that this book

is about is a function of power and institutional support. As feminist academics, we need to recognize that we too have power within the institutions
where we work and that we are responsible for the climate that we create or
foster for other more vulnerable, differently situated or less privileged
women. The piece that is the hardest and makes this chapter so difficult to
write is that much of the chill that lesbians experience comes from other
women. It comes from our feminist colleagues, often in ways that replicate
or reinforce institutional practices. As well, some of the chill is experienced
between lesbians, among whom tensions around outness and assimilation
can be exceedingly strong and exceedingly damaging. These issues are discussed below under the heading "Feminists Chills."

Institutional Chills

Lesbians were almost, if not totally, undetectable at an institutional level at
Western. We were not recognized as a target group for hiring or promotion
for faculty or staff or for student recruitment.

> *My suggestion at a faculty meeting that we should include out lesbians and gays
> in the list of students whom we wanted to recruit was greeted with guffaws and
> snickers.*

It was not seen as important to include lesbians on departmental, faculty, or
university committees. Lesbian perspectives were not specifically sought;
lesbians were not consulted on important initiatives within the University.
Very little lesbian content was included in course materials and there were
no courses devoted to lesbian or lesbian and gay studies. Our partners and
children were not recognized for the purposes of health benefits.[19] It was as
if we did not exist.

When the institution does not acknowledge the existence of an oppressed group and the members of that group are not making themselves
felt, marginalization is probably the key issue for that group. At this stage,
oppression largely takes the form of omission; the more virulent and active
hate practices are usually only unleashed when the group begins to become
more publicly identifiable and starts to make demands of the institution.
Given that lesbians were very much at the undetectable stage,[20] we did not
experience the overt and vicious lesbian hating that no doubt lies barely below the surface. Ignoring lesbians and lesbian issues is a form of lesbian hating, but a more passive form, and I think many of us chose to stifle ourselves
in order to avoid more direct and harsh forms. In many ways, marginalization can feel easier and safer to live with. The presumption of heterosexuality, itself an oppressive practice, makes being publicly identifiable as a lesbian difficult to initiate and difficult to sustain.

Other oppressive practices flow from the presumption of heterosexuality and add to the chill for lesbians. The social chatter about weekend and non-work activities that can in some circumstances be congenial is often alienating and oppressive for lesbians. Lesbians who are not out usually remain silent during these conversations or, alternatively, they may feel compelled to "heterosexualize" their activities or to make up stories so that they do not stand out through their silences. But even for those of us who are out, these conversations can be oppressive. I do not want to give my colleagues, particularly my non-feminist and male colleagues, access to my lesbian life or culture; I do not want to indulge their interest in knowing who we are and what we do. For me, this is not about privacy, this is about lesbian space. We know that we are the subject of speculation and gossip, and the tales of others' comments and questions relayed back to us are disconcerting with respect to the teller as well as the original source. While there is a tension here between our desire for inclusion and our resistance to allowing others access to us, inclusivity and access are not synonymous. The inclusivity is about being acknowledged and responded to as lesbians; the resistance to access is about ensuring separate space and reflects our concerns about appropriation and voyeurism.

Out lesbians are not usually subjected to the sexualizing and demeaning comments that our heterosexual female, or closeted lesbian, colleagues face. We experience a different type of sexualization, much of which takes place behind our backs. Clothes and self presentation can be extremely loaded for lesbians. There is a great deal of implicit and explicit pressure to conform to female stereotypes.

> My first experience of lesbian chill at the university that I recognized and remember as such was a comment from a senior administrator when I attended an end of term gathering, after I was hired but before I had actually started. His passing, gratuitous comment that he preferred my hair when it was longer sent shivers up my spine. I doubt that he made any conscious lesbian connection with my short hair, but I certainly did and he definitely was telling me he preferred me to look more "feminine."
>
> I was clearly the most "casually" dressed of the women in my department. I only ever wore pants, usually with a jacket, while my women colleagues almost always wore skirts or dresses when they taught. I looked different from the other women and always felt that this was noted and seen negatively.

There is a constant threat of violence, both implicit and explicit, ranging from anti-lesbian graffiti to obscene phone calls.

> The first time I spoke as a lesbian in the University was at a reading group of feminist students. Subsequently the word must have spread because quite soon after that I received 3 or 4 obscene phone calls (of the heavy breathing variety). Coincidence? I think not.

And there is the construct of the "good lesbian/bad lesbian," a dichotomy fostered by the institution and having the effect of isolating and discrediting activist lesbians. This can happen where there are some "out" lesbians, that is, women who are known by their colleagues to be lesbian, who fit very nicely and comfortably into the institution, without causing problems, without making others feel uncomfortable, without making an "issue" of their lesbianism. The acceptance of these lesbians is often used against more active, "in your face" lesbians who are then characterized as the "problem." The institution feels smug in its ability to get along with "lesbians;" the difficulties presented by the activist are individualized with the assertion that it is she who is difficult and a denial that it has anything to do with her being a lesbian.

Feminist Chills

The feminist chill can take many forms. We have already talked about the apparent absence of lesbians and lesbian issues and the heterosexual presumption operating in the reports that gave rise to this book. These are part of what makes the climate chilly for us. To a large extent, lesbian issues are ignored unless lesbians raise them and then when we do we are perceived as always and only putting lesbians at the centre. Out and active, political lesbians are seen as too angry, too aggressive, too hostile; we are seen as stereotypical dykes by those for whom this is a label of discomfort or dislike, not pride.

Some heterosexual feminists look to us for approval or absolution for their heterosexuality: to tell them we understand why they remain in sexual relationships with men; to assure them that their heterosexuality does not detract from or contradict their feminism; to confirm that the men they are involved with are different; to affirm their place beside us on the "lesbian continuum." They tell us that they are no different from us, that they experience the same forms of oppression that we do, that they do not avail themselves of their heterosexual privilege, or that they don't even have it. They resent us and feel "excluded" when we make our own space.

At the other extreme, our feminist colleagues sometimes disown us or critically distance themselves from us. The fears of heterosexual women that someone might think they are a lesbian are disheartening and oppressive.

> *I was at a conference recently at which a feminist showed a strongly lesbian positive cartoon in the course of her talk. It was wonderfully affirming for me and I was just thinking how brave she was to do it. But that thought was only momentary, it lasted only until her statement that she loved this cartoon but her husband hated it. What the cartoon gave, the statement more than took away. It was not only that I no longer felt wonderful and affirmed; I now felt betrayed and undermined.*

Feminists and other women participate in the stereotyping, devaluing, isolation and re-victimization that create the chilly climate for lesbians. In some ways, these forms of lesbian chill are more on the surface in the feminist academic community than in the university at large because lesbians and lesbian issues, while often ignored, are not totally obscured. This means that the omissions and mistakes are also more obvious. Lesbians are at a different stage within the institution of feminism than within the institution of the university. We have higher expectations and are more hopeful that the climate within feminism will warm. This requires all of us to take responsibility for the ways in which we contribute to the chilly climate for other women and to work to ensure that women from all oppressed groups have full access to the institutions of which we are part and to support their full inclusion and activism within those institutions.

The invitation to do this book chapter was such an act of accountability and support and we bask in the warmth of it. At the same time, we want to acknowledge that this was a hard piece for us to write and no doubt a hard piece for the authors to read.

Notes

1 I am always careful when I describe myself as "coming out" or "out" in the law school to recognize that "outness" in an academic institution is an ephemeral concept. Coming out is an ongoing process and that moment when one summons every ounce of energy and utters those words "as a lesbian . . ." is just that, a moment. Those present hear the statement and the word spreads, but not to everyone and not to those (mostly students) who enter the institution at a later date.

2 Why I was not out at Western is not as easy a question to answer as one might think. I could say that homophobia kept me quiet about my sexual identity, at least with respect to my work-related activities. But it is not as simple as that. The full force of homophobia is not unleashed until one publicly identifies as a lesbian. I had a gut feeling, however, that it was not safe to be out at Western, at least not until I had tenure.

3 "Preface," p. 4.

4 The *Backhouse Report*, written in 1987 and 1988, was first released in April 1988 (see chapter 3). The author notes that she did not examine these forms of discrimination: "Not until 1988 did various federal programs begin to require the collection and reporting of data on race and disability" p. 62. This raises an issue that I shall return to, which is the unavailability of statistical information.

5 See "Conclusion," p. 359.

6 There are, of course, lesbians who do not "pass" visually as heterosexual, and for these lesbians the costs are even higher than for those who are not so publicly identifiable as lesbians.

7 Constance Backhouse, Roma Harris, Gillian Michell and Alison Wylie, "The Chilly Climate for Faculty Women at Western," first released in November 1989, and included here as chapter 4, p. 98.

8 Ibid., p. 125.

9 Ibid.

10 Ibid., p. 125-26.

11 Ibid., p. 102-103.

12 Ibid., p. 110.

13 Alison Wylie, "A Response to Some Criticisms of the *Chilly Climate Report*," Appendix B, chapter 5, p. 160.

14 Ibid., p. 163.

15 I must emphasize that I recognize the inability of many to be out in the workplace (or elsewhere) given the lesbian hating that exists. These comments are not a condemnation of those who cannot speak as lesbians, but rather an attempt to give a context for my own complicity in the marginalization of lesbians in the *Chilly Climate Report*.

16 See chapter 5.

17 This is why we speak largely in the past tense in reference to our experiences at Western. I left in the early 1990s, because my contract was not renewed; Claire Young left in the early 1990s to teach at a different university.

18 Alison Wylie, "The Contents of Activism on 'Climate' Issues," chapter 2, p. 38.

19 We understand that Western was one of the last universities to extend benefits to lesbian and gay partners; the revised policy was instituted on July 1, 1994.

20 A few of us — faculty, staff and students — were "out" to varying degrees, but there certainly was no identifiable lesbian presence or activism at Western.

12

Conclusion

Alison Wylie

I. On Inconclusion

Much has happened in universities and colleges across Canada since 1986 when Sheila McIntyre first circulated her "Memo." The impetus provided by the external requirements of the Federal Contractors Program and by advocacy within post-secondary educational institutions has made these especially exciting years where equity is concerned. Most Canadian colleges and universities now have formal employment equity policies in place and most have committees or task forces and, in many cases, professional staff who are responsible for designing and implementing these policies. These policies and associated programs affirm a commitment to employment equity not only for women but for all four federally designated target groups: in the language of these policies they include women, "visible minorities,"[1] Native people, and people with disabilities. Typically they call for data collection which provides, in some cases for the first time, valuable information about the representation and location of members of these target groups in college and university institutions. Sometimes as part of these employment equity initiatives, and sometimes independently, the university or college task forces charged with investigating and improving the employment status of under-represented groups also undertake to document workplace conditions; the report on the status of women mandated by the President at the University of Saskatchewan, *Reinventing Our Legacy*, is a striking case in point. An increasing number of institutions are also developing equity initiatives in other areas, e.g., through policies and procedures on sexual and racial harassment, mentoring and peer support programs, services for students and sometimes staff with disabilities, services and support groups for returning students, for students of Aboriginal ancestry, for gay and lesbian students, and for students from a range of other ethnic and religious backgrounds. Frequently, too, the stated goals of the employment equity programs developed by colleges and universities include education and other initiatives that hold the promise of fostering a more inclusive institutional culture.

At the same time, however, it seems unavoidable that these gains have not been without cost. In many contexts overt hostility to equity policies and principles has intensified at precisely the moment when these have shown most potential to change our academic and teaching institutions. While disaffection with the requirements of data collection and goal setting was certainly evident when plans for equity programs were on the drawing board, it seems to have taken increasingly intransigent and vocal forms as these programs have become a fixture in our universities and colleges. On one hand, the sharply defensive tone of critics of equity programs is one indication that they have begun to have an impact. On the other hand, we seem to be in imminent danger of losing at least as much ground as we have gained through the establishment of formal, institutional, commitments to equity.

In discussing the project of this collection with contributors and members of the Chilly Collective, I have been struck by a divided sense of optimism and of frustration, even despair, at the ways in which equity initiatives are being circumvented and undermined even as they are being instituted. A recurrent theme in these discussions has been concern that the backlash against equity initiatives is deepening, and seems to be attracting supporters who may have been sympathetic to the cause of equity under other conditions, and so long as it had no substantial impact on their own practices. Such colleagues are swayed by the arguments of those who insist that, at a time of increasing financial constraint, equity is an unaffordable luxury. And they are influenced by challenges to the principles underpinning equity programs which represent equity policies and programs as inimical to the rights conferred by principles of free speech and academic freedom.[2]

Abstract rights of freedom of speech and of academic freedom are invoked in academic contexts as a trump card by critics of university and college equity policies that address climate issues (e.g., policies that construe equity as including rights to work, teach, and learn in an environment free of harassment). Restrictions on sexist, racist, ablist, or homophobic language and practice, for example, are decried as "weapons of intimidation and mind control"[3] that are used to harass university faculty;[4] indeed, the appearance of anti-racism and anti-sexism policies is described by some as indicative of an imminent slide into "Iron Curtain"-style violations of fundamental rights to free speech and academic freedom.[5] Questions about the cost of such exercises of freedom for those who are demeaned by racist, sexist, homophobic, or ablist "speech" (for example) are thus effectively side-lined;[6] it is the abstract principle that matters, not the specifics of systemic inequities which substantially affect the capacity to exercise such rights. Also lost in these polarized debates is any sustained consideration of the responsibilities that might be understood to devolve on those whose institutional status and gender, race, and class position (for example), confers on their "speech" an authority which ensures that it will have a disproportionate impact on others. What is often at stake when issues of freedom in speech and in academic inquiry become a central focus for debate on our campuses is the threat that newly instituted equity programs may actually change the conditions of privilege that have been reinforced by traditional hiring practices, conditions of employment, and teaching and research practice.

I write this conclusion, then, at an especially unsettled moment where equity issues are concerned, particularly as they bear on the workplace environment in Canadian colleges and universities. This is the first sense in which this is a conclusion which cannot provide closure or, as one member of the Chilly Collective put it, why it must be "a wrap up that cannot be a wrap up." The essays collected here are interventions into a process of institutional and societal change that is ongoing; they raise issues that are, in every respect, unresolved.

There is a second and related sense in which this conclusion cannot be a conclusion that was noted by virtually everyone involved in writing, assembling, reviewing, and discussing this collection. As the contributors themselves make clear, each essay was born of a dynamic process of dialogue and activism which is as open ended and unresolved as the conditions they address. The essays themselves are, in a sense, a palimpsest of experiential accounts that have temporal depth and pragmatic specificity. More than this, they are self- and mutually transforming. Individual authors frequently respond to one another: they take up projects that are inspired both by the strengths and the shortcomings of work that has gone before; their own understanding of climate issues is transformed in the process of building on the work of others. In addition, these projects are defined by the contexts of activism in which they arise; they are themselves acts of intervention that are quite directly and continuously (re)shaped by the impact they have, or fail to have, as catalysts for change. There is, then, no unifying summary to be given of what these essays have achieved, of where "we" stand with respect to climate issues. The diversity of voices and standpoints represented, while still woefully narrow in range, mark a deliberate, and increasingly clearly articulated, resistance to any stance that would impose closure. It is to be hoped that these essays will be a catalyst, in their flaws and incompleteness as much as in their substantive contributions, for further research and activism on climate issues.

In what follows I consider, in more detail, how work on climate issues has unfolded in the context of equity initiatives in one university setting: that of the University of Western Ontario, where the project of this collection began and the Chilly Collective took shape. By all accounts Western is in no sense unique either in the difficulties posed by its workplace environment for some members of the university community, or in the commitment, energy, and imagination of those who have made a positive difference in this environment. I offer this discussion, then, as a reflection on developments which illustrate, in the particularities of one institution, some of the general remarks I have made about the nature of the stopping point at which we tentatively close this collection. There is much to be done if we are to understand what mitigates or intensifies chilliness in college and university environments, and how best to realize greater respect and support for diversity in these contexts.

II. Freezes and Thaws on the Equity Front

Equity Initiatives and Climate Issues

In the six years since the *Backhouse Report* was circulated initiatives have been taken in many of the areas identified as particularly pressing in the petition supporting this *Report* that was presented to the President by Western's Caucus on Women's Issues (the Women's Caucus). As required by the Federal Contractors Program, a formal commitment has been made to employment equity; an institutional policy on employment equity was adopted in November 1988,[7] and a standing committee on employment equity was established in 1989-90. One of the first tasks addressed by this committee and a newly appointed Employment Equity Officer was that of establishing, through a work-force "census," a detailed profile of all categories of employees on campus with respect to the four federally designated target groups. This census was to provide the basis for a formal employment equity plan, the effectiveness of which would be monitored by an ongoing program of data collection. In addition, the information gathered in these connections was to be included in annual reports to the President, which it was expected the President would release to the University community. In all this the University moved quickly to comply with the requirements of the Federal Contractors Program.

Beyond compliance, it was heartening that the President's Office and Employment Equity Officer undertook wide consultation about the structure and membership of the President's Standing Committee for Employment Equity (PSCEE). As required by regulation, this Committee included representatives of the four federally designated target groups and of a wide range of employee constituencies; it also included part-time employees and graduate students, as well as those represented by employee unions and associations. This was encouraging for those active on women's issues inasmuch as the Women's Caucus petition had particularly emphasized the need to focus on the concerns of part-time employees. Moreover, the first person elected as the chair of PSCEE (May 1989-June 1992) was Carol Agòcs, a widely respected expert on equity programs in a range of employment contexts. She had long argued the need, where equity programs are concerned, for broadly consultative processes of change that address not just formal policies and organizational systems, but also the workplace environment.[8]

Most important, however, from the outset the PSCEE adopted a course of action which reflected a recognition that, to be effective, Western's employment equity program must establish, in the university community as a whole, what the Committee described in its first annual report as "a higher level of awareness and sensitivity . . . regarding the subtle forms of unequal treatment and discrimination and the attitudinal barriers that impair the productivity and job satisfaction of designated group members."[9] In this spirit, the Committee moved immediately to establish five task forces, each of which would involve as many members of the university community as possible in the work of the Committee. These included: 1) a "communication" task force, responsible for "informing the university community about Employment Equity"; 2) a "data" task force that would develop the necessary employment equity database; 3) a task force responsible for reviewing employment policies, practices, and procedures; 4) a task force on "bias-free communication" which would work to "rais[e] awareness of subtle forms of unequal treatment and promot[e] equity in communication"; and 5) a "career support systems" task force which would coordinate efforts to provide "career-related information, mentoring and support to members of the four designated groups working at Western."[10] All of these were active by the end of the first year of the Committee's operation. The *First Annual Report* of PSCEE, which was completed in October 1990 and published in an abridged form in *Western News* in January 1991, describes the remarkable range of initiatives that these task forces had already undertaken in their first year, or had planned for the future. The sense of energy and excitement generated by PSCEE in these first few years was enormously gratifying for many who had worked on equity issues in relative isolation and with little public recognition in the past.

The *First Annual Report*: Steps Forward

One of the most active of the task forces set up in 1989-90 was that responsible for establishing the work-force database required for setting the goals of an "Employment Equity Work Plan," a crucial component of compliance with the requirements of the Federal Contractors Program. In April 1990, this task force conducted a University-wide census of all employees to establish the representation of target-group members at Western. The response rate described in the preliminary report on this census the following fall was impressive, although significantly better for regular full-time employees than for those in part-time and temporary positions. Just under three-quarters of all employees returned their surveys; 81% of regular full-time employees and over half of those in other categories of employment (part time, temporary, and casual employees).[11]

The preliminary analysis of these survey returns showed that standard patterns of workplace segregation for women are instantiated at Western. Women are disproportionately well represented among temporary and part-time employees (75%), and in non-academic and non-unionized staff positions; they account for 80% of employees eligible for membership in the Staff Association (UWOSA, the group representing clerical workers), almost half of those eligible to join the Professional and Managerial Association (PMA), and 42% of those eligible for union membership. By contrast, women constitute just 20% of regular, full-time faculty, less than half their representation in any other category of regular full-time employment at Western.[12]

Employees who identified themselves as "visible minorities" and as "persons with disabilities" have no substantial representation in any category of regular, full-time employment at Western. In fact, while "visible minorities" accounted for 7% of the total work force at Western in 1990, their reported representation in the part-time work force was more than four times greater than in the regular full-time work force (5% compared to 22%); they are best represented, among regular full-time employees, as faculty (all ranks combined).[13] A different pattern was reported for people with disabilities; they make up just 3% of the overall work force, but are better represented in unionized positions and among faculty (5% and 4% respectively) than in staff and professional-managerial categories of employment. Unions similarly include a larger proportion of people reporting a language other than English as their "first language" than other employee groups.[14] Such a small number of employees identified themselves as of "Canadian Aboriginal ancestry" that no breakdown by employment category could be reported; they account for just 12 of the 3,759 employees who returned census forms, or .3% of survey respondents.[15] The preliminary report provided no data on the number of women who face situations of "multiple jeopardy" as members of other target groups (i.e., women who have disabilities and/or are also members of "visible minorities" or of the First Nations).

Although little detail was available by the end of the first year on more fine-grained patterns of distribution of target-group members,[16] the 1990 *Report* did include a discussion of the low representation of women in the ranks of senior and tenured faculty based on data available from sources other than the census.[17] Evidently women "constitute over half of the incumbents of lecturer and instructor positions" but "only four percent of full professors," a long-established pattern in Canadian universities and at Western.[18] Although the authors of the *First Annual Report* note that there had been some improvement in the rates at which women received "career appointments" from 1988-89 to 1989-90 (i.e., tenured or tenurable appointments, as opposed to limited-term or part-time positions), they observe that women remain disproportionately concentrated in the lowest and most vulnerable faculty ranks. In the full text of the *Report*, the PSCEE concluded that "the data provide little foundation for the [administration's] claim that 'women faculty are rapidly advancing through the academic ranks' (The University of Western Ontario, June 1990, p. 7)."[19] They argue, moreover, that this situation is cause for concern, given that any gains made in the overall representation of women among faculty might well be eroded by impending financial cuts; in 1989-90 "75 percent of men, but only 37 percent of women who hold full time faculty positions at Western, are in career ranks that are likely to be fully protected from cut-backs (full and associate professorships)."[20]

By this logic, the data summarized in the *First Annual Report* establish, more generally, that "visible minorities," as well as women in all categories of employment, are disproportionately vulnerable to economic retrenchment given that their strongest representation is typically in part-time, temporary, and non-unionized positions.[21]

The Federal Contractors Program requires a "work-force audit" to determine where target-group members are underrepresented compared with federal and provincial statistics on their availability (in the region, nationally and provincially, and in the relevant segments of the work force). The results of such an audit are the basis for identifying areas in which action must be taken to improve the employment record of the institution. In line with this, at the end of its first year of operation the PSCEE emphasized the need to move quickly toward the development of concrete employment equity goals and specific timetables for realizing them. While it was too early to give any very detailed assessment of where equity initiatives would be needed,[22] the *First Annual Report* of the PSCEE did include a lengthy discussion of "Issues that Have Emerged from In Camera Sessions and Reviews of Documents."[23] Significantly, Western's PSCEE is said to be unique in including, in its work-force audit questionnaire, not only questions designed to collect the demographic information required by federal regulation, but also several open-ended questions asking respondents' about their experiences as employees. In the section summarizing these responses,[24] and elsewhere, the PSCEE stressed the importance of addressing issues relating to workplace environment and culture, for example: "inhospitable working environment[s] for members of designated groups"; "inequitable and adverse working conditions."[25]

The concerns about workplace climate reported by PSCEE are quite striking, considered in light of the experiences described in the various reports on climate issues that had been drafted at Western and elsewhere in the late 1980s. Altogether 19% of all women, and fully 41% of faculty women responding to Western's workplace census reported that they had "experienced disadvantage based on [their] gender"; this was true, as well, for 22% of those who identified as "visible minorities," and 34% of those with disabilities (again, no data are presented to indicate reporting rates for women in these latter categories).[26] The authors of this *First Annual Report* (in both its original form and the "Abridged" publication) comment on the sorts of conditions that might give rise to these responses. They note that "insensitive attitudes and intolerance of difference, expressed in language and behaviour, contribute to a working environment that many women, minorities, and people with disabilities perceive as detrimental."[27] They then turn to a discussion of the impact that such practices can be expected to have on the ability of the University to attract and retain minority-group members and women, especially at senior levels. Where women faculty are concerned, one group for which relatively detailed data were available, the PSCEE argued that the University must not only "seriously examine" the reasons for losing promising women candidates to other schools and for failing to "retain some of the qualified women it hires," but must ask why women are under-represented among applicants for its advertised positions wherever this is cited by administrators and hiring committees as a reason for their failure to appoint women.[28]

Climate issues figure centrally in the PSCEE's assessment both of the problems facing the University in this connection and of the prospects for finding solutions to them:

> The essential point here is that the underrepresentation of women on Western's faculty does not result simply from an absence of women 'in the pipeline'. . . . The nature of the offers of employment Western extends to women, and the kind of working environment women find when they do accept positions here, are two factors that are amenable to change initiatives and that affect rates of representation of women on faculty.[29]

Evidently the *in camera* testimony offered the PSCEE by women employees provided some insights about the features of the workplace environment that might be at issue here. The full version of the *First Annual Report* includes a summary of the concerns and notes that they closely parallel those "identified in the scholarly literature on gender discrimination in universities and other types of organizations throughout North America" and, indeed, by the *Chilly Climate Report*.[30] In fact, the *Chilly Climate Report* is identified as a resource on which the PSCEE drew in seeking an understanding of "climate issues affecting women on campus,"[31] and the response of the senior administration to this *Report* is listed as one of the issues requiring attention where workplace environment is concerned: "This response was profoundly disappointing to women who have experienced unequal treatment or harassment, in that it implied a denial of their experience and a lack of administrative commitment to gender equality."[32]

A parallel but more general argument was made in connection with workplace environment issues for "visible minorities" for whom no comparably detailed breakdown of rank and status was available.[33] The PSCEE warned that "employment equity initiatives ... will be hampered" to the extent that administrative responses to issues of race and ethnicity contribute to the perception that the University is an inhospitable environment for minorities. Perhaps most telling, the Committee prefaces this discussion with the observation that "the race relations climate on campus has been damaged during 1989-90 by the continuing controversy regarding academic racism" generated by the Rushton affair.[34]

The *Report* also includes a consideration of issues of access that restrict the participation of people with disabilities in the workplace; the ways in which advertising and the assessment of credentials for many jobs may systematically disadvantage "visible minorities," immigrants, and any whose first language is not English; the "very low representation of Native people in the work force" and declining support for Native students; and the workplace conditions that affect part-time faculty and teaching assistants.[35] In setting an agenda for future work on equity at Western, then, the 1989-90 PSCEE made it clear that a fuller investigation of, and improvements in, the workplace environment would have to be given a high priority.[36]

This concern with climate issues was consistent with, and seemed to closely inform, the emphasis that the PSCEE put on the need for a program of education, as had been initiated by the Equity in Communication and Bias-free Communication Task Forces. In fact, the PSCEE argued that education and communication are an integral part of the goal setting process:

> The Committee proposes that the process of setting goals should grow out of an educational and training initiative developed by the Employment Equity Officer and the Committee. The analysis of Western's employment

equity data will provide a basis for identifying issues and setting priorities for the University as a whole, and for goal-setting at the unit level. The goal setting process will begin with briefings about federal regulations, provincial legislation, and University policy on human rights and employment equity, as well as results of the employment equity census and relevant availability data. These information sessions will involve deans, officers and representatives of the employee associations and unions, and members of committees responsible for personnel decision-making.

The information and discussion sessions are the first step in the goal setting exercise, in which each unit will be asked to develop realistic targets and timetables for increasing the representation of each designated group that is presently underrepresented.[37]

As described in more detail in the full text of the *First Annual Report*, this "educational" agenda was broadly conceived not just as a matter of informing the university community about the legal and institutional requirements of the new Employment Equity Program, but of raising awareness about equity issues in ways that might engage everyone in the process of developing and implementing an "Employment Equity Work Plan." In principle, at least, this process might, in itself, help to make the workplace environment more hospitable for target-group members whose interests and concerns are little understood by majority groups on campus. Moreover, it might help to ensure that a commitment to improve the workplace environment would be a component of the emerging equity work plan.

To this end, the Task Force on Communication brought in several high-profile speakers on equity issues (Glenda Simms, Jeanette Lavell, Georges Erasmus), while that on Career Support began collaborative work with the Women's Caucus on what was initially described as a proposal for a "mentoring" program. And the task force on Bias-free Communication produced a series of six columns, published in *Western News*, on "cultural and social issues involved in communicating across lines of gender, race, ethnicity, and disability," and undertook to develop a draft policy and educational pamphlet on equity in communication. One of the published columns was an enormously witty guide to sub-varieties of the species "dinosaurus academicus" which drew considerable good-humoured comment.[38] It was members of this task force, the chair of PSCEE, and the Employment Equity Officer who collaborated most actively with the Women's Caucus in the production of the *Chilly Climate* video; by the time the PSCEE drafted its *First Annual Report* the video had been funded and was in production.

In short, there was a lot to be optimistic about, two years into the development of an official employment equity program at Western. A number of aspects of this program addressed exactly the issues which had been raised by those concerned with the chilly climate for women, and addressed them in much broader terms than the *Backhouse Report* or the *Chilly Climate Report* had been able to do. The PSCEE undertook to educate itself about these issues as they affected not only women in a wide range of employment categories, but also "visible minorities," people with disabilities, members of the First Nations, immigrants, and employees whose first language was not English.[39]

To this end, the PSCEE solicited written and oral submissions and advice from individuals and organizations, on campus and off, whose experience might help inform the design of the equity program. And in response to what they learned, they were quite explicit on the point that formal compliance would not be enough on its own. An effective employment equity program at Western would have to undertake to change the conditions that play a role in producing and perpetuating systemic inequity, conditions which are familiar in universities and colleges across North America. Finally, the PSCEE had very quickly taken a number of promising initiatives that were designed to address these climate issues. *Western News'* coverage of the activities of the Employment Equity Committee and Office in 1989 and 1990 ran headlines like, "Process Gathering Momentum,"[40] and "Western Aims to Go Beyond Compliance."[41] As a further measure of this optimism, it was striking that those responding to an internal survey of Women's Caucus members — a "Report Card on Employment Equity" distributed in the spring of 1990 — gave consistently high grades to the PSCEE on various measures of "commitment," "communication," and "action." Indeed, these Caucus members gave the PSCEE a much more positive assessment than they gave the senior administration, which they regarded, for the most part, as insensitive to equity issues.[42]

Formulating an Employment Equity Workplan:
Emerging Resistance to Equity Initiatives

The work of the Committee has continued apace. An Equity Services Office was created in September 1991, incorporating, in one location and administrative unit, several existing staff. As Leela MadhavaRau describes (in chapter 10), a Race Relations Policy had been established the previous September (1990), and she was appointed as Race Relations Officer in June 1991.[43] An Aboriginal Council was developed, and the creation of a position for an Aboriginal Services Coordinator was initiated under a provincial grant. This coordinator, and an equity data analyst serving the office as a whole, have since been appointed, and these new positions, as well as the existing Sexual Harassment Officers and Employment Equity Officer, have been integrated into the new Department of Equity Services with their own office and facilities. There has been considerable work done to develop an audit of Western's physical plant and to assess conditions of access for those with disabilities. The Employment Equity Committee and Officer have undertaken an extensive program of training sessions with administrators and unit heads, as well as a number of widely advertised public sessions on employment equity (in the fall of 1992), and a video working group has been actively engaged in producing a series of training videos that will facilitate this process. In April 1991, a well-attended provincial conference on "Remedies for Racism and Sexism in Colleges and Universities" was held at Fanshawe College, jointly sponsored by employment equity committees at Fanshawe and Western, working with the Ontario Anti-Racism Secretariat, the Ontario Women's Directorate, and the Ministry of Colleges and Universities. The *Chilly Climate* video had its premiere at this conference, and was then distributed free to all colleges and universities in Ontario (a provision of the provincial funding for this project). It has subsequently been marketed widely in Canada and the United States; proceeds from sales of the video are divided between the Women's Caucus and the PSCEE, and are to be used to fund future "employment equity change agent projects."[44]

With expansion and refinement of the work-force database, it was possible to begin to make comparisons with external statistics on the availability of target-group members and determine where equity initiatives are needed at Western.[45] Although the summary of these data prepared for the *Second Report* of the PSCEE was not available to the university community until April 1993, the process of goal setting was initiated in 1992-93.[46]

Consistent with the commitment to broad "stakeholder involvement," there was strong emphasis on the need for departments and other administrative units to take responsibility for setting their own equity goals and timetables for the elimination of barriers in "employment decision making" and the workplace climate, for education on equity issues, and for changing the "numerical representation of members of the four designated groups" (i.e., by recruiting and hiring target-group members).[47] By October 1993, the President was in a position to present an "Employment Equity Work Plan" to the Senate,[48] and in April 1994 it was announced that Western had passed its first "compliance review" by the Federal Contractors Program.[49]

It is too early to tell how effective this equity program will be in the long term and whether, in particular, it will have an impact on the workplace environment. While the formal process of developing a work plan has met federal requirements, there have been some serious setbacks where climate and other initiatives are concerned; highly vocal resistance to equity policies and programs for change has increased as an abstract institutional commitment has begun to take concrete form. There are a number of causes for concern.

For one thing, the *Second Report* was presented to the President in June 1992, but despite repeated assurances of its imminent release, as indicated above, the abridged and updated version did not appear until April 1993, long after unit-level decision makers and committees had begun the process of setting equity goals and timetables; the first of three target dates for which goals were to be set was 1993 (the others were 1995 and 2000). Evidently problems had been discovered in the work-force database where information about salaries was concerned; this emerged in the course of running regression analyses designed to identify pay inequities among faculty, an agreement reached when the requirements of provincial pay equity legislation were addressed for women staff, union, and PMA members, and faculty were declared a male-dominated job class. It was agreed that the *Report* would be released without salary information, and at the time of writing (two and a half years after the *Second Report* was completed) the matter of identifying and resolving pay inequities for women faculty has not been settled.[50]

In the interim, campus-wide training sessions were held in the fall of 1992. These were designed to educate the full spectrum of employees at Western about equity issues and about the federal regulations and campus policies governing Western's equity program. They were not intended to provide information about the profile of Western's work force and, given their scope, they could not address the implications of these policies for different employee groups. Response to these sessions was evidently quite mixed, and attendance varied a great deal by employee group, at least in part because administrative and unionized employees were required to participate, but faculty attended on a voluntary basis. While a range of other information sessions were held for administrators and unit heads (e.g., Deans and department Chairs), plans for a broader program of equity education for faculty were to be developed at the level of departments and faculties as part of the process of creating an equity work plan; educational and hiring goals were to be formulated at the same time. In practice this meant that most non-administrative members of academic work units entered the process of goal setting with scant training on equity issues; relatively few of those sitting on departmental appointments committees, or voting on goals and timetables in department meetings had had any but the most superficial contact with the training process. In some cases the outcome was encouraging, but in many the process was excruciating for those few target-group members and their supporters who found themselves in the position of having to defend, explain, educate, or (depending on their view of the matter) dissociate themselves from the process.

With limited education on equity issues, and anxiety evidently mounting about the threat of "reverse discrimination," a number of highly critical reactions against the employment equity program and policy began to appear in *Western News*. In one which appeared in mid-November 1992, two members of the Faculty of Social Science took, as their point of departure, a critique of information about the status of women faculty that had been released by the Provost in an annual report to the Senate in late October 1992.[51] They objected that a decline in the rates at which women were being appointed to faculty positions, reported by the Provost, was not statistically significant.[52] Evidently the Provost had explained this discrepancy at the time, in answer to a question from the floor; on his account the apparent decrease of 10% in entry-level appointments reflected an error which had resulted in inflated figures for earlier years (i.e., the earlier figures did not distinguish between different types of first-time appointments). The decrease was indeed "not significant," but not just in a statistical sense; the later (lower) figures more accurately represented the rate at which women were being recruited to career, as opposed to limited-term appointments (see discussion of the *First Annual Report*, above). These critics went on, however, to make explicit the sorts of arguments the PSCEE had been at pains to counter when it had insisted, in the *First Annual Report*, that the failure to attract a strong candidate pool of women is not an adequate defence for failure to hire women into faculty positions. They argued that male and female candidates for faculty positions must be assumed to be equally motivated to apply for jobs; therefore a requirement to hire women above the level of their representation in actual applicant pools constitutes a "require[ment to] hire less qualified females at the expense of more qualified males."[53] And this, they insist,

> would not only constitute discrimination against men but also contravene the Conditions of Appointment document of this university, which states in the preamble ". . . the obligation of the university to appoint, promote, and grant tenure to members of the faculty regardless of race, sex, religion or politics." Indeed, the preamble goes on to tell us what the criterion should be, namely, "to appoint, promote and grant tenure to members of the faculty on the basis of merit."[54]

The only response to this letter which appeared in *Western News* was a rejoinder published by a member of the English Department who concluded her critique of the presumptions made about the "qualifications" of women candidates with the following:

> I would like to close by saying that I'm tired of reading in various locations around this university that I am less qualified than the equivalent male (whoever that mythical being might be). I think I can probably speak for all the "unqualified" recently-hired women on campus when I say that it is time this tired argument was left behind. When I look at my female colleagues, most of whom did not have working spouses to ease their way through graduate school, nor spouses who did laundry, child-care and cooking detail while typing and retyping the academic's thesis, I see heavily overworked women trying to sit on too many committees, teach and counsel far too many students, and carry on a research program with too

few hours. I do not see underqualified people and no Chi-square or slight-
ing remark will convince me otherwise.[55]

Judging from the concerns expressed by those who said they had "experienced disadvantage on the basis of gender," in response to the census questionnaire,[56] this response captured the frustrations of many women on campus, including women staff and managers of all kinds, as well as women
faculty.

But perhaps as worrisome as these assumptions about the qualifications
of women faculty who are hired was the apparent unfamiliarity of the authors of the original critique with the literature on employment patterns for
women in academic settings, and with the terms and conditions of the
federal regulations governing institutional employment equity programs
like that which was being developed at Western. It is important to be clear
just what "entry-level faculty positions" are at issue when the claim is made
that women show higher rates of appointment to such positions than men,
relative to the relevant candidate pools. Women still show disproportionately high rates of (entry-level) appointment to limited-term, untenurable
positions. And even when women do better than men in appointments to
probationary (tenure-stream) positions, the problem remains that this advantage is systematically undercut as new cohorts of appointees move up
the ranks, into tenured and more senior positions.[57] This was one aspect of
the "pipeline problem" on which the PSCEE had focused in their *First Annual Report*, and it was central, again, in the *Second Report*, although both reports also draw attention to ways in which many academic units had failed
to do all they could *even to recruit* qualified women, let alone retain and promote them (see below). As the author of the letter of rebuttal suggests, the
attitudes expressed by critics of employment equity do nothing to encourage women to stay in the employment pipeline once they do get through the
training pipeline and secure positions.

In addition, however, such critics often seem unaware that employment
equity programs in Canada are legally empowered to institute forward-
looking strategies for changing the representation of the four designated
target groups among employees, to bring it up to the level at which target-
group members are available in the work force as a whole. In an extended
internal discussion about whether, or how, to respond to critics of employment equity, the 1992-93 Executive of the Women's Caucus decided that the
time had come when the need for education on equity policies and principles that such reactions so often demonstrate should be addressed by the
President's Office or one of its designates in the area of employment equity,
not by representatives of the target groups in question:

> It is properly the responsibility of [the President] and/or the Employment
> Equity committee and office to provide ... clarification of the terms of our
> institutional commitment to equity, for the community as a whole. .... Cer-
> tainly [recent exchanges in *Western News*] seem to indicate a pressing need
> for some such intervention ... education in the area of employment equity
> is now the responsibility of various institutional bodies and officers.[58]

No institutional response was issued to the growing number of letters
disputing the efficacy of the University's commitments to equity which appeared in *Western News*, with increasing regularity, through the period
when the *Second Report* was being reviewed and the process of "goal setting" was set in motion (1992-94).

When the "Abridged and Updated" version of the *Second Report* was
published in *Western News* in April 1993, its summary of the census data
provided a sobering, if not unexpected, picture of workplace segregation
and under-representation for the four target groups in many areas of employment. These data supported, in the details they provided, the general
profile outlined in the *First Annual Report* and the equity concerns raised in
this connection.[59] The number of employees reporting "Aboriginal ancestry" at Western now stood at 13 (up from 12), and was substantially lower
than their representation in the relevant external labour force: "Aboriginal
people represent 1.2% of the labour force in London, and .7% of the Ontario
labour force," compared to .3% of those employed at Western.[60] People with
disabilities were also "very under-represented in staff and faculty positions
relative to their presence in the Ontario work force"[61] for all occupational
levels documented by the PSCEE.[62] The 3.4% representation of "visible
minorities" among administrative staff at Western was comparable to the
London work force, but less than half that of Ontario.[63] Finally, the *Second
Report* included a breakdown by gender of target-group categories which
showed that a third of "visible minority" employees at Western were wom-
en in 1993, and that they were disproportionately concentrated in staff positions.[64]

Overall, women are better represented in supervisory and middle-
ranked administrative positions at Western than in the external work force,
but under-represented among senior administrators and faculty, and in
unionized positions. In fact, where non-unionized staff positions are concerned, the area in which "visible minority" women are concentrated, the
Second Report describes "a pattern of job ghettos for women, with 70% of
women in the UWOSA constituency concentrated in clerical jobs — 90% of
which are held by women."[65] Among women faculty, fewer than five who
held full-time positions in 1993 identified as "visible minorities";[66] as the
published *Report* describes the situation, "women who are also members of
"visible minorities" are nearly absent from the faculty."[67] Overall, women

faculty account for just 17.2% of those eligible for membership in Western's Faculty Association (i.e., regular full-time faculty), compared to 21.1% of faculty in Ontario and 20.8% in all Canadian universities.[68] Most striking, the 4.3% representation of women among Full Professors at Western is substantially lower than that reported for other Ontario and Canadian universities (7% and 7.3% respectively).[69] Moreover, *contra* the fears expressed by the critics of equity initiatives at Western, the *Second Report* points out that while nearly half of new faculty appointments made in 1990-91 went to women, "men continue to be more likely than women to be offered probationary or tenured positions"; 40% of appointments to men were probationary or tenured, compared to 24% of those made to women.[70] Not surprisingly, the proportion of women holding untenured, limited-term appointments continues to be much higher than for men: 39% of women, compared to 16% of men, held such contracts, while 61% of women were tenured, compared to 84% of men.[71]

The comparison with other universities and with external availability statistics is also striking where "visible minority" faculty are concerned. "Visible minorities" constitute 4.5% of tenured faculty members and 8% of probationary appointments at Western, while their "current rate of availability" in Ontario is reported to be 10.2%. Although, by comparison with women, the proportion of tenured faculty or Full Professors who identified as "visible minorities" (largely male) is closer to their overall representation among faculty (i.e., the segregation by rank is not so clear cut),[72] like women, faculty who identified themselves as "visible minorities" also tend to be concentrated in untenured positions. By extension of the concerns raised in the *First Annual Report* and restated in *Second Report*, this means that they, too, are disproportionately vulnerable to economic retrenchment.[73]

Reflecting on these census figures and the results of comparison with various forms of "availability" data, the authors of the *Second Report* responded to a "frustration" evidently expressed to the PSCEE by administrators and colleagues who feel that there simply are not adequate resources available to be effective in implementing equity goals.[74] In what the local media described as a "politely worded" statement to the effect that "the University of Western Ontario could be doing more with the resources it has to address the under-representation of women, "visible minorities," Aboriginal and disabled persons,"[75] authors of the *Second Report* observe that:

> The absence of resources to take advantage of the availability of these individuals [members of target groups who could be recruited for positions at Western] is one of the consequences of the funding crisis at Western. But it also reflects the fact that the resources that are available are being used to support priorities other than increasing the representation of qualified designated group members in faculty positions. . . . [Q]ualified individuals

in faculty positions at other universities, or in limited term positions at Western, have indicated that they are available to be recruited or retained, but resources have been used to make other appointments instead.[76]

Reiterating a point made in the *First Annual Report*, the authors of this *Report* go on to observe that such instances "undermine the claim that a shortage of qualified designated group members 'in the pipeline' explains the failure to improve their representation in faculty positions at Western." They conclude with the observation that "such instances contribute to scepticism about the commitment of academic decision-makers at the University to remedy the under-representation of designated groups."[77]

A Deepening Chill?

It is perhaps unsurprising that Western had not done as well as it might (to paraphrase a statement that closes the section quoted above),[78] given the combination of a laudable commitment to engage all "stakeholders" in the process of setting and implementing equity goals, and the vocal resistance to such initiatives that has emerged with increasing insistence in the last several years, especially among faculty. Evidently Western's experience is by no means unique, especially in contexts where a commitment has been made to develop and implement equity goals using a broadly consultative approach. Drawing on the experience at York, where "top-down" processes of goal setting were also rejected in favour of a process of unit-level goal setting, Ellen Baar argues that if such approaches are to work (if broad compliance is to be realized), there must be a structure of incentives in place which ensure that more is at stake than "reputation" and privilege when setting employment equity goals.[79] She argues for a model of "communitarian regulation" in which it is in every unit's best interest to ensure not only its own compliance but that of other units; each must be, in some sense, a "hostage to all others."[80] At Western it would seem that not even reputation was at stake for many units. The public controversies that focused on the Race Relations Policy and on sexual harassment policies, for example, seem to have created a climate in which "reputation" was, for some, enhanced by resistance to proposed changes in hiring practices or in other aspects of the workplace environment. Certainly, a vocal contingent of the most privileged stakeholders at Western have made it clear that they will tolerate no interference with the "freedoms" and privileges they currently enjoy. From early on in the process of data collection and goal setting, public discussion of equity issues had been dominated by reactions against the "temptation to debase standards,"[81] "political correctness,"[82] and "bogus multiculturalism."[83] In an especially timely and compelling public address arranged by the Employment Equity Committee and the Advisory Committee on Race

Relations in March 1993, Stephen Lewis made a strong case that "those involved in employment equity initiatives should not lose hope when faced
with the inevitable backlash such programs cause."[84] At this juncture, however, the backlash was just gathering momentum.

By the following fall the debate over academic racism, which the PSCEE
felt had "damaged" the race relations climate at Western in 1989-90,[85] had
taken the decidedly non-academic form of a protracted dispute about the
new Race Relations Policy.[86] As described by MadhavaRau (in chapter 10),
the original policy had been sent back into review in February 1993, and the
revisions which emerged through a long process of debate in the fall and
winter of 1993-94[87] seem to have pleased no one but the most outspoken
critics of equity initiatives on campus. One especially vocal critic conceded
that the new draft policy may be acceptable only because it "will probably
do no harm — all that one can reasonably expect from something that is undesirable in principle."[88] His assessment that the Race Relations Policy had
been effectively gutted is precisely what had alarmed those who had hoped
to see employment equity accompanied by a strong anti-racism policy and
program of education on campus. In a letter expressing "grave concerns"
about the proposed policy six months earlier, seven faculty and staff noted a
number of ways in which the objectives of educating the university community had been subordinated to a legalistic procedure which systematically
reproduces the power inequities existing within the institution.[89] This drew
a rebuttal to the effect that, in recommending race relations training for
those in "positions of responsibility," these advocates of a stronger policy
were imposing a "condition of... ideological indoctrination in 'political
correctness.' "[90] In this atmosphere it was perhaps to have been expected, in
retrospect, that the proposal for a formal policy and set of guidelines on
bias-free communication would be scuttled at both Senate and Faculty
Council levels; it was sent back to committee in 1991-92 and has still not
resurfaced, despite the PSCEE's strong endorsement of the need for Western
to adopt and implement a policy on Equity in Communication.[91]

On another front, the provincial proposal for a policy of "zero tolerance" for sexual harassment (also discussed in chapter 10) exacerbated an
ongoing debate about ways in which existing sexual harassment policies
could be, and allegedly have been, used to harass and victimize male faculty. In an extended "Dialogue" piece entitled, "What's Wrong with Racial
and Sexual Harassment?," a professor at King's College (an affiliate of Western, not governed by Western's policies on sexual harassment, race relations, or employment equity) compared the dangers of the new Race Relations Policy and a sexual harassment policy that was then under review at
his college; he argued that such policies provide the occasion for
"witchhunts" by women students who, in launching "groundless accusa-

tions of sexual harassment," exploit what they know to be conditions of "irrationality and prejudice against men."[92] The most dangerous and "prevalent" form of harassment, in his view, is "administrative." His further discussion makes it clear that by this he means specifically administrative harassment of male faculty members accused of misconduct by malicious and self-serving female students; the issue of racial harassment quickly drops out of the discussion. Two weeks later, this critic of anti-harassment policies followed up his original discussion with a letter to the editor in which he reported that he had received enormous support from colleagues who had urged him to elaborate on two topics: "the need for a policy to contain administrative harassment and the inclusion of prostitution in the proposed *Harassment in the Workplace Policy*."[93] He had space, he said, to pursue only the latter issue and in this connection asked, "Who knows whether the female partner in [a] *delinquence a deux* was not soliciting and was not offering her body for some kind of advancement?" This follows a general reference to situations in which it is assumed (unfairly in his view) that a male professor involved in a sexual relationship with a woman student or staff member must be "guilty" (he must have "initiated the contact" and have caused the woman to "suffer") because of the woman's "dependent status."[94]

If the PSCEE was right in its 1991 assessment that "insensitive attitudes and intolerance of difference ... contribute to a working environment that many [target-group members] perceive as detrimental,"[95] these reactions to the Race Relations and Sexual Harassment Policies will have done nothing to reassure women and "visible minorities" that the University offers them an hospitable environment.[96] Through this period (1992-93) there was, as well, a running debate about the provisions for "special accommodation" for students with disabilities (specifically students with learning disabilities) which made it clear to many readers that the effective integration of people with disabilities into Western's student body and work force would require much more than the assurance of physical access, as important as this is.[97] There were also public debates for and against "accommodation" on other fronts. In one instance, despite initial resistance, eloquent and ultimately persuasive arguments were made for responding positively to a request by Muslim students for a prayer room on campus.[98] In another, a deeply divisive dispute erupted in connection with the advertisement for a controversial speaker on the Middle East sponsored by a "Palestinian solidarity committee," the Canadians Concerned for the Middle East.[99]

In some cases these public exchanges have been thoughtful and constructive discussions which may well have educated the university community about the experiences, concerns, and needs of those whose interests were at issue. In others, however, they have been dominated by defensive assertions of the right "not to know" described so powerfully by Bruce Feldthusen (chapter 9). It is a sad irony indeed that, in a community of educators, there should be such trenchant resistance to the very proposal that education on equity issues — on issues of racism, sexism, and ablism (as a beginning) — might be necessary, given the profile of Western's work force and the nature of the institution.[100]

It is also worrisome that in defending the right to maintain and express or enact familiar attitudes and privileges, these debates frequently reaffirm just the sorts of inaccurate and demeaning stereotypes that a substantial number of respondents to the work-force census identified as at the root of practices that they feel have put them at a disadvantage. PSCEE's *Second Report* provides a great deal of detail on these responses, including summaries of the concerns raised not only by women but also by employees who identified as "visible minorities" (including, for these purposes, those of Aboriginal ancestry) or as having disabilities, and those for whom English was not their first language. "Visible minorities" employed in faculty, staff, and administrative/managerial positions describe experiences of exclusion from communication networks, and of finding themselves subject to "excessive concern and sarcasm expressed overtly and covertly about [their] abilities to deliver . . . typical stereotypes."[101] For some these attitudes translate into the assumption that they are not capable of or interested in promotion or professional development, resulting in persistent under-utilization of their experience, skills, and talents. Those with disabilities describe co-workers as "impatient," as having "difficulty understanding" their capabilities as much as their limitations.[102] And altogether 355 women — 19% of women employed at Western, 5.4% of whom identified as having disabilities or belonging to a "visible minority" group — report a broad range of experiences in which they felt their gender had been a disadvantage, nearly half of which the *Second Report* describes as having to do with "workplace climate" issues.[103] These include a sense of not being taken seriously and of being marginalized in social situations and professional contexts, concerns with differential work loads and inequitable compensation and, most striking, the frustration that, as women, they are expected to take these inequities and indignities in stride — "to accept sexism [lewd remarks, belittling remarks, etc.] because they mean no harm by it."[104] It is sexist attitudes and stereotypes of this last sort which are most powerfully reinforced when the critics of equity initiatives condemn policies that would make us all accountable for the harm done by exclusionary and demeaning attitudes, speech, and practices.

III. Looking Forward

By all accounts, the situation at Western is not unusual in any respect. As Stephen Lewis warned, news from universities and colleges across the country makes it clear that equity policies and programs are under assault even as they gain the firmest institutional foothold they have ever had in Canadian universities. Often efforts to address climate issues seem to be the most contentious aspects of these efforts to make change, as the recent course of events at the University of Victoria makes painfully clear.[105]

It is the very volatility of debates about workplace climate that is mobilizing further work on these issues. For example, the Canadian Women's Studies Association has initiated an ambitious project of "investigating the production of, and reactions to, chilly climate reports on post-secondary education campuses across Canada" as these affect "all women and marginalized peoples" in these institutions.[106] And at Western, the proceeds from sales of the *Chilly Climate* video are being used as seed funding for a new video project on the backlash against equity initiatives that we have witnessed across Canada.

One thing that both gains and setbacks in this area make clear, however, is the central and continuing importance of climate issues; it is increasingly on this front that the battle for equity is being fought. We offer these reports on how climate issues have been addressed as one point of departure for this necessary work. It is our conviction that it is more important now than ever to speak out about the practices that create multiply chilly workplace environments and to show how everyone loses when these marginalize, in different ways and with differing effects, a very wide range of people who might otherwise be making significant contributions to our universities and colleges. Taken together, women, people of Aboriginal ancestry, members of the enormous range of groups identified as "visible minorities," people with disabilities, gays and lesbians, and members of ethnic or cultural and religious minorities constitute a clear majority of the Canadian population. As a community and as a nation we cannot afford the attitudes and practices that compromise the full involvement of any of these constituencies in an area of such vital importance to us all as post-secondary education. Our prospects for success in what Stephen Lewis described so powerfully as a "global struggle [for] equality and freedom from racism and sexism"[107] depend fundamentally on our ability to make change in the institutional climate that such so-called "minority" groups encounter in our universities and colleges. It depends fundamentally on our ability to educate ourselves and one another in the richest sense of the term.

Notes

1 In what follows I use the problematic language of "visible minorities" in reference to the terms of federally and institutionally mandated equity policies. See n. 1, chapter 2, for a discussion of why the terminology of "minority" is problematic. That of "visible" is equally problematic, as ablist and as presupposing that lack of colour, "whiteness," is the unmarked normative term in a racialist symbolic and political economy. For a recent discussion of "whiteness" as a racialist construct, see Ruth Frankenberg, *White Women, Race Matters: The Social Construction of Whiteness* (Minneapolis: University of Minnesota Press, 1993), e.g., p. 6, 194-205.

2 In a discussion of how such debates have unfolded in another context (over racism and allegations of censorship in publication), Marelene Nourbese Philip provides an incisive analysis of how appeals to abstract rights to speech are used to redefine and displace the terms of debate about substantive equity of access and opportunity. Policies designed to make a positive difference in the opportunities writers of colour have to exercise rights of speech are decried as inimical to these rights considered in the abstract, without reference to structuring systems of oppression and disenfranchisement. Marelene Nourbese Philip, "The Disappearing Debate: Racism and Censorship," in Libby Scheier, Sarah Sheard, and Eleanor Wachtel, eds., *Language in Her Eye* (Toronto: Coach House Press, 1990), p. 209-19.

3 Doreen Kimura, "SAFS Concerns, Goals Reiterated by President," *Western News*, April 2, 1992. See also, for example, Robert Fulford, "The Ongoing Assault on Academic Freedom," *The Globe and Mail*, May 11, 1994, p. C1.

The acronym SAFS stands for "Society for Academic Freedom and Scholarship," a group that promotes "academic freedom in teaching, research, and scholarship" and the maintenance of "standards of excellence in hiring and promotion of university faculty" (SAFS Statement of Goals), over against equity programs and other initiatives that they understand to erode the essential meritocracy of the academy. See, for example, "Provincial Society of Scholars: Group to Defend Academic Freedom," *Western News*, March 19, 1992, p. 5. SAFS produces its own newsletter, *Society for Academic Freedom and Scholarship Newsletter*, and its goals and affiliations are described in the news coverage of a conference SAFS members organized in March 1993 on the "University in Jeopardy." See, for example, "Concerns Voiced about New Iron Curtain," "Clash of Views on Equity Issues," and " 'Bogus Multiculturalism' Affects U.S. Universities," all in *Western News*, March 18, 1993, p. 7. See also Krishna Rau and Clive Thompson, "Hate 101," *This Magazine*, March/April 1995, p. 18-24.

4 Doreen Kimura, "A Very Real Threat," *The London Free Press*, November 4, 1992.

5 "Concerns Voiced about New Iron Curtain."

6 One critique along these lines is a discussion of SAFS that appeared at the time the society was first taking shape: Carol Agòcs, "Academic Freedom, Equity — 'Complementary Values,' " *Western News*, March 26, 1992.

7 The full statement of policy pertaining to the Employment Equity Program is included as Appendix A in the *Second Annual Report of the President's Standing Committee for Employment Equity*, prepared by Carol Agòcs, Chair, PSCEE, with the assistance of the Employment Equity Office, Department of Equity Services, and in consultation with the President's Standing Committee for Employment Equity. It was presented to the President in June 1992 (London: Office of the President, Western), p. 29-30.

8 See, for example: Carol Agòcs, "Affirmative Action, Canadian Style: A Reconnaissance," *Canadian Public Policy*, 12 (1986): 148-62; Carol Agòcs, "Implementing Employment Equity: The Role of Participation in Organizational Change," in W. Lafferty and E. Rosenstein, eds., *International Handbook of Participation in Organizations* (Toronto: Oxford University Press, 1992), chap. 1; and Carol Agòcs, Catherine Burr and Felicity Somerset, *Employment Equity: Co-operative Strategies for Organizational Change* (Scarborough Ontario: Prentice-Hall Canada, 1992).

9 PSCEE, "Abridged Version of the *First Annual Report* of the President's Standing Committee for Employment Equity, October 1990," *Western News Supplement*, January 31, 1991, p. S2.

10 Ibid., p. S2-3.
11 Ibid., p. S3. See also "Employment Equity: Full-time Faculty, Staff Response to Census at
   80%," *Western News*, May 26, 1990, p. 6. Note that the figures published in the "Abridged Version of the *First Annual Report*" cited here are all slightly higher than those reported in the
   unabridged version of the *First Annual Report of the President's Standing Committee for Employment Equity*, submitted by the PSCEE to the President in October 1990 (London: Office of the
   President, Western). The full *Report* provides a summary of response rates in two tables. The
   first of these (Table 1.1) reports the rate of response for "all employees surveyed" (i.e., all who
   were at Western in April 1990), while the second (Table 1.2) summarizes these results for "current employees"; those "who were employees of the University when the census was mailed
   out, and for whom no notice of termination had been processed when data were retrieved for
   analysis" (*First Annual Report*, p. 19). The response rates are slightly higher in the second
   table, as corrected for employees who had left Western between the time the census form was
   sent out and the responses analyzed, but still 1-3% lower in each broad employee category
   than was reported three months later, in January. The figures presented in the published report are for "current employees" (i.e., they were based on Table 1.2), and presumably they
   were updated to include responses received between October 1990 and January 1991.
12 PSCEE, "Abridged Version of the *First Annual Report*," p. S3.
13 PSCEE, *First Annual Report*, p. 18, Table 2.2.
14 Ibid. While 25% of all respondents said that English was not their first language, between
   37% and 53% of the membership of two major unions at Western were in this group.
15 Ibid., p. S3.
16 The employment categories for which data were reported in the *First Annual Report* were
   regular full time (faculty, those eligible for membership in the Professional Managerial Association, the Western Staff Association, and the unions), casual weekly, and temporary
   monthly. Little information was given on the distribution of target-group members
   through ranks or occupations within these broad categories of employment.
17 PSCEE, *First Annual Report*, p. 21-22. In Appendix J, a series of six tables, based on *Western
   Facts*, summarizes the information available on the representation of women among full-
   time faculty (by faculty and rank), students (graduate and undergraduate), and administrative staff. Such information was not available for any other target group.
18 PSCEE, "Abridged Version of the *First Annual Report*," p. S3. See also chapters 2 and 3.
19 PSCEE, *First Annual Report*, p. 21.
20 Ibid., p. S4.
21 The *Second Report* of the PSCEE would later indicate that this was especially true for visible
   minority women; see below.
22 At this point analysis of the census data was in its preliminary stages; it was too early to attempt meaningful comparisons with baseline statistics on the representation of target-
   group members in the relevant candidate pools and in segments of the work force employed outside the University. Such comparisons were reported two years later in the *Second Report of the President's Standing Committee for Employment Equity*, submitted to the
   President in June 1992.
23 PSCEE, *First Annual Report*, p. 20-27.
24 Issues raised in response to census questions, workplace experiences, and in presentations
   and briefs solicited by the Committee were discussed, in the published version of this *Report*, under the heading "Summary of Issues Identified by the Committee"; PSCEE, *First
   Annual Report*, p. S2-S3.
25 Ibid., p. S4.
26 Ibid., p. S3.
27 Ibid., p. S4.
28 Ibid.
29 PSCEE, *First Annual Report*, p. 24.

30 Ibid., p. 22-23.

31 Ibid., p. 22.

32 Ibid., p. 23.

33 Presumably these data were not made available because of concerns about confidentiality, given the small number of employees who identified as members of this target group.

34 PSCEE, "Abridged Version of the *First Annual Report*," p. S4.

35 PSCEE, *First Annual Report*, p. 25-27, and PSCEE, "Abridged Version of the *First Annual Report*," p. S4.

36 PSCEE, "Abridged Version of the *First Annual Report*," p. S4.

37 Ibid., p. S4-5.

38 Sarah J. Shorten, "Homo Academicus," *Western News*, March 29, 1990, p. 7.

39 Although this fact-finding process did, to some extent, broaden the scope of concern defined by federal regulations, with its focus on just four target groups there was, so far as I know, no investigation of the effects of homophobia, anti-semitism, or stereotyping and intolerance toward other ethnic and cultural or religious minorities, to name a few areas in which there has been active debate at Western in recent years (see below).

40 *Western News*, November 16, 1989, p. 1.

41 Ibid., p. 6.

42 This survey was distributed to all members of the Women's Caucus in April 1990 and asked for an assessment of employment equity initiatives in three areas: as undertaken by their own work units, by the senior administration, and by the employment equity officer and the PSCEE. The same questions were asked in each case, and focused on the main areas identified for action both by the Federal Contractors Guidelines and in the employment equity policy adopted at Western. This survey drew a 30% response rate. As such, the sample is clearly too small to support any general conclusions about how women viewed the equity program at Western in its various manifestations. The results are interesting, however, inasmuch as those motivated to respond would seem likely to be women who are active on equity issues and, perhaps, those most disaffected with the situation they encountered. Given that we could expect a critical bias from such a sample, it is striking that the grades Caucus respondents gave their own work units varied considerably, and yet there is a high degree of consistency in their negative assessment of the senior administration. While a number of respondents indicated that they knew too little about the activities of the Employment Equity Committee and Office to assess them, those who did answer questions about the PSCEE rated it very highly. The results of the survey are presented in "1990 Caucus Report on Employment Equity: Preliminary Summary of Results," July 1990, Archives of Western's Caucus on Women's Issues, London.

43 See "Race and Ethnocultural Relations — Draft UWO Policy Circulated," *Western News*, December 7, 1989, p. 1, 8, and "Race Relations: Revisions Made in Draft Policy," *Western News*, April 26, 1990, p. 1, 6. For a history of the formation and review of this policy, see M.W. Westmacott (Chair), "Report of the Race Relations Policy Review Committee," *Western News Supplement*, September 16, 1993, p. S2-S4.

44 PSCEE, *Second Report*, p. 8.

45 A summary of the census data and these comparisons was presented in the *Second Report of the President's Standing Committee for Employment Equity* in June 1992, but was not published until April the following year. It appeared as "Second Report of the President's Standing Committee for Employment Equity, June 1992 (Abridged and Updated March 1993)," *Western News Supplement*, April 22, 1993, p. S1-S4.

46 Jim Anderson, "Employment Equity Plan Sets Actions, Objectives," *Western News*, October 28, 1993, p. 1-2.

47 PSCEE, "Second Report," p. S3. It is important to note that this decentralized process is not required by the Federal Contractors Guidelines. It was a quite innovative strategy adopted by the PSCEE; the hope was that if individual units formulated their own goals,

the commitment to equity, and the goals themselves, would be more meaningful than if imposed from outside. Evidently a similar approach was adopted at York University, and is described in some detail by Ellen Baar ("Using Accountable Self Regulation to Achieve Employment Equity in Universities," *Canadian Woman Studies*, 12, 3 [1992]: 46-52). She notes that, as at Western, "top-down" models were avoided as incompatible with the collegial decision making and decentralized hiring practices typical of academic units (p. 48).

48 "Employment Equity Work Plan for the University of Western Ontario," *Western News Supplement*, February 3, 1994, p. S1-S4.

49 "Employment Equity Work Gets Federal Endorsement," *Western News*, April 7, 1994, p. 6.

50 PSCEE, *Second Report*, "Exhibit C."

51 Provost Thomas J. Collins, "Provost's Statistical Summary Report: Regular Full-Time Faculty Appointments and Recruitment Activities Effective July 2, 1991 to July 1, 1992," Senate Agenda, October 21, 1992, Exhibit 6, Appendix 1, p. 2.

52 Stephen J. Lupker and Clive Seligman, "Women, Applicant Pool, and Employment Equity," *Western News*, November 12, 1992, p. 13.

53 Ibid.

54 Ibid.

55 M.J. Toswell, "Tired of Reading About 'Less Qualified Women,'" *Western News*, November 26, 1992, p. 13.

56 PSCEE, *First Annual Report*, p. 22-26, and PSCEE, *Second Report*, Appendix D, p. 6-25.

57 See discussion of this literature in chapter 2.

58 Internal memo to the President and Executive of Western's Caucus on Women's Issues, November 19, 1992, Archives of Western's Caucus on Women's Issues, London.

59 While the patterns of distribution across general categories of employment seem unchanged, the figures reported in the *Second Report* are lower in most cases. For example, the overall representation of visible minorities in Western's work force is reported as 4.4% overall in 1993, compared with 7% in 1991; people with disabilities were reported to be 2.1% of the work force in 1993, but 3% in 1991. The reported representation of women and of people of Aboriginal ancestry was essentially unchanged.

This difference in reported figures reflects, in part, the results of renewed efforts to increase the rate of response to the census: "over two hundred employees were added to the data base [since 1990]." In addition, however, in the *Second Report* the base used in reporting the percentage of target-group members represented in various employee categories is the *total number of employees* in these categories (i.e., the total number to whom census forms were, or could have been, sent), not the total number of employees who responded to the survey. In the *First Annual Report*, the percentages reported for target-group members are of employees in various categories who returned their census forms. Where, for example, 77.9% of regular full-time employees returned surveys, this means there was approximately a 20% difference between the base used to calculate representation figures given for such employees in the *Second Report* and that used in the *First Annual Report* (this would, of course, vary with the rate at which employees in different categories of full-time employment returned census forms). The rationale for using this larger base was that the "analysis of designated group representation for purposes of compliance with the Federal Contractors Program is intended to be based on the total work force of an organization"; thus, the figures reported in the *Second Report* are, in effect, minimum numbers of individuals in each target group employed in various capacities at Western. The reason some of the figures for women remain essentially unchanged is because "the sex of an individual is identified in every employee record on the human resource data base" so that analysis by sex was not dependent on data generated by the work-force census. Human resources data were not available for visible minorities, employees of Aboriginal ancestry, or employees with disabilities (PSCEE, *Second Report*, p. S3).

60 PSCEE, *"Second Report* — Abridged and Updated," p. S4.

61 Ibid., p. S2.

62 Ibid., p. S4.
63 Ibid., p. S4. Compare 3.4% of administrative staff at Western who identified themselves as "visible minorities" in 1990-91 with 3.9% in London's work force and 8.5% in Ontario.
64 Ibid. Altogether 74% of "visible minority" women were eligible for membership in the Western Staff Association, compared with 58% of women who were not members of this target group.
65 PCSEE, *Second Annual Report*, p. 4.
66 Ibid., p. 5.
67 PSCEE, "*Second Report* — Abridged and Updated," p. S2.
68 Ibid.
69 PSCEE, *Second Report*, p. 5, 32,
70 PSCEE, "*Second Report* — Abridged and Updated," p. S2.
71 Ibid.
72 Altogether 5.3% of faculty members at Western identified as visible minorities: 4.5% of tenured faculty and 5.9% of Full Professors were visible minorities. A much larger proportion of Western's faculty were women: 18.6%. But just 10.3% of tenured faculty were women, and 4.3% of Full Professors were women (PSCEE, *Second Report*, p. 5, and Table 6a, p. 32).
73 While 4.5% of tenured faculty identified as visible minorities, 8.2% of those holding probationary appointments and 5.7% of those holding limited-term appointments were visible minorities. The skew for women was greater, with women holding more than three times the proportion of limited-term appointments as they did tenured positions (36.2% compared to 10.3%, respectively) (PSCEE, *Second Report*, p. 5, and Table 6a, p. 32).
74 "*Second Report* — Abridged and Updated," p. S3.
75 Stephen Northfield, "Employment Equity: Politely Worded Report Says Western Has a Long Way to Go," *The London Free Press*, April 22, 1993, p. B2.
76 PSCEE, "*Second Report* — Abridged and Updated," p. S3.
77 Ibid.
78 Ibid. The wording of the statement referred to here is as follows: "if there was sustained commitment by decision-makers, improvement would be slow because of resource limitations and low turn-over, however it could be better than it has been."
79 Ellen Baar, "Accountable Self Regulation."
80 Ibid., p. 51.
81 Douglas N. Jackson, "Must Resist 'Temptation to Debase Standards,'" letter to the editor, *Western News*, April 2, 1992, p. 4.
82 "Concerns Voiced about New Iron Curtain," p. 7.
83 "'Bogus Multiculturalism' Affects U.S. Universities," p. 7.
84 "Equity Programs Will Prevail Over Backlash, Predicts Lewis," *Western News*, March 18, 1993, p. 5-6.
85 PSCEE, "Abridged Version of the *First Annual Report*," p. S4.
86 See chapter 8.
87 These were originally proposed in Westmacott, "Report of the Race Relations Policy Review Committee."
88 Kenneth H.W. Hilborn, "Probably Will Do No Harm if Honestly Interpreted," *Western News*, April 21, 1994.
89 Frances Bauer, Mike Atkinson, Constance Backhouse, Anne Cummings, Nancy Kendall, Bonnie MacLachlan, Leela MadhavaRau, Gillian Michell, Shirley Murray, and Aniko Varpalotai, "Grave Concerns Regarding Proposed Race Relations Policy," *Western News*, April 14, 1994, p. 11.
90 Kenneth H.W. Hilborn, "Urges Expanded Knowledge of History, Traditional Values," *Western News*, October 28, 1993, p. 17.
91 PSCEE, *Second Report*, p. 20.

92 Heinz-Joachim Klatt, "What's Wrong with Racial and Sexual Harassment?" *Western News*, October 28, 1993, p. 16.

93 H.-J. Klatt, "Harassment in Workplace: Policies and 'Assumptions,'" *Western News*, November 11, 1993, p. 13.

94 Ibid.

95 PSCEE, *First Annual Report*, p. S4.

96 It is especially sobering, as a faculty member, to note that several of the most outspoken critics of the Race Relations Policy, and of employment equity generally, now sit on the Executive of the Western Faculty Association.

97 For a recent example, see Steve Lupker, "Faculty and UWO Policy on Special Accommodation," *Western News*, September 16, 1993, p. 14.

98 This was ultimately granted, and one of the most thoughtful discussions of implicit institutional bias to appear in *Western News* was published by Michael P. Carroll, "Universalistic Policies Can Be Shaped by Cultural Biases," *Western News*, February 3, 1994, p. 12.

99 See, for example, G.B. Rollman, A. Goldschlager, E.L. Medzon, H. Merskey, and B.D. Singer, "Agreement to Settle Sets 'A Disturbing Precedent,'" *Western News*, March 17, 1994, p. 11, and Office of the President and Vice-Chancellor, "An Open Letter to the Arab/Palestinian Community of the University of Western Ontario and the City of London," *Western News*, March 3, 1993, p. 3.

100 See Bruce Feldthusen, "Question: Is Something Wrong with This Picture?" *Western News*, October 14, 1993, p. 13. Feldthusen's letter to the editor is brief and very much to the point. It runs as follows:
    "Picture this:
    "Western's entire faculty is meeting. We are the meritocracy. We are mostly men. In fact, we are mostly men of middle age or beyond. And we are, men and women alike, overwhelmingly white-skinned. The topic of discussion is racism. We are determining what can and what cannot be defined as racist in the way that suits us best. We are deciding what, if anything, to do about systemic racism at the university. We are deciding what racism complaint procedures will protect us best. We are in agreement. We are not racist.
    "Is something wrong with this picture?"

101 PSCEE, *Second Report*, p. 19-21. Altogether 22% of visible minorities who responded to the census reported disadvantages, slightly more among those employed in administrative and staff positions than among faculty (p. 7). Employees who were identified as of Aboriginal heritage were included among visible minorities in the discussion of reports of disadvantage, for reasons of confidentiality given their small numbers.

102 Ibid., p. 24.

103 PSCEE, "*Second Report* — Abridged and Updated," p. S4, and *Second Report*, p. 8-19. It is striking, in fact, how closely the categories and the content of the responses summarized here parallel those reported by the authors of the 1989 *Chilly Climate Report*. This earlier *Report* concerned a sample that was just 10% of that reported by the PSCEE, and covered only women faculty. See chapters 3 and 4.

104 Ibid., p. 11.

105 See, in particular, Beth Bilson and Thomas R. Berger, "Report of the Review Committee into the Political Science Department," prepared for the President of the University of Victoria, January 21, 1994. Bilson and Berger describe how the concerns raised in an internal investigation of "ways and means of making the department more supportive to women" (p. 10) became a matter of national debate.

106 Susan Prentice, "Canadian Women's Studies Association Chilly Climate Project," memo circulated to all Canadian post-secondary institutions, April 20, 1994.

107 "Equity Programs," p. 5.

Epilogue
Studying Science, Playing Politics[1]

Deborah Skilliter

We should be heartened by the increasing numbers of women and members (both men and women) of a range of excluded groups who are now entering the college and university training pipeline. Their presence marks an important step toward realizing the goals of full equality of access to and employment in institutions of higher education. As many of the contributors to this collection point out, however, our commitment to equity, and any gains we make in realizing it, will be systematically undercut if the working and learning environment that these students encounter remains disproportionately chilly, imposing barriers to full participation which rob us of their talents and contributions. In the discussion with which we close—an essay that appeared in The Globe and Mail just as we were completing this collection—Deborah Skilliter describes in clear and uncompromising detail the decidedly chilly climate that altogether too many students still encounter in college and university classrooms. As indicated by the editor's note that accompanied Skilliter's piece when it first appeared, she was a fourth-year geology student at Saint Mary's University in Halifax at the time she wrote about her classroom experiences.

Some weeks after Skilliter's essay appeared, Andrea Schluter published a further discussion of the issues that Skilliter raises. As Schluter observes, the need for such public naming of "blatant sexism and harassment" cannot be overemphasized.[2] Often, she says, "people don't really know what transpires in the revered halls of academic science,"[3] and when they do learn of experiences like Skilliter's, they may assume that they are isolated anomalies, given improvements in the representation of women in colleges and universities. If anything, Schluter argues, Skilliter understates the problem: "often the discrimination, the undermining of women's power and esteem, is much more insidious than her article illustrated."[4] It is symptomatic of deeply entrenched sexism in science and, to varying degrees, in most other disciplines taught or practised in our universities and colleges. For this reason, Schluter argues, "unfortunately, Ms. Skilliter's experience is not exceptional."[5]

387

Schluter's assessment is widely shared by those who are concerned by evidence that women continue to disappear from the training pipeline even as their represen- tation in college and university programs shows steady improvement.[6] Despite years of activism on these issues, the flood of reports on the status of women in higher education continues unabated and testifies to an unsupportable cost in the loss of trained talent. And, increasingly, these reports address questions about the impact of a learning and working environment that remains hostile not only to women, but to a great many others as well. We close, then, with an acknowledge- ment of how much remains to be done. So long as students encounter the sorts of demeaning and alienating practices described here, the culture created by chilly- making attitudes and practices reproduces itself, undermining yet another genera- tion of potential scholars and teachers.

– Eds.

I'd been thinking of a career in science for about four years when I broached the subject of studying geology in university to my highschool guidance counselor.

"You wouldn't be any good at it," he opined. "Besides women don't be- long in science."

Dutifully, I enrolled in an arts program, but still felt a little wistful about geology. That summer I worked as a field assistant on a geological mapping project in Cape Breton. The project geologist — a woman — and I talked about the experiences of women studying science while we hammered at rocks amid clouds of black flies. She presented me with the novel idea that women could have careers in science. She also exploded my fear that sci- ence was beyond my mental capacities. Geology has traditionally been a man's field, but she encouraged me to find my place.

I made the switch.

I quickly learned that women were far from welcome in the lab. Two of the men in my geology class decided to make me the target of a series of more and more threatening practical "jokes" combined with a constant bar- rage of insulting remarks about women in general. I quickly learned to wear jeans on campus after an incident in which my skirt was yanked over my ears while I stood talking with some classmates. One day I returned to my microscope to find the specimen replaced by condom. I decided that I'd had enough.

It didn't occur to me that the University might have some means of deal- ing with the problem. The only thing I could think of was to threaten to in- volve the police. This didn't so much reduce the level of harassment as change its style. From now on I was regarded as a "feminist with fangs."

Despite all this, the Geology Department had started to feel like home to me, mostly because of the encouragement I got from the professors and because of the small classes. But I still felt nervous about Chemistry and Math because of my shaky background and the huge classes.

I was slightly reassured when the Chemistry Professor, Dr. Jekyll (not his real name), suggested in the first class that the $95 textbook was really worth the money because it was written by a female and that women in science needed more role models.

A few weeks into the first semester, several incidents began to make me uneasy. A young woman passed in an assignment unstapled. Dr. Jekyll threw the unstapled assignment into the air and beckoned the woman to come forward and retrieve the pages that were now strewn about the front of the classroom. Reluctantly, the woman began collecting her papers. While she was walking back to her desk, Dr. Jekyll exclaimed, "My, you're cute when you blush."

Shortly into second semester, we began a unit on the properties of light. Dr. Jekyll asked for a "volunteer" to demonstrate the reflectivity of light. These "volunteers" were actually conscripts and were generally female. By now the class had become somewhat wary of the call for volunteers and there was intense scrutiny of shoelaces and notebooks. He singled out a woman and began to explain.

"We are able to see Eve because light reflects off her. Light reflects off her head. Light reflects off her ears. Light reflects off her eyes, and my, what beautiful eyes she has! Light reflects off her seductive lips, and light reflects off her A-HEMS."

This was accompanied by loud mock throat clearing. I heard a suppressed noise of protest from a woman sitting behind me. We exchanged sympathetic glances. My first thought was to get out of the classroom as quickly as possible and hope not to have to return. My second thought was that this style of teaching shouldn't be allowed to continue.

Eventually I tracked down the phone number of the University's advisor on sexual-harassment complaints and then spent several days agonizing over whether or not I should phone. I discussed it at home and was advised to forget about it. What right did I have to question the lecturing style of a Professor? I should simply go to class, take notes and leave. Ignore comments that were unrelated to Chemistry.

I tried this approach without success. I was unable to concentrate on the course material. I kept waiting for Dr. Jekyll to drop the next bomb, and was in a constant state of anxiety that I could be the next "volunteer." I dialled the number.

The adviser assured me that my complaint was valid. I knew this, but I had a purpose in visiting her office: I wanted out. I was able, with the adviser's assistance, to transfer into another section of the same subject. Within days, I was happily settled into my new class.

But not without cost. All the bureaucratic wrangling involved in changing classes had eaten into time I should have been spending studying. I had several hours of work to catch up on and I had developed an intense hatred and fear of Chemistry.

The academic year has come to a close and I am left with lots of questions. I've realized that behaviour like Dr. Jekyll's is fairly common. It has also occurred to me that Dr. Jekyll is unconscious of the impact his classroom power games have on his students. Or it may be that he doesn't care.

During exams I literally bumped into Dr. Jekyll in the hallway. He asked to speak to me. Fighting down a mixture of panic and anger, I tried to make my escape. He would have none of it. "This won't take a minute," he said, then proceeded to offer what he called an "apology." He liked, he said, to use everyday examples when he taught, to help students better understand the subject. This sounded to me more like self-justification than an apology. But all I could think of was that I just wanted to get away. Fast.

Afterwards it bothered me that he could have identified me so easily from a class of close to 100 students when my complaint was supposed to have been confidential. It also bothered me that even what passed for an apology was something imposed on me against my will.

Was my guidance counselor right? Do I belong in the world of science? I think I do. But I think that those who teach the subject have to consider the power they have. For this to happen means that science has to change, and I plan to be a part of that change.

Notes

1 This discussion was originally published in *The Globe and Mail*, June 13, 1994. Permission to reprint it here has been granted by the author.
2 Andrea Schluter, "By 'Liberating' Science, We Can Expand Its Boundaries," *The Globe and Mail*, August 24, 1994, p. A20.
3 Ibid.
4 Ibid.
5 Ibid.
6 See, for example, Sheila Widnall, "AAAS Presidential Lecture: Voices from the Pipeline," *Science*, 241 (1988): 1740-45, and also the annual *Science* features on "Women in Science" (beginning in 1992).